A BOY IN TEREZÍN

ALSO BY Debórah Dwork

The Terezín Album of Mariánka Zadikow

Voices and Views: A History of the Holocaust

Children With A Star: Jewish Youth in Nazi Europe

War Is Good for Babies and Other Young Children

ALSO BY Debórah Dwork and Robert Jan van Pelt

Flight from the Reich: Refugee Jews, 1933–1946

Holocaust: A History

Auschwitz

A Boy in Terezín

The Private Diary of Pavel Weiner,
April 1944–April 1945

Pavel Weiner

TRANSLATED FROM THE CZECH by Paul (Pavel) Weiner
AND EDITED BY Karen Weiner

WITH INTRODUCTION AND NOTES BY Debórah Dwork

 Northwestern University Press • Evanston, Illinois

Northwestern University Press
www.nupress.northwestern.edu

Printed in the United States of America

10 9 8 7 6 5 4 3 2 1

Library of Congress Cataloging-in-Publication Data

Weiner, Pavel, 1931–2010.
    A boy in Terezin : the private diary of Pavel Weiner, April 1944–April 1945 /
  Pavel Weiner ; translated from the Czech by Paul (Pavel) Weiner and edited by
  Karen Weiner ; with introduction and notes by Deborah Dwork.
      p. cm.
    Includes index.
    ISBN 978-0-8101-2779-1 (cloth : alk. paper)
      1. Weiner, Pavel, 1931–2010—Diaries. 2. Holocaust, Jewish (1939–1945)—Czech
  Republic—Terezín (Severočeský kraj)—Personal narratives. 3. Theresienstadt
  (Concentration camp) 4. Jewish children in the Holocaust—Czech Republic—
  Terezín (Severočeský kraj)—Diaries. 5. Concentration camp inmates—Czech
  Republic—Terezín (Severočeský kraj)—Diaries. 6. Jews—Czech Republic—
  Diaries. I. Weiner, Karen. II. Dwork, Deborah. III. Title.
  DS135.C97W449 2012
  940.53′18092—dc23
  [B]

                                                                    2011024544

I dedicate the publication of this diary to the memory of my father and my grandmother Valy, who truly define strength in the face of adversity; to the memory of my uncle Hanuš and grandfather Ludvík, whom I tragically never had the chance to meet; to Franta Maier, whose leadership and love helped my father through this most difficult time; and to the boys of Room 7—my extended "Nešarim family" and the many boys who left on transports and never returned.

—*Karen Weiner*

CONTENTS

List of Illustrations   ix

Acknowledgments   xi

Introduction by Debórah Dwork   xiii

DIARY   3

Appendixes

Boys in Room 7 Mentioned in the Diary   231

Pavel's Family   233

Persons Mentioned Frequently in the Diary   234

Glossary of Camp Terms   236

Index   239

ILLUSTRATIONS

1. Weiner family, Prague, circa 1934 — xiv

2. Hanuš Weiner, Prague, circa 1939 — xv

3. Pavel Weiner, Prague, circa 1939 — xv

4. Pavel and Hanuš Weiner, Prague, 1934 — xvi

5. Pavel and Hanuš Weiner, February 1936 — xvi

6. Diary entries, May 14 and 15, 1944 — xxv

7. Valy Weiner (née Stein) family with Ludvík Weiner, July 1926 — xxvii

8. Letter from Hermine Stein in Auschwitz-Birkenau to her daughter Valy Weiner in Terezín, circa March 1944 — xxviii

9. *Nešar* cover, March 7, 1944 — xxxii

10. *Nešar* contents page, March 7, 1944 — xxxii

11. Page in *Nešar*, March 7, 1944 — xxxiii

12. First page of "Tomáš Masaryk" (article by Pavel Weiner in *Nešar*, March 7, 1944) — xxxiii

13. Paul Weiner's "Nešarim Soccer Chronicle" — xxxiv

14. Title page of Pavel Weiner's "Nešarim Soccer Chronicle" — xxxv

15. The personification of victory — xxxvi

16. Cover page of the first volume of the diary ("Diary I, 4 April – 13 May 1944, Weiner Pavel") — 5

17. First page of "Diary I" — 6

18. Broadside diary page, with Pavel's illustration to mark
    the end of June 1944   80

19. Diary entry from September 13, 1944   152

20. Title page of the sixth notebook, October 1944   180

21. Cookie shapes (from Pavel's diary, November 1, 1944)   187

22. Layout of the bakery in which Pavel worked (from
    Pavel's diary, November 1, 1944)   188

23. Plan of room and vestibule (from Pavel's diary,
    November 2, 1944)   190

24. Poem written by Pavel on his thirteenth birthday,
    November 13, 1944   196

25. Pavel's drawing of a vase with flowers in honor of his
    thirteenth birthday   197

26. Layout of the main warehouse (first of two drawings
    from Pavel's diary, November 16, 1944)   199

27. Layout of the main warehouse (second of two drawings
    from Pavel's diary, November 16, 1944)   200

28. Last page of Pavel's diary, April 22, 1945   228

ACKNOWLEDGMENTS

I am deeply grateful for this opportunity to make my father's dream of documenting his experiences come true. The project would not have been possible without the vision, hard work, and commitment of so many people. First, a special thank you goes to Tatyana McAuley, without whom the diary would not be where it is today. Her recognition of its historical and personal value got the wheels turning, and her dedicated research into the boys of Room 7 was invaluable. It has been a pleasure to work with and learn from Debórah Dwork, whose interest in the diary and persistence in bringing it to the public have fueled the project to completion. I am grateful for the expertise and dedication of the staff at Northwestern University Press, and particularly for the patience and skill of Anne Gendler, managing editor, and Alma Reising, copy editor, as we prepared the diary for publication. I thank Henry L. Carrigan Jr., senior editor and assistant director, for taking on the diary for publication and Marianne Jankowski, art director, and Peter Raccuglia, assistant acquisitions editor, for their hard work and creativity. I acknowledge the work of Tomáš Federovič, a historian at the Terezín Memorial, whose article on my father's diary provided a wonderful stepping-off point; Steven Sernett for his database research; and Marjorie Glazer, a volunteer at the Strassler Center for Holocaust and Genocide Studies, who brought an eye for English grammar to the translated text. Of course, I could not have completed this project without the insight of the remaining "boys" of Room 7, and I especially recognize the dedication and patience of Franta Maier, Michael Gruenbaum, and Erich Spitz as they responded to my seemingly endless queries. Many thanks go to Zuzana Justman, Danielle and George Vago, Sonja Rotenberg, Edgar Knobloch, John Freund, and Edgar Krasa for their collective help with translation and/or descriptions of life in Terezín. I am thankful too for the family history passed on to me by my great-uncle, Eric Stein. And, most important, I am forever grateful to my father, Paul Weiner, who had the foresight to eloquently document such a turbulent time in his life and the willingness to share that history with all of us.

—Karen Weiner

One of the pleasures of finishing a project is that it provides an opportunity to express appreciation for those who helped. I am delighted to thank Karen Weiner, whose partner on this project I became. I thank, too, Steven Sernett at the Terezín Digital Resource Center, who scoured the databases in search of information about people Pavel mentioned. And I am hugely grateful for the commitment of many at Northwestern University Press. It is due to their dedication that the project became a product. Hats off, in alphabetical order, to: Henry L. Carrigan Jr., senior editor and assistant director; Anne Gendler, managing editor; Marianne Jankowski, art director; Peter Raccuglia, assistant acquisitions editor; and Alma Reising, copy editor. Most of all, I appreciate every minute Paul Weiner spent with me, recording his history, pondering my questions, and helping me understand the boy he had been. His life is a golden thread in the weaving of history.

—Debórah Dwork

INTRODUCTION

Debórah Dwork

"Now after having spent two years in Terezín, I deeply regret that I haven't kept a diary from the beginning," twelve-year-old Pavel Weiner began his record of his third and last year as a prisoner in the transit camp the Germans called the model ghetto of Theresienstadt and the inmates called by its Czech town name. It was a place where, Pavel explained, "one gets to know the harder side of life; one's mother doesn't keep you pampered. One tends to see things with eyes wide open." Referring to another boy, Pavel continued: "I realize that Sasha's undertaking of writing a diary is good and, therefore, I have decided to write one myself. I hope that I will be successful and that my diary will fulfill its purpose." Alexandr (Sasha) Schweinburg was deported to Auschwitz later that year; he perished and his diary disappeared. Their fate was all too typical.[1] Thanks to luck and fortuitous circumstances, Pavel and his diary survived—Pavel a survivor of the Holocaust and his diary a precious record of his daily life and the history of the camp.

Pavel Weiner, nicknamed Pajík in Terezín, was born in Prague (then the capital of Czechoslovakia, now of the Czech Republic) on Friday, November 13, 1931. "We led a very comfortable middle-class Jewish life," he recalled seventy years after that existence was permanently shattered. "By 'we' I mean my father, whose name was Ludvík, and my mother, whose name was Valy, and my older brother, four years older brother, Handa."[2] Ludvík, a businessman, worked for his sister Olga's husband, Otomar Sušický, in his leather wholesale enterprise. The two families lived in the center of the city in a five-story building, owned by Otomar, with a view of the river. Like most families of their socioeconomic class, the Weiner family employed a maid and the boys had a German governess. And, like many middle-class Jews in Prague, their Jewish identity functioned on multiple levels. On the one hand,

COURTESY KAREN WEINER

Weiner family: Valy (née Stein), Pavel, Ludvík, and Hanuš, Prague, circa 1934

they saw themselves as Czechs, and their Jewish practice, Paul (as he was called in the United States) recalled, "was limited to observing the high holidays." Yet, the family social network was composed of "mostly Jewish friends and relatives."[3]

Theirs was a typical family life of that time, place, and milieu. Ludvík and Valy, Paul remembered, "were social democrats. They belonged to liberal clubs. We went on vacations as a family. In summer we rented a villa near Prague, usually with some friends doing the same thing. In the wintertime, we went skiing." Hanuš, known as Handa, was a studious boy who did well in school. Pavel played the piano, accordion, and recorder. In Paul's memory, "It was really a happy eleven years of my childhood."[4] And he is correct: no matter what troubles, or quarrels, or tensions there may have been, those were ordinary difficulties which, in retrospect, were insignificant.

Adolf Hitler and the Nazi party had come to power in Germany in 1933, but Prague was not Berlin and democratic Czechoslovakia hardly the Third Reich. For the Weiners, as for many Czech Jews, the Germans' march into the perimeter of Czechoslovakia known as the

Hanuš Weiner, Prague, circa 1939   *Pavel Weiner, Prague, circa 1939*

Sudetenland in 1938 dealt a crushing blow. "One of the first, most dramatic experiences was the Munich crisis in 1938 when there was the possibility that Czechoslovakia may be invaded by Germans," Paul remembered.

Britain, France, and Italy avoided that possibility by handing the Sudetenland to Germany in the hope of "peace for our time," as the British prime minister Neville Chamberlain put it after meeting with Hitler in Munich. Their appeasement effort also handed the Nazi regime power over the Jews in that area, and in any case delayed invasion for merely half a year. The Sudetenland became part of the greater German Reich; Czechoslovakia's other lands, Bohemia and Moravia, as yet had not. But the Czechs, ready to wage war against Germany before Munich, now lost the courage to hold on to what was left. Resolutely anti-German, President Edvard Beneš resigned. So did the rest of the country. The leading liberal daily spoke for many on October 4, 1938: "If we cannot sing with the angels, we shall howl with the wolves." Force, not law, ruled the world; the Czechs would do well to find their place among the powerful. Therefore, the paper concluded, "Let us seek—we have no other choice—accommodation with Germany."[5] The new president, Emil Hácha, tried to do just that.

Hitler demanded no less. Prague must take orders from Berlin on matters of foreign policy; Czechoslovakia must reduce its army, limit freedom of the press, adjust its economy to suit German needs, and introduce anti-Jewish legislation.[6] In March 1939, Hácha was summoned to Berlin to sign a German-drafted declaration stating that

Pavel and Hanuš Weiner, Prague, 1934

Pavel and Hanuš Weiner, February 1936

"the Czechoslovak President . . . confidently placed the fate of the Czech people and country in the hands of the Führer of the German Reich."[7] The German army marched in the next day, imposing a "protectorate" upon the remaining Czech lands of Bohemia and Moravia.[8] The Nazis and their "Jewish Question" and their systems to "solve" that "problem" gripped the country.

"Things got pretty bad," Paul recalled. The ordinary routines of the Weiners' daily life disappeared as edict followed edict. Paul remembered being "kicked out of school," that "we couldn't go to the movies," and being forced "to sit in the back of the streetcar." Nevertheless, "unfortunately, except for my [maternal] uncle and some cousins, the whole family remained in Czechoslovakia." His father felt "that he was born here and that his roots are here, and things will pass over."[9] These sentiments were shared by many. Their closest friends, the Kürschner and Knobloch families, did not emigrate either. The Kürschners may have felt as Ludvík did. Another factor shaped the Knoblochs' decision: Dr. Knobloch, a city coroner, was gentile; Mrs. Knobloch a Jew. "They didn't feel it necessary to emigrate," Paul explained.[10] The mixed marriage protected Mrs. Knobloch and the children; thus privileged, she was in a position to send parcels to the Weiner family when they were deported to Terezín. Ties of family and friendship counted for a lot during that time. As Pavel recounted in his diary, Mrs. Knobloch's brother, Dr. Rudolf Bergmann, also did his best to help the Weiners, through his position in the Terezín Jewish administration.

Deportation of Jews from Prague began at the end of 1941, and from that point the Weiners "were aware that it is looming," Paul recalled. They entrusted their silverware, jewelry, and other valuables to gentile friends. "We hoped that we would be delayed," Paul remembered, but "in May [1942] we were summoned to a transport: AU1."[11] The Trade Fair Palace served as a central deportation point. Every transport was numbered and each deportee wore a number on a string around the neck. Pavel's number was 908. That marked the end of the world Pavel knew. "Our life was shaken apart."[12]

At that point, the Germans did not yet employ cattle cars to deport Jews from Prague to Terezín. They left in ordinary passenger trains, and if gentile neighbors and Jews who for the moment remained in Prague were deceived, so were those on the transports. They, like all of Prague's Jews, did not want to leave their homes, their city, and the world that they knew. But they had no idea what awaited them just fifty kilometers away. The train stopped at the small town of Bohušovice. Everyone was ordered off and marched under Czech gendarme guard to the transit camp the Germans called Theresienstadt.

What was Theresienstadt? What purpose did it serve? In the spring of 1942 the Germans evidently made an important decision. They had murdered millions of Jews in the east. Western Europe's Jews must now be dealt with. But how? Perhaps someone suggested an annihilation facility in Belgium or France, but if so the idea got nowhere. Western Europe's Jews would be sent east.[13]

This created a new logistical difficulty of moving many Jews over long distances. In the Soviet Union, *Einsatzgruppen* (specially designated murder squads) killed Jews on the spot. There was no need to collect and ship people to annihilation centers. In Poland, ghettos served as storage pens. The distances to the camps were short and the authorities coordinated their activities. The situation was more complicated in the west, where there were no closed ghettos and Jews had long been integrated into society. Local sensibilities might be offended. Cattle cars in the central train station would not do. So the Germans sent Jews by third-class rail to an isolated transit camp within the country—and thence east. Thus, all except the—by then—rather routine initial deportation was screened from public view. No direct connection existed between the capital cities of Western Europe and the new necropolises in the east.

The transit camps served another function as well. The often-competing agencies involved in the "Final Solution" shared a common policy of Judeocide, but each had its own agenda, priorities, and schedule. A roundup in Paris, for example, was not always coordinated properly with the maximum "legal" dispossession of Jewish property, the military's demand that week on the railways, or the current killing capacity in the death camps. Germans used the transit camps as holding pens for Jews until the gas chambers of Sobibór or Birkenau could accommodate them and empty railway cars could move them, thus maximizing the efficiency of the annihilation system.

Finally, the transit camps aided German subterfuge: these were permanent settlements, they implied. In the case of Theresienstadt, the implicit was explicit. *The Führer Gives the Jews a Town* proclaimed the title of a Nazi propaganda film about that transit camp. The Germans' perversions notwithstanding, transit camps were not stable, merry communities but temporary, wretched stopovers on the way east. Indeed, many of the people photographed by the Germans had been deported and killed by the time the film was shown.

The Germans considered a number of options before they settled on Terezín. Prague's fifth district might have done nicely as a ghetto, but the Germans' desire for secrecy superseded the advantages of easy access. A number of other Bohemian and Moravian towns presented possibilities.[14] None so perfectly met the Germans' needs as the fortified garrison town of Terezín, where the Gestapo had set up its central prison in the local "Small Fortress" shortly after the Germans occupied the country.[15] Built for military purposes in the 1780s by the Austrian emperor Joseph II and named in honor of his mother, Maria Theresa, Theresienstadt was formally transformed into a transit camp in February 1942 by Reinhard Heydrich, head of the Reich Security Main Office and Heinrich Himmler's right-hand man. By his order, the small walled city not far from Prague was evacuated of its thirty-seven hundred inhabitants and a "Jewish settlement" or "old people's ghetto" was officially established.[16]

A first transport of 342 young Jewish men, mostly construction workers, left Prague on November 24, 1941. Almost before they could begin their work, two transports of women, children, and elderly persons arrived. A second building detail was shipped in on December 4.[17] Their job was to prepare for an influx of thousands. The newly established camp administration had far greater responsibilities. Like the Jewish Councils organized elsewhere, the Terezín Ältestenrat (Council of Elders) was composed of prominent Jewish men designated by the Germans to carry out their orders and to deal with the myriad problems of a community under duress. The council oversaw housing allocations, food distribution, hygiene services, medical care, and youth services; they established and maintained children's homes, cookhouses, a laundry facility, a library, a central bakery, thirty-six clinics, hundreds of sickrooms, and thousands of sickbeds. Created to "govern" the Jews, the German-imposed Ältestenrat had many responsibilities and great authority within the community but no power outside it and no leverage at all with the Nazis.[18] In addition to the difficulties all Jewish Councils faced in occupied Europe, the Ältestenrat in Terezín had the particular challenge of dealing with a community separated by language and culture, composed as it was of large numbers of Jews from Germany, Czechoslovakia, and Austria as well as, in smaller numbers, the Netherlands, Denmark, France, and elsewhere.

Arriving in May 1942, the Weiner family faced a streamlined reception system. The Germans shoved the deportees into *die Schleuse* (the sluice). At that time, the term referred to the absorption depot located

in the dank, subterranean dungeons of the town walls. Later, when
deportations from Terezín to the east became increasingly common,
die Schleuse or *Schleusky* meant any processing point for incoming or
outgoing transports. There they sat anxiously awaiting the Germans'
next move. Assigned to living quarters, families found themselves
torn asunder. Ludvík and Handa were assigned to men's barracks.
"I ended up with my mother in Dresdner barracks," Paul recalled, "a
pretty miserable place. Cold and unfriendly."[19] Pavel did not remain
there long; he was soon moved to room 7 in L417, building number
17 on the fourth lengthwise street, the *Kinderheim* (children's home)
for Czech boys.[20]

Terezín was a transit camp. But it was unique in the Nazi system. It
was, the Germans claimed, a place where they, in their compassion,
sent elderly Jews unfit for the "hard labor" all the Jews "resettled" in
Poland were to do. Thus Terezín helped to perpetuate the myth dis-
seminated by Hitler's regime that the long trains of deported Jews
were chugging along to agricultural settlements in the east, not to
death camps. To avoid embarrassing questions, highly decorated or
severely disabled war veterans also were eligible for Theresienstadt,
as were a certain number of very well known Jews.[21] Terezín, however,
was hardly a settlement or a ghetto. As the statistics show, it was simply
another transit center. Of the 141,162 Jews shipped in, 88,202 sub-
sequently were deported east; 276 were handed over to the Gestapo
and disappeared; 33,456 died; 1,623 were released to neutral countries (1,200 to Switzerland and 423 to Sweden) in 1945; 31 were let
go; 764 escaped; and 16,832 remained when the camp was liberated,
including 22 unregistered children born there.[22]

Oddly enough, the purely theoretical construction of Terezín as
a stable community had an effect on the inmates. In his diary Pavel
consistently used the term "ghetto" rather than "transit camp," reflecting his perception of Terezín as a place where Jews were to live, not
a stopover to the east. Despite the constant threat of the deportation
trains, lack of food and hygiene, and omnipresent disease, the Jewish
inhabitants created an intellectual and cultural life for both adults and
children. Child welfare was taken especially seriously. The first German-
appointed Elder of the Jews, Jakob Edelstein, and indeed the entire
Council of Elders believed that this task was central to their mission.

Children accounted for about 10 percent of the population of
Theresienstadt. The Germans (happily) took little notice of them,
leaving their governance to Edelstein and his council. They estab-

lished a *Jugendfuersorge* (youth welfare department) to safeguard the children's health and to continue their education despite the Germans' draconian prohibitions. To that end, the Jewish administrators supported the policy of instituting separate children's homes. Beginning in mid-1942, the majority of children over the age of four were placed in a *Kinderheim*. At that time many of the Jewish leaders were Zionists, and they had the idea that this collective life would help to instill the values of Zionism while protecting the children from the worst of the brutality of life at Terezín. In more prosaic ways, too, the youth welfare department sought to improve conditions for children. Their living quarters were less crowded than those of the adults. Late in the summer of 1942 the department prevailed upon the Germans to allow the children to use the courtyards and gardens, and they even were permitted to play on the fortifications of the city. Within a few months the council opened a children's kitchen that provided more and better-quality food, and early in 1943 it established a children's hospital.[23]

The most outstanding work of the department, however, was its support of clandestine classes. Secret study circles were established, and many of the *madrichim* (youth leaders or counselors) and *Betreueren* and *Betreuerinnen* (male and female child care workers) in the *Kinderheim* were devoted to the cause of education. For them, as for the children, it was an act of faith in the future. "We [the boys in room 7] lived a very, very special life thanks to our *madrich*, Franta Maier," Paul reminisced. "Strict" but "very caring," and barely a decade older than the eleven-to-thirteen-year-olds for whom he was responsible, Franta embraced his duties. "He excelled in soccer; he organized the *heim* performances. He kept us busy; he kept us occupied. We didn't have too much time to do any mischief or even to think about the conditions." Franta nurtured "a camaraderie in the *heim*," and he supervised "the excellent instruction we got."[24]

Pavel's diary is grounded in the *heim*. Opened on July 8, 1942, room 7 was home to forty-one youngsters. The population fluctuated with transports into and deportations out of Terezín. The boys and their teachers and *Betreuerinnen* march across the diary pages. Pavel wrote about boys standing guard as others participated in classes held in the L417 attic; the subjects they studied; books they read; and topics they discussed. With the idea that the educational program prepared the youngsters for reentry into the school system, they were tested in every subject: math, physics, Hebrew, Czech literature, geography, and history. This degree of dedication called for a high level of organization, and the structure of the *heim* emerges clearly through Pavel's entries. Franta held *Apel* (assembly) as often as twice a day, usually in room 7 but sometimes elsewhere, to check the barracks and tell the boys what the program would be. They had daytime activities: room cleanup, classes, sports, rehearsals. And evening activities: performances for each other, a lecture by one boy to the others, and bedtime readings by Franta.[25]

If the *heim* offered much to the boys, the rich cultural life of Terezín did too. Initially forbidden by the Germans, the arts gained ground when they realized that performances, shows, and lectures suited their propaganda program: to showcase Terezín as a functioning, unexceptional city with a stable population and a normal civic life. Eventually, they went to great lengths to perpetuate this myth. Starting in the summer of 1943 a coffeehouse, bank, post office, and even a petty crimes court were opened. Stores sold goods robbed from the newly arriving inmates. (Sometimes people re-purchased their own possessions.) Art and music in particular flourished. "They give out tickets for a Beethoven concert, which I unfortunately miss," Pavel wrote in the very first diary entry (April 4, 1944). Nearly a year later (January 6, 1945), he remained just as engaged. "Yesterday, I was at a concert, Beethoven. The hall was overfilled and there was good reason. I could hardly have found concerts of this type in Prague."

The camp boasted five cabaret groups, several small orchestras, a "municipal" orchestra of thirty-five musicians, and a jazz band. A number of operas were produced, including Bedřich Smetana's *Bartered Bride*. "During *Apel*, I find out that tomorrow the opera *The Bartered Bride* will be performed for the entire School!" (meaning all of L417), Pavel exclaimed one Sunday (July 23, 1944). A jazz band and solo concerts by singers and virtuosi also were popular. One man began a puppet theater; two dramatists, Gustav Schorsch and Josef Taussig, entertained young people with lectures, poetry recitations, and literature readings; and Mozart's opera *Bastien and Bastienne* was produced for the children's enjoyment. "Handa gives me a ticket for the opera *Bastien and Bastienne,* which will take place at eight o'clock in the Magdeburg Barracks," Pavel wrote happily on August 5, 1944. "It is amazing!"[26]

The young people themselves participated in these ventures. The composer Karel Reiner worked with children, choreographer Kamila

Rosenbaum interpreted Jan Karafiát's "Fire-Flies" as a dance-play for children (it was shown nearly thirty times), and best known of all, the conductor Rafael Schächter trained a children's choir and produced the enormously popular opera *Brundibár*. Composed by Hans Krása with libretto by Adolf Hoffmeister in Prague in 1938, its first performance was presented as a gift to Ota (also called Moritz) Freudenfeld, director of the Jewish orphanage in Prague, on the occasion of his fiftieth birthday that year. Freudenfeld's son Rudolf, a gifted amateur musician and one of the L417 educators, conducted fifty-five performances of *Brundibár* in Terezín.[27]

The *heim* and the efforts of the *Jugendfuersorge* shielded Pavel from much of the misery in Terezín, but nothing could protect him from the worst of it, or core ethical dilemmas that arose from being trapped in the Germans' net. "After such a long time, we again hear the dreaded word, TRANSPORT!" Pavel lamented on May 11, 1944. "What an awful word. This word means knapsacks, suitcases, and hunched Jewish figures underneath them. Why? Just because the Germans want it, and on account of that, thousands of miserable people must leave their bundle and go away into the mist. Yes, this is transport."
Everyone focused on who would be on the list. Pavel noted the effect of the announcement: "Of course, the good mood sinks below freezing point. I have difficulties consoling Mother. I don't succeed because I myself am disturbed." Three boys from room 7 were included, prompting Pavel's comment the next day: "I am unhappy. Everything else becomes secondary." Pavel described the ordeal (May 14). Elderly inmates were targeted. They "get tangled up in carts [taking them to the train] . . . , old grandmothers stumble over luggage. In brief, it is hell on earth. If all this didn't appear to me as if it were a dream, most likely it would shatter me." Still, Pavel reflected, "this is nothing compared to what is to follow." Tasked to help the deportees, the room 7 boys went from barracks to barracks. "A lot of old people wait to leave their homes with knapsacks in front of them. . . . The hunched figures fearfully entrust their luggage to us. The luggage is not well packed and at least half falls apart. We are dripping with sweat. After loading the luggage, we start moving. Behind us, a sad procession of people drags on. People have now lost all human signs and resemble outlaws. We drag slowly along. . . . We push our cart like a mighty stream of water. Such a scene cannot be depicted with a pen alone." The mentally ill were targeted too, "almost half

the [Kavalierka] barracks," where they were quartered. "There, it is the worst."

The Weiner family was struck too. They learned the following day that "Aunt and Uncle Sušický are in the transport." Olga and Otomar were two of the 7,503 people shipped to Auschwitz in three convoys over a four-day period, from May 15 to 18, 1944. Only 389 survived. Olga and Otomar were not among them.

No one knew where the transports went or what these destinations signified. But, miserable as life in Terezín most assuredly was, no one wished to leave the familiar. Thus the system of *reklamace,* reclaiming people from deportation, was born. The designated deportees and their families besieged the Jewish administration and anyone they thought might be powerful enough to intervene on their behalf. Take someone else! they beseeched. If *reklamace* offered marked inmates a glimmer of hope for a reprieve, it fomented turmoil in the camp. "There is a big chaos involving all kinds of *reklamace* and swindles. Nobody is safe," Pavel worried (May 14).

Nobody was safe in any case. When Pavel heard that "all men in the age group of eighteen to fifty must leave on a transport for a work camp in Germany," he was not worried: "it does not concern my family" (September [23], 1944). False comfort. The first words he heard the next morning were, "Do you know that the age bracket has been increased to sixteen to fifty-five?" Pavel felt "as if someone has shot me." Father and brother were on the list. Desperate, Pavel "urge[d] Father to go and see Dr. Bergmann to get out of the transport." Handa and Ludvík were confined to the *Schleusky* while Valy tried her best at *reklamace.* To no avail. In the evening of September 26, he was "able to get into the *Schleusky* to talk with Father and Handa, perhaps for the last time." He meant for the last time until Germany's defeat, not for the last time in his life. He had no idea that transport might mean death. The family agreed on a postwar plan to regain contact. Still, Pavel broke down as he said good-bye. "With my father it goes well, but when Handa comes I don't know why, but I start crying and so does my mother" (September [25]). Nor was the *heim* a source of comfort: "All counselors go, which means so will Franta. The whole education program will collapse because [professors] Zwicker, Kohn, and Eisinger are going. I am completely distraught" (September [24]).

The transports pitted inmates against each other at key moments; the scarcities of camp existence pushed them to antisocial behaviors every day. Need trumped former ethics. People who never would

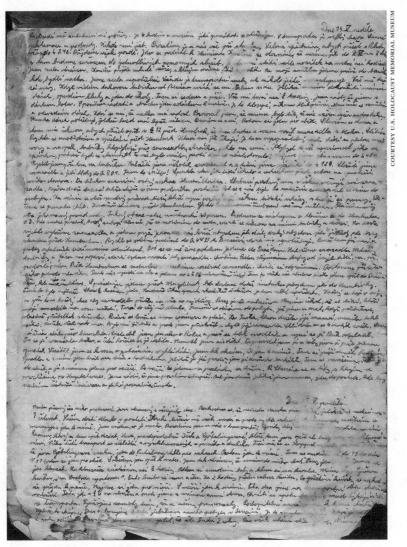

Diary entries, May 14 and 15, 1944

have stolen from a group enterprise in normal life took advantage of every opportunity to *schlojs*, or purloin, what they could in Terezín. The situation reshaped morality. Working in the camp gardens in August 1944, Pavel was determined "to get a good assignment, which means that I will be able to *schlojs*." He understood that this practice prevailed although it meant less food for the community. "Such is the real attitude toward work in Terezín" (August 3). He understood, too, that it would not do at home: "This could never have happened to me in Prague" (August 10). Yet, eating the fruits of a *schlojs,* he observed (August 4), "In Terezín, one gets joy out of every little swindle."

In time, Pavel turned to *schlojs*-ing whatever he could, wherever he went. His loot included paper for his diary (August 30).

Closely written in tiny script on different sizes and types of paper, Pavel's diary provides a youngster's view of important events in the history of the camp.[28] Soon after he began to write, the *Kommandantur* (the German camp administration) embarked upon the *Verschönerung* (beautification campaign), in anticipation of an International Red Cross visit. For some time, the Germans had faced diplomatic difficulties and public relations questions that the regime wished to quell. Two representatives of the German Red Cross, accompanied by Adolf Eichmann and a couple of others from the Reich Security Main Office, had visited Terezín in June 1943. The Red Cross delegates reported to the International Red Cross, which passed on their observations to the World Jewish Congress. Do inmates remain, or are they sent elsewhere? the World Jewish Congress asked the International Red Cross. No one knew. Growing concerned that this question would gain currency, the Germans deported Jews from Terezín to Auschwitz, where they were quartered in a separate family camp (BIIb) hastily established for them in September. There the Terezín deportees were held as evidence against reports of mass murder. Specially privileged, these inmates were spared the customary selection process, they wore their own clothes, and they were not assigned to slave labor squads. During the first days of March 1944 the Germans ordered them to write postcards to relatives, to prove their safe arrival in the east. The cards were dated March 25, but the Jews who had written them had been killed on March 7. They had served their purpose.[29]

The Germans moved too soon. By spring 1944, it was clear that the Reich was losing the war, and more foreign diplomats and international welfare organizations began to ask about the fate of the Jews. In response to deteriorating foreign relations, the Germans agreed to permit a delegation of the International Red Cross to visit Theresienstadt in June 1944. Anticipating questions from the delegation about deportation, the Germans dispatched the three May transports—carrying Olga and Otomar Sušický among the 7,503—to refill the family camp in Birkenau. If worst came to worst, and a visit to Birkenau were

COURTESY KAREN WEINER

Valy Weiner (née Stein) family with Ludvík Weiner, July 1926: Zikmund Stein (Valy's father), Trude Stein (Valy's sister), Eric Stein (Valy's brother), Ludvík Weiner, Valy Weiner, and Hermine Stein (Valy's mother)

Pavel's maternal grandparents (Valy's parents) Zikmund and Hermine and his maternal aunt Trude were deported to Terezín. When the Germans occupied Czechoslovakia his maternal uncle Eric Stein fled just days before the Nazis came after him; he managed to reach the United States. Trude died in Terezín in July 1943. Pavel's grandparents were deported to Auschwitz in September. Hermine was forced to write to her daughter to tell of her safe arrival. She and her husband were killed thereafter.

demanded, a group of deportees from Theresienstadt would be on hand.

As the Germans orchestrated their plan in Auschwitz, preparations moved forward in Terezín. "What is interesting is *Verschönerung*," Pavel observed (June 9). "The route through which the commission will be taken has been set. The route leads through our hall and gym, which have been cleanly painted and scrubbed. Only lower surfaces of the houses have been painted. During the day of the commission, there will be a luxurious lunch. *This* is Terezín!"

The Germans held a dress rehearsal on June 16. Pavel thought "the Red Cross Commission is expected. Everything is in tiptop shape," until "suddenly, fourteen Germans barge into the barracks" and he realized "this must not be the right commission." Still, the show went on. "In front of the School, the boys grab me and tell me to go singing with them, which I do." Franta explained that "when the commission arrives we must sing German songs. We are learning 'O, Tannenbaum

Letter from Hermine Stein in Auschwitz-Birkenau to her daughter Valy Weiner in Terezín, circa early March 1944

By the time Valy received the letter her mother had been forced to write to prove her safe arrival, Hermine and her husband had been killed.

[Oh, Christmas tree]' and several others, but we are not doing too well." The boys are told to go on the carousel and swings that had just been erected for the Red Cross visit. "I go so many times that I get dizzy. Then, we throw the ball and finally the commission arrives. Obviously, they are satisfied with the well-behaved playing children."[30]

Pavel described the final touches of the campaign. June 22: "*Verschönerung* reaches the highest point today. Each table has its own flowerpot. The sidewalks are washed and therefore we cannot even walk on them. Everything is in tiptop order." The delegation arrived the next day. For lunch, he reported, "We have tongue, mashed potatoes, onions, and cucumber salad! Today, the transport numbers

don't exist. [Council of Elders chairman] Eppstein leads the commission and drives in his own car! There is *Apel* with instruction to
have all rooms in order. I go for lunch and I'm lucky that I get a good
piece of tongue. The commission is already in. . . . The children must
scream 'Onkel Rahm, schön wieder sardinen? [Uncle Rahm, again
sardines?]' as he passes by. . . . Everything is spotless in the *heim*. . . .
Brundibár is being played throughout the day. . . . SS men Haindl
and Bergel are in civilian clothes today. On the *bašta* [the green area
atop the town's broad rampart walls used as playing fields], there
are matches going on and everybody is waiting for the commission.
The *Ghettowache* [the Jewish ghetto police] wear gloves today. All the
people are watching the commission."

This was theater of the absurd taken to the extreme. Karl Rahm
was the Nazi commandant of Terezín. After the war, he was charged
with crimes against humanity and executed. SS officers Karl Bergel
and Rudolf Haindl gloried in the power they wielded in uniform.
Never would the children have addressed the commandant, and neither Bergel nor Haindl would have dreamed of appearing without
uniform. As Pavel remarked, "Eppstein spoke French and played out
the comedy well."

Terezín was the only Holocaust camp outside observers ever entered and, when it came to it, it was not much of a delegation. The
entire company comprised three people: two Danes representing
the Foreign Office and the Ministry of Health, and one Swiss, the
deputy head of the International Red Cross, who came in place of his
superior who said he had to make another trip just then. The Swedish embassy was invited to send a representative, but declined as the
visit conflicted with a national holiday.[31] Nor did the commission ask
difficult questions, either that day or afterward. By July 1944 it was
clear to the Germans that the second lot of Jews in the family camp
would not be needed either. The family camp was dismantled; those
found "unfit for work" were gassed and the rest were sent on to slave
labor sites.

If the International Red Cross failed to ask questions, Terezín artists used their talent to try to communicate information. "I learn that
the painters Ungar, Haas, Fritta, and two others were arrested and,
with their families, taken to the Small Fortress," Pavel confided to his
diary on July 17, 1944. "It is probably because they painted pictures
showing Terezín people and then sold them." His few lines open the
door to the notorious "painters' affair." Otto Ungar, Leo Haas, and

Fritz Taussig (known as Bedřich Fritta), whom Pavel mentions, and Norbert Troller and Ferdinand Bloch, whom he does not, were assigned to the *Zeichenstube* (graphics department). This gave them access to art supplies and license to visit nearly all parts of the camp. The artists created a pictorial record of the misery of Terezín daily life and their drawings, passed through Czech gendarmes, traveled to the outside world. As Pavel heard, Ungar, Haas, Taussig, and Bloch were brought to SS headquarters in Terezín, where they were interrogated by no less a person than Adolf Eichmann, which indicates how seriously the Nazis took the artists' work.

Bloch and Taussig perished before liberation; Ungar died of dysentery soon afterward. Haas and Troller survived, as did many of all five artists' works. They had hidden drawings in Terezín, in addition to those smuggled out, to serve as a record of the Germans' atrocities. "Inside are SS officers Haindl and Burger from Prague, as well as the gendarmes. They are looking for the paintings," Pavel continued the next day. Fortunately, they did not find them. Recovered after the war, a number hang in museums today, a testament to the conditions some 140,000 endured.[32]

Perhaps to refute the artists' work, perhaps to counter the increasing volume of news about the Germans' concentration camps, the Ministry of Propaganda in Berlin ordered Rahm to exploit inmate talent to produce a film about Terezín: *The Führer Gives the Jews a Town.* "Today, they are making a film, for which SS officer Haindl selects people who look like 'typical' Jews," Pavel reported on August 16. "It is a masquerade directed by Gerron, a former film director." Kurt Gerron, a famous stage and film actor and director, and a Terezín inmate, was charged by Rahm to do the job. A whole-cloth fabrication, the film—twenty-three minutes of which survive—showed Terezín precisely as the Germans wished the world to see it: a happy, thriving community which, thanks to Hitler's generosity, enjoyed a separate but equal existence in their own pretty town. To that end, Gerron staged performances for the camera. "Today, assignments are made for filming as spectators in *Brundibár,*" Pavel wrote on August 20. "By chance I'm assigned." And he added: "This whole filming is a comedy, as is everything in Terezín." He well understood the charade. "At the post office, the film people are filming Jews as they walk out with packages," he recorded some days later (August 26). "When the filming is over, Gerron, who is directing it, tells the people who are carrying packages: 'Bitte es tut mir leit aber die Paketen geben Sie zuruck [I am sorry but please return the parcels].'" Pavel's bemusement vanished when Gerron staged a soccer game for his movie (September 1): "I see long lines of old people, youngsters, and invalids who are forced to go watch the soccer match, Sparta vs. Jugendfuersorge. It will be filmed and two thousand people will have to watch and scream under the supervision of the SS." That, Pavel concluded, "is not funny." He was right. In fact, nothing about the initiative was harmless comedy. Most of the people Gerron filmed were deported and murdered. Gerron and his wife, Olga, were too. Serving the Nazis availed him nought.[33]

Deportation signaled disaster. Indeed, the very idea that a transport train might travel to safety was unimaginable. "The weirdest transport ever was the transport to Switzerland" (in February 1945), Pavel recalled in one of his last diary entries (April 15). "Out of nowhere, the news spread that twelve hundred people from Terezín will go to Switzerland." Although the inmates did not credit it, the rumor was true. Himmler realized that Germany would lose the war, and he—ever loyal to the regime—pursued a number of initiatives in the hope of gaining better terms for the Reich. Believing his party's propaganda about the power Jews wielded, these were Jews-for-sale deals which, he imagined, would show the Nazis as pragmatists with whom the Allies (in the west; he held no such illusions about the U.S.S.R.) could negotiate productively. Himmler did not want any questions about missing family members. Thus Pavel and his mother "were not even given consideration because only whole families or singles could go." The transport was to include twelve hundred. To fill it, "about fifty-one hundred people received summonses. Most of them, however, didn't believe the Germans and didn't expect anything good from them. More have refused than have accepted." In the end, 1,210 inmates left Terezín on February 5, 1945. For them, the war ended a few months early.

Months, even weeks, made a difference. Another series of negotiations between Himmler and the Swedish count Folke Bernadotte, a diplomat and the head of the Swedish Red Cross during the war, led to the release of the 423 Danish Jews in Terezín.[34] "I hear the world-shaking news: the Danes are going home at eight o'clock this evening," Pavel rejoiced on April 15. "When we look out of the window, we see Swedish soldiers. They are all smiling and one of them waves a closed fist at us indicating that we should not despair. I am delirious with joy!" Buses painted white with a large red cross on each side to

Nešar *cover, March 7, 1944*

Nešar *contents page, March 7, 1944; note that three of the four articles are by Pavel Weiner*

ensure instant recognition as noncombatant vehicles stood ready to evacuate the Danes. Ambulances flanked the buses. And they were needed. For a number of prisoners, malnourished and ill, evacuation just weeks before Germany surrendered (May 8, 1945) meant the difference between life and death. For Pavel, it was a taste "of Freedom."

If Pavel's diary served solely to provide a boy's perspective on events of historical significance, it would be a remarkable document. It does more than that, however. No one was keeping records of the internal lives of youngsters; there is no archive of material on how they perceived the world they inhabited and the strategies they employed to manage it. Thus, every child's diary that survived is a rare and very valuable historical source. Through the pages of Pavel's journal, we learn about the daily life of a young boy in a Nazi transit camp. We learn about his hopes and fears, his ambitions and his worries. He reported what loomed large for him and we read how he negotiated the difficulties he faced.

Food, education, *Nešar* (the magazine he founded and edited), its competition, *Rim, Rim, Rim,* his parents, the boys in room 7, and his *madrich,* Franta Maier, claim his first entry (April 4, 1944). And he pursued these topics throughout the year. Indeed, reading his discus-

Page in Nešar *(March 7, 1944) showing a photograph of Tomáš Masaryk (first president of the newly founded Czechoslovakia after World War I)*

First page of *"Tomáš Masaryk" (article by Pavel Weiner in* Nešar, *March 7, 1944)*

sions of meals and snacks, one would think that food was abundant in Terezín. Yet it is precisely because it was *not* that Pavel focused on it. Always on the lookout for a second helping or some variety in the endlessly repetitive and meager diet, Pavel managed the utterly improbable: he left Terezín with more flesh on his bones than when he entered. Similarly, he was fiercely determined to continue his education. The Jewish administration policies and practices supported his ambitions, as did the social culture of the camp in general and his parents in particular. Still, the energy and drive came from him. He reported in detail on the subjects he studied and the private lessons he enjoyed. His parents paid with food for English-language tutorials and piano instruction for him, and he begged his mother to teach him French. No matter how much he did, he worried that it was not enough. "Two years of my life have been lost," he lamented on August 4, 1944. "If I were in Prague, I would be going to theaters, I would read, I would write. But here I have no materials, no opportunity, and no freedom." He resolved: "I will start leading a new life. . . . I will study, read, and study some more."

Yet, as his diary records, not only had he been studying and reading, he had been writing, too. He had founded a magazine that, as the room 7 boys called themselves *nešarim* (eagles), he named *Nešar.*

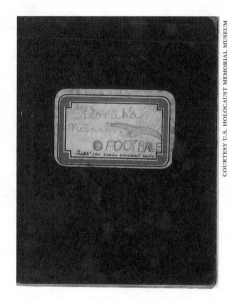

Pavel Weiner's "Nešarim Soccer Chronicle,"
with a picture of the boys' emblem, a soaring
eagle

Producing the illustrated magazine channeled his energy: writing articles, serving as editor, and encouraging other boys to produce material for it. "I am glad my exams are over and I can devote all my time to *Nešar*," he wrote on April 4, 1944. "Today I am experiencing a serious crisis with the magazine. There are very few contributions and my head is empty. However, I manage to write two articles: 'Death on the Ship' and 'The Sick Man.'" Work on the magazine at one and the same time prompted him to pay attention to life in Terezín in order to write about it and, busy with creative production, inured him to it.[35]

The endeavor lurched from struggle to struggle—for good pieces, for readership, for drawings—yet Pavel managed to produce thirteen issues.[36] He spoke of it with pride sixty-five years later. *Nešar*, he said, was like the *New York Review of Books*. The competition, *Rim, Rim, Rim*, was the *New York Post*. One aimed for high culture; the other was popular for its sports reports.[37] The initiative reflected his goals and ambitions. Despite incarceration, and notwithstanding the human resources problem of persuading others to participate and the practical obstacles of obtaining paper and writing instruments, Pavel pressed forward. He set his sights on "life after." And in the meantime, he sought to produce some simulacrum of normality.

The Germans' construction of Terezín as a model ghetto served Pavel well in this regard. One of the institutions their fantasy supported was the camp library. Opened in the fall of 1942, it initially

COURTESY U.S. HOLOCAUST MEMORIAL MUSEUM

Title page of Pavel Weiner's "Nešarim Soccer Chronicle"

"Nešarim" is written in Hebrew; the English word "GOAL!" headlines the picture of a point as it is scored; the magazine title *Rim, Rim, Rim* runs across the left corner; and the cheer "Tempo Nešarim!" ("Go, go, go, Nešarim!") is at the bottom right.

held some five thousand volumes. The collection grew to over fifty thousand as the regime shipped books to Terezín from closed and confiscated Jewish libraries and private collections. Possibly the only library in greater Germany to offer works by banned Jewish authors (it held nearly six hundred copies of the beloved and banned poet Heinrich Heine's poems), the Terezín collection covered a wide range of subjects.[38] Pavel turned to the camp library to research articles, for books to read, and in search of a quiet place to study. As Pavel's diary indicates, others did too. "I suggest to Leo Beran [another room 7 boy] that we write an article together," he reported on April 5, 1944. "We go to the library, which is crowded. I find an encyclopedia and after a short search, I locate an entry on 'World War.' I think it is a good source for our article." In Terezín, as elsewhere, youngsters sometimes had to fight for the books they wanted. "I go to the library to borrow a French book," he recorded (April 20). "I have to argue in the library, but finally they lend me a book. Immediately, I hurry to my mother. We study for about half an hour. I have to study the new vocabulary."

Dedicated as Pavel was to education and *Nešar*, he was equally enthusiastic about soccer. No star player, he was passionate about the sport nevertheless, eagerly joining pickup games on the *bašta* and happily cheering the teams he favored. The administrative departments and Zionist organizations in Terezín fielded their own squads,

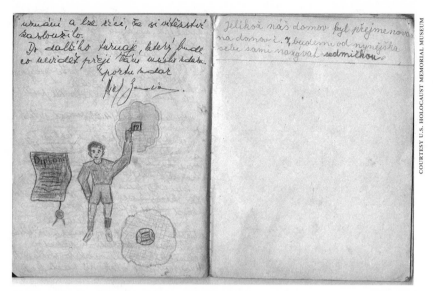

The personification of victory (with a Star of David on the boy's shirt)

and Pavel noted the scores of dozens of matches. By September he had grown so determined to improve as a player that he sought a coach. "After a short while playing with a rag ball, I return home with Mangl [a room 7 friend]. We make our beds and agree that today we have to find a coach." Both talent and equipment were required. "We like Soridek from Hagibor, who also owns a ball," he observed with satisfaction (September 7). It turned out that Soridek had no ball. Disappointed but undaunted, the boys went through a series of leads before, Pavel reported, "we manage to get Mr. Heller to be our coach" (September 13).

If food, education, *Nešar,* and soccer kept Pavel occupied, his relationships with the other boys, Franta, his parents, and his mother in particular, were the lifeblood of his existence. In 1944, Pavel quarreled regularly with everybody. The boy who emerges from the diary was nothing like the even-tempered, good-natured, well-liked adult he became. He adored Franta, and felt slighted when the *madrich* appeared to favor another. He sought friendship, and felt hurt when the other boy seemed to choose someone else's company. His father annoyed him, even while Pavel worried mightily about his health. And he fought with his mother about everything: what he ate; what he wore; what he did; what *she* did; what *she* said. Yet he wanted nothing more than her love and approval. "I go to my mother's in order to study French. When I arrive at my mother's, she refuses to teach me. I am very angry," he raged (April 29). The underlying cause of his distress tumbled out. "It comes to a point when even my mother doesn't believe in me. I feel miserable. It affects my whole disposition. I feel totally abandoned. The worst is when I have an argument with my parents. I am unhappy." Yet, "I don't listen to my mother."

He was, after all, an adolescent. He suffered from the mood swings, self-doubts, and self-absorption so characteristic of that stage of life. Then too, he was incarcerated with no release date in view, and he craved freedom. Working in the central warehouse in the fall of 1944, he had the opportunity to "leave the Ghetto. I look above, on the ground, and all around. I look at the horses, at the bicycles, at the mud, at the German signs, at the sky, at the buildings, in short, at everything. Even then, I cannot grasp it all. Freedom is something else than sitting around in the Ghetto. Freedom is something one fights for and dies for!" (November 30). The language reflects his age, but it also captures his situation. Pavel had no freedom. Indeed, he barely had any space to himself at all. Trapped behind the camp walls, he lived in a room crammed with boys: three-tiered bunks lined the walls, and a table with wooden benches ran down the center. "The small living space has a great effect on me," he lamented (April 29, 1944).

Pavel lived on two levels, at once absorbing the horror of camp existence and focusing on other matters, or at least internally moving himself away from that assault. After hearing about a transport, he wrote, "I meet my parents and go for a walk with them. We talk about the question of transports. We admire the beauty of Terezín's nature" (May 11, 1944). Describing nightmarish scenes as the elderly and mentally ill prepare for deportation, he shifted in a few lines from "It is the worst" to "I am so bored that I go to Mother's and write in my diary. I meet Gustl [a room 7 boy] and I go to play rag ball with him in the yard" (May 14). Did he observe faithfully or was he comforting himself with the observation: "Soon, all traces of the transport disappear and everything comes back to normal" (May 18)? And when his father and brother were deported, he admitted with astonishing honesty, "I can't wait until they start loading because I want to have all the farewells behind me." Trapped in the maelstrom, he realized that "the situation keeps changing and so do my emotions" (September [25]).

Pavel's diary lays bare the maturation of a twelve-year-old boy through his Bar Mitzvah year at a particular time and in a particular place. As he neared his thirteenth birthday, he began to actualize his insights into actions. Perhaps age accounted for this development. Possibly it was due to events. In one month, from September 27 through October 28, the Germans shipped 18,422 people to Auschwitz. Pavel and his mother were spared because she worked in the *Glimmer* (mica) industry, which the Germans considered essential to their war effort. The deportations emptied the camp and Pavel, still subject to adolescent turmoil, nevertheless gained greater perspective. "The impact of the circumstances affects one so much that one doesn't know what he is doing and tends to vent one's feelings to the nearest person—in my case, it is my mother even though I love her." He began to outgrow the urge to express his anxiety as anger. "This argument quiets down shortly because love toward Mother overtakes me and I calm down." At core, he acknowledged (October 14), "I see in my mother the only friend I have."

It was a pivotal realization. Describing his mother, Pavel's words and tone changed. "I feel sorry for her that she works so hard," he wrote the next day. He walked "through the empty streets." Despair overwhelmed him. "I can see only darkness and in this darkness there is only one bright spot and that is my mother." They continued to quarrel, of course. But he had begun to grow up. The adult this young person would become glimmers in his entries. "I'm only thirteen years old and I can already independently form my views about the world," he reflected on New Year's Eve, 1944. "I have grasped what life is about, which is the principal matter and also the most difficult one."

The now much reduced camp population worked and waited during the winter and early spring of 1945. They yearned for the end, and they feared the Germans would murder them, leaving no one alive to tell what had transpired in Terezín. News about the front traveled quickly. Pavel followed the Soviets' advance from the east and the Allies in the west. "Now the Allies have occupied all of Germany and Austria, all the way to Leipzig," he exulted on April 15. "Now, the end can be expected at any minute. The mood here is marvelous." Still, he was concerned. "The Germans are furious. I only hope that they will not take out their last anger on us." Happily, they did not.

Trainloads of ill and emaciated survivors of death and labor camps arrived in Terezín, shipped west by the Germans that spring. "The people from the transports have brought with them some awful news which we cannot believe: All children twelve years and under and all people sixty-five years and older have been gassed. Only those capable of work were not killed. What are our grandmother and grandfather doing, and all the boys from Room 7?" Pavel worried in his last diary entry on April 22, 1945.

The Germans fled Terezín and the International Red Cross took the camp under its protection. Pavel and his mother returned to Prague. He had his diary and issues of *Nešar* with him.

Pavel and Valy waited for Ludvík and Handa in vain. Ludvík had died in Kaufering, a subcamp of Dachau, in December 1944; Handa, with him until the end, shortly thereafter, in January 1945.

Pavel forgot about his diary in the maelstrom of the postwar period. Busy with reconstructing their lives, he and his mother had far more pressing matters on their minds. But Valy put the diary and *Nešar* issues away for safekeeping. And they were kept safe: Paul rediscovered his papers in 1979 when he moved Valy from Washington, D.C., to New York, where he and his wife and daughter lived. No one, he recalled decades later, was more astonished than he. Translating his diary into English took Paul many years and, as it is his work, adds another layer of authenticity to the voice we read. When Paul died in January 2010, his daughter, Karen Weiner, took on her father's task. Preparing the diary for publication, she deleted repetitions. But the text remains the adult Paul's translation of Pavel's original text. And the original documents, gifted by Paul to the United States Holocaust Memorial Museum, are now safe forever.

Notes

1. There is some confusion in the literature with regard to the statistics pertaining to children. Thus, for example, in the epilogue to the very lovely . . . *I Never Saw Another Butterfly* . . . (New York: Schocken, 1978), Jiří Weil notes that "there were 15,000 of them [children] and 100 came back" (61). An entire page (81) is devoted to the presentation of this statistic. Above a child's drawing of a flower and a butterfly the following information appears: "A total of around 15,000 children under the age of 15 passed through Terezín. Of these, around 100 came back." From these sentences it would be logical to assume that approximately 15,000 children were deported to Theresienstadt, and only 100 survived. Many writers have made that deduction, and these figures are often adduced. For instance, Inge Auerbacher explains in her autobiographical memoir, *I Am a Star* (New York: Prentice-Hall, 1986): "Of fifteen thousand children imprisoned in Terezín between 1941 and 1945, about 100 survived. I am one of them" (1). The introduction to *Terezín,* published by the Council of Jewish Communities in

the Czech Lands (Prague, 1965), offers a variation on these figures: "The transports [out of Terezín, to the east] included also 15,000 children, of whom less than 150 returned" (5).

This interpretation is incorrect. In *Theresienstadt 1941–1945: Das Antlitz einer Zwangsgemeinschaft* (Tübingen: J. C. B. Mohr/Paul Siebeck, 1960), H. G. Adler presents a different set of figures which, coincidentally, help to explain the source of the original error (see 37–60). According to Adler, 6,588 children were transported out of Theresienstadt and of those only 100 lived to see liberation; Adler believed that all of the survivors were between fourteen and sixteen years old. However, 7,407 children under the age of fifteen were transported into Theresienstadt. Furthermore, a certain number (probably quite small) were born in the transit center. An entire transport of children from Białystok mysteriously arrived in Theresienstadt and not so mysteriously disappeared again. Adler figured that the Białystok children brought the total number to about 10,000 youngsters. To this, he added 2,000 to account for the fifteen- and sixteen-year-olds. In other words, according to Adler, there were 12,000 children in Theresienstadt at one time or another. At the end of October 1944, there were 819 children still in Terezín; more arrived thereafter. When Terezín was liberated, there were 1,633 children under fifteen years old (572–73). See also Zdenek Lederer, *Ghetto Theresienstadt* (London: Edward Goldston, 1953), 263.

2. Paul Weiner, oral history conducted by Debórah Dwork, New York, N.Y., January 7 and 11, 2010.

3. Ibid.

4. Ibid.

5. Quoted in Vojtech Mastny, *The Czechs Under Nazi Rule: The Failure of National Resistance, 1939–42* (New York and London: Columbia University Press, 1971), 21.

6. See Debórah Dwork and Robert Jan van Pelt, *Holocaust* (New York: W. W. Norton, 2002), 135–45.

7. U.S. Department of State, *Documents on German Foreign Policy, 1918–1945*, series D, 12 vols. (Washington, D.C.: U.S. Government Printing Office, 1949–62), 4:270.

8. Ibid., 4:283ff.

9. Oral history of Paul Weiner.

10. Ibid.

11. Ibid.

12. Ibid.

13. Peter Longerich, *Politik der Vernichtung: Eine Gesamtdarstellung der nationalsozialistischen Judenverfolgung* (Munich: Piper, 1998), 493ff., 513ff.

14. Lederer, *Ghetto Theresienstadt*, 13–14.

15. Miroslava Benešová, Vojtěch Blodig, and Marek Poloncarz, *The Small Fortress Terezín, 1940–1945* (Terezín: Terezín Memorial, 1996); Táňa Kulišova, *Terezín, Little Fortress* (Prague: Union of Anti-Fascist Fighters, 1953).

16. Raul Hilberg, *The Destruction of the European Jews* (New Haven and London: Yale University Press, 2003), 2:430ff.

17. Lederer, *Ghetto Theresienstadt*, 14–15.

18. See, among others, Ruth Bondy, *"Elder of the Jews": Jakob Edelstein of Theresienstadt* (New York: Grove Press, 1989), 252–65.

19. Oral history of Paul Weiner.

20. See Thelma Gruenbaum, *Nešarim: Child Survivors of Terezín* (London and Portland, Ore.: Vallentine Mitchell, 2004) for interviews of surviving room 7 boys.

21. See Hilberg, *Destruction of the European Jews,* 2:430ff.; Lederer, *Ghetto Theresienstadt,* 8ff.

22. Adler, *Theresienstadt,* 47–48; see also Adler's extended discussion of these statistics (37ff.).

23. Adler, *Theresienstadt,* 547–48, 560, 562; Council of Jewish Communities, *Terezín,* 78, 93; Lederer, *Ghetto Theresienstadt,* 41, 47, 97, 132–33, 137. Rabbi Leo Baeck was the last head of the *Jugendfuersorge.* For a first-hand account by Gonda Redlich, head of the *Jugendfuersorge,* see Saul S. Friedman, ed., *The Terezín Diary of Gonda Redlich* (Lexington: University Press of Kentucky, 1992).

24. Oral history of Paul Weiner.

25. For more on Jewish child life in transit camps in general, and Terezín in particular, see Debórah Dwork, *Children with a Star: Jewish Youth in Nazi Europe* (New Haven and London: Yale University Press, 1991), 113–53. See also Hannelore Brenner, *The Girls of Room 28: Friendship, Hope, and Survival in Theresienstadt* (New York: Schocken Books, 2009), for a discussion of the Czech girls' counterpart *heim.*

26. For more about music in Terezín, see Joža Karas, *Music in Terezín, 1941–1945* (New York: Beaufort Books, 1985), and Mariánka May and Debórah Dwork, *The Terezín Album of Mariánka Zadikow* (Chicago and London: University of Chicago Press, 2008).

27. See, among others, Rebecca Rovit, "The 'Brundibár' Project: Memorializing Theresienstadt Children's Opera," *Performing Arts Journal* 22, no. 2 (May 2000), 111–22.

28. For a study of the diary, see Tomáš Fedorovič, "Deník Pavla Weinera," *Terezínské listy* (Prague: Památník Terezín, 2003), 63–88.

29. See Debórah Dwork and Robert Jan van Pelt, *Auschwitz* (New York: W. W. Norton, 2008), 340–41; Nili Keren, "The Family Camp," in *Anatomy of the Auschwitz Death Camp,* ed. Yisrael Gutman and Michael Berenbaum, 428–40 (Bloomington: Indiana University Press, 1994).

30. For another first-person discussion of the beautification campaign, see Philipp Manes, *As If It Were Life: A WWII Diary from the Theresienstadt Ghetto,* ed. Ben Barkow and Klaus Leist, 167–76 (New York: Palgrave Macmillan, 2009).

31. Jean-Claude Favez, *The Red Cross and the Holocaust* (Cambridge: Cambridge University Press, 1999), 43–45, 72–74.

32. For more on the artists and the painters' affair, see Anne Dutlinger, ed., *Art, Music, and Education as Strategies for Survival: Theresienstadt, 1941–1945* (New York and London: Herodias, 2001); Gerald Green, *The Artists of Terezín* (New York: Hawthorn Books, 1978); Marjorie Lamberti, "Making Art in the Terezín Concentration Camp," *New England Review* 17, no. 4 (Fall 1995), 104–11; Massachusetts College of Art, *Seeing Through "Paradise": Artists and the Terezín Concentration Camp* (Boston: Massachusetts College of Art, 1991). Leo Haas and Norbert Troller wrote about their ordeal: Leo Haas, "The Affair of the Painters of Terezín," in Council of Jewish Communities in the Czech Lands, *Terezín,* 156–61; Norbert Troller, *Theresienstadt: Hitler's Gift to the Jews* (Chapel Hill and London: University of North Carolina Press, 1991).

33. See Hans Hofer, "The Film About Terezín," in Council of Jewish Communities in the Czech Lands, *Terezín,* 181–84.

34. For more on this, see Sune Persson, "Folke Bernadotte and the White Buses," in *"Bystanders" to the Holocaust: A Re-evaluation,* ed. David Cesarani and Paul A. Levine, 237–68 (London and Portland, Ore.: Frank Cass, 2002).

35. See Marie Rút Křížková, Kurt Jiří Kotouč, and Zdeněk Ornest, eds., *We Are Children Just the Same: "Vedem," the Secret Magazine of the Boys of Terezín* (Philadelphia and Jerusalem: The Jewish Publication Society, 1995), to learn about *Vedem,* the magazine edited by Petr Ginz in room 1 of L417.

36. According to a poem by Jiří Bloch (Blecha) written at the time, *Nešar* ran to thirteen issues. I thank Michael (Míša) Gruenbaum for sending me a copy of Jiří Bloch's poem, which would have been lost like Sasha Schweinburg's diary but for Míša. "When I was in Terezín I scribbled this poem into a small notebook and after we were liberated I carried it with me along with other 'souvenirs' when we traveled from Prague through Paris to Cuba and finally to the USA," Míša explained to me. When the surviving room 7 boys decided to hold the first *nešarim* reunion, he "sent it to Hanuš Holzer who lives in Switzerland and he, together with Erich Spitz who lives in France, had it printed and made into a small booklet. We asked Helga Hoskova to make some illustrations for it and they became part of the booklet" (email communication, August 26, 2010). Míša no longer recalls how he came to see the poem originally or what the original looked like.

37. Oral history of Paul Weiner.

38. For more on the library, see George E. Berkley, *Hitler's Gift: The Story of Theresienstadt* (Boston: Branden Books, 1993), 139–40; Miriam Intrator, "Avenues of Intellectual Resistance in the Ghetto Theresienstadt: Escape Through the Ghetto Central Library, Reading, Storytelling, and Lecturing" (M.A. thesis, University of North Carolina, Chapel Hill, April 2003).

A BOY IN TEREZÍN

DIARY of PAVEL WEINER

WRITTEN IN TEREZÍN

April 1944 to April 1945

A Note on the Text

The text of the diary is Paul Weiner's translation from the original Czech; it was then edited by Karen Weiner to delete unclear references, repetitions, and illegible sentences. Edits also include corrections of misspelled, awkward, and transposed words, but the content of the diary has been preserved throughout. Bracketed text within the diary indicates Debórah Dwork's insertions (to identify people, correct dates, or supply translations). The exceptions to this practice are bracketed question marks, questioned words, or indications of illegible or missing words; these notes were inserted by Paul Weiner when he translated his childhood diary. Paul Weiner's editorial insertions while translating the diary are identified by his initials.

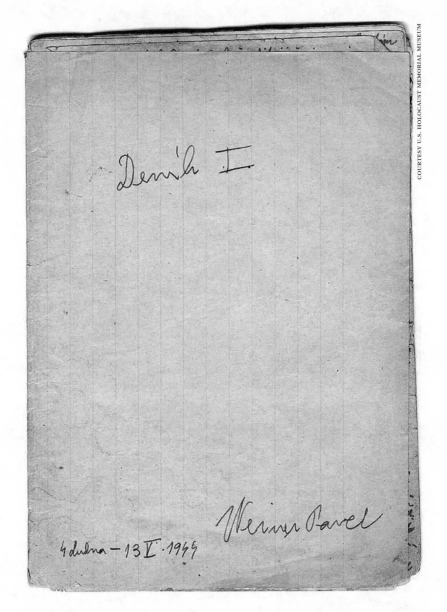

Cover page of the first volume of the diary: "Diary I, 4 April – 13 May 1944, Weiner Pavel"

Pavel recorded his diary in a series of notebooks. He wrote his surname first, as customary in central Europe.

Vydržet ! ! !

Úterý dne 4. dubna 1944.

First page of "Diary I"; note the closely written text

Volume 1

Introduction

Now after having spent two years in Terezín, I deeply regret that I haven't kept a diary from the beginning. Wouldn't it be the best remembrance of a life which is characterized in a very harsh light? Terezín offers the best opportunity to keep up a diary. Here one gets to know the harder side of life; one's mother doesn't keep you pampered. One tends to see things with eyes wide open. I realize that Sasha's[1] undertaking of writing a diary is good and, therefore, I have decided to write one myself. I hope that I will be successful and that my diary will fulfill its purpose! Let's keep it up!!!

Let's keep it up!!!

Tuesday, 4 April 1944

Today the daylight savings time goes into effect. At midnight we reset the clock by one hour. The only disadvantage is that today is housekeeping and we have to get up at six o'clock regardless of the new time. That means five o'clock daylight time. We are saved by Mrs. Mautner,[2] who lets us sleep until seven. I don't know why, but Mrs. Mautner is very angry and hurries us. We receive ten tickets for bathing, but I am not interested because I have a cold. I am glad my exams are over

1. Born May 8, 1930, Alexandr Schweinburg (nicknamed Sasha or Sása) was assigned number 532 and deported with transport L on December 10, 1941, from Prague to Terezín. He was among the room 7 boys selected for deportation to Auschwitz with convoy En (his number: 1313) on October 10, 1944. Alexandr did not survive.
2. Marie Mautner (b. June 18, 1908) served as an assistant to Franta Maier (see note 4), the *madrich* (counselor or youth leader) of room 7. Mother of Jiří and Pavel Mautner (see note 61), she was deported with her sons from Tábor to Terezín on transport Bz; her number: 247. Assigned number 246, Mrs. Mautner was shipped to Auschwitz with her sons on October 12, 1944, with transport Eq. She did not survive.

and I can devote all my time to *Nešar*.[3] Today I am experiencing a serious crisis with the magazine. There are very few contributions and my head is empty. However, I manage to write two articles: "Death on the Ship" and "The Sick Man." When housekeeping is over, I get a coupon for the washroom for 12:30. I don't go though, because my father advises against it. I spend the morning listening to exams in class 2B. I find out that I am not missing much. As was previously agreed, I am supposed to bring lunch for my mother. First, I visit my father and I can see that his health has improved because he went to see a doctor. The whole morning it is raining heavily. Later, I pick up my luncheon dishes in the barracks. There is a very long food line at the Hannover Barracks. I join the line in the back and I watch old women. I leave through the back entrance so I can deliver the lunch to my mother as quickly as possible. I find her all alone. She refuses the lunch and therefore I return it. She stuffs my pockets full with matzos. I am a bit scared that they will catch me, but all turns out well. As always, I do my English homework five minutes before the lesson starts. I am interrupted by Franta's[4] arrival. It just happens that he is in a good mood. We agree on who is going to do the scrubbing. Franta announces that this evening we will have a phonograph performance. We have to be in bed by nine o'clock. They give out tickets for a Beethoven concert, which I unfortunately miss. I finish my English homework and learn the vocabulary. I want to go to the library to write something, but it is closed. When I return, I get ready for my lesson, which, to my delight, takes place. I chat with Sasha about Lion[5] and about the diary. I am surprised by a Christmas cake, which we receive as a special ration in the *heim* [home, meaning room 7]. I chat with Brenner[6] and start to write my diary. Unfortunately, I have

3. One of the two magazines written by the boys in room 7, *Nešar* was edited by Pavel. The U.S. Holocaust Memorial Museum collection holds two issues of *Nešar*, one of which is a "special" on the Nešarim soccer team (see illustrations on pages xxxiv–xxxvi).

4. František Maier (called Franta) was the beloved *madrich* of the room 7 boys. Born on May 17, 1922, Franta was just shy of his twentieth birthday when he was deported on March 19, 1942, from his hometown of Brno (Brünn in German) to Terezín on transport Ac (his number: 935). Sent to Auschwitz on September 28, 1944, on transport Ek (number 505), Franta survived to be liberated in the subcamp of Gleiwitz. He immigrated to the United States after the war. According to Paul's later recollections (see the introduction), Franta's discipline, affection, and attentiveness protected the room 7 boys from much of the misery of Terezín daily life.

5. Pavel Lion, a room 7 boy, was born on July 24, 1930. Deported from Prague to Terezín with transport M (his number: 27) on December 14, 1941, he was sent to Auschwitz with convoy Eq (number 406) on October 12, 1944. He did not survive.

6. Hanuš Brenner, nicknamed Brena, was born on December 16, 1929. He was deported from Prague to Terezín on December 17, 1941, with transport N and assigned num-

to finish because Franta comes to give an exam in singing. During the exam I get angry because Franta keeps saying that I have lost my pitch. I am very worried, but I pass the exam. After the exam, I go with Lamm[7] for *geback* [pastry]. I have my dinner and then write in my diary. After that, I talk with my parents about Prague. Unfortunately, it is only an illusion and a memory. I should point out that I am not on speaking terms with Kalíšek.[8] He is now very indifferent. Nothing noteworthy happens today. I accompany my father home. Some boys start to disgust me—for example, Kapr,[9] Kalíšek, and Pedro.[10] I am very disgusted that *Rim, Rim*[11] is all written up. We must get on the ball! Shortly before nine o'clock, Franta announces the cancellation of the phonograph concert. He has to go to a meeting and asks us to go to bed. I chat with Kalíšek. Soon Franta returns to announce housekeeping reforms. Kalíšek gets three days of housekeeping. In bed I finish writing an article called "Prisoner." When the lights are turned off, I cough heavily and feel cold. In fifteen minutes I fall asleep.

Wednesday, 5 April 1944

Alarm today is at seven a.m. Mrs. Mautner wakes us up. I want to stay in bed because I have a headache, but I am not allowed. I am not sorry once I get up, as outside it is warm and pleasant. I have to confess that today I do not air my bed linen. Last night I was assigned to housekeeping, but fortunately it is called off. I am worried about the magazine, and I bring the contributions to Brenner. It is evident

ber 513. A room 7 boy, he was sent on to Auschwitz (convoy Eo; number 948) nearly three years later, on October 6, 1944, where he perished.

7. A room 7 boy, Bedřich Lamm was born on January 23, 1930, and deported from Olomouc (Olmütz in German) to Terezín with transport AAm (his number: 654) on July 4, 1942. He was sent to Auschwitz on May 18, 1944, with convoy Eb as number 634. Bedřich did not survive.

8. Karel Klein, called Kalíšek or Kalí, was one of Pavel's dearest friends among the room 7 boys. Born July 11, 1931, Kalíšek (number 222) was deported from Plzeň (Pilsen in German) to Terezín on January 26, 1942, with transport T. He, number 708, was sent to Auschwitz with convoy Ev on October 28, 1944; he did not survive.

9. Jiří Ruzek, called Kapr (carp), was born on March 14, 1931. He was assigned number 968 and deported from Prague to Terezín with transport N on December 17, 1941. Assigned to room 7, Kapr survived to be liberated in Terezín. He returned to Prague and remained in Czechoslovakia after the war.

10. Born in Prague on September 17, 1930, Petr Lederer (nicknamed Pedro) was deported to Terezín on December 10, 1941, with transport L (his number: 317). He was assigned to room 7 and was liberated in Terezín. Pedro returned to Prague, studied textile engineering, and remained in Czechoslovakia.

11. Pavel refers to the other magazine produced in room 7 as *Rim, Rim* or simply *Rim*.

that Brenner doesn't feel like writing. He does not agree with the contributions but nevertheless, he promises to write three articles. I doubt that I will ever see them. *Apel* [assembly, from the German *Appell*] is more or less uneventful. A little disagreement occurs between Robin[12] and me because he refuses to write an article called "Book." I would be glad if the editorial staff was reduced. *Nešar* does not need any critics. I suggest to Leo Beran[13] that we write an article together. He accepts and therefore we go to the library, which is crowded. I find an encyclopedia and after a short search, I locate an entry on "World War." I think it is a good source for our article. At noon I go for lunch, which consists of potatoes and *tunke* [thin gravy with no nutritional value]. I am not satisfied with it. I am finding out that Kalíšek is a false friend. I will talk to him, but I don't feel close to him anymore. I discuss the importance of language with Sasha. I like him and want to ask for his advice. He is not as flighty as others. I go to Brenner, but he still doesn't have one single article. I'm furious with him! If I could, I would write everything myself. Housekeeping is again canceled. During *Apel,* they give out tickets to a Beethoven concert and I manage to get one. After *Apel,* we have a rehearsal for *Nebuchadnezar.* It doesn't interest me much. At three o'clock the concert starts. I pick myself up and hurry with Sasha into the Hamburg Barracks. For a while we roam through the barracks and soon we find the room where the concert takes place. I get into an argument with one of the boys. At the concert, B. Koff plays the piano and H. Taussig the violin.[14] They play "Spring Sonata" and "Thirty-two Variations." It is quite short and I have heard better playing before. At four o'clock,

12. Robin (officially Robert Herz), his brother Macek (see entry for May 13, 1944), and their parents were deported to Terezín on March 29, 1942, with transport Ae (his number: 998) from Brno. Robin (nicknamed Biblu) was assigned to room 7; Macek, eleven months older, was in the room next door. Robin, Macek, and Jan Strebinger (Gorila; see note 27) were shipped to Auschwitz with convoy Eb (Robin's number: 380) on May 18, 1944, and were among those force-marched west when the Germans abandoned Auschwitz in January 1945. Robin and Jan were liberated by the American Seventy-first Infantry Division in Gunskirchen, a subcamp of Mauthausen (Austria) on May 4, 1945. Macek was no longer with them, but he survived as well; their parents did not. Robin immigrated to Canada in 1948.

13. Leo Beran (b. September 14, 1930), called Leoš, was assigned number 285 and shipped from Třebíč to Terezín with convoy Av on May 18, 1942. A room 7 boy, he died, presumably in Auschwitz, to which he was sent on October 23, 1944, with transport Et (his number: 1106), along with his mother and sister (see also note 160).

14. Heinrich Taussig was born October 20, 1923. A member of the Terezín Quartet, he was deported in 1944 to Auschwitz, where he died.

I return to the *heim* with Sasha and Beran. We discuss food. I laze around, and then I get dressed, take my diary and fountain pen and go to my father. He is on his way to get supper. I ask my father to fill my pen with ink and I get my wish. My father gives me a *buchta* [bun or roll, typically with jam filling] to bring to my mother and then leaves for supper. My mother is not at home. The women in Mother's barracks complain that I have not as yet shown them the magazines. I have to do so. I'm told that my mother is in the bathhouse. Sure enough, I meet her there. We go together for dinner and we talk a little. For dinner we have soup and a small *geback*. It seems that I will learn French with my mother. I'm delighted! Soon my father arrives. We have a good Linzer tart. Handa[15] also arrives. We decide to go for a walk, and then we make tea and leave. We discuss the overall stay in Terezín. Via a detour, I return to the School.[16] I am quite sad; I would like to tear myself apart. I hate the world around me, particularly Robin, Brenner, Kalíšek, and Gustl.[17] They laugh at me, particularly Kalíšek, because of my thinking. Envy! Robin doesn't keep his word to write an article. Brenner hasn't even written his first article. I think that I will write it myself. If I make up my mind, I can do it. I'll have to. Now there will be a rehearsal for the play *Nebuchadnezar*. I have an argument with Gustl. After the rehearsal, there should have been a reading from the poet Wolker,[18] but it doesn't happen. While thinking, I fall asleep.

Thursday, 6 April 1944

Yesterday Franta promised us that we could stay longer in bed today. Because of Mrs. Mautner's mistake, it doesn't happen that way. She comes to wake us up but then agrees that we can stay in bed until eight. I don't have house duty! After I put my things in order, I drop in on Brenner. I am pleasantly surprised as he has started to write.

15. Pavel's older brother, Hanuš, nicknamed Handa (b. June 9, 1927).

16. Pavel called L417, the children's home for Czech boys, "the School" in his diary. The building had functioned as a school prior to the establishment of the Ghetto.

17. Gustl Stein (also called Gustav, Gusta, and Gustla) was born on August 10, 1930, and deported to Terezín from Plzeň on transport S (his number: 440). A room 7 boy, he was shipped to Auschwitz on October 6, 1944, with convoy Eo, number 871. Gustl did not survive.

18. Jiří Wolker (b. March 29, 1900) was a well-known Czech poet and playwright and a founding member of the Communist Party of Czechoslovakia. He died at a very young age (on January 3, 1924) from lung disease.

He already has two articles written. Progress! He promises to write more. Since Gustl had an argument with Herz about a shelf, I have to return his shelf to Gustl. I have a big *bordel* [from the German *bordell*, or brothel; meaning a big mess or uproar] on my shelf. I have to find a new one. I have a sharp but short discussion with Robin about writing an article. It is successful because he decides to go to the library to write. Since Franta does not show up at *Apel*, it is canceled. Later on I decide to go to the library. I intend to write about the history of Serbia. Because the library doesn't have anything about it, I borrow the biography of Antonín Dvořák instead. I exchange two books: *The Count of Monte Christo* and *Desert and* [illegible]. I also ask about borrowing a French textbook. At noon, I return to the School to find that a surprise *Apel* has been called for the whole School. Everybody is already there. Otík[19] blows his horn again. He cancels all festivities and musical performances relating to the end of the semester. Really, it is disappointing to me because I had a chance to receive a prize. As always, I have bad luck. I go for lunch: barley and hamburgers. I save the barley for dinner. After lunch, I go to play soccer. I continue to have sharp pains in my back and left side. I think it is a strained muscle. I make up with Gustl. Kalíšek, however, ignores me and speaks only with Kapr and Grizzly,[20] who returned last night. During the soccer game, I argue with Brenner and Kapr, who are making fun of me. I keep telling myself that I'll have my revenge in another discipline. I find out from Brenner that he still hasn't written an article. I'm furious when I see him calmly playing soccer! The magazine must be ready!! After the soccer game we are called to *Apel*. Franta is not satisfied with it. We read a story by Wolker. It is marvelous, but we don't finish it. Later, I go to play soccer again. I realize that I have become a real soccer "crazy." The editorial staff of *Rim, Rim* annoys me. We must not be pushed around! At five o'clock, I finish playing soccer. I go for supper (*geback*) and I eat it immediately. I bring supper for my mother. At her barracks we eat crepes that are just average. For

19. Otto Klein (b. February 21, 1921), also called Ota and Otík, served as the director of L417. Otík (number 220) was deported from Prague to Terezín with transport J on December 4, 1941, and shipped to Auschwitz three years later with transport Ek (his number: 2306) on September 28, 1944. Liberated in Auschwitz, Otík returned to Prague and worked as a sociologist at the Czechoslovak Academy of Sciences after the war. He died in Paris in 1968.

20. Petr Rindler (b. February 28, 1930), called Grizzly by the room 7 boys, was deported from Prague to Terezín with transport V on January 30, 1942. He was sent on convoy Er to Auschwitz on October 16, 1944. Petr did not survive.

a while I talk with my parents and write my diary, but then I hurry to the *heim* because at eight there is to be a lecture on graphology. Unfortunately, it is canceled. It is a beautiful evening so I go for a walk with Kalíšek and then I go to the *heim*.

Friday, 7 April 1944

Yesterday, it was decided that we could sleep until eight o'clock. Unfortunately, I have house duty, so I still have to get up at 7:45. The weather is not very nice. I have to clean the halls. Due to lack of time I can't air my bed linen. I go to Brenner, who is writing an article. *Apel* was delayed and Franta reminds us that the usual Friday tidiness inspection will take place. It is rumored that a new education program is being organized.[21] After *Apel,* I want to go with the boys to the library. Unfortunately, it is closed until Sunday noon. I return to the *heim* empty-handed. Childishly, I am looking forward to eating a *buchta* filled with cream. The importance of food in Terezín! I don't go for lunch but send Kikina[22] for it. The *buchta* is just so-so. After lunch, I go to Brenner and dictate the magazine article. Finally, we finish it. Now to bind it and illustrate it and my week's work will be finished! We decide that I will go with Zweig[23] for hot water to get washed. Because there is no running water at L408, we have to go all the way to the Magdeburg Barracks. We stand in line for about twenty minutes but it pays off. I wash myself very nicely. I clean my shelf and change into clean clothes. I'm already prepared for the tidiness check. Meanwhile, Gustla finishes the cover and binds the magazine. I am shocked by what Elihu[24] has to say. He says that he will no longer do the illustrations for us; he will work for another magazine. I don't know what to

21. By "program," Pavel means scheduled activities or lessons.

22. Jiří Repper (b. November 13, 1930), called Kikina by the room 7 boys, was deported from his hometown of Brno with convoy Ai (his number: 125) on April 8, 1942, to Terezín, where he remained. Toward the end of the war he contracted meningitis and encephalitis, which was treated by medication smuggled into the camp by a Czech gendarme. Kikina survived and immigrated to Israel (1949) and then to the United States (1952).

23. Gustav Zweig (b. July 31, 1930), nicknamed Tuti or Tutinek by the room 7 boys, was deported on April 8, 1942, from his hometown of Brno to Terezín as number 659 on transport Ai. He was sent to Auschwitz (transport En; number 516) on October 4, 1944, where he died.

24. Gabriel Mühlstein (b. September 18, 1930), whom the room 7 boys called Eli or Elihu, was deported from Prague to Terezín with convoy N (his number: 902) on December 17, 1941. He was shipped to Auschwitz on October 16, 1944, with transport Er (number 1131). Eli did not survive.

do. Shortly, I make up with Gustla. However, with Kalíšek I'm still not on speaking terms. I have a feeling that *Rim, Rim* is up to something, as Hermann[25] and Lion walk around like peacocks. I have to wait until the evening. During the Friday check, nothing special happens except that we talk about an introduction for the Passover celebration that will take place at nine o'clock. Later, I go for two soups because Kopperl[26] gave me his. I go to Mother's, and I am taking the magazines with me. The ninth issue is not so successful. For this reason, I am in a bad mood and I don't behave well toward my parents. My father cannot walk at all. I'm very worried. Hope for our freedom slowly vanishes. I return to the *heim*, where I just loaf around and read the book *Six Heroes from Nome*. The whole day bores me. I can't wait to go to sleep. Finally, Franta arrives and tells us a few stories. They are good! After the festivities tonight, something world-shaking happens: Lion comes out with *Rim, Rim*. I think it will make a good impression, but Lion will not be able to keep it up for long. I keep reminding myself about the end of my article "Envy," and with new energy I'm preparing myself for a fight with the competition. There is a reading of *Rim, Rim* and it's only fair. I am surprised by Gorila's[27] article, "The Will." Perhaps today *Nešar* and *Rim, Rim* are equal. Then I read *Nešar*. I think that two of my articles are successful. At eleven o'clock, I fall asleep. This day has provided me with great awareness.

Saturday, 8 April 1944

On Saturdays we can sleep as long as we wish. I wake up at seven. I open the book, *Six Heroes from Nome,* and read. The book is so-so. At

25. Jan Hermann (b. January 18, 1930), officially known also as Hanuš and nicknamed Mustang or Kuzma by the room 7 boys, was assigned number 596 and deported from Prague on July 2, 1942, with convoy AAl. He was sent to Auschwitz with transport Ev (number 693) on October 28, 1944. Jan did not survive.

26. Rudolf Kopperl (b. July 27, 1930) was called Krysa by the room 7 boys. Deported from České Budějovice (Budweis in German) on April 18, 1942 (number 868 on convoy Akb), Rudolf was sent to Auschwitz with transport Er (number 1003) on October 16, 1944. He did not survive.

27. Jan Strebinger (b. February 7, 1931; listed in the Terezín registry as Jan Hans) was born in Bratislava and, with his parents, moved to Brno and then Prague when the Germans annexed Austria in 1939. Jan (numbered 969) and his parents were deported to Terezín on transport M. Jan, nicknamed Gorila, and Robin Herz were close friends in room 7, and the relationship continued when Robin, Robin's brother Macek, and Gorila were shipped to Auschwitz with transport Eb (Gorila's number: 238) on May 18, 1944. Gorila's parents perished; he and the two Herz brothers survived. Jan and Robin were liberated together in Gunskirchen. A year later (1946), Jan immigrated to England and then to Brazil.

nine o'clock, my mother comes. She brings with her lots of clothing. She has stopped in the attic to bring me my spring clothing. She brings my knickerbockers suit and a pair of running shoes. The weather is beautiful; the sun is warm. I insist on putting on my knee socks. As far as I am concerned, I am right, but I let my mother talk me out of it. After I get dressed, Professor Zwicker[28] arrives and writes down the age of every boy. I hope to get all Excellents. After, I go for a walk with Kalíšek. I should point out that there was an alarm in the School today because of SS Rahm's visit.[29] He was accompanied by the entire Jewish Council. However, he went only into Room 1. There is a rumor that there will be a regular playground installed in our yard. I set out with Kalíšek across the park. We again see Rahm going to the Kavalier Barracks. We are joined by Lion and Herz and we follow in Rahm's footsteps. Rahm goes all over Terezín, including to the ramparts. Of course, we follow him. Soon, we stop following and go for lunch. Today we have farfel and salami. I take the lunch to Mother's, but I am in a bad mood. Mrs. Roubíček gives me a book, but I don't like it and I immediately return it. I return to the *heim* very angry because I am not allowed to wear my knee socks. In this respect, my mother is beyond improvement! I can see that all the children are wearing knee socks—even Tuti and Sasha have them on. My anger reaches such intensity that I pick myself up and hurry to tell my mother that I am going home to put on my suit with knee socks. And I do it! I think that my mother will be shocked, but I have to do it. At home I change into my spring suit and, full of anger, I go for a walk with Kalíšek. Originally, I wanted to go to my mother's, but Kalíšek convinces me just to go for a walk. We walk all the way to the Jaeger Barracks. I feel wonderful. It's a beautiful spring day. We meet Hermann, Gustl, and Pedro. We crawl into a glass house and we play there. We spend a pleasant afternoon. At four o'clock, I go to the *heim*. I stop at my mother's and I announce that I'm going to a soccer game. My mother objects, but I don't listen. I go to the Dresdner Barracks;

28. Bruno Zwicker, Ph.D. (b. February 17, 1907[?]), was deported from Brno to Terezín on March 29, 1942, with transport Ae. Professor Zwicker taught history and geography in Terezín. He was sent to Auschwitz with convoy Ek on September 28, 1944; he did not survive.

29. Three SS officers served as commandant of Terezín: Siegfried Seidl, until July 1943; Anton Burger, July 1943–February 1944; and Karl Rahm, February 1944–May 5, 1945. Pavel wrote his diary during Rahm's regime. Rahm fled Terezín in May 1945. Captured by American forces in Austria, he was extradited to Czechoslovakia, charged with crimes against humanity, and executed on April 30, 1947.

the match is between [illegible] and Hagibor Praha and between Jugendfuersorge[30] and Kadr. Jugendfuersorge loses 4:1. I hurry to my
mother's to have my dinner, but the mood is sad. My father can walk
only with a cane. I feel sorry for him. Soon I return to the *heim* and I
feel sad.

Friday, 14 April 1944

I got my report card today and I have all Excellents and three Sat-
isfactories! I don't know how it happened, but I have not written in
my diary for six days. During these six days a lot of things have happened. I was worried about my magazine, but as it turns out, the worries were needless. I had arguments with many boys, such as Kalíšek,
with whom I have already made up. But with Herz it is serious. Every
day he becomes more obnoxious. He kisses Franta's ass. He is not at
all concerned about the magazine. This should not concern me. He
does not even know what's in the tenth issue. It is not my fault. If he
were to come to me nicely, I would explain to him everything but I
don't speak to him at all. I don't care. Another thing that occurred
was an exam with Berman.[31] I was accepted to play the recorder, but I
didn't pass the singing because I was awfully hoarse. Some idiot, who
didn't even know how to play the piano well, gave me the exam. I feel
dejected. My father's state of health scares me. He cannot walk well
and he doesn't hear well. I feel sorry for him and at the same time
I'm furious because it has to be *my* dad who is stricken. Every evening,
I get furious and I return to the *heim* with disgust. Now, I realize that
I behave badly and that I better shape up. I don't know whether I'll
succeed. Also, I have started to learn French. It turns out quite well.
I must keep it up and I must not pay attention to the mocking of

30. Many departments, groups of workers, and Zionist factions in Terezín fielded soccer
teams. The Jugendfuersorge team (Jufa for short) mentioned here represented the youth
welfare department. See also note 34.

31. Bass-baritone Karel Berman (1919–95) was a key figure in the musical life of Terezín. Deported from Prague to the Lípa camp on January 16, 1942, Karel was one of 120
men pulled out of that camp and sent, via Prague, on the Cv transport to Terezín (March
6, 1943). Karel worked as a corpse carrier during the day and performed in musical productions in the evening. Among his many activities, he sang in Bedřich Smetana's opera
The Bartered Bride and Verdi's *Requiem,* mounted Vilém Blodek's opera *In the Well,* and
conducted a girls' chorus. Shipped to Auschwitz on September 28, 1944, Karel survived
and was liberated in Allach. He remained in Czechoslovakia after the war, attended the
Prague Conservatory, and enjoyed an illustrious career as an opera singer, stage director,
and member of the Czech National Theater in Prague.

others. I am looking forward to *Nešar* being ready. I spend the afternoon with Brenner. In the course of our English lesson, I find out that Dr. Jelínková[32] doesn't agree with the original prizes. She offers us unbelievable prizes. I figure that we will learn nothing from her lesson. I return to the *heim* for the usual Friday *Apel*. It is announced there that on Sunday L417 will be evacuated. Later in the evening there is another *Apel*. I take *Nešar* and go to my mother. Eli agrees to do the illustrations for *Nešar*. His magazine will not materialize. Again, I am upset by my father's state of health. I go home. Details for the L417 evacuation are given during the evening *Apel*. A reading of *Nešar* follows. Its tenth issue is met with average success. *Rim, Rim* is also read. I can see the difference between the two magazines. Ours is better, as something is missing in *Rim, Rim*. Beran's article, "World War," causes uproar. Gorila asks Beran sarcastically from where he copied it. Soon I fall asleep.

Saturday, 15 April 1944

I wake at about seven o'clock. I shoot the breeze with Kalíšek. I am becoming aware that it is impossible to argue with one's neighbor in Terezín. I read a book. Again, the weather is beautiful. It is Saturday and we are allowed to sleep longer. At about 8:30, my mother arrives. I don't know why, but I renege on my promise to behave well toward my parents. Again, I get into an argument with my mother. She says that I should put on my knickers suit. She blames me for being unfriendly and picky toward my father. She says that last night he could not walk home because he got completely blinded. I am touched and I get tears in my eyes. I am in mental turmoil; I don't feel like doing anything. Soon, my mother leaves. I go for a walk with Kalíšek, and then to my mother's for lunch. I am petrified about my father's state of health. I go to a soccer match but I am not interested today. I feel some pins and needles in my left cheek. I have a head cold. I get depressed by the thought of having to move tomorrow into the Hamburg Barracks because of the evacuation. Soon, I return to the *heim*. I go for supper, but I have no appetite. I put my overcoat on. I am cold, but I walk slowly to my mother's. I am afraid that my mother will make me feel remorseful. I want to leave early. I bring home a hot water bottle. My father walks very badly. At home, I collapse on

---

32. Dr. Jelínková taught English in Terezín.

my bed. I forgot to mention that I have not been on speaking terms with Robin for some time now. This afternoon I helped Franta build a cubicle in the attic and Robin was there also. I called him names and we started to fight. I got beaten up. Robin poured lime all over me and messed up my whole suit. Then I kicked him and hurried to the *heim*. Angrily, I took my fountain pen and very carefully I dripped ink on Robin's bed. Robin got furious! I finished the seed of destruction. Now at night, while I am lying in bed, Robin shows up angrily and does the same thing to me. I don't go for it and we begin to fight again. This time, I beat the hell out of him! He tells me that he no longer wants to be on the editorial staff. I behave very coolly. From then on, we don't talk. I get my stuff ready for the move. I'm all packed, thanks to my mother's help. I fall asleep with a thermos bottle on my cheek.

Sunday, 16 April 1944

In the past few days, it was decided that we have to move to the Hamburg Barracks because the School is being disinfected. The move is today. We are supposed to stay in the Hamburg Barracks for two weeks. We wake up at 7:30. I have everything ready. I only have to make my bedroll. By noon L417 must be empty. The disinfection begins immediately and it will last until Wednesday. Afterward they will paint. My cheeks don't hurt me any more. I am healthy, after all. I find out that the suitcases that stay behind must be left open. Since I don't have a lock, I have to get one from my mother. I also don't have any string for my bedroll. Otherwise, I am all packed. I run to the barracks for these things. I get some real motherly love. Mother ignores my previous insults and is concerned about me as if nothing had happened. I am not washed yet when I manage to load my things on the cart in an organized manner. I take with me almost all my things—some food and some bric-a-brac. Finally, the cart gets going. Again, the weather is beautiful. Just a delight! I feel as if I were some kind of an immigrant. Finally, we stop in our new place to stay. Unlike during the last few days, I am in a good mood. We enter the Hamburg Barracks yard and stop there. Guards are assigned to watch the carts. We go in alphabetical order to report in the Office 76. After we are assigned Room 86, we go to the basement to pick up our straw mattresses and bring them to our assigned room. Each of us takes a place. Franta has arranged it all. I let it be known that I want to sleep next to Furcht,[33] Gustl, and Beran. A space along the wall near the window is assigned to us. It is a pretty good spot. I take four mattresses which, however, are taken away from me. I don't care. I make my bedroll and arrange all my things. The first thing I do is to get washed up. I find out there are excellent bathhouses here. Afterward, I set out for my mother's. I crawl through the window and I have my lunch. In the afternoon we go to the ramparts. I also play handball. We have a lot of *Apels;* otherwise, nothing much happens. At night I get all washed in the bathhouse. It is a sheer delight! Afterward, I fall asleep, a healthy sleep, even though I lie on the floor.

Soccer scores of the day: Jugendfuersorge 6: Electricians 2, Sparta: [illegible] 4:2, Kadr: Spedice[34] [scores missing].

Monday and Tuesday, 17 and 18 April 1944

Because I forgot my diary at the School, I have to combine the events of the last two days. It doesn't matter because both days were spent in "exile." I have little space and few things. On Monday morning, I wake up and I can't believe how well I slept. We stay in bed until eight o'clock. There are about twenty of us here. Other boys sleep with their parents. The fleas don't bite me any more. I air my stuff in a nearby window and then I get washed. There is *Apel* in the yard at 8:30. These *Apels* are useless because nobody can hear a thing. I'm near my mother's and I take advantage of it by spending a lot of time there. I study French. Otherwise, nothing happens. Later I go for lunch—it is farfel, which I like. After lunch, I go to the Hamburg Barracks for a while, just to loaf around. I have been neglecting *Nešar.* I have to get to work on it even without Biblu. Later, there is another *Apel.* We go to the ramparts where we play various games and I read *The Human Lot.* This book is well written, but it doesn't hold my attention. I borrow a pair of sneakers to play handball with Bäumel.[35] After a long struggle, I win 10:7. I am late and therefore I miss my mother's

33. Valtr Furcht (b. July 16, 1931), nicknamed Duch by his friends in room 7, was given number 914 and sent on convey AAe from Prague to Terezín on June 20, 1942. Shipped on transport Eq (number 1258) to Auschwitz, Duch did not survive.

34. Groups of workers that fielded teams included the haulers (*Spedice*) and the electricians (*Elektra*).

35. Erich (also spelled Erik) Bäumel, born August 16, 1931, was assigned number 603 on transport M from Prague to Terezín (December 14, 1941). Erich was one of the room 7 boys shipped with convoy Er (his number: 119) on October 16, 1944, to Auschwitz. He did not survive.

work break. My mother works in a noodle factory and she is on an afternoon shift. The evening is long without my mother. I bring her supper but I don't stay long because I go to the barracks for supper. We have bread pudding. I walk my father home because he continues to complain that he can't see in the dark. The doctors say that he has an inflammation of the nerves and lacks vitamins. All he needs is a good diet and he will be cured. Last night on the way home he could see well, but as soon as he came home he got another attack. I return to the Hamburg Barracks, where in the yard we play soccer against the Dutchmen. I finish playing at about nine o'clock. At night I have diarrhea. I went to the bathroom once during the day and I go twice during the night. It is very stupid because where I'm staying is completely dark at night. After washing myself in the bathhouse, I go to bed and soon I fall asleep.

Tuesday I wake up at seven. I slept quite well. Again we stay in bed until eight and I get up at the designated time. There is yet another *Apel*. This gets on my nerves. The weather is not as nice as on Monday. I go to the library with Beran for a French lesson. Later we go to the barracks so that I can study with my mother. I go for lunch and afterward nothing happens. The entire afternoon we spend at the ramparts. In the evening, my father and I go to see a cabaret performance by Schwenk.[36] It is mediocre. Some jokes are quite good by making fun of everybody. My father feels quite well. In the evening I do not wash myself. Tonight in bed Franta reads to us *The Human Lot*, but during the reading I fall asleep.

Wednesday, 19 April 1944

Today L417 is supposed to reopen and all our things have to come out. Professor Kohn[37] takes over our division. Already, the night before, there was *Apel* which dealt with the move. The move to air the School is scheduled for noon. It is a very "convenient time." At nine o'clock, there is *Apel* with Franta. At 11:30, we will have to assemble

36. Cabaret artist Karel Svenk (also spelled Schwenk) was a member of one of the early construction details. His former career at the Club for Wasted Talent in Prague stood him in good stead in Terezín, where he used his biting irony to mock camp life. Deported to Auschwitz in September 1944, Svenk was sent on to work in a factory in Meuselwitz near Leipzig. He died there in early April 1945.

37. Antonín Kohn (b. June 22, 1898) was deported from Prague to Terezín with transport X on February 12, 1942. He taught mathematics in the camp until he was shipped to Auschwitz with convoy Ek on September 28, 1944. He did not survive.

at our homerooms. He doesn't want to subject himself to others' commands. He quite correctly asserts that for us it is not healthy to breathe the gas in the School and tells us to finish things up as soon as possible. Because Kalíšek is sick, Franta asks me to go to his mother and tell her to come to the School at 11:30. With my luck, I am told also to have my hair cut. Despite a lot of complaints, I do as I am told. First, I go to my mother's for a key. From there I go to Mrs. Klein.[38] Immediately, Mrs. Klein asks me to stay longer with Kalíšek. Because there is nothing seriously wrong with him, I climb to his bed and talk with him at length. The time passes quickly. Later I hurry to the Hamburg Barracks for lunch (potatoes and spinach). The lines there are very long. I hurry so that I will be in time for the departure, but my hurry is useless. It is a typical Jewish punctuality. Departure doesn't take place until noon, in front of the house with some instructions. We go together to the School. We find a big mess. I pack quickly. The luggage must be brought to the attic. It is very difficult to transport the luggage when the attic is so crowded. Soon all is finished. I'm leaving the "good old" Room 7. It's about three o'clock and I wander slowly to the Hamburg Barracks. Because I have no dishes, I can't take any soup. I go for supper to my mother. On the way, I run into my father, who is returning from the bakery because Rahm was there. When I arrive at the bakery, Rahm is leaving on his bike [motorcycle]. I go inside the bakery to see my mother. We talk for a while, but when I tell her that I had no soup, she gets very angry. We soon make up. I return to my father and we talk for an hour. I want to go to the library, but it is closed. Instead, I go to the *heim* and play soccer. I'm neglecting the magazine! This week it will not be published. At about nine, I go to bed. I'm reading *The Human Lot* and I soon fall asleep.

Thursday, 20 April 1944

Today I am determined to tell the whole Room 7 to go to hell and to spend the morning with my mother. First, I go to fetch the marmalade. I stand in line for a long time.

I'm not taking part at all in helping around the School. First, I go to the library to borrow a French book. I have to argue in the library, but finally they lend me a book. Immediately, I hurry to my mother. We study for about half an hour. I have to study the new vocabulary.

38. Kalíšek's mother.

I have a small argument with Mother because I want to copy all the words, which would delay fetching my lunch. It's cold outside and therefore I don't feel like going. Finally I go. I have to return to the library because I left my meal card there as a deposit. After lunch, I talk with my parents. My father is complaining about his chest and leg pain. I continue to worry a lot about him. Because there is *Apel* at 1:30, I have to go home. As always, *Apel* is worthless. Later, I play with a tennis ball in the yard. I'm furious with myself that I'm forced to play with this dirty, miserable ball. Because of this damn ball, I am not getting anywhere. I am neglecting the magazine. When I see *Rim, Rim* almost ready, I'm very sad. Grizzly wants to do everything by himself. He wants to type our magazine all by himself. I can't tolerate it! I cannot be put to shame in front of the whole *heim*. I realize at last that it would serve me best if I applied myself more to mental activities. Therefore, I quit playing with the ball and I go home to write in my diary. Time passes quickly. Soon, Bäumel arrives and is looking for someone with whom he can play ball. My stupid self goes with him. I don't mind that I reneged on my promise, but I'm destroying both my shoes and my knees. When I finish, I go for my supper as well as for Mother's. I bring both to the bakery, where my father is already waiting. I am in a bad mood. Nothing tastes good and I don't talk. I soon return home and write in my diary. Again, I have diarrhea tonight. At nine, I go to bed and, after some joking around with Beran, I soon fall asleep.

Friday, 21 April 1944

When I wake up, the first thing I hear is about the disappearance of two boys from the Ghetto. They are from our School and their names are Belov and Thein. They must have a great deal of courage. Belov is said to have escaped once before but he was caught. We stay in bed until eight. When I get up, I'm determined to spend the morning in the library, and so I go there with Beran. I do my English lesson, I study French, and I write in the diary from the previous day. I enjoy learning French very much. At about 11:45, I go with Lappert[39] to the School. I'm looking forward to having a *buchta* with cream. I take out my lunch and go to my mother's. I'm forced to leave the barracks

---

39. Jindřich Lappert (b. January 10, 1931) was assigned number 959 on transport W from Prague to Terezín on February 8, 1942. Like so many other room 7 boys, he was sent to Auschwitz with convoy Er on October 16, 1944. His number: 119. Jindřich did not survive.

soon, however, because there is *Apel* in the attic at 11:30. I have to mention the important news that my father finally got his injection of Bethuna and I think that he is getting better. I am very pleased. Unfortunately, I am neglecting the magazine. *Apel* today concerns the escape of the two boys and for this reason all the boys from the Hamburg Barracks must move to us. Boys from Room 7 will move at six o'clock. Sasha and Koko[40] have to move in between us, which results in much pushing. I notice the consequences at night. After *Apel*, I go for bread to pay for my lesson. I am studying English with Dr. Jelínková. Now the lessons have become more expensive, asking for twenty-eight days a payment of one-quarter to one-half a loaf of bread, 4½ dkg of margarine and 2 dkg of sugar. I cannot accept such conditions! On my way to the *heim*, I crawl through the window, but Franta catches me and I have to pick up stones in front of the Hannover Barracks. Franta is very obnoxious to me. Afterward, I go to my lesson. We want to get out of it, but we don't succeed. On my return home, I pick up supper for my mother and for me. When I go to my mother at the bakery, my father is there too. We eat fried potatoes and then I go to the barracks with him. There, we talk for a while. Later we set out to the square where there is a concert. I say good-bye to my father and run into Gustla. We walk through Terezín. Gustl goes to his mother and then I go home where I spend the evening doing nothing. *Rim, Rim* has been published. Franta clearly favors it. Lion says that *Rim, Rim* will undertake a big attack on *Nešar*. Suddenly, he disappears from the room. The main feature of the magazine is the so-called "Answer to *Nešar*." It attacks me and ridicules my articles. Actually, I will write this amazing article into my diary. It will be a good remembrance of my comrades, Lion and Kokošek. I am really stunned. The boys are, of course, laughing at me. I am thinking of revenge. I am afraid we are going to lose Herz. We cannot be put to shame. I ignore Franta's reading and I fall asleep thinking of my so-called comrades. This day has left a powerful impression on me.

Saturday, 22 April 1944

I sleep very badly because other boys have moved into our room, so we have to lie lengthwise. It is very stupid. I'm still devastated from

40. Petr Heller (b. August 5, 1931), nicknamed Kokošek or Koko, was deported with transport M from Prague to Terezín on December 14, 1942. A room 7 boy, he was sent to Auschwitz with convoy Er on October 10, 1944. Koko did not survive.

the previous evening. At about nine o'clock, I get up. All the boys are
arguing over Lion's article about me. The entire editorial staff of *Rim,
Rim* is very obnoxious to me. I have decided that I will not write a
reply to *Rim, Rim*. It would spoil our magazine. We now have to get
to work with new energy! While still in a bad mood, I write an article called "Courage." I think that it will be successful. I try to reach
others. I will go to Gustl to visit Kalíšek and Brenner. There is *Apel*,
after which something happens for which I have been waiting a long
time. Grizzly comes to me and, showing puzzling calmness, tells me:
"I'm quitting *Nešar*." I accept it very coolly. Obviously, Lion has drawn
Grizzly to his side. Now Grizzly is going to tell him all our secrets. In
misery, one gets to know people. Immediately, I inform Gustl, who
is still quite interested in *Nešar*. He keeps reminding us that we are
in a mess! I calm him down. I am not so concerned about Grizzly's
article, but rather it is a matter of pride. We go to see Kalíšek. He
promises that he will write some kind of article. I think that Kalíšek
will be faithful to us. Next, we go to see Brenner, who is still in bed. I
show him *Rim, Rim*. He is equally unconcerned and he promises that
he will write the article "Death on the Ship." Later, I go with Gustl to
the library. I don't stay there long. I go for lunch, but in Hamburg
they are not giving out food. I go then to L216, where they give out
barley. Finally, I find lunch at 2KK. I bring the lunch to my mother's.
I have a ticket for a bath, but I don't use it. My father is walking better after the injections, and I am pleased. At about 1:30, I go home. I
keep forgetting about *Apel*. Fortunately, two boys warn me that *Apel* is
taking place and therefore I escape to my mother's without notice. I
laze around for a while. At 2:30, I return home. I find the boys reading with Franta. I apologize for missing *Apel*. Everyone is laughing at
me. They are reading *Island Within Us*. It is marvelous! It describes
three generations in a family. The first is an old Reb named Chaim.
He has a son named Ephraim. He is like his father. The Reb becomes
a winemaker and his son rejects the business and moves to Germany.
He changes his name and has a son named Tobias. Finally, Ephraim
concludes that he is not behaving correctly. He studies, joins the
army, and allows himself to be christened. We finish reading when
Tobias, depressed because of the death of his son, says "Shema Yisrael" ["Hear O Israel"—the first words of the most important Jewish
prayer]. After the reading, I go to fetch my supper and then return
to Mother's. I hear that Handa will start going to the *Landwirtschaft*

[agriculture department][41] probably only because of my father's contacts. I go to a soccer match between Kadr and WW. The score is 3:1. I again have diarrhea. After the soccer match, I return to Mother's. She walks my father home and I write the article "Modern Story" while she is gone. When my mother returns, I cuddle with her for a while and then I go home. I ignore the boys. So far, we have an article from Mustang and one from Huppert.[42] As far as I am concerned, Huppert is a good boy, as yet unspoiled. I go to bed. I keep thinking to myself that the boys in our room are becoming indifferent. Then, I fall asleep.

Sunday, 23 April 1944

I slept very badly. The fleas have never bitten me like this before. They kept me awake for about an hour. I'm determined to wash myself halfway up today. I do so and I feel much refreshed. After putting things in order, I'm forced to go to Kalíšek for his contribution to the magazine. He wrote an article called "Into the Other Life." It is an average story. Robin moved back into the *heim*.[43] I still don't like him. There is *Apel* again. Nothing of importance is being transacted. I'm recognizing that Franta is pulling away from me and therefore I no longer like him. I could write whole sagas about my relationship with Franta. After *Apel* there is again this mock [?] program. We are studying physics but I am not interested. During the program, I finish the article "Modern Story." I believe its theme is original even though I got it from Handa. After all, one doesn't become smart overnight! Soon I flee the program. I go to the library, where I write my diary and

41. Working for the agriculture department was prized employment because it offered the opportunity to purloin produce.

42. Pavel Huppert was born on September 28, 1931, in Katowice (Poland) and moved with his parents and brother to Moravská Ostrava the following year only to return to Katowice when German troops marched into Ostrava in March 1939. When Germany attacked Poland in September, the Huppert family fled and then split up, with the father going to Teheran (Iran) and the mother and sons to Prague. Divorced along the way, Pavel's mother remarried. The new family of four was deported from Prague to Terezín on transport Cv in March 1943 (his number: 547). Both boys were placed in L417, but in different classrooms. All four were shipped to Auschwitz; Pavel, his brother, and mother with convoy Eq (his number: 808) on October 12, 1944. Pavel and his brother were sent on to the Dachau subcamp Kaufering, where Pavel's brother died. Liberated in May 1945, Pavel was reunited with his mother and stepfather. They immigrated to Australia, where Pavel's biological father joined his son.

43. Robin had been living with his brother in another room for some time.

study French. At 1:30, I return to the *heim*. There is *Apel* and afterward a reading of *Island Within Us*. Soon we break up and go to watch soccer matches—it's Jugendfuersorge vs. Praga and Elektra vs. Spedice. Before the soccer matches, however, I had to go to the library for a *menaška* [meal ticket] stop with Kalíšek and we went together to the *Menagedienst* [meal service department] to get a temporary card. Only then I go to the matches, which I enjoy. The score of the first match is 1:1 and the score of the second is 2:2. At seven I go to the barracks, but my parents are not there. They return shortly and I accompany my father home. I go to bed early and during the reading I once again fall asleep. There was nothing special about this day.

Monday, 24 April 1944

I slept pretty well but I am afflicted with a certain mental anguish. I am worried about the magazine. It seems as if both my body and my brain are turning into stone. It's an awful state. I don't feel like doing anything. I feel that I am at odds with almost the whole *heim*. I get up and get washed. After I finish putting things in order, I throw myself on the mattress and do absolutely nothing. Suddenly, Franta asks who would like to be an instructor for the game "Treasure Hunt." I volunteer along with Gustl. Kokošek, Gorila, Herz, Jila,[44] and I agree on the rules of the game. We will make chalk marks and we will place clues. First we have to find chalk. We look all over and finally we find some in the *Materialverwaltung* [supply department]. We immediately set out to do the job. Our route goes through L306 and the blocks, where we hide an instruction saying to go to Backergasse 3. From there the path winds through the barracks, and at the door in BV [probably *Bauverwaltung*, the building supplies department] another note directs the route to the gate in the laundry room, where we plan to have additional arrows. However, this we cannot do, and therefore, we put arrows at the *Entwesung* [delousing station]. From the crossing, the route goes through the Kavalier Barracks, the *Stadtpark* [town park], and all the way to the nursery. There we hide a note with instructions to go to L128, and from there arrows lead to the Bahnhofstrasse. Yet another note directs the hunt to the food storage building. Final instructions, placed in Neuegasse, lead back

44. Arnošt Jilovsky (b. July 31, 1931), nicknamed Jila by the room 7 boys, was deported from Prague to Terezín on July 2, 1942, with convoy Dp (his number: 10). Jila was shipped to Auschwitz on transport Et (number 23) in October 1944. He did not survive.

to the Kavalier Barracks. A series of arrows lead to the "treasure"!
. . . At eleven o'clock, we all return home. I take my lunch and rest
for a while on the mattress. Afterward I go to Mrs. Stein[45] to pick up
Gustl, but he is not there. I find him at home and we go together to
look at the arrows. We lengthen the route by going around the Hannover Barracks. Later I go to my father. I watch him defending an old
woman. He has no paper [probably to be used during the treasure
hunt: PW]. I again go to inspect the arrows. I come home, where the
boys are reading. Later, there is the game. Our group has the longest
"route" and therefore we lose. At four o'clock, I return to the *heim*
very dirty. I get washed at the pump. Then I go for supper and to my
parents. There I get angry because my mother won't let me go to the
concert. I soon return home. One hears rumors about transports,
which would be very disagreeable. At home I write in my diary. Later
I play handball doubles in the yard. At nine, I get washed, which feels
marvelous after today's activity. Then I go to bed in darkness and fall
asleep. I really didn't enjoy this day.

Tuesday, 25 April 1944

Already I'm sleeping better. The fleas no longer bite me. I don't go
to get washed up because I have no towel today. I decide to go with
Gustl to see Brenner. It's worth mentioning that I saw a naked woman
there washing herself! I turned away bashfully. We talk with Brena
and I give him my opinion on submitting an article to *Rim, Rim* that
answers their accusations about me. I could then rub it in front of
their eyes for accepting my writing. I give him paper and articles
and then leave for the library where Gustl is writing the article "The
Miner." I study French until 11:30. I go for lunch and then just re-
lax in my bed. Suddenly my father taps on the windowpane and says
to pick up a new French textbook. I go and get it. It's just average.
Then I return home and the afternoon is not very significant. I go
with my mother to her barracks. I'm somehow mad and I pick myself
up and return to the *heim*. I write my diary and then I go for a walk
with Lamm. My parents go for a walk with the Kürschners.[46] I want to
bring the contributions to Brena, but I don't feel like going. Instead,
I play handball with Gustl and then I go to bed. While Franta is read-

45. Gustl Stein's mother.
46. Family friends from Prague.

ing to us, I fall asleep. These days spent in the Hamburg Barracks are not noteworthy.

Wednesday, 26 April 1944

I wake up at seven o'clock. We are getting up quite early these days. Because I didn't get a chance to write my diary, I want to summarize what's interesting. The most important thing is that I'm writing the magazine, which will come out this evening. I have an argument with Springer.[47] It culminates in my getting two days of house arrest which, however, I don't follow at all. Franta is very angry at me. In the evening, he reads *Nešar*. It's quite a big hit! *Rim, Rim* is furious that I beat them out! Yet, I have never been as unhappy as I am today. I realize that the boys and Franta are unfaithful. I can barely fall asleep.

Thursday, 27 April 1944

Another day. We wake up at seven o'clock and get up at eight. After we put things in order, there is *Apel*. I was assigned to go to the barber and I immediately go there with Kopperl. The barber is not in L609 and therefore I go to have my hair cut by Mr. Neumann. Because it is *Grunt* [general cleanup] there, he will not cut hair until next week. I return home with Kopperl. Because I don't feel like going to the program, I go on the ramparts and there I work—that is to say, I bask—until 11:30. I return to the School and go for lunch. After lunch I play *hlavicky* [head soccer] in the yard, which I have to interrupt on account of *Apel*. Franta announces that he would like to have something like scout groups in the *heim*. So far there will be only one group and he will announce in the evening who has been assigned to that group. Then we go to the roof of the Kavalier Barracks,[48] but we cannot get in. We go around the barracks and then we lie down on the slope where there is a group of small children. Kopperl asks me if I want to go swimming with him at 5:30. Of course, I agree. For a while I just lie around Kavalierka. Then we go past the *cvokarna* [slang for a mental hospital], where a young boy tells us what goes on inside.

47. František Springer (b. March 9, 1931), called Franta, was deported to Terezín with transport U from Brno on January 28, 1942; he was assigned number 911. A room 7 boy, he was shipped to Auschwitz on October 10, 1944: number 1313 on transport En. Franta did not survive.

48. Also called Kavalierka, the Kavalier Barracks were used to house the mentally ill.

We want to write a play but we don't have much ambition. I have supper at my mother's. I only have a piece of bread because it is too late. At home, I wait for Kopperl. He comes out all tired and announces that he got confused and the ticket for swimming is for 6:45. I go back to my mother. I again have to bring with me my French textbook. Otherwise nothing of interest happens. I have to visit Springer and ask him to write an article. The magazine makes me quite nervous. At the assigned hour I go swimming. It is marvelous! I swim nicely, and then I return to Mother's. Soon, however, I go home with my father, who is walking much better. At home, I just lie around. I'm angry at Grizzly and Herz for their insincerity. They are through with me and I'm through with them. I really don't care because I really don't need such a friendship. We soon go to bed and Franta gives us the names of the boys who are assigned into the scout group and they are as follows: Springer, Lappert, Tuti, Míša,[49] Kopperl, the Götzlinger brothers,[50] Bäumel, Huppert, and me. Franta asks me very strangely if the company is good enough for me. There are some good friends of mine in it (for example: Huppert, Springer, Kopperl, and sometimes Tuti). I would prefer to be with Gustl, Kalíšek, and others. But I do want to belong to a group. I think that Gustl and Kalíšek would not be interested in belonging, whereas the ones whom Franta chose are interested. I have to think about it.

Friday, 28 April 1944

We are supposed to get up at 6:45, but I don't feel like it. Franta has to work really hard to get the blanket off me. I'm still so sleepy. After tidying things up, I make up my mind to visit Springer, who is sick, but I don't know where he is staying. First, I go to [illegible], but he is

49. Michael Gruenbaum (b. August 23, 1930), or Míša, lived with his parents and sister in Prague when the Germans invaded in March 1939. His father, a successful lawyer, was arrested by the Germans in October 1941, incarcerated in Pankrac Prison in Prague and transferred to the Small Fortress in Terezín, where he was killed in December 1941. Míša and his mother and sister were deported to Terezín in November 1942 on transport Cc from Prague, numbered 978, 977, and 979, respectively. Míša was assigned to room 7. All three remained in Terezín to be liberated in April 1945. Míša later immigrated to Cuba and then to the United States.

50. Felix (b. December 12, 1928) and Pavel (b. September 3, 1930; nicknamed Pudlina) Götzlinger were assigned numbers 174 and 175, respectively, and deported from Olomouc to Terezín with transport Aam on July 4, 1942. Both joined room 7 and both were sent to Auschwitz on the Er transport of October 16, 1944, Felix numbered 1338 and Pavel 1339. Neither survived.

not there. Then, I go to Slunce, the house where my father lives, but
Franta Springer is not there. I go to where his mother stays. There,
I am told that she actually lives elsewhere. I go there next, but I am
told that Mrs. Springer has moved away. I go to *Evidenz* [the registry
office] and I am told that she is at Q501 so I finally go there. If I
hadn't met his mother in the yard, I would never have found Franta
Springer, who is lying in bed. He is glad to see me and we talk until
ten o'clock, the time of the program. He promises that he will write
something and that I should bring him a copy of *Nešar*. I go home,
where the program has already started. We have Irenka.[51] She doesn't
notice me come in. After the boring lesson, I go to play in the yard.
We play soccer against Jestrabi [the Hawks]. I play but I put the ball
in my own net. Afterward, there is *Apel*, where nothing important
happens. Then, I go again to play soccer until two o'clock. I have to
leave because Kopperl shot a bomb right into my testicles. It hurts
very much. I lie down on the bunk and, together with other boys, we
call Jelínková bad names. I'm cutting today's lesson. I go with Beran
to the library and there I write my diary and study French. I did not
take my meal dish with me, so I have to dash from Hamburg back to
L216, where I try to borrow Handa's dish. Handa is not home, but
somebody lends it to me. I hurry to Hamburg. There, I eat my supper
and then I hurry to my mother's. I am in a good mood. After dinner, I
talk with my father and have a French lesson with my mother. I think
I am making good progress! Back at home, we read *Rim, Rim*. I think
it is better than others and I am heartbroken. Zebulon[52] is staying
with us overnight. It seems that *Rim* is again attracting the boys' readership. Then Zebulon is telling us about Faust while I fall asleep.

Saturday, 29 April 1944

I'm still heartbroken about *Rim, Rim*. I keep seeing in front of my eyes
that the *Nešar* magazine will go bust. I don't know how I'll manage. I
think that it is the greatest mental struggle that I have ever been in.
After all, it is the first work of my life which will demonstrate whether
I can cross the deep precipice of life. Now, I'm finding myself on the

51. Irena Seidlerová (b. February 16, 1926) was deported from Prague to Terezín with
transport Cv on March 6, 1943. She served as an assistant to Franta Maier and survived to
be liberated in Terezín.
52. Zebulon Ehrlich was a teacher in the Jewish primary school in Prague and served as
a *madrich* in L417.

sharpest curve. In bed, I study French. Suddenly, my mother arrives
and brings boots and stockings to be fixed. Afterward, I again study
French. I am mentally depressed. The small living space has a great
effect on me. I am distraught. My mood is spoiled. I want to go to my
mother's and study there. I stay at home though because I am afraid
of being absent for *Apel*. During *Apel*, I am criticized because I am
not washed, and so I have to leave to get washed. However, because
the washroom is closed, this is not an option. Therefore, I go to my
mother's in order to study French. When I arrive at my mother's, she
refuses to teach me. I am very angry. It comes to a point when even
my mother doesn't believe in me. I feel miserable. It affects my whole
disposition. I feel totally abandoned. The worst is when I have an argument with my parents. I am unhappy. I don't listen to my mother.
Finally, I go to have lunch. I am so angry that I don't even go with
my lunch to my mother's. For lunch I have to go to L216. I get a full
dish of noodles. I'm pleased. What a strange pleasure. At home, I am
boasting with my salami and noodles and I am warming it up. I think
that I will cut the salami into the noodles. I can't do anything. I cannot write the magazine. At 2:30 we run into Heini Maier.[53] He seems
to be a nice guy. We agree to meet every Sunday and Wednesday. I go
and watch soccer. It is a tremendous match, full of exciting moments.
At seven o'clock, I return to the *heim* in a better mood. I heard today
that one woman from the barracks wanted to hang herself. At home,
I discuss with Beran and Sasha the subject of suicide and the question
of what one lives for. This question interests me very much. I go to
bed and Franta again confronts me. Various subjects are being discussed. It is an evening of silence and I reluctantly fall asleep.

Sunday, 30 April 1944

I wake up at 6:30. Because there is *Grunt* we must get up early today. I'm still sleepy. We have to take everything out and surprisingly
there is not much confusion. Because I have to guard L417 at eight
o'clock, I'm forced to interrupt all my magazine work. I don't know
whether it will be ready. I go to guard with ten other boys and, once
there, we get very bored. I am the guard on the big yard. It is really

---

53. Heinrich (or Heini) Maier (b. November 27, 1925) was deported on transport J
from Prague on December 4, 1941. He served as a Hebrew instructor in Terezín. Shipped
to Auschwitz with convoy Bk on September 28, 1944, Heini did not survive.

quite useless because both exits are closed. I complain to Rudla.[54] Afterward, I go to Franta's cottage to shoot the breeze. I'm again castigated by Franta that I do not guard. I roam through the whole School. I stay in Room 1 because they have the fire on. Afterward, I have an argument with Beneš.[55] I go to the attic and there we talk for about an hour. Rudla Weil arrives and says that we all will have to be on duty again. Therefore, I go out to the small yard. There, I play soccer with Pepek Stadler and Sasha, using a tin can. At noon, I can finally go home. I have to hurry to get lunch at Hamburg. I'm pleased that I arrive just when they are dishing out the food. I find out that Sparta, the team where I play defense, is playing against Slavie today at four o'clock. We have quite a match ahead of us. I go with *buchta* and cream to my mother's. She keeps the *buchta* for supper and gives me a cup of potato salad. It is very good. My father is walking almost normally. The injections help him a lot. I go home with a feeling of pleasure. However, I must go back to my mother's to get my shorts. I immediately return and go to the yard. It is said that *Apel* will not take place today. At home, I change into the uniform—we have blue shorts and red shirts. At four o'clock, I go to the *bašta* [the green area atop the broad rampart walls used as playing fields] and I arrive just in time. We are scheduled to take the field. Everybody laughs at us. The match is two sixteen-minute halves. I play well and I defend well. I think that I will make the team. But the match ends with our loss of 4:0. After the match, I go to my dad for ink and then I return to the *heim*. I have quite a bit of work ahead of me and I also want to go and play more soccer. But first I eat a *buchta* and then I go for supper (spinach, potatoes, and *geback*). I want to write an article, but I'm not quite successful. I go to visit the boys in the Dresdner Barracks, where a match between Jugendfuersorge and Rapid is taking place. The first goal is scored against Jufa [Jugendfuersorge]. Franta is hit in the nose and the game is interrupted. Afterward, Jufa starts equalizing and winning. In the second half, Franta faints. He is not healthy. The final score is 7:2 in favor of Jufa. After the match, I go home. I forgot to mention that I inquired about work in the garden today. I'm sup-

54. Rudolf (or Rudla) Weil (b. January 27, 1914) was deported from Kladno to Terezín on February 22, 1942, with transport Y. Pavel knew him as a temporary (and unpopular) room 7 *madrich*. Rudla was shipped on to Auschwitz with convoy Ek on September 28, 1944. He did not survive.

55. Jiří Beneš (b. April 3, 1931) was assigned number 355 and deported on transport M from Prague to Terezín on December 14, 1941. A room 7 boy, Jiří was sent to Auschwitz on May 15, 1944, with convoy Dz; he was number 147. He did not survive.

posed to see Mr. Prager. I meet my father and I tell him everything. At home, I write an article and my diary. I am in a good mood. Franta doesn't sleep with us. Because there is a big ruckus, the lights go out soon and I fall asleep.

MAY
Monday, 1 May 1944

I wake up in a mental turmoil. It is raw outside, not at all like the first of May. Franta did not sleep in the *heim* last night. I'm somehow in a bad mood. After we put things in order, there is *Apel.* Again, I am assigned to guard the School. I am unhappy that I will not be able to devote any time to the magazine once again. I go and complain to Otík, who rebuffs me. I don't want to go anywhere. I have a lot of things to do ahead of me and now everything is spoiled. At nine o'clock, we go to L417. I am assigned to guard the small yard. Since I don't enjoy it, I go to the big gate instead. In the meantime, the bunks are being put up in our *heim.* I stay at the big gate until eleven o'clock and afterward I go to my mother's so that she will come with me to see Mr. Prager about the garden. I arrive at the barracks and my mother isn't there. I go to look for her at Hannover, but I don't find her there either. Finally, we meet but she has no time to go with me, which makes me so angry that I lose my desire for the whole thing. I return to the School. Our watch is soon over and I go for lunch. By chance, I get into the front of the line. With the lunch, I go to my mother's, where the same spectacle repeats itself. But Handa is there. It comes to a point where my mother promises that she will go to complain about me to Franta and that I will not be able to play soccer. I take the potatoes with me and leave. On the way home, I regret that I have messed everything up. I am again enticed and go to play soccer. I return home on account of *Apel.* Again, I have the watch from four to eight o'clock and I bitterly protest. Franta arrives and is mad. He asks everyone if they want to go and I make a dumb face. Franta pours out his anger at me. After *Apel,* I am totally unable to do any mental work. Again, I go to play on the *bašta.* Because the ball liner bursts, I have to return home. Soon, I have to take up my duty. I go with the boys to L417 and I take with me my diary and papers. My first spot is at the gate. I go for supper and I eat a dumpling from my hand. I am asked by Kokošek whether I wouldn't want to watch the gate, and I agree. I write an article entitled "Beggar." I warm up the potatoes and I have to borrow some margarine. Afterward, I go to the School with Huppert and we walk around. In about five days we will have to move. It doesn't look as if the magazine will come out. I roam around the yard and at eight o'clock, I go home with Majošek.[56] I do nothing at home and with disgust I go to sleep.

Tuesday, 2 May 1944

We have to get up at six o'clock on account of *Grunt*. A man named Vogel[57] has been assigned to be our teacher. Vogel goes to get washed up and therefore I can stay in bed. I am soon finished with carrying things out. I want to go to my mother and make up with her. In the interim, I sit in the hall and there I finish my article "Beggar" and write my diary. I then go to my mother's. I ask her if she would give me a lesson and she says "yes." For a while I sit and watch her do the laundry. It is quite certain that the magazine will not come out. I keep thinking about how it could fold. Now, the time is ripe for it to happen. I go to the library for a French textbook, but they don't want to lend it to me. Therefore, I study there for a while and then go home. Already, they are carrying things inside and therefore, I follow suit. After having taken things in, I go to Mother with the new textbook. It's quite good. I write out vocabulary from four lessons and it goes quite well. After the lesson, I go for lunch. I notice that Eli is standing in front of the line, which is very long. I want to join him, but Eli refuses. I therefore go to the back of the line and I stand there for about twenty minutes. The *strouhanka* [farfel] is not worth the wait. I'm in a hurry because I have a bathing ticket for 12:30. I forgot to mention that I already made up with Mother. I'm very glad that I accepted to go to the garden in L410 three times a week, on Tuesday and Friday afternoons and on Thursday mornings. I am no longer angry. After lunch, I go to the bathhouse. On the way I meet Pudlina.

56. Martin Mayer (b. November 19, 1930) and his parents and sister lived in Brno. Deported with transport Ac (his number: 995) to Terezín on March 19, 1942, Majošek (as he was called) lived in the Dresdner Barracks until L417 was set up to accommodate youngsters. Majošek and his family were among the 1210 Terezín inmates who, as part of a Jews-for-sale deal struck by SS Reichsführer Heinrich Himmler, were sent to safety in Switzerland (February 5, 1945). The family returned to Czechoslovakia after the war; Majošek studied at the University of Brno and became a scientist. He, his wife, and two children left for West Germany in the wake of the Prague Spring (1968).

57. Vogel was assigned to be the teacher while the boys were temporarily away from the *heim*.

We have to wait in front of the Vrchlabi Barracks.[58] The bath is good and then I go home. From the time of my arrival until three o'clock, nothing happens. At three o'clock, we have English lessons. I want to cut them. However, I enjoy the lessons. I again pay with bread. After the lesson, I go to Kalíšek. I climb on his bed, and we talk about moving. His grandmother knows mine. I spend about an hour there. I am in a big hurry because at six o'clock, we have a meeting in front of L216 with Heini. I go for supper and afterward I go to my mother's. I don't find any food there and, therefore, I go to see her in the bakery. The *Getak* [slang for ghetto—i.e., Jewish—police] won't let me in, but I slip by. Father is there with Handa. I eat *krem* [cream?] there. Since I don't have time, I go to L216. I call the boys and go with them. Heini is already waiting there. We go to celebrate the first of May. I don't enjoy the festivities because the whole atmosphere is Zionistic. After the festivities, we go with a ball on the *bašta* and we play three sets of volleyball. Then, we watch the match between Skid and Wien. It ends in a tie of 4:4. After the match, I write an article at home called "Death on the Ship," and I soon fall asleep.

Wednesday, 3 May 1944

Wake-up today is at seven o'clock. I go to see my mother in the barracks after cleanup. At nine o'clock is *Apel,* and at ten o'clock is a rehearsal for singing. I take my diary and papers. I eat and I take with me a little chair to write in the yard. I am so involved in writing "Death on the Ship" that I don't realize it is already nine o'clock. I say the hell with the whole *Apel,* and I stay at my mother's. I don't give a damn about the *heim.* Already for some time now, Franta is indifferent to me. No wonder; it is his fault! I spend the day thinking about the magazine. I only lack desire. It will fold. I don't know, but I cannot do a thing. Let's see what happens. At 9:30, I return to the *heim* and I learn that Vogel has tested singing during *Apel.* Because I was not there, I was not assigned to anything. The rest of the morning, I am idle. The only thing of interest is that I visit Holzer[59] in the sick

58. The Vrchlabi Barracks housed a hospital.

59. Hanuš Holzer (b. June 29, 1929) and his parents were deported from Prague to Terezín with transport V on January 30, 1942 (his number: 85). Extraburt (Hanuš's nickname) was assigned to the Hamburg Barracks until L417 was organized. He and his family remained in Terezín to be liberated in April 1945 and they returned to Prague. When the Soviet tanks rolled in to quell the Prague Spring, Extraburt and his wife and infant son made their way to Switzerland, where they settled.

ward and he is very happy to see me. I tell him to write an article and
he promises to do so. Because they give out lunch, I go for it. There
are potatoes with *tunke*. I go with the lunch to my mother's and I eat
there.

Thursday, 4 May 1944

We get up at the normal hour. Because I am told to report to the garden at 7:30, I have to hurry so that I will not miss it. At the assigned
time, I am at L410, where there is a meeting place. Our squad leader
is an old man named Schwarzbart,[60] and there are also several women.
The garden is divided into three sections. They are very nice. Almost
everything seems to grow there. First, they divide the assignments
and I am assigned to make flowerpots. I don't like this work very
much. Soon, Schwarzbart comes and throws out all the pots. Outside
it is very nasty and cold and, for this reason, we excuse ourselves and
go home for coats and pants. When we return, the work seems to go
much better. Then, we throw dirt onto piles. I look where everything
is, so at the appropriate time, I will *schlojs* [purloin] it. Because of the
cold, we are dismissed at eleven o'clock and I go home. I have the
feeling that today, for the first time in my life, I have worked! If I were
at home in Prague, I would not be able to do this. In the Hamburg
Barracks, I immediately get lunch and I take it to my mother. There,
I stay about an hour. I still have problems with the magazine. It has to
come out on Friday and we haven't started writing it! After lunch, I
go with Gustl to give Brena and Kalíšek some contributions. We have
to hurry on account of *Apel*. After *Apel*, I have to go to the barber. On
the way, I stop at the School, where I am detained because of an argument about a tennis ball between the boys in Room 5 and the Dutch.
At four o'clock, I finally get to the barber, who doesn't want to take
me. Therefore, I have to return home. I go again to the *bašta* to watch
a soccer match between the Nešarim and the Dragons which ends
with a score of 2:0. After the match, I go home and there Kopperl
and I throw balls. I realize it is getting late and therefore I have to go
to Mother at the bakery. My mother says that the noodles will not be
ready until seven o'clock. I return to the *heim* again and play soccer

---

60. Julius Schwarzbart (b. June 21, 1899) was deported from Brno with transport Af on
March 31, 1942. He worked in youth agriculture and was Pavel's supervisor in the garden.
Shipped to Auschwitz with convoy Ex on October 19, 1944, Julius Schwarzbart did not
survive.

in the yard. During the game, we are asked to go with a cart to the Magdeburg Barracks for blankets. I sit on top of the cart. After the blankets are loaded, I climb all the way to the top. At home, I want to again play soccer, but it doesn't happen because it is already 7:30. I go to Mother's to eat the noodles and then I go with my father to L313. He doesn't have any ink and I go chasing after it. By chance, Handa sits in the office of L218 and he gives me ink, which makes me very happy. It's already 8:30 and I return home. I forgot to write my diary and I really don't know if I can remember. At home, I go to bed and I soon fall asleep.

Friday, 5 May 1944

I slept very badly, as the fleas were biting me. I wake up at 5:45 and I am very sleepy. I write my diary. I realize that today is the date when the magazine is supposed to come out. There is *Grunt* and everything has to be carried out. After *Grunt*, I go to my mother's and I am surprised because we have received a package from Prague from the [illegible name]. It contains eggs, flour, *buchty*, and more. Immediately I am in better spirits. I'm scolded, however, that I didn't have my hair cut. My mother says I look like a rabbi. I promise that I will have my hair cut today. However, I keep thinking about the magazine, which is more important. So far, I have the following articles: "The First of May," "The Beggar's Hand," "Are We Different?" and "The Snowy Expanse of Graves." What's still missing is "The Journey Through Poland," for which I rely on Huppert. Brenner comes and we walk together to the library to write the magazine. He does not have anything written as yet and I have to lend him my pen. We are writing with great speed. By the time we leave, we have three and a half articles fully written, and I'm very pleased. I can see that when one wants something, one can succeed. I think that everything will actually be ready on time. We agree to meet again in one hour. I run in order to get my lunch and I take the lunch to Mother's. We argue a lot. I really don't want to describe it all here in my diary. I take a towel and go to the barber but they tell me that they will not cut hair until tomorrow. I'm getting angry at myself. In half an hour we have an assembly in the garden. Brenner is already there. We finish writing the fourth article. I am in a hurry to be there by two o'clock. I'm in charge of one lawn, and I like it quite a bit. But then I prune and I mess it up. I was invited by Springer to his Bar Mitzvah. I didn't know that the invitation will have its consequences. I'm dirty and I go back to the library. There, with Brenner, we write for the magazine. Unfortunately, Franta sees us and we get a talking to. I feel very lousy and I say to myself, "That's how it is!" We finish the fourth article though and that's all that counts. Now, I have to get Gustl to write the article "The Journey" and everything will be ready. I stagger into the barracks and my father is already there. I complain that I feel crummy. My father takes my temperature and unfortunately I have 37.8 degrees [Celsius]. It is dumb. I immediately go to bed and lie down. There, I finish making lines and numbers. Gustl has a headache so he cannot write. Huppert hurries and writes two articles. He really is dependable! I feel lousy and I have a headache. I am sorry that we don't have covers for the magazine. *Rim* is ready. There is a rehearsal of *Nebuchadnezar* and I fall asleep during it. I wake up only while *Rim* is read. It's not very good, just all sports. *Nešar* is not being read because I pretend to sleep. I wonder, "After all, why am I involved in this magazine?" My thoughts no longer please me. The whole magazine doesn't please me. I don't even know when I fall asleep. I forgot that I listened to Sasha's speech. I no longer want to be his friend.

Saturday, 6 May 1944

When I wake up, nothing hurts me anymore. I take my temperature and have 37.3 degrees. Mother gets me up and I wonder why she is so concerned. I don't understand it. I have a bath and read *Nešar*. I don't enjoy it. It's no longer what it used to be. After reading, the doctor arrives. I'm supposed to stay in bed. Soon Mother arrives and says that I should lie down at her place. Another incident occurs because Mother wants to wait for me. She departs full of anger. Later, I get dressed and go to her barracks. We are angry at each other. I sit on the bed and I am bored. I have no appetite for food. After lunch, I take my shoes off and crawl into bed. I continue arguing with Mother. I cannot write out the details of all the arguments. I look through a Russian dictionary. Soon we make up. I take my temperature again and I no longer have any fever. Afterward, I try a crossword puzzle. I again have an encounter with Mother because she claims that she has no fleas, and I read Czech literature and thus I spend the whole afternoon. I eat nothing for supper. I'm very bored. At seven o'clock, there is a cabaret called "Bonke Gruppe." I go to the specified place. It is something amazing. In particular, [illegible] surprises me. The jokes are marvelous. At nine o'clock, I must leave. I meet Gustl, who calls me to the washroom, where I see a naked woman! Is it indiscreet? Father is very concerned about me to the extent that it is harmful. I go home with Gustl and Leo, where I lie down and quickly fall asleep.

Sunday, 7 May 1944

I wake up at the normal time but I feel weak from yesterday. While I'm still in bed, my mother arrives and says she is sick and she is going to bed. She says that I should bring medicine to her, and I promise to do that. At nine o'clock, we are supposed to have *Apel,* but I don't go. Again, I have a tremendous diarrhea. I get involved in an incident with Vogel, because he will not allow me to go to my mother. I win and I run off to Mother's, but I return at once. Vogel lectures about atoms, neutrons, etc. I don't enjoy it much. After the program is over, I go for lunch. We have *buchty* with cream. I want to save the *buchty* for Mother's Day. The whole business of gifts concerns me. Afterward, I go to Mother's. I want to play soccer tomorrow. My mother will not allow me but says that she will think about it. I don't know how it will turn out. I spend no time on the magazine today. When I see Grizzly and Herz, my stomach turns over. I keep taking it easy, and I am allowed to go outside only for purpose. There is *Apel* and then I go to the barber. On the way, I stop at the School. I cannot understand why everything takes so long. Nothing is being done there. I have an awful diarrhea today. At the barber, my hair is cut by a very obnoxious woman. Nevertheless, I'm glad it is finally cut. After the barber, I go to watch soccer. Since I don't enjoy it, I leave and go home. I hurry to the *bašta,* even though I am not allowed, because there is a match at 4:45 between the Hawks and Hollandia. Now I am sorry. The match ends in a tie of 3:3. I leave and go for supper, where they serve *geback.* Again, I keep it. Somehow I feel sick to my stomach. I hurry to Mother's. There, Mother decides firmly that she will not allow me to play soccer. I am unhappy and I argue a lot. Again, I have to go to the bathroom; it is the fifth time today. I have the shivers and I feel dizzy. I take my temperature and, lo and behold, I have 37.4 degrees. Now, I no longer can insist on playing soccer. I go home and I take two pills. At home, I maintain that I have 37.6 degrees temperature because I want to get into bed. However, I don't manage to do this. I can see now what egotists the other boys are. They very calmly fight near my bed and throw my things off my bench. I have to go again twice to the bathroom. I feel worse than yesterday. Very tired, I soon succumb to sleep.

Monday, 8 May 1944

I wake up and I have a feeling of a peculiar weakness. I stay in bed. I take my temperature and have 37.1 degrees. Soon, my father arrives and he is very concerned. I'm supposed to go to Mother's, but I feel very strange and dizzy. I can see how the boys don't behave like friends. I say to myself that I will be exactly like them. Then, suddenly, comes world-shaking news—we have to move out. First, I think that we are moving back to L417 and I start packing my things. But, later it turns out that it is only to the first floor. The *sichy* [elderly sick people] are moving to the main floor, because according to Rahm's edict, L504 will become Terezín's *Siechenheim* [nursing home]. I take it relatively calmly. I pack up and go to Mother's. Again I am examined by the doctor and he comes to the conclusion that I have a stomach flu. He prescribes some zwieback. Then, I lie down on Mother's bed and I am bored. I don't eat anything for lunch. At noon, my mother lies down next to me, and I fall into an unhealthy sleep. However, I sleep nevertheless. I wake up at four o'clock. Now I know what it is to be sick in Terezín. Gustl arrives; how I envy those who are healthy. He says that we are not going to be moving until seven o'clock. Those who can move should do so; otherwise we will be moved to the attic. I leave it to fate. I read Czech literature and other things. Then Handa runs in and says that he injured his hand and has to get a tetanus shot. My mother is all excited and sends Father after him. It is marvelous on the part of both. I continue staying in bed and being bored. Gustl arrives and tells me that I have been moved to the sick ward. I can't believe that if somebody were to tell me such news, I would accept it with such indifference. Perhaps this is the good, or the bad, side of Terezín? Soon, I gather myself and go home. Again, Father accompanies me. I really don't know whether it's necessary or whether it is true fatherly love. I am convinced that it is the latter. I make it to the *heim* and to the second floor with difficulty. Now I no longer have a permanent home. However, I realize that I am staying in a nice room. There are ten spots there and five of these are from Room 7. I am staying next to Lappert in a double block [bunk bed]. I have to get myself a straw mattress. I am glad that I am in the sick ward. I lie down and I already feel remarkably better. It is also great fun to be here. I fall asleep quite late.

Tuesday, 9 May 1944

I slept wonderfully. The good environment and gaiety have a good effect on me. Really, I am not at all sick any longer. I don't miss anything and I feel better than yesterday. The only thing that I do is wash myself quickly. Breakfast is brought to me in bed. It is really marvelous! Again, I feel the sincere care of my father. When he had to go to the ground floor, it was okay, but now that I am fortunately all cured and revitalized, for him to drag himself to the second floor is no small undertaking. Indeed, I could kick myself that I am so indebted to my father. I always keep telling myself that my behavior will improve, but I never manage to do it—at least not until now!

There is another doctor visit. My diarrhea has improved significantly. I went to the bathroom only once. For the purpose of the visit, I pretend and tell them I went more often because I want to stay at the sick ward and there is no place for me in the *heim*. I am properly looked over and I must stay in bed. This is the only thing that keeps me here because I am bored by not doing anything. At noon, my father comes to visit me, but I refuse his meal. I feel sorry for my mother! She toils the whole morning with food and I just refuse it. It is quite inconsiderate of me! After lunch, I just laze around in bed. I'm leaving the magazine to its fate because it no longer entertains me. I don't feel like working any more on my articles. I don't know how it's going to turn out. Thus I spend the whole afternoon until my father arrives and brings me food. I like spending the day the way I did today. However, in one word it was . . . inactive. In the evening, the lights go out at 9:30 and I fall asleep out of boredom.

Wednesday, 10 May 1944

I wake up because I have to go to the bathroom. I cannot hold food and I have very fluid stool. Afterward, however, I feel quite well and with blessed laziness I lie down on the bed. I read Shakespeare. Nothing, however, lasts forever. My laziness stops entertaining me. When I think that on Sunday is Mother's Day and I don't have anything or don't know what the magazine is doing, I feel like jumping out of bed and that's exactly what I do. Dr. Klein releases me at one o'clock.

This, however, changes my whole day. I am glad that I am able to get up and I even get a ration of crackers. Gustl came to visit me only once. In the *heim*, all disputes are straightened out about where I belong and about arguments that started during moving. Sasha came to visit me only once too. I get dressed, go for lunch, and then to Mother's. I feel like I have risen from the dead. I eat my lunch at Mother's, but soon get into an argument with her. For this reason, I pack up and leave. I am awfully weak. I hardly crawl up to the second floor. It is oppressively warm, which only adds to my inactivity. I worry about Mother's Day. I want to write an article in order to accomplish something. However, I don't know how or when. I loiter around. I get a brainstorm to start a new competition. It involves illustrations from books and one must guess from which book they come. There are approximately sixteen illustrations. I meet Pepík and I roam around with him. Afterward, I return to the *heim*. I get saved by lack of time because it is already time for supper. A question keeps coming up in my mind: "What type of person is my mother?" With the question unanswered, I enter the barracks. I don't know how it came about, but I start preaching to my mother. Whoever is going to read this will be surprised, but unfortunately it is the truth. I blame Mother and tell her that she keeps picking on me. Since there is a meeting at one o'clock, I have to say good-bye to her, full of anger and spite. But before my departure, I make up with Mother by promising her that I will improve my behavior. With shame and my head down, I go to the *bašta*. At the meeting, we read and sing and learn how to make knots. Overall, it does not please me. Because I have no concept of time, I stay on the *bašta* and watch a match of handball. I return to Mother's and there it starts again . . . It is already 8:45. Mother scolds me. I'm unhappy. Already I have reneged on my promise. I go home and everything is dull, as always. I lie down and I soon fall asleep. It was a boring day.

Thursday, 11 May 1944

I wake up at seven o'clock. I don't want to wash up, but I am forced to do so. I am glad that my bed is already made up and that I can indulge in my laziness and wait for the doctor's visit. It turns out that I must be completely healthy, because they allow me to get up. I'm glad! I get dressed, I attend to the necessary things and go for lunch and then to my mother's. I am in a good mood, and my mother and

I reminisce about our last night's spat, but more on the promise we made to each other. We joke, and I haven't felt so well for a long time. I sit outside and study French. Father is not the same as he used to be. He talks, and we sit as one whole family, with Handa, in front of the barracks. Nothing lasts forever, particularly joy and happiness.

We go with Mother for Father's suit and, after such a long time, we again hear the dreaded word, TRANSPORT! What an awful word. This word means knapsacks, suitcases, and hunched Jewish figures underneath them. Why? Just because the Germans want it, and on account of that, thousands of miserable people must leave their bundle and go away into the mist. Yes, this is transport.

Of course, the good mood sinks below freezing point. I have difficulties consoling Mother. I don't succeed because I myself am disturbed. I go home to visit Holzer, then upstairs, and then again to my mother's. There I have a snack and we talk awhile. Afterward, I go and have my supper. Then, more news. At a time, yet to be determined, we will be moving from Hamburg, possibly to the School. I am distraught. Transport . . . moving. Another version is that we will move into BV. At any rate, there will be *Apel* at six o'clock. First I go to Mother's but soon it is six o'clock and therefore I return home. At home, of course, *Apel* doesn't take place, but Mrs. Mautner tells us that tomorrow at seven o'clock in the morning we are moving into L417. I'm glad that it turned out at least this well. I meet my parents and go for a walk with them. We talk about the question of transports. We admire the beauty of Terezín's nature. Because time passes quickly we have to part, and each one of us goes his own way. I go to Hamburg and I again feel very tired. I pack my things and go to bed, where I soon succumb to sleep.

Friday, 12 May 1944

I wake up because there is turmoil in the room. It is already 6:30 and therefore I get up quickly. I don't have any time to wash up. Everybody is up already. My mother arrives and asks whether I need her. I say no because Mother is not quite healthy as yet. I do everything by myself. I have already packed up my bedroll. At last, they call us that the cart is ready. I have a heavy bundle because I have all kinds of things inside. Only with difficulty, I drag it downstairs. I feel weak. I don't have any strength to walk up the steps. I feel like walking on air. The cart starts moving. Room 7 is supposed to serve as the moving department. I can hardly keep up with the boys. Finally we stop in front of the School and we carry our luggage upstairs. Nothing really has changed. The room is empty except for bunks. Because I am assigned to assistance duty, I have to return with the cart to Hamburg. The boys run but I cannot keep up with them. I linger behind. In Hamburg, I load everything up and then return to L417. The scene is replayed. Franta says to find a mattress beater and for this reason I go to Mother's. I get it and soon return to the School where the boys are gathered. Mrs. Mautner arrives and announces that she is in the transport. I feel sorry for Jirka and Palka.[61] Franta is heartbroken. Then the spaces are assigned and I get a spot with Kalíšek in the middle level in what used to be second block. Franta says Kalíšek should get a better spot because he is recovering from a sickness. I don't care about the space, but it is a matter of principle. I'm angry at Kalíšek. He comes in like a king and, even when he is healthy, he does nothing. I can see that Gustl is his best friend. I go and beat the mattresses. My mind isn't in it though. I've lost one of my mattresses. I look for it in the yard, in the attic, in fact everywhere, but I cannot find it. I am distraught and I look for another mattress which may be left over. Finally, everything clears up; Franta took it because he says it belongs to him and it suits him well. I can't offer anything to contradict him. Instead, I pick up Kikina's mattress, which is pretty bad. However, I am happy that at last I have two mattresses. I make up my bundle in which I pack everything. I take my meal dish and go for lunch. I see long lines and therefore I let Grizzly pick up my lunch. This proves to be fateful. With lunch, I go to Mother's. So far only the Mautner brothers and Beneš are in the transport. I talk for awhile with my parents and then I sit in the yard and write my diary. I remember the garden and I want to go to work. First I go home, but there I learn that Franta does not want us to go to work. It's two o'clock, the time for *Apel,* which ends in excitement over an announcement that at four o'clock there will be an inspection by Otík. We are told to be clean and washed up. Then we're dismissed and we talk in the *heim,* and throw the ball around. I go and wash myself in the newly refurbished washroom. This makes me feel great. After getting washed, I

61. Jiří (b. February 21, 1930; nicknamed Jirka) and Pavel (b. March 23, 1942; nicknamed Palka) Mautner were deported with transport Bz from Tábor to Terezín on November 12, 1942; Jiří numbered 248 and Pavel 249. They were assigned to room 7, and their mother was Franta Maier's assistant. Jirka and Palka were shipped to Auschwitz with convoy Eq on October 12, 1944, now numbered 247 and 248. Both perished.

take the ball outside and throw it around. Because it is late, we are told that there will be no *Apel.* I go to the barracks for my *menaška* and my meal dish. I cannot find my mother or the *menaška.* I try to remember where it could be. Then it strikes me that Grizzly must not have returned it to me after lunch. I quickly run to Grizzly, but he is not there. I look for him in the School, but he is not there either. Then I go to *Kinderkuche* [the kitchen where the children's meals are prepared], to L403, to the barracks. He is not any of those places either—so I go to L48, to Dr. Bauer, where I'm not allowed to enter, and then again to the School and to the kitchen, but my *menaška* for supper is nowhere to be found. It starts to bore me and I say to hell with the dumplings and go to Mother's instead. There I have my dinner. Fortunately, Handa got more dumplings and Mother has done some more cooking. I'm really worried about the gift. Now, in the time of transports, nobody cares about it. Because my mother goes to the washroom, I'm forced to go home. On the way I meet Kopperl, who tells me that the following are on the transport list: Bäumel, Gorila, and Huppert. In total, all people in the A.K. transport get the summons. I am unhappy. Everything else becomes secondary. I forgot to say that at noon there was an air raid which lasted half an hour and that we also had to clean the attic. At home I challenge Lappert to a game. He agrees. We go to his mother and we tease a little girl. It is getting late and therefore we return home. I go to bed and, despite my heavy cough, I fall asleep before the lights go out.

Saturday, 13 May 1944

I sleep well in the new surroundings. It is Saturday and therefore we can sleep longer. I'm glad that I have found my *menaška.* It was lying on my bed. I don't have the patience to stay in bed, however, so I get dressed and hurry to Mother's. Everything concerns the transport. It is dreadful. I am scared of *reklamace* [attempts to get out of a transport] because we may be called.[62] Meanwhile, we haven't heard anything. I go to my father to fill my pen and then I go to Mother's. Now we are friendly again. I go in the yard and there I write my diary and also an article. I like it there and I stay until lunch. I find out that

62. This sentence reflects Pavel's worry that if others are able to get out of the transport, his family may be put on the list instead. See the introduction for more on how *reklamace* pitted the inmates against each other.

Lamm is in the transport but not Bäumel. The Mautners are also in it. Herz must go without his brother, Macek. Even though I am not on speaking terms with him, I don't wish all this on him. I go with my lunch to Mother's, where we have another argument. I am very bored. Therefore, I decide that I will make a rag ball. I immediately go to my father for rags and a stocking. I arrive at Mother's, but she tells me that she has no time to make a ball. Again, I blame her and perhaps rightfully so. I therefore start to make the ball myself and I am doing it quite well. I am angry at my mother, who finally comes and finishes the ball for me. It is marvelous. I immediately put it to use by playing with it with Petr. I play with him excellently. I forgot to mention that when I went for lunch, I was promised by Hermann that he would make a gift for me by four o'clock tomorrow. I am delighted. After playing with the ball, I go for supper. It's *geback* again. When I return to the barracks, my father asks whether I already have a gift. I say no. Father sees that others have their own gifts and he talks to me very sharply. I start crying; in desperation it occurred.

[Rest of this day is left blank or is missing: PW.]

Volume 2

Sunday, 14 May 1944

I wake up while someone is pulling on my blanket. It is six o'clock and we have to go and help the needy ones. In the transport, there is a big chaos involving all kinds of *reklamace* and swindles. Nobody is safe. I am in a big hurry so that I will arrive on time to L218 with the boys. However, we come late. I go to see Heini. We learn that we are supposed to go to three houses in BV and there we will be assigned to individual assistant services. It is boring to stand next to stretchers for the dead for what feels like ten hours. I'm quite bored. Finally, a young girl arrives with whom we are supposed to go and help. As my bad luck may have it, we go directly to the barracks where my mother lives. We are absolutely not needed. Everywhere there is noise of the transport, but no one as yet starts loading. Everything is unnerving me. When I see Beran's old grandmother, my heart aches. I leave the boys and go to the School because I have to finish the gift for my mother. There, I sit down and write. It takes me just about half an hour. I'm pleased that I have finished the gift. With a feeling of joy and fear, I go and deliver the gift to my mother. It is stupid to wish someone well here in Terezín. At long last, I dare to give the present to my mother. I think that she is pleased. I noticed that my mother was sorry she didn't get anything last night. Mother seems to need a gift because she immediately is in a better mood. I talk with her and then I go for lunch. I stop at the *heim* and there I'm told to be again in front of Hamburg at 11:30 to haul luggage from the blocks using a cart. I quickly eat my lunch and hurry to Hamburg. The boys are already waiting for me. There is an indescribable commotion there. People get tangled up in carts and vice versa, old grandmothers stumble over luggage. In brief, it is hell on earth. If all this didn't appear to me as if it were a dream, most likely it would shatter me. This is nothing compared to what is to follow. First we push the cart to L409. I keep thinking about my grandmother. We load some luggage and go to L129. We unload and go to Q501. There it all begins! A lot of old people wait to leave their homes with knapsacks in front of them. A sharp order by the *Hausalter* [house chairman] can be heard through the noise. The hunched figures fearfully entrust their luggage to us. The luggage is not well packed and at least half falls apart. We are dripping with sweat. After loading the luggage, we start moving. Behind us, a sad procession of people drags on. People have now lost all human signs and resemble outlaws. We drag slowly along. At last, we stop in front of Hamburg. We push our cart like a mighty stream of water. Such a scene cannot be depicted with a pen alone. We push through the crowd and into the Hamburg Barracks. The *Ordnung Dienst* [*Ordnungsdienst:* the inmate police force][63] don't let us in; everyone is afraid of the Germans. I don't even look back to see whether the old men and women are still dragging behind us. In the yard, we quickly unload the luggage and depart. Someone screams at us to keep going and someone else tells us to go another way. In spite of this, we soon appear outside of Hamburg. We go quickly to look in Q611 whether Beneš needs us. Beneš is no longer there and we must ignore the pleas of others. Sweat continues to drip off me. We push on to the Dresdner Barracks. We load the luggage belonging to Míša's grandmother. On the way, we accept suitcases from other people. In front of the Hamburg Barracks, we stop to separate the luggage and we rest for a while. Another young man joins us. He jumps on the cart and we go to L506. There, everything is packed up and so we return to Dresdner, where there is nothing to load. With the empty cart, we go to the front of Magdeburg, where we get further instructions to go to Kavalierka. There, it is the worst. Almost half of the barracks is going on the transport. Many old men and women are waiting in the yard. There is a tremendous disorder there. Everybody is concerned about his or her belongings and, at the same time, everyone wants their luggage to be loaded on the cart as quickly as possible. Soon everything is loaded up. We have to wait until the people who have their luggage on the cart line up. This, of course, takes a long time. Finally, we start moving. We are almost near the gate when an old woman runs—I should say limps—toward us. She is just saying goodbye to someone she knows and she cries. She wants to take along

---

63. The German-imposed Jewish governance structure included many departments, among them the *Ordnungsdienst;* Jewish inmates served as policemen to maintain order. They thus wielded authority over other Jews, but had no power vis-à-vis the Germans.

the bag that her friend carried for her. However, she cannot manage with only two hands. I feel sorry for her and therefore I jump toward her and grab her luggage. It consists of four small bags. The old lady continues to mumble something. I could overhear something about God and why she had prayed all her life but now God is abandoning her. Then, one of her bags breaks and all of the mustard spills out. I can't do anything about it. I accompany her, but I have to leave her at the gate. I return to the cart and help with unloading. I am so bored that I go to Mother's and write in my diary. I meet Gustl and I go to play rag ball with him in the yard. Because it is getting late, I go back to the barracks to have supper. Father goes to work and I go with Mother for dinner. After dinner, Mother and I go for a walk behind Ovčín and we stop at my father's, who joins us for a walk along Haupt-strasse. We are glad that for a while we are safe. Then, I go home. I go to bed where I soon fall asleep, partly due to fatigue but also simply due to the realization of life here.

Monday, 15 May 1944

I am disgusted by yesterday's events. I decide that I will not help today because I don't want to get upset. I stay in bed quite long. However, staying in bed bores me and therefore I get up, I get dressed and washed and I go to Mother's. I am curious as to what is happening. As of now, the following are in the transport from our *heim:* Gorila (who is trying for reclamation), Lamm (who is in again), Herz, and most likely Išík [see Jiří Lekner, appendix, page 231] and the Götzlingers (who are in it again but are trying to be reclaimed). In all, this third transport consists of people who were reclaimed from the first and the second ones. Since I don't know yet whether the Götzlingers will be out of the transport, I go to the *Verteilungstelle* [distribution center] for my knapsack. Then, I go to Mother's. There, I am bored until eleven o'clock, at which time I go for lunch. With lunch, I return to Mother's. However, I'm so disgusted that I don't have any appetite. I soon go home and go sliding. I stay on the slide for half an hour. Then, I take off my shoes and lie down on the bunk. I read a book I have borrowed, *Jan Svobodak as a Reporter.* I finish the whole book in two hours, and then I decide to go to Mother's, but first I go to supper and with supper I return to Mother's. Considering that it is "transport time," both of us are in a surprisingly good mood. Father goes to work at 5:30, and therefore I am alone with Mother. We talk for a while about things concerning the transport. I take advantage of the privacy and study French with my mother, who, for obvious reasons, doesn't have much desire to do this. I fully understand. Today is our second anniversary in Terezín. It is a sad anniversary. When I left Prague two years ago, I certainly did not believe that I would be here for two years. However, time continues to pass by. Suddenly, we have bad news. We study no more than twenty minutes when Father arrives and announces that Aunt [Olga] and Uncle [Otomar] Sušický are in the transport. Mother, of course, stops giving me the lesson and immediately goes to the Sušickýs. One doesn't have one minute of peace here. Immediately, everything is upside down. My parents go into offices [perhaps to get the Sušickýs reclaimed: PW], and I return to the *heim*. Vera Schlesingerová[64] is in the transport and Franta will most likely go with her. In addition, Lamm again receives the summons. I give him sugar. He's just leaving and he is completely alone. There are many people I know in the transport. At home, I cannot think about anything but the transport. Now, life in the *heim* is entirely different. Since everybody is in bed already, I join them. My things are in a big mess. For a while, I read about Mozart. Because the lights go out, I lie down and soon I succumb to sleep.

Tuesday, 16 May 1944

I wake up and I am all sweated up. The mood in the *heim* is depressing. Again, I find it distasteful to help out and therefore I lie idly in bed. Soon, I am bored and so I get up. Again, I don't air my bed linen and I don't even wash up. I decide that I will go to Mother's. First, however, I take my rag ball and go to play a game even though my shoes are torn. After the game, I'm very bored. I go to Mother's. As always, there is great commotion there. Little Míša still sleeps over there. Since I have not written my diary for the fourteenth of May, I sit down and write it. When I finish writing it I go for lunch, but I have to stop at home for my dishes. There are long lines, but my turn comes up soon. I go to Mother's with lunch. I find many people there with many *bonky* [rumors]. It is impossible to write about them

64. Vera Schlesingerová (b. September 22, 1919) was assigned number 429 and deported from Prague to Terezín with transport M on December 14, 1941. Franta Maier was her boyfriend, and both were shipped to Auschwitz, as Pavel indicates, but they did not leave on the same transport, or at this time. Franta was sent to Auschwitz on convoy Ek on September 28, 1944 (see diary entries for September 24–26) and Vera on transport Em (her number: 1077) on October 1. She survived to be liberated at the Kudowa labor camp.

because things change every minute. I go back and fetch lunch for my mother. Mother's desire for food makes me angry. When she sees some soup, immediately she takes it. I already want to go home when Mrs. Fried offers Mother some leftover soup. Mother, of course, accepts it. My anger has no limits! I scold her and I insult her that she is a beggar. I'm so angry that I leave and go home to L417. There Sasha catches up with me and asks me why I haven't been going to lessons. He says that I should go today. I resolutely refuse. Sasha blames me that I have an excuse all the time. Partly he's right. He wants me to pay for the lessons that we did not even take. As I see it, it's sheer stupidity. I prefer to play *okenka* [a children's game]. I play until I notice that my shoe is richer by one more hole. For supper, it is again soup and I bring it to my mother. There I find out some more news: the German Jews made a *smelina*[65] during the transport. They gave five hundred German Jews to the Czechs for inclusion in the second transport so they would get it over with, and now for the third transport, they want this favor back. For this reason, everybody who has been reclaimed must be given back to the transport. The whole transport will consist of seven thousand people. In all, it is rumored that Terezín will be liquidated. Then nothing really matters. Mother goes to help Aunt Olga and I go home. Nothing particularly exciting happens at home. I have a play-fight with Sasha. It comes to a point when Hermann takes a pillow and Sasha has me in a hold. I make fun of it on Sasha's account. I go to bed and soon fall asleep.

Wednesday, 17 May 1944

Today, the third transport is being loaded. I don't care and I stay in bed until 8:30. Then I go to Mother. The transports interest me only superficially. I don't want the boys to go in the transports, but it's better they than I. Something unpleasant has happened to Peterka. It is being hushed up. Still there is gossip. I will describe just the minimum here: When I come to my mother, we have a big argument. Mother behaves strangely, maybe because of the transports. She is very stubborn. [Illegible word.] She cares only about cooking and about my upbringing, but not about my enjoyment. It upsets me very much. For this reason, I am testy on other things. I am so unhappy

65. Pavel's use of the term *smelina,* a trick for personal gain, expresses the mutual distrust between Czech and German Jews.

that I leave Mother early. Later, I am sorry about what I have done, but then I do it all over again. I go home and I waste the rest of the afternoon talking to the boys in the *heim*. I notice that my coat has disappeared from the bunk where other coats are lying. I think quickly; I spot a similar coat with a label: "Míša Gruenbaum." I don't know what to do. Míša is in the transport and must have packed my coat. I run to Míša, but he is not there. I don't know how to get inside the Hamburg Barracks. By chance I run into Hermann, who has a pass. I get the blue and red ribbon which allows me to enter the *Schlojska* [slang for *die Schleuse* or *Schleusky,* the processing center for incoming and outgoing transports] in the Hamburg Barracks. After much unpacking, the Gruenbaums take out my coat. I take the coat and go to the Sušickýs to say good-bye. Then I go for my supper. The potato soup really bores me. On the way I run into the boys who have a cart. I decide that I will also help. First, I run quickly to my mother to eat my supper and then I rush to the Hamburg Barracks. It's very crowded with everyone trying to get inside. I meet my Aunt Olga. I bring the luggage to the right room. However, my aunt cannot find her luggage. I have to look for it in the yard. A woman comes to me in the yard with a red band and takes my band under the pretext that Rahm is coming and he will throw me out. This does not embarrass me. I go home for a new band, but I don't return to the *Schleusky.* I find out that Rahm will make the whole transport walk in front of him at the Hamburg Barracks and with a motion of his glove he will change the fate of many people. He will pick primarily workers, Mr. Lechner among them. At home we talk about the Ghetto's leaders. The transport is already finished. However, people are still being called. With this method, about eight hundred people have been reclaimed. Rahm is pretty good. My eyes are closing, so I go to bed. Then Franta arrives and announces that Rahm was at Room 1, which was very disorderly. He made a big *bordel.* For this reason, we have to get up tomorrow at 6:30 and there will be a big *Grunt.*

Thursday, 18 May 1944

I get up at the usual time. It is exactly 6:30 when I beat and brush the mattress. Soon I'm finished with *Grunt.* We also have to scrub and we are not supposed to leave the *heim.* I comply for a while and read a book, but when they start scrubbing we have to carry water pails and therefore Kokošek and I leave for the barracks. I take my diary with me. Soon, all traces of the transport disappear and everything comes back to normal. People disappear, but one never loses those one knows. I'm glad that the majority of our boys have been reclaimed from the transport. Huppert is out [of the transport] and so is Išík. At least we are not losing the contributors to *Nešar*. Now everything concerning the magazine bores me though. It is said that *Rim, Rim* will probably come out soon. I learn from Kokošek that Herz is sending sarcastic regards to me and to Gustl. I don't wish that he is leaving on the transport but I'm glad I'm getting rid of him. I had another argument with Gustl, but it does not have deep roots. However, Kalíšek gets on my nerves because he doesn't pay attention to me. I go to my mother's, but I don't stay too long. My mother pays attention only to her work and I'm supposed to bore myself there and therefore I leave. At home, I start writing my diary, but I lose all desire when I see that the boys are playing in the yard. Unfortunately, the game is almost over. I go sliding in the gym,[66] where they are preparing the nursery. It isn't ready yet and Leošek[67] doesn't permit sliding in the gym. In a short while, Leošek rushes in and makes us stand in a row. We pretend to be innocent. This doesn't help us though, because as punishment we have to go and clean up the small yard. Soon we are through with the work and we go back to the yard, where they are just finishing a game of *okenka*. We start to play a new match. I play pretty well despite the poor shoes, and I endure to the end. I finish third. I am all sweated up and therefore I go upstairs. I put myself in order and then I go for lunch. Springer still has my dish. Because there is a long line, we play a game of doubles of *česka* [a version of handball]. Today's lunch is potatoes with *tunke*. With lunch, I go to Mother, who keeps the potatoes and gives me burned farfel. I don't know how, but we start arguing again. We insult each other. I go and fetch lunch for my mother. At *Nachschup* [second helpings] I bring to my mother a full pot of soup, which is clear, of course. Again, I needle my mother. She looks awfully bad. However, insults come freely out of my mouth. After this incident, I return home. I don't even go upstairs, but directly into the yard. I want to write in my diary, but the lure of the ball

66. Previously used as a school, L417 had a gym in the basement. Stairs from the main level led down to it. The space was used primarily as a theater and for concerts and meetings during the ghetto era.

67. Leo Demner (b. June 17, 1919) was deported on December 4, 1941, from Prague to Terezín on transport J. He served as an assistant to Ota Klein. Shipped to Auschwitz with convoy Ek on September 28, 1944, Leo survived and was liberated in Taucha.

is stronger. They are just finishing a game of *česka*. We choose four teams. I am on Pudlina's. We play and we lose. I enjoy the play and I work really hard to do well. All together we play two matches and I'm bushed. I don't watch the time. At five o'clock is *Apel* and therefore we have to finish. I get washed up. *Apel* doesn't take place, but instead we go to help carry down suitcases from the large attic to the small one. I have three suitcases and it is quite hard work. Then I go for dinner and to Mother. There, again, is a very bad mood. I don't know why, but we start arguing again. It gets so bad that I return to the *heim* early. At home, I accept the boys' invitation and go play *okenka*. I play until 8:30, and then I sit down and write my diary. I have to finish quickly because Franta suddenly arrives and tells us that the do-nothing life will soon be over. The lights go out. In darkness, I go to bed but I am still up when Išík and Míša return from the *Schleusky*. I want to wait up for Huppert, but I fall asleep.

Friday, 19 May 1944

I had bad dreams last night. I feel relieved when I wake up. It is 6:30. For a while I read, but soon Franta arrives and I have to get up. He says that one life is over and another one is starting. He screams at us, maybe because he is upset from the departure of his parents. I am angry at Kalíšek because I work hard in place of him and he wants to have all the benefits. I no longer like him or Gustl. I feel abandoned. Immediately, in the morning I notice that I am missing a *dekada* [food ration] that I had on my little table. I believe that it has something to do with the theft of Lion's onions. They must be stealing here. I am without margarine and I tell this to Franta. Tutinek asks me to carry some baskets up to the small attic. I do as he wishes. Franta warns us about inventory [?]. He is angry that the *Kofferlager* [suitcase storage room] has not been organized. I go to the attic and Franta asks me about something in a sarcastic tone. There is *Apel,* which seems to be the gateway to our new life. Everything has to be in tiptop shape. The next *Apel* will be at 11:30. There are two groups assigned to help in keeping the place clean. I am not assigned, but at eleven o'clock I will help Franta with the luggage. Franta asks me about my *dekada*—nobody knows anything and Franta uses this opportunity to give us a lecture about honesty. After *Apel,* the boys go to work, but I go to the yard to play *okenka.* The game is pretty boring and so I quit. It is eleven o'clock, the time for my duty. Franta, however, arrives and announces that he has to leave. For this reason, I go again to play. My eye is still sore from the last match. This new game is boring and I quit. There is another *Apel*. Otík tells us what I already expected: transport, moving, saving of furniture, beginning of the programs and nothing else. After *Apel*, I go to eat lunch. Finally, the lunch is good: *buchty* with cream! I do what I said I would do and I don't go to Mother's at noon. Instead, I watch the boys play cards. Today is Friday and there is supposed to be a cleanliness inspection, but I go to work, which excuses me. Before leaving, I have an argument on account of the lessons. Sasha wants me to pay for English lessons I didn't take. I give him all my bread. Before going home, I want to stop at Dr. Jelínková's. However, I meet Pepek, who says that Jelínková doesn't teach today. I hurry to get to the garden where the lineup is at two o'clock. Our squad leader is Ilse and our supervisor is Schwarzbart. He is an old man. He keeps scolding me for sitting on the lawn. However, I am protected by Ilse. Then we are supposed to water the garden. The time passes quickly and soon it is five o'clock, the end of our work. I volunteer to cut lilacs. I can see that something will come out of it. I ask Schwarzbart if he could give me some lilacs, but he says not before the end of the work. We work speedily until 5:30, at which time we carry the lilacs in our arms to BV. Everyone envies us. In BV it doesn't look like any lilacs will be left for me. I dare to ask. Schwarzbart says to go around the garden and somebody there should give me some. I hurry to the garden with Spulka.[68] Some girl cuts little pieces of lilacs for us. I'm very dirty and sweaty. I put the lilacs under my coat and go to the School. There, I arrange the lilacs and put a band around them. I go for dinner and take the lilacs to Mother. I hope that this will make it easier for us to make up. I was not mistaken. Mother is overjoyed. She gives me a lot to eat, and I am so full that I have cramps. Everybody is glad that we have squeaked out of the transport. After washing dishes, I go for a walk with Mother. Then my parents come to see my living quarters. They are not very satisfied and soon go home. I write my diary until the time when Franta arrives

68. Erich Spitz (b. March 27, 1931) was deported from Brno to Terezín with his parents a few days after his eleventh birthday, March 31, 1942, on transport Af (his number: 398). Separated from his father upon arrival, Spulka, as he was called, and his mother were assigned to the Dresdner Barracks, where he was quartered until L417 was organized in July. Erich and his parents remained in Terezín and returned to Brno after the war. In Hungary at the time of the Hungarian Revolution in 1956, Spulka decided not to return to Czechoslovakia and made his way to France.

and says that, if we go to bed on time, he will read to us. He is in a very good mood. Finally, I get a chance to wash up. It is really needed! Then I go to bed and write my diary.

Saturday, 20 May 1944

It is Saturday, the day when we can sleep until seven o'clock. In bed, immediately after waking, I hear that whoever wants to train on the *bašta* can go. Quick as lightning, I get dressed and watch the ball being inflated and tied up. At approximately 7:30, we set out to the *bašta*. For a while we kick shots at the goalie, but Franta soon arrives. We make our usual run. Somehow, I must have slept deeply because I have a headache. After the run, we line up for gymnastics. After gymnastics Majošek arrives; I was supposed to play in his place. Then we start playing a real match, but I don't participate. Franta promises that we will switch around. At ten o'clock we have to be at the garden *Apel* in L410. I play but I am soon replaced by a substitute, so I play for only ten minutes and I have to go home. On the way I stop at Mother's. I go with Gustl to L410. *Apel* is overall meaningless. Prager, Altman, and Schwarzbart talk about work and cleanliness, correctness, and honesty. Prager throws Spulka out of the garden. It is about eleven o'clock and there is supposed to be another *Apel,* which, however, doesn't take place. Around noon I go to Jelínková with Sasha for lessons. Everything is locked up and therefore I go for lunch instead. While I eat, something unpleasant happens to me; I drop a piece of salami on the ground. Very nonchalantly, I wash it off in my soup. Water is, after all, water. Because there is supposed to be *Apel* at one o'clock, I must leave. It is raining and very muddy outside, which doesn't do any good for my shoes. I have an argument with Father. He gives me a *menášek* [serving dish] to bring to the barracks. I take it there and then I hurry home. There is another *Apel.* After *Apel,* I go with Sasha to Jelínková and we agree to a lesson on Monday between 4:30 and 5:30 and the same time on Thursdays. Sasha and I needle each other because we have to give up *body* [points/meal coupons?: PW] and a *menášek.* I go to Mother for the *body* and with them I return home, bringing my flute with me. Then I go to Q609 to Berman for the music. At home, I practice for about forty-five minutes and afterward I play cards with the boys. Because it is getting late, I go for supper. At six o'clock, there is a meeting with Heini. I don't like today's meeting at all. We sing, Heini tells us stories, and we make knots. I leave the meeting gladly. I am supposed to go to Mother's, but I go instead to play *okenka,* which doesn't please me. At nine o'clock I go home and soon am off to bed.

Sunday, 21 May 1944

Today the new "normal" life really starts. We get up at 6:30 because at nine, the normal program starts. Franta is his old self and pays a lot of attention to order. I have all my school supplies packed in my suitcase, but my pen screeches something awful. The notebook which I bought at [?] is in the attic. Franta tells me that I must not keep my bread unwrapped. Therefore, I go to Mother, who is at the doctor. I give her my whole loaf of bread. I look through the suitcase to see if I have my notebook there, but I cannot find a thing. I have to hurry because at 8:45 there is *Apel.* And, I have to go to the attic, which, of course, is locked up. By chance, Otík opens it up for us and I look through the knapsack (I don't have any keys for the bag). I don't find anything there, either. I become desperate. After all, I have to have a notebook for the first day of the program! I quickly make a decision. I race to Mother's for a key, and then I go into Mother's bag and I find the key there. I quickly run home. Thanks to Kata,[69] I am able to get into the attic. Finally, I find the sought-after notebook and I immediately go to Room 5, where the program is being held. I can see that everyone enters work with new zest. There are only nine of us. For the first hour, we have Eisinger[70] for Czech. We learn about verse and it interests me a lot. In the course of the lesson, Kohn arrives and dictates the schedule. The second lesson is on the geography of Scandinavia taught by Zwicker. He is always good. Then, the beginners have English. I go upstairs and I teach Springer algebra. Soon, there is a lesson in Hebrew. Surprisingly, I like it this time. Nevertheless, I'm glad when the instruction is over. Now, I can see what an advan-

---

69. Katerina Fuchs (b. May 16, 1921), called Kata, was assigned number 571 on transport M and deported from Prague on December 14, 1941. She served as an assistant to Franta Maier until she was shipped on to Auschwitz with convoy En (her number: 751) on October 4, 1944. She survived to be liberated at the concentration camp at Mauthausen. Kata returned to Prague after the war.

70. Professor Valtr Eisinger (b. May 27, 1913) was deported on transport U from Brno to Terezín on January 28, 1942. He served as the *madrich* in room 1 of L417, an inspiration to the hundreds of thirteen-to-fifteen-year-old boys quartered there between 1942 and 1944. Deported to Auschwitz with convoy Ek on September 28, 1944, Valtr Eisinger did not survive.

tage it is to have an orderly notebook and pen. One can really learn. For lunch, we have *buchty* and cream. I go to Mother's but I must soon leave because there will be *Apel* at one o'clock. Surprisingly, this one actually takes place. After it, I cannot recall what I did. I recall only that I received "*fuska*" [Czech colloquial word for an extra job] to write notes on what our class had done. I got a notebook for it. I write my diary. I notice that Franta is nice to me when he wants something from me. Tuti wants a pen from me, but I won't lend him one. I go outside in the yard to play with a big ball. Because I have a lesson at five o'clock, however, I have to finish. I like the lesson very much. We talk past the ending time and then I go to my mother's with supper. There, Mr. Berman tells me that tomorrow at seven o'clock will be a rehearsal in the brewery's attic. I am petrified because I have never as yet practiced with Jindra. I put myself together and hurry home, but on the way I stop at the Vrchlabi Barracks, where I look at the owls who have settled there. I quickly go to see Jindra, who, however, is not there. I stop at Handa's, who is lying on the roof. I have to return home and again write my diary. At 8:45, I again go to see Jindra, who again is not there. I don't know what to do. Franta arrives and announces that if we will be in bed by nine o'clock, he will read to us. Tonight, Kalíšek is sleeping next to me. We go to get washed together. We have a lot of things to tell each other, particularly he to me. Soon, Franta arrives and reads the story "Prophet Elias" from the book *Stories from the Ghetto*. My eyes are closing. Because there are several pages missing, Franta has to stop. Soon, despite my bad cough, I fall asleep.

Monday, 22 May 1944

Franta's voice wakes me up and it makes me jump. I really don't feel like getting up, but I am forced to. I put things in order. It is raining outside. Immediately after cleanup, I go to Jindra, who, however, is still sleeping. I am really mad, but nothing can be done about it. There is *Apel*. I give Franta my notebook. We must sign a paper that deals with behavior in the School. Then comes the program. Our first lesson is English today. For the first fifteen minutes, I am alone with Springer. For me, it is pretty boring. The second hour is Judaism, where we repeat old material. Today, I am particularly sharp. However, I feel awfully cold. The third lesson, mathematics with Professor Kohn, is held in the attic. As always, he is very interesting. The fourth lesson is history and we learn about the colonization of villages and about Jan Luxemburg.[71] I'm not very interested today and, therefore, when I am called on, my thoughts are somewhere else. Finally, the lesson is over and I go upstairs, where I find out that I am supposed to go to Jindra at four o'clock. I summarize the subject material of all classes for Franta. I am kowtowing to him. It is 12:30 when I go to Mother's. We have a small argument, which passes over quickly. I have lunch and fly home. Really, now I don't have any time to spend with Mother. *Apel* is at 1:45. As always, it is worthless. Afterward, we all sit down and Franta reads us a book by Kruif entitled *Should Generals Die in Bed?* I cannot concentrate. Afterward, the program continues with a repetition of physics. We make fun of Irenka. After the program, we go home. I sew on buttons and then I study some kind of laws of scouting. Then, we do our homework. I am tested by Franta and my answers are all good. I go to Jindra, who is still not there. Now, I am desperate. I return to the *heim,* but immediately I go to L218. I wait there for about half an hour and I discover for myself my music scores. Finally, Jindra arrives and we practice. We're doing quite well, but all moves too slowly. At approximately 5:30 I return home, where there is another meeting with Heini. He reads "Posleda"[?] to us until about 6:45. Afterward, I rush to have supper with Mother, where I find out that we have received a parcel from the Knoblochs.[72] I immediately eat the cracklings. I meet Jindra in front of BV and we go together to the brewery, where we find Berman. We immediately start to play. Partly because of stage fright and partly because I cannot play so fast, I did not do very well. I don't feel upset, however, because everything can be improved upon. I go to Mother's for supper, but because she is about to have a bath, I return home and write my diary. Franta arrives and we talk for a while about state constitutions. I recognize Kalíšek to be a false friend. I feel sleepy. I go to bed and fall asleep. I have an ugly dream about our School burning down. I don't know what consequences this will have.

Tuesday, Wednesday, Thursday, 23, 24, 25 May 1944

Because these past days I had neither the time nor the inclination, I have not written my diary. I don't think it will matter if I combine

---

71. Jan Luxemburg (1296–1356), eldest son of Holy Roman Emperor Henry VII, became the count of Luxembourg in 1309 and was elected king of Bohemia in 1310, and thus one of the seven prince-electors of the Holy Roman Empire.

72. The Knoblochs and the Weiners were friends in Prague. Mrs. Knobloch was Jewish; her husband was not. This protected her from deportation.

the events of these days. The most important thing is that I don't feel like doing anything, not even working on the magazine. This has something to do with my preoccupation with playing soccer! We play a match that we win two to nothing, but unfortunately the ball which I had borrowed from Room 5 breaks. I continue to play *česka* in the yard and I have a faithful companion in Gustl. I am now in top form. Thus, I entirely neglect my parents. I arrive in the barracks for only half an hour. I am always concerned about my mother and, on the way to the *heim*, I feel guilty. I keep seeing in front of me her ill-looking and worried face that arouses in me simultaneously superstitious fear and pain. I don't know how to crack this chestnut. The answer arrives on the evening of the twenty-fifth. And this is how it happened: In the morning we have work in the garden and then program in the afternoon. Therefore, I only spend half an hour at Mother's and I can see that my mother feels bad about it. In the afternoon we have program until five o'clock and then I do something I shouldn't have done. Like an idiot, I go to play *česka* in the yard. I make a magnificent effort and beat Gustl 10:3, but isn't all this worthless? I meet Brenner, who wonders why I would want to see Mother rather than attend a meeting. I quickly run to Mother's and again this worried face appears. Mother is now sick; she suffers from a disease similar to my father's. I feel that I am the worst child in the world when I tell her that I have to leave again. Inside, I am confused—should I stay or should I leave? I leave. . . .

I don't like the meeting at all. It is quite obvious that Heini is trying to brainwash us with Zionism. I don't feel comfortable in the Zionist circle. It seems that as a Zionist, people will consider me inferior. This is the reason why I am not a Zionist. I'm glad when the meeting is over and I quickly run to Mother's but unfortunately she is not at home. Now it comes to me how I'm harming others by playing with that miserable ball. I don't feel like doing anything. Why is the magazine going bankrupt? It is only because of playing ball. I keep telling myself that I must not be destroyed by a ball. I must not play for two days, and only then in moderation. Dejectedly, I walk through town looking for my parents, whom I don't find. I return to the *heim*. There, I see again how Lion is working hard on the magazine, but I close my eyes and then, like a madman, I run to the safety of my mother. How pleased I am to see Mother's worried look! Just one little kiss is enough to make me happy and to improve my depressed mood. Being with her is being in a different world where one doesn't play *česka* continuously. At home, I find things in a big mess and many of my things, such as my socks, have disappeared. I go to bed and I fall asleep soon.

Friday, 26 May 1944

For several days when I awake I am completely sweated up. Obviously, it is on account of weakness. Today, I am again sweated and I am very sleepy. I stay in bed longer and Mrs. Mautner immediately punishes me by telling me I have to go to bed by six o'clock. Soon this punishment is canceled, even without my asking. I go to Mother's, whom I don't reach at home. I sit down and do my English homework. After I finish, I go to the School for *Apel*. I see on my bed a bundle of linen that was returned to me from my last delivery to the laundry. After *Apel*, we are dismissed to go to the program. The first lesson is Jelínková. We are reading *Happy Prince* in English. During the break, I cannot find my margarine. Most likely, somebody again must have made a "mistake" [meant sarcastically?: PW] and taken it. However, I am wrong since I find it later. The second lesson is history: Jan Luxemburg and the university. After the lesson, I walk along with Zwicker and we talk. On Fridays, we have only two lessons. At home, I sit down and finish writing my diary. Because it is eleven o'clock, I go for lunch and with it to my mother's so that I can spend more time with my parents. We have *buchty* with cream. There is a good mood prevailing at Mother's and I don't feel sorry that I arrived early. I go for *Nachschup* for my mother, and then at one o'clock I return home for *Apel*, during which it is announced that at six o'clock there will be a cleanliness inspection. Because we were inattentive, we have to stand. I don't care for how long other boys have to stand because I have to go to the garden at 1:30. However, while I'm waiting, I have an argument with Kalíšek, after which we leave for work. I am assigned to a group of weeders. I don't like this work at all. We work on a lawn where there are some seeded carrots and a lot of weeds. All the time, Schwarzbart screams at us and tells us that he should throw us out. Perhaps he is right. Afterward, we do some watering of whatever is freshly seeded. I'm glad when the work is finished. In the street, I feel embarrassed that I'm wearing two different socks. At home, Gustl really gets to me by blaming me that I have lost his spoon. It doesn't help that I search for it; the spoon is gone. Because of the inspection at six o'clock, I go first to Mother's. There, I change and get washed up and I am clean as a whistle. Then I go back to the School. *Rim, Rim* magazine has come out. It gets on my nerves. During *Apel*, the diary of the *heim* is read, but we have to fin-

ish because Otík arrives. He tells us that we ask for too much. I think
he is full of hot air. We are dismissed and, for a while, I look over the
heim with interest. I forgot to mention that Father has gotten sick; he
has a headache and a cold. I go to Father's, where I meet my mother.
I completely forget to eat my supper. Mother asks me if I had my supper and, for the first time in my life, I lie to her. I'm sure that Mother
knows that I am lying, but she doesn't say a thing. We leave Father's
place and go to Mother's barracks. There, she sews a button for me
and then, after a long lapse of time, we study French together. I have
forgotten a lot so we go through three lessons. Because it is getting
late, I go home. At the *heim,* I am upset with questions about whether
Nešar has been published. I write my diary and then I crawl into bed
where *Rim, Rim* is being read. It is quite good actually.

Saturday, 27 May 1944

When I awake today, I am no longer as sweated up as on previous
mornings. We can stay in bed longer today. I write my diary, and when
I finish I just lie idly in bed. The calm is interrupted by Mother's arrival. It is ugly outside, but nevertheless Mother wants me to go with
her to the attic to take out our summer stuff. I am missing many
things and Mother misses one [?], Mother changes my linen so now
I am all clean. Then, she leaves and we are on good terms. I am missing my *menaška* and I immediately realize that it is at Mother's. Franta
starts screaming that things are in a mess. During *Apel* today, there is
a tremendous *bordel.* As punishment, we have to stay home from six
o'clock on, and at 5:30 there will be another *Apel.* I hurry to get my
menaška at Mother's; the mood is no longer good. Mother is cooking
and has no time to give me a French lesson. I spend about half an
hour there and then I go to soccer. It is pretty good. I am there until
seven o'clock and I am quite angry. When I return to Mother's, we
have an awful argument. I will not even describe the details. At any
rate, we go for a walk and everything repeats itself. Mother says that
I'm bad, which makes me so angry that I pick myself up and go home.
I think that now my world and life are lost.

JUNE
[No date shown: PW.]

Now, this week has been one of my worst. Constantly I am besieged
with questions as to what *Nešar* is doing and I keep answering that it

will come out, even though I know that it will not. I am filled with dread, thinking that my first life work has been destroyed. In addition, my diary has not been written. I have decided that I'm not going to use the current system of writing my diary. From now on, I will write out only the most important facts and omit meaningless details. What has happened this week? Overall, a lot, and at the same time, nothing. Many things happened and then immediately disappeared. I had an argument with Mother that lasted until Monday evening. In the evening, I was completely distraught. I sat with my mother in total mental abandonment and I started to cry. This had an effect on my mother, and vice versa. We immediately made up and the following day, everything was in order. Quieter days followed. I practiced my flute and I got a ball which, unfortunately, had a leak. The life of the *heim* has consisted of programs, which have been somewhat entertaining. Then, I played hooky from the garden and, as a result, I was thrown out along with three other boys. I was glad, but Mother was angry. I play less soccer now because my shoes are torn. This, however, is not the cause for having not written anything over the past few days. These days have all been similar until Tuesday—a day of great events in the life of Terezín. First, in the afternoon I received notice of a package with sardines. Franta and Kata also got one so I picked it up for them as well. Mother and Father were very happy because they found out that Father's and grandfather's names were mistakenly on the list of "undeliverables." Since the mistake has been corrected, we can expect more packages from Uncle Erich, who is living in the USA. I went immediately to the post office, where I had to stand in line for a long time. Then, Handa arrived and said that he also got notices for two packages. Secondly, it has been confirmed that the expected invasion has occurred in Northern France. There is a good mood everywhere and we all hope that by 13 November, my birthday, we will be home in Prague. Tonight, we open the tin of sardines. Because I have a ticket to the "Music of Youth" concert, I leave. I go to the new hall called Orel [Eagle]. And I like the performance very much, particularly "Ledec." In the evening, Franta is reading us Seifert[73] when I fall asleep.

Wednesday, 7 June 1944

Today is the usual program which, I must be frank, does not entertain me much now. By chance, today we have three lessons. I am teed off

---

73. Jaroslav Seifert, Czech journalist, translator, and poet, was awarded the Nobel Prize for literature in 1984.

that we are not allowed to go to the big yard. The *Verschönerung* [beautification program] is slowly coming to an end. Our gym is all decorated and, for this reason, Rahm comes to visit us in the morning. For the last three Sundays, Mother has had a day off and yesterday she started the morning shift. For this reason, I don't go to have lunch with her. During the noon *Apel*, Franta tells us that today we will study. For a week, I haven't written the program into the notebook. I have to rewrite everything so that Franta can test us. It takes me a good long while and afterward I study. I listen to the examinations of others. The whole afternoon passes by in this way. The *tercie* [third form in a *gymnasium*, an academic high school] ended up well. Then, I go for a lesson where I make fun of Jelínková. After, I go to Mother's. I am nervous because I have a meeting at six o'clock. Mother is angry. I don't like the meeting. I return to Mother's, where the mood is bad. I don't feel like studying French and therefore I return home where Franta is reading to us. Very tired, I soon fall asleep.

Thursday, 8 June 1944

I wake up with a headache that disappears during the morning "quarter hour" [exercise?: PW], which is pretty good. Today I have *Zimmerka* [room cleanup duty]. Kalíšek and I clean up while the rest go to the garden. During this time, I also write my diary. I decide again that I will be writing shorter entries. Afterward I want to go to play *česka*, but I don't go because I must make up notebooks for Franta. Later, the gardeners return with lettuce. I feel bad now that I was thrown out of the garden. I try to reach Otík to reaccept me. Kalíšek is buddying more with Gustl and actually both of them are quite obnoxious to me. Meanwhile, I have a good feeling, that certain pleasure which tells me that I will be celebrating my next birthday in Prague. The English are attacking strategically piece by piece along a front that is four hundred kilometers long. It is really marvelous. The *Verschönerung* is over and the park opens up. It has benches on which, unfortunately, we cannot sit because of nasty weather. Mother is at work so I stay at home for lunch. Since I have room duty, I have to again put the *heim* in order. In the afternoon, we have a program that is not interesting at all. Today is my brother's birthday eve. I am mad that I have so much work to do. I dread the program for the evening. First, there is my room duty. Secondly, I want to be at Mother's, and thirdly, I have an examination at Berman's. Finally, and fourthly, I also have a meeting with Heini. I really don't know how I am supposed to do all these things. I go to Mother's and she is doing a lot of good things for Handa. I feel bad that I cannot stay longer. I decide that I will not go to the meeting. Instead, I go with Jirka to see Berman. Despite my stage fright, I play the cantata and the examination turns out quite well. I return home where I stand guard. At 7:45, Kalíšek comes to take my place and I go to Mother's. I catch Handa while he is leaving and I congratulate him on his seventeenth birthday [the following day, June 9: PW]. I give him my sardines, as I have plenty to eat. Then my parents walk me home. Mrs. Mautner reads us Čapek[74] and I fall asleep during her reading.

Friday, 9 June 1944

Today is meaningful only on account of the evening *Apel*. The morning is monotonous, the same as all others—the usual *Apels* and then programs. What is interesting is *Verschönerung*. The route through which the commission will be taken has been set. The route leads through our hall and gym, which have been cleanly painted and scrubbed. Only lower surfaces of the houses have been painted. During the day of the commission, there will be a luxurious lunch. *This* is Terezín! In today's program we only have three hours. The remaining hour I do nothing. I go for a *buchta* with cream. For the whole afternoon, until four o'clock, I walk around. I meet with Sasha and I decide that I will tell everybody that *Nešar* has folded. It is really true. During *Apel*, Franta also asks me how *Nešar* is doing and I tell him that it no longer exists. I'm glad that I have gotten it off my chest. Then I go to Mother's where the mood is good. I'm mad that I have a meeting at 7:30. I have dinner and then I go with my father to the *bašta*. Father walks me home at seven o'clock. I finish my diary and then I go to a meeting which I don't enjoy much. Then *Rim, Rim* comes out. I go to bed and Franta reads us a story during which I fall asleep.

Saturday, 10 June 1944

We are supposed to have soccer practice today, but since we don't have a ball we cannot go. We stay in bed for a long time and I read.

74. Karel Čapek (1890–1938) was a hugely popular and influential Czech author. Identified by the Gestapo as its Czech "public enemy #2," Čapek died of pneumonia shortly after the Germans annexed the Sudetenland.

We have to get up on account of the German commission. I completely forget that I have to go to Jindra. After we put things in tiptop shape, Franta tells us that we are free from 9:30 on. At 1:30, there will be another *Apel,* which I realize I must attend. I study French and then I do my homework. Soon I go for lunch. I get a ration of yeast, and for lunch there is salami and potatoes which I bake. Then, I go to Mother's and I bring her all my food. Mother has morning shift and therefore I return home. There is *Apel,* and, afterward, Franta reads to us. I'm looking forward to spending the afternoon at Mother's. I am welcomed there, but she has no time to give me lessons in French. She makes dumplings and I very patiently wait, but when it takes too long I say the hell with it and I start to insult Mother that she doesn't know how to do anything else but cook. The idea of lessons is gone. I am very mad. Outside, it's raining. I go for supper and then I return to Mother's. I don't feel like eating, but my mother forces me to do so. Slowly, I become sorry that I got angry at her, but I don't let on. We go for a walk. The subject of our discussion is our living quarters. I blame my parents for not managing to get a flat. It obviously affects my father. He is in a bad mood and says, while he is sitting in the park, that he will never again be happy. It makes me very angry to hear this. Afterward, I go home where I lie down and fall asleep.

Monday, 12 June 1944

The morning is uneventful. However, the evening is interesting because I play outside with the ball. The ball falls into the L414 garden. That garden is locked and therefore I have to sneak at ten o'clock into the garden, but I come out empty-handed. While doing this, I am written up for coming in late. I don't think that much will come of it though. In the evening comes Arna Meisl and we are told that tomorrow we may volunteer for all-day garden work. I fall asleep.

Tuesday, 13 June 1944

In the morning, I wake up with a feeling of indecision as to whether to go to the garden or not. I therefore go to Mother's, who tells me to do what I want, but she advises me not to go if I want to study. At home, I learn that the whole third form volunteers have to work in the garden all day. Lion and I decide that it would not be a bad idea to start some kind of a study group. This makes up my mind. I go with Lion to Mother's. The conversation comes to the subject of magazines. Lion asks me the question for which I have been waiting a long time . . . whether I would like to contribute to *Rim, Rim.* He says that no one can write the kind of articles that I write and that it would be a pity if they stopped appearing. I tell him I will think it over. I really would like to do it, but something is telling me that I cannot abandon *Nešar.* I don't catch Mother at her home and, therefore, I go back to mine. I volunteer to go to the garden, but Kohn doesn't want to let us go. Children born in 1931 probably will not be allowed to work in the garden. I cut the program and go to consult with Franta. He is on our side. With lunch I go to Mother's. There is continuous uncertainty as to whether I can get into the garden. Kohn calls us in and tries to convince us to think it over. At home, I notice that I have lost my *menaška* again so I am forced to go with Kalíšek to the *Menagekartenstelle* [meal ticket distribution office]. After a long search, I get a replacement ticket. At six o'clock, we learn that we probably won't be accepted to work in the garden. In the evening, I go with Father to the *bašta* and then home to sleep.

Wednesday, 14 June 1944

Nothing of interest has occurred today. The only thing that has been definitely decided is that I will not go to the garden, not even to the garden in L410 because we have been working poorly there. Undoubtedly, this is Otík's idea. Our "professors" wouldn't permit it. In the morning, we have again program. At 12:30, the *Läusedoktor* [lice doctor] arrives. He comes to the conclusion that my head is dirty. Mrs. Mautner wants to wash my head with KUPREX, but I know that it is useless. It's no wonder that my scalp is dirty since we don't go to the bathhouse. Even though I am annoyed, I go and wash myself. Our *heim* looks pretty good now. Everybody has a shelf for bric-a-brac, for food, for wash utensils and for clothing. Every day we are awaiting the Red Cross visit. Just this morning, Bloch[75] brought me the lost *menaška.* Now, I even have a replacement that I am not going to use. In the afternoon, I have my English lesson. I have it only because I want to educate myself. Jelínková is now so obnoxious to me that, if I could find someone better, I would stop taking lessons from her. In the evening, we have a meeting with Heini in L218, and today I like it. It lasts until 8:45, at which time I go to Mother's and there I study

75. Jiří Bloch (b. December 20, 1930) was assigned number 589 on transport G from Brno on December 2, 1941. Nicknamed Blecha (bedbug) by the room 7 boys, he was deported to Auschwitz with convoy En on October 4, 1944. His number: 1261. Jiří did not survive.

French. I am making great progress in this language! I continue to study. Then I go home, lie down and fall asleep.

Thursday, 15 June 1944

In the morning, we don't have the program that we usually have on Thursdays because the gardeners go to the garden. I spend the morning writing my diary and studying French. At about 11:30, I go for lunch. Normally I wouldn't mention lunch, but today I have to. I give the *Menagedienste* the found meal ticket. The woman has in front of her a list of lost meal tickets and when she sees mine, she immediately stops the line. She asks me whether I have lost my meal ticket. First, I tell her "no," but then I say "yes" and I pull out of my pocket the replacement ticket. She says to go and straighten it out with Mr. Basser, which I do. He takes both meal tickets from me and says that I should come for lunch at 12:30. Downhearted, I return home. I am furious. At home my mother tells me off. And, I remember something else. When I am at Mother's, Mrs. Fried announces that my father's room in L313 is being inspected by the gendarmes [Czech rural police]. We immediately go to L313. My father says that some Pole, a horse driver, has been bringing in two sacks of cigarettes hidden in ashes. The Polish man lives in L313. At the same time, the Jaeger Barracks are being inspected. In L313, we learn that they did not even go to my father's room. All of L313 is surrounded by the *Ghettowache* [Jewish ghetto police] and by gendarmes. Nobody is allowed to go in or out. Soon I leave Mother's place, and at home the whole place is filled with talk of *pruser* [scandal]. SS officer Haindl[76] has inspected nude women in the Ústecký Barracks. Soon, I go for lunch. There something mysterious happens. I obtain tickets and I go for lunch when suddenly the *Menagedienst* people notice that they are missing a coupon. Everybody thinks that I have played a trick. After lengthy explanations, I say what is probably the truth—that the previous mess service had already cut off the coupons. On this basis, I finally get my lunch.

Soon the gendarmes leave L313. During the afternoon *Apel*, there is a tremendous *pruser*. Franta throws things off shelves. He doesn't

---

76. SS Officer Rudolf Haindl, formerly an electrician from Vienna, enjoyed inspiring fear and anxiety, jumping upon inmates unexpectedly, peering through binoculars at the agricultural details in the fields, touring the streets in his car, and tearing into a frenzy when he caught someone with a cigarette. He fled Terezín in early May, but was arrested in Salzburg in 1947 and hanged in Litoměřice in September 1948.

want to let us play soccer at five o'clock because there is another *Apel* at 5:30. I go to the program. During the break, I beg Franta to let us play. We get permission only as long as *Apel* will take place at six o'clock. The boys agree. I cut my second lesson short because I have to go for the meal ticket. I get it. During the fourth period, we have a test in Judaism in which I'm not doing too well. Then I go to the *bašta*. I'm sure that we will lose. Today I am playing badly compared to other times when I am the best player. The half-time score is 2:0. The goals against us start piling up and we end with a score of 8:0. I am teed off because Tuti told me that I was responsible for all the goals. At home, he tells me that he really didn't mean it. As a punishment, because we were not home by six o'clock, the whole *heim* has to stay in from eight o'clock on. We have to straighten up our shelves during that period. I am very tired and therefore I soon fall asleep.

Friday, 16 June 1944

The morning is entirely uneventful. During the free period, I study. Today the Red Cross Commission is expected. Everything is in tiptop shape. We go to the program and, for the second period, we have Irenka. She asks what magnetic inflection is and I answer "declination" and she promptly throws me out. In fact, I'm glad. I spend the hour studying. Mother already works as a helper in the bakery and for this she gets a lot of bread. Now, she has a shift so I can no longer have lunch with her. We have farfel for lunch. It is a fact that the visitors have arrived. The *Stadtkapelle* [town orchestra][77] has been playing since noon. It is Friday, the day on which we have to get washed in the afternoon. I also change my clothes and then I go to Mother's. She is in a good mood and I want to learn. First, we go on several errands together and then we study. Mother is quite satisfied with me. Suddenly, fourteen Germans barge into the barracks. This must not be the right commission. First Rahm enters and he points to things. Also present are Guenther[78] and the representative of the Protek-

77. The *Stadtkapelle* presented concerts in the musical pavilion in the town park on the Terezín square. It was established by Peter Deutsch (b. 1901), formerly conductor of the Royal Orchestra in Copenhagen, who was deported to Terezín in October 1943.

78. As Adolf Eichmann's representative in Bohemia, SS Major Hans Guenther was head of the Central Office of Jewish Emigration in Prague and oversaw the forced removal and annihilation of Czech Jews.

torat Frank.[79] They walk through the whole barracks and look under bedding to see if there are mattresses there. From there they go to the bakery. It is a real comedy. It is 4:30, and therefore I have to return home. In front of the School, the boys grab me and tell me to go singing with them, which I do. Franta sits at the pavilion and we are instructed that when the commission arrives we must sing German songs. We are learning "O, Tannenbaum" and several others, but we are not doing too well. We are told to ride the carousel and go on the swings [play equipment erected for the beautification campaign]. I go so many times that I get all dizzy. Then, we throw the ball and finally the commission arrives. Obviously, they are satisfied with the well-behaved playing children. It is six o'clock. I go to Jindra to practice and at 6:30 we must go to Berman. They don't want to tune our flutes and we are not in the best form. We go to Berman and I have no stage fright. Amazingly, we don't mess up too much. I still feel dizzy from the carousel and I go to Mother's. I study French with my father and he is very satisfied with me. Because it is already nine o'clock, I go home with my father and I soon fall asleep.

Saturday, 17 June 1944

Today is Saturday and therefore we have to go for practice. Since it is nasty outside though, we don't go. We stay in bed until nine o'clock and then we put things in order. At noon, I go for lunch and in the afternoon I am bored. Very conveniently, Father arrives and he offers to go for a walk with me, to which I agree. We walk through Terezín and we both admire the relative beauty of this town. When I think about it—my arrival in Terezín and Terezín then and now—there has been a tremendous change. There are benches everywhere and the houses are neat. On the other hand, when I look through the windows of Kavalierka, I see people—old people, all crowded together, and the true impression of Terezín comes back to me. For the Germans, this is just a small detail. The commission ordered that the children be regularly instructed and that we must have vegetables and other benefits twice a week. There is *Apel*, after which we are free until 9:30. I gather my French material and go to Mother's. Mother,

---

79. An early and enthusiastic Nazi, Karl Hermann Frank (1898–1946) became the most powerful official in Bohemia and Moravia. Brought to justice after the war, Frank was hanged for war crimes in general and for his role in the annihilation of the people of Lidice in particular.

as always, cooks and has no time for me. I spend the whole afternoon on my own there. This tees me off something awful and I hurry home. At eight o'clock, I have a test with Berman in the Adler Eagle House. I go there but there is *Schopfung* [?] and, therefore, I have to wait for such a long time. Jindra is also there. I'm struck with stage fright, even though I know I will be playing in front of a very small audience. In the end, I play well and everybody likes it. At home, during Franta's reading, I fall asleep.

Sunday, 18 June 1944

This morning is very festive. Outside it is beautiful, but soon the weather turns and it starts raining off and on until the evening. Truly, it is a pity that we cannot enjoy the summer. I'm looking forward to the afternoon matches: Beavers vs. Nešarim, Czechs vs. Moravia vs. Berlin, Vienna vs. Prague. But the program today is quite dumb. Mother has afternoon shift. Barracks #7 has to move. There is a danger that my mother may have to move also. There are supposed to be ninety-seven people in each barracks. I go with lunch to Mother's. There it is as always. I go home and our next program is practical mathematics. It's raining outside. I argue with Sasha on account of English. I want to go to watch soccer and therefore I want to cut my class. I go to my father and we happen to stop at the barracks when Witr[80] brings the news that the barracks must be emptied by ten o'clock. The news spreads fast throughout the whole barracks. It is being decided who is moving for good to Dresdner Barracks and who will go only for two days to Hannover Barracks. We go to Mother, who left work on account of the move, and she starts to pack. She's all upset and angry. I go to get hold of a cart, which I manage to bring from the bakery. I feel proud as I organize everything. I am angry at Mother's awkwardness. It starts raining. My father is really trying hard. It is a dreadful comedy! And, I make fun of all this. Then, I go to L313 and there, my father unloads everything. I get angry because everybody takes such a long time. The *Ghettowache* is already giving us hell and Mother is angry at me. I am furious that Mother promises the cart to Mrs. Bremschová. I want to go home, but nevertheless we go to the barracks that

---

80. Born September 28, 1930, Petr Witrofsky was deported on January 30, 1942, from Prague to Terezín with transport V; he was number 966. He was assigned to room 7; the boys nicknamed him Witr. Petr was shipped to Auschwitz on November 23, 1944, in transport Et (his number: 524). He did not survive.

is now almost empty. I say good-bye to Mother and want to go home, but I change my mind and go to the attic. Mother has a pretty good space. Then, I go to the barracks again to make up with Mother. I am really bushed. At 9:45, when I arrive home, the boys are already in bed. I undress quickly, get washed and fall asleep.

Tuesday, 20 June 1944

There is supposed to be *Grunt* today. I sleep heavily and we all over-sleep. Mother has already settled with all her things in L313. In the barracks, the bunks are all set up, although very poorly. In the morning there is a program, and in the afternoon there are soccer matches. We play against team Blauweiss [a Zionist youth movement]. I play in borrowed soccer boots from Išík. It turns out to be a fateful mistake because they are heavy and I can't play well at all. In spite of this, we lose only 3:2. It is a good achievement. Otherwise, nothing is happening. We receive a ration of 35 dkg of marmalade, which I keep. The following morning there is a program. In the newly formed "school" is a sign saying "vacation." It is funny!! With lunch, I go to Mother's. During *Apel*, I have a mess on my shelf and I am castigated. Then the scrubbing starts. The lost soccer boot is found and I give it to Išík. We receive a very good package from the Schwarzes. I go to the *bašta* to watch a match between the Eagles and the Hawks. The result is 8:1! Then, I run for supper. I don't stay too long at Mother's because I have a meeting at 6:45. During the meeting we have an Olympiad, which I win. Afterward Heini reads us Čapek. After the meeting I go to Mother's, from where I depart very soon. And at home I write my diary.

Wednesday, 21 June 1944

I wake up from a heavy sleep and I am dizzy. Today, Mother is moving back to her barracks. It is stupidly arranged now. In the middle there is a row of bunks and near the windows there are *einzliky* [single bunks]. My mother's place is the same as before. During *Apel*, I get into trouble because my shoes are dirty. Franta continues to be ever more obnoxious to me. Most likely, he is mad at me. Even though I have a headache and I am generally feeling lousy, I go to help my mother move. My help comes in handy. I bang the dirt out of her bed linen. I feel quite lousy and I'm excused from the program for three lessons. On the way home, there is a short air raid. After lunch I go to Mother's, and after the afternoon *Apel*, we are forced to study.

I rewrite the study material. I don't learn anything because the examinations are not going to take place for some time. At five o'clock, there is *Apel* by Otík, which is entirely meaningless. On Friday, the Red Cross Commission will arrive again. One can't believe what is going on. Beautiful apartments are made, Eppstein[81] gets a car, the children must sing, in the offices there are signs saying "Wahrend der Arbeit Rauchen Verboten [Smoking Prohibited During Work]," and Rahm has entirely changed. Everyone gets a ration of one liverwurst today. I have decided that I will participate in literature class. I will probably write stories with Kalíšek, who has already "published" his book. I'm not on very good terms now with Kalíšek. It is the same thing with Gustl. At my parents', I learn that Handa has an infection of the middle ear and that Father is not doing well. My mother has quite a lot to worry about. She had a night shift and she slept for only three hours in the afternoon and therefore she is quite bushed. Nevertheless, we study French together and I'm doing quite well. In the evening, I have a minor argument with her with no great consequences and we soon make up. Father walks me home. He is a poor man. At home, I get washed under the pump because the washroom is being fixed. I lie down and soon thereafter I fall asleep.

Thursday, 22 June 1944

I have the whole morning free, which I spend writing "Parents and Children." My mother arrives at my place and asks me to go to the attic with her. Somehow, it happens that we have an argument and overall I'm in a lousy mood. I go to the barracks with Mother. *Verschönerung* reaches the highest point today. Each table has its own flowerpot. The sidewalks are washed and therefore we cannot even walk on them. Everything is in tiptop order. A new library is being set up. I go for lunch and with it to my mother. It is strange that Kalíšek got into the garden and I did not. I soon go home. In the afternoon, there is *Apel* and then a program, which is very boring. The fourth period is dropped. At approximately 5:30, I go to Mother's, but I don't find her home. I spend a while listening to the band and then I go again to Mother's, and this time I find her at home. I study French a while, and then I go with my parents to the barracks where I study with my father. The mood is quite good. At about nine o'clock, I go home and

81. Dr. Paul Eppstein (1901–44) was a professor of sociology and (1940) executive director of the Reich Association of Jews in Germany. Deported to Terezín in January 1943, he replaced Jakob Edelstein as chairman of the Council of Elders. See also note 129.

in bed I read Čapek. After playing with Kalíšek in the bunk, I soon
fall asleep.

Friday, 23 June 1944

Today is the day of the Red Cross Commission. It is dumb that I have
room duty and Kalíšek has garden work in the afternoon. It is strange
that Kalíšek again got into the garden and I did not. We beg Mrs.
Mautner to have my room duty changed with somebody else and
I get into an argument with Kalíšek. During *Apel,* Franta finds my
dirty shoes on the shelf and therefore I have to clean the whole shelf.
Franta is obviously quite mad at me. Today lunch is being given between ten and twelve. We have tongue, mashed potatoes, onions, and
cucumber salad! Today, the transport numbers don't exist. Eppstein
leads the commission and drives in his own car! There is *Apel* with instruction to have all rooms in order. I go for lunch and I'm lucky that
I get a good piece of tongue. The commission is already in. Himmler[82] didn't come. Eppstein is leading the commission. The children
must scream "Onkel Rahm, schön wieder sardinen? [Uncle Rahm,
again sardines?]" as he passes by. During the afternoon *Apel,* I have
another problem with Franta. Kalíšek goes to the garden and I have to
sit around at home. I sulk over my "fate." Everything is spotless in the
heim. Mrs. Mautner is moved by my excellent neatness and she lets me
go out for two hours. The commission consists of approximately ten
men. *Brundibár*[83] [Czech children's opera] is being played throughout the day. The band is playing. SS men Haindl and Bergel[84] are in

82. Heinrich Himmler (1900–1945), a devout believer in Hitler and the Nazi party,
joined the SS in 1925 and patiently consolidated his power. Rewarded with the title SS
Reichsführer, Himmler employed all the resources available to him to effect the murder
of the Jewish people. Himmler was arrested after the war, but committed suicide before
interrogation.

83. The Czech children's opera *Brundibár* was composed in 1938 by Hans Krása, with
libretto by Adolf Hoffmeister. It was performed for the first time in July 1941 in Prague,
in honor of the fiftieth birthday of the director of the Jewish orphanage, Ota (also called
Moritz) Freudenfeld (see note 93). The story features children, and spins a morality tale
of good defeating evil. Both cast and potential audience were deported in the following
months and years, and *Brundibár* premiered in Terezín in September 1943. It met with
huge success. For the spectators, the children represented hope in the future, and the
youngsters vanquished the evil Brundibár (who had come to represent Hitler). Tragically,
however, by war's end nearly all the children who had played in the opera with its big chorus had been shipped to annihilation camps in the east.

84. SS Lieutenant Karl Bergel, formerly a hairdresser from Dortmund, served as camp
inspector under Commandant Siegfried Seidl and was feared for his brutality. Bergel fled
Terezín after the war. He was charged, tried in absentia, and condemned to death.

civilian clothes today. On the *bašta*, there are matches going on and everybody is waiting for the commission. The *Ghettowache* wear gloves today. All the people are watching the commission. On the *bašta*, I play tennis with a tennis ball. The commission is expected in the School. We are forced to read, but the visitors go only to see Room 1. At 6:30, I leave for Mother's. Supper is given out until seven o'clock. There, they are telling all kinds of rumors about the commission, which in the meantime, has departed. It is said that the president of the Red Cross was here, as were some Ghetto experts. Eppstein spoke French and played out the comedy well. Afterward, I go to the barracks and we sit around quite pleasantly. At nine o'clock, I return home. I don't want to wash myself but something tells me I should. When I am in bed, Franta comes and tells me again that I should write something. Then I play in the bunk with Kalíšek and we both fall asleep.

Saturday, 24 June 1944

I am late in writing my diary and therefore I didn't write Saturday. This afternoon the Ghetto observed "quiet time" to acknowledge the success of Friday's commission. A dinner party and a concert were held for all *partaky* [squad leaders] connected with the *Verschönerung*. There was also a concert. In the morning, I write my diary. My mother keeps cooking at my father's. It is quite nice there! In the afternoon, I go to Mother's and then to the *bašta*. During the evening, nothing happens.

Sunday, 25 June 1944

We have an arranged match with Skid III for six o'clock in the morning. The preparation was done yesterday evening. Kalíšek doesn't want to get up at 5:30. By sheer coincidence, I wake up. We go into the empty streets. We play on the *bašta* for two hours. We lose 12:4. Afterward, Brenner practices with us and it is quite good. At approximately nine o'clock, we go home. For the first time in a while, the weather is nice. At home, I put things in order and go to Mother's. Tomorrow, I have to send out my laundry and therefore I leave. Mother works the afternoon shift, so I can devote the rest of the day fully to my father. After lunch, I go to the *bašta*, and then to my father's. I am missing my *menášek*. I look for it and I find it at Handa's. Today, for the first time in the history of Terezín, we observe English Sunday [Whit Sunday]. Many residents walk through the Ghetto. It is truly very beautiful. I go for a walk with my father. We stop at the *Stadtkapelle*, which today plays particularly well. I'm amazed what the Jews can do. For dinner we have two gingerbreads. We are taken by all the beauty. After the band ends, I go to soccer—Sparta is playing against Praha and the result is 3:1. At eight o'clock, the band plays again. This time it plays Czech folk songs that receive applause. At nine o'clock, I go home. I get washed and I fall asleep feeling that I have spent this day as if I were in Prague. But, sadly, it is just an illusion. Franta is not reading tonight. So ends the first day that resembles a little bit—just a little bit—the day of freedom.

Monday, 26 June 1944

I'm looking forward to the match against the Eagles. We should win! After a three-day break, the program is starting again. I have an argument with Kalíšek and I tell him that he prefers Gustl as a friend over me. That is enough. I'm in a bad mood. After *Apel*, there is a program and that lasts until noon. I change my bed linen and then I go with a bad lunch to Mother's and to L313. Father has really changed. He already runs like a Sokol [member of a Czech nationalistic fitness movement] and he is entirely different. I learn that Handa, who behaves strangely toward me, went to see Prager on account of the garden. Prager said that he has no objection to accepting me in the garden and that I should bring a note from Otík. I have 50 percent of the battle won! At home, there is *Apel* and a rehearsal for the new *nesev* [Hebrew-language entertainment program]. Franta has turned and now favors me. Most likely he will want something from me. I have to run after Šmudla[85] and Otík, whom I unfortunately don't reach. For this reason, I go to Zebulon. Hebrew bores me and I seem to provoke Zebulon. Today, on account of the match, I cannot write anything. However, we don't have a ball. Nevertheless we go at 4:45 to the *bašta*. It is awfully hot today but the match goes pretty well. At half-time we lead 1:0 and then we win 3:0. As a result of this win, we are assured of leading the division! Afterward, I take a shower. Barefoot and without a shirt, I go to my father, where I have dinner. I get dressed because it

---

85. Arnošt Klauber (b. April 4, 1921), nicknamed Šmudla, was deported on January 26, 1942, from Plzeň to Terezín on transport T (his number: 308). Šmudla served as the *madrich* for room 5 in L417 until he was shipped to Auschwitz on September 28, 1944, with convoy Ek as number 396. He survived to be liberated in Gleiwitz and, returning to Czechoslovakia after the war, remained there.

starts raining, and this prevents us from going for a walk. I study with Father. Before nine o'clock, I go home, where I change my linen and, after a thorough washing, I go to bed. Franta is reading us *The Hope*, which deals with the Spanish Revolution. I fall asleep.

Tuesday, 27 June 1944

Today there is *Grunt*, but I don't clean my mattress. I'm not on good terms with Kalíšek anymore. Again it is awfully hot. I tell Gustl about the garden because today the decision will be made regarding my acceptance. I speak with Šmudla, who tells me that I must have Otík's permission. It doesn't look good. During the second break in the program, I go after Otík, whom I catch near the church. At long last, he gives me his approval, but only together with Gustl, and I'm very happy. We have a test in physics about magnetism, which I think I messed up. After the program, I go to Šmudla, who writes a note for me to give to Prager. I have won! With lunch, I go to Mother's. She says that there is only one spot open in the garden. After the afternoon's *Apel*, I get a ticket to bathing where I go at two o'clock. It is unbearably hot and it's drizzling. Most likely there will be a thunderstorm, which is what actually happens. After bathing, I go to Prager, but he is not there. I notice a commission that consists of ten uniformed SS men. One of them uses a cane. He is an invalid. I wonder what it must be like now, for example, in Berlin or even in Prague. Why is there this war? Because two empires don't get along, we have to sit around in Terezín?——Why?——At the *Jugendfuersorge* office, I have better luck. I find Prager and he dictates a letter that takes twenty minutes. Finally, he's finished. He's quite nice to me and assigns me to L410. However, he assigns Gustl to Kavalierka. I immediately go and tell the news to Mother. The mood is good. At six o'clock, I have a meeting with Heini and I don't go to Mother's. During the meeting, they read us something Zionistic (dumb!) and then we have a minor mental Olympiad. Afterward, I go with Kalíšek for a walk. In the evening, I don't go to get washed and I listen to Franta's reading. I fall asleep.

Tuesday [Wednesday], 28 June 1944

I am looking forward to working in the garden. Today has not offered anything worth thinking about. Everything goes easily. I wake up in the morning and everything moves at a normal speed. In the morning, we again have a program, after which I go for a while to L313. We receive a pretty good package from Budějovice,[86] only it was very poorly packaged so that much has spilled out in transit. Food is food, nevertheless. Mother tells me that I have an exam at 8:30 already with the orchestra. I'm looking forward to it. At home after *Apel*, Franta is reading to us *The Hope* again. It is wild. After reading, by chance I run into Jindra. We have an English lesson and I try to pay with half a loaf of bread, but the teacher doesn't want it. During the whole lesson, we just giggle. I really want to cut it, but I don't have the courage to do so. I go to L313 and people there are not in a good mood. After a dreadful supper, I leave. At eight o'clock, I go to Orel [the new hall]. Schächter,[87] Fried, Prager, and others are already there. It seems that Schächter doesn't like it and doesn't want to show it in public. I start playing at nine o'clock with three violins and cello. It is not very pretty. We finish at 10:30 and Jindra takes me home. Because of the heat, I cannot fall asleep for a long time. Finally I am overcome by a stronger [there is a break in the text: PW].

Thursday, 29 June 1944

The noise of the boys who go to practice wakes me up. I'm looking forward to the morning in the garden. I cannot sleep from six to seven so I write my diary. Then, I get up and go to the garden. Unfortunately, it rains and I don't know whether they will let us go home. Schwarzbart accepts me nonchalantly. I am amazed how everything has grown in the garden. I have missed the lettuce, but there are a lot of other vegetables there. First we water the cucumbers and, while doing this, I take a raspberry and also a little bit of currant. I decided not to *schlojs*. Because it starts raining and the boys have returned from the manure place, Schwarzbart sends us home. I don't feel like going home and therefore I go to Schwarzbart and ask him whether I

---

86. České Budějovice: a city in southern Bohemia.

87. A towering figure in the musical life of Terezín, Rafael Schächter was born in Brăila, Romania, in May 1905 and was killed in Auschwitz in October 1944. A choral conductor and a pianist, Schächter brought his passion for music and organizational talent to his productions in Terezín. He established informal singing evenings and choral performances and mounted a number of operas, including Smetana's *Bartered Bride* and *The Kiss* and Mozart's *The Marriage of Figaro* and *The Magic Flute*. His decision in early 1943 to mount Verdi's *Requiem*—a Catholic Mass for the dead to be sung by Jewish prisoners—caused some controversy in the camp.

can stay. He agrees. It is decided that I will go to Kreta for parsley. I'm looking forward to it. Kreta is an enormous field full of vegetables. There, I again can see the countryside far and wide. I feel the loneliness and I know I better turn away. I have a chat with Handa. We pick parsley and put it in cases. We pass by the gendarmes. When we carry vegetables, the old people just pounce on us. We get a ration of parsley which I take to my mother. We also receive a package for the Sušickýs, who have left on the transport. I go to pay for the package and I bring it home with my father. The package is not very good. Actually, it is from strangers. There is *Apel* and then a program. We have Zebulon and I have tremendous dislike for Hebrew. I'm quite fresh toward Zebulon and everybody laughs. We make fun of everything. I am forced to sit at another table but I don't care. The other two lessons go quite well. Šmudla is there. I go with Gustl. Šmudla wants to keep us there until 7:30, and he wants to dictate to us the theme starting from Abraham all the way to Restoration. However, he calls it off. I go for a walk and then have dinner at Mother's. We are not on good terms again. I go to the *bašta,* but have to return home on account of Franta's *Apel* at eight o'clock. We talk and practice. Afterward, there is reading and I go to get washed up. In the bathhouse, I have an argument with Beran. During reading, I fall asleep.

Friday, 30 June 1944

I don't feel like getting up at six o'clock. However, it is to no avail because Tuti hasn't shown up. I use the time to write my diary and put things in order. I'm looking forward to going to the garden this afternoon. During *Apel,* Franta throws everything off my shelf. During program, we have geography and then physics. I get a very good grade on the quiz. I'm making fun of Irenka. Soon I go for lunch and take it to my father since Mother is working her shift. I leave soon. In the afternoon, I go to the garden. It's raining and I'm assigned to hay. At the co-op[88] we have to wait but finally we start moving. We go past the gendarmes and then through a field path around by the army hospital. I see wounded soldiers. Truly I cannot believe that just behind Terezín there are such woods. We cross the state road and we approach the town of Litoměřice. On the state road it is completely different and, for me, it feels very strange. Actually I haven't seen things

88. Storage site for harvested crops to be shipped to Germany.

like this for the last two years. Finally we stop in a wide field. It is marvelous. We pull hay and we put it into piles. In the near distance, I see the outlines of houses and the steeples of Litoměřice. I take it all in as if it were a dream. What I would like to do most would be to run away. I think how two years of my youth are now spoiled! At the end of the work, we get caught in a downpour. Therefore, we go home again by way of the curvy field road. Again we pass by a gendarme, who counts us as if we were pigs; yes, I am back in Terezín.———We return to the co-op for a lineup. I go home and get washed up. We don't receive any rations today. At Mother's, I have a luxurious dinner. We have *pomazanka* [radish cheese spread] with eggs. Then I go to a concert in the town hall by Berman. He sings marvelously, but by the end of the songs I am always half asleep. At home, we continue with our supper. I fill myself tremendously. Back at the School, I cannot do anything. I go to see the cabaret by Room 6, which has gotten new boys because Room 2 has been liquidated. Then I go to bed, where I have another argument with Kalíšek. It is awfully hot in the room and Kalíšek is sick. I tell him not to call me names, or else I will not talk to him. Obviously, he does not take it to heart.

[Illustration showing the end of the month of June: PW.]

Broadside diary page, with Pavel's illustration to mark the end of June

JULY
Saturday, 1 July 1944

I wake up very early. I first study French and then write my diary. Today, I want to carry out my plan, which is to write a book that will most likely be called "Stories from the Ghetto." So far, in bed I write the introduction, titled "If . . . ." Now I have to make sure it doesn't turn out the same way as the magazine. We soon have to get up. There is no *Apel* this morning. I am offered a game titled "Smelina." It is a Terezín invention that resembles "Business" [Czech version of "Monopoly"]. I play until noon. After *Apel,* I go and play *německá* [a ball game]. The rest of the afternoon I spend by myself and I don't take any supper. I go to Mother in L313. I'm in a bad mood and I'm trying hard to leave as early as possible. I do so in ten minutes, and I go to watch a soccer match between Sparta and Jugendfuersorge (score 5:3). At home, I again play "Smelina," but soon I go to bed and fall asleep.

Sunday, 2 July 1944

Nothing has happened. Life passes by like a lazy river; nothing occurs and still so much is going on. My greatest desire is to write down everything on paper. An opportunity arises as *Rim, Rim* has undertaken a competition of literary content. There are five themes and I have a good chance to win. The afternoon is largely uneventful. Mother is on her shift, and in the evening, I go with my father to watch a soccer match, Elektra vs. Kadr (score 2:2). After the match we go and sit down on a bench behind L504. It is marvelous there. We study French and then we listen to a musical group that is playing extremely well. They are playing Czech songs. At home, I lie down and listen to the reading. Its content is about the execution of some Communist. I no longer talk to Kalíšek. I ask him to give me something to drink and he gives it to someone else. He has now lost whatever little feeling of friendship I had for him.

Monday, 3 July 1944

The morning passes by normally. Again, we have the program. Tuti lectures about Judaism. One day doesn't differ from another. Something heavy is hanging over us. I am indifferent to everything. We are called in by Franta, who says that there will be some important meeting, and it turns out to be correct. Five boys have to move out of the *heim* because of social considerations. The chosen are Sasha, Beran, Majošek, Seiner,[89] and Hermann. Only as a result of Franta's intervention is the matter deferred. I go with Father to the *bašta*, where we are scheduled for three matches. We also have a choir rehearsal. Today I find out that Grizzly's mother has died.

Tuesday, 4 July 1944

There is *Grunt* today and therefore we get up at six o'clock. After beating out our mattresses and doing general housekeeping, I write my diary. I keep thinking about Grizzly's mother. She had been crippled for the last ten years and then got a brain tumor and pneumonia. It is really a blessing for her. Grizzly sleeps at his father's and I haven't seen him for the last two days. We have again a program and I am again making fun of Irenka. Father brings me lunch and I don't stay very long at my mother's. I am looking forward to going to the garden. I forgot to mention something: during the morning *Apel*, Franta got mad and threw down the whole cupboard full of food. Among many glasses full of margarine and milk, one victim was also my sugar, which spilled. Franta quite gracefully asked whose sugar it was. What followed then I already mentioned. During the afternoon *Apel*, I get a ticket for a package of four lessons. I have a big schedule for the afternoon. First, I have to go to the garden, then to the pool, and, at five o'clock, I will play soccer against Terezín and I still don't have any boots. I'll manage. We go to the garden and I go with Mrs. Kienová to Kreta for parsley. I see Handa there. We go back to the garden and I hear how other boys have stolen currants. I don't see any obstacle so I start eating a currant. We then have to go to garden #1 and there it really starts. I water with a small pot so that I can pass by the strawberries as frequently as possible. I take about five strawberries. Ilse tells us to pick up apples that have fallen off the trees and are lying among the strawberries. I take approximately twenty strawberries. At four o'clock, I have to go to the pool. I must be acting very awkwardly and, on the way home, Ilse catches me and asks me whether I have stolen anything. I deny it. She then asks me to leave.

89. Jindřich Seiner [possibly Steiner] (b. August 29, 1930) was assigned number 138 and deported from Prague to Terezín on transport Ck on December 22, 1941. A room 7 boy, Jindřich was shipped to Auschwitz on October 6, 1944, with convoy Eo; his number: 749. He did not survive.

I am quite upset. As I learn later, about 150 strawberries got lost. This will be a big scandal! At home I quickly change clothing, and I hurry to the pool. I don't like it there at all. The big boys are making huge waves so that nobody can swim. Then, I go in my uniform to the *bašta*. Soon my parents arrive to watch me play. They are out of luck because team Terezín didn't bring the ball and the match is postponed indefinitely. I stay a while on the *bašta* and then I go to Mother's. I have supper there and talk with my parents. The political news is excellent. However, we are still in Terezín. It is said that there is a scandal on account of five hundred stolen loaves of bread. At home, I get washed and Franta is reading to us, but I fall asleep. I am tired mainly because of the oppressive heat but also because of being exposed to the *schlojs* experience. Today, I have realized many interesting facts about Terezín.

Wednesday, 5 July 1944

I wake up with the idea that I don't have the draft of the "Letter" for today's first lesson. Then, I have to write an article for the *Rim, Rim* competition. I therefore quickly get dressed and make my bed, and then sit in the yard to write. Gustl joins me. I don't participate in housekeeping. When I finish the article, I go upstairs. I have an incident with Mrs. Mautner because I left my boots on the bench. The consequences become known during the morning *Apel*. Franta, as a punishment, assigns me to clean the toilets with Pudlina. By sheer luck, the bathroom is being cleaned by a *hajzlbaba* [slang for a woman toilet cleaner] so that I'm finished and can join the program. My composition is liked by everyone. Gustl submitted some nonsense. The remaining two lessons are called off. Mrs. Rindlero-vá's[90] funeral is today. As a matter of principle, I refuse to go. Instead, I go to play with Gustl. After fifteen minutes I go to have lunch with my father, who takes me along because he knows the cook in L210. Lunch is good. The afternoon is entirely uneventful. I stay on the bunk and study French. I have to ease off French because I am getting it confused with English. I feel pain in my bladder. I have to continually go to the bathroom. The exams at the school are called off. I go to my parents and then for a meeting with Heini. There a game is being played, which I win. In the evening, there is a rehearsal of

90. The mother of Petr Rindler (Grizzly).

nesev, celebrating the second anniversary of our School. Then, I go and get washed and fall asleep. Most likely, I will no longer talk with Kalíšek.

Thursday, 6 July 1944

I wake up very late. I have to go to the garden. There is no work for us and therefore we have to go pick linden blossoms. It is quite dumb and it is awfully hot. We go to the lineup, where it is decided who goes into what group. We want to go to the Bohušovice tree lanes; instead we are assigned to linden trees on the square. We go there at once. The work is boring. I climb a tree and I pick blossoms. We pick all the way from the *Komandatura* [SS camp headquarters] along all of L3 block, and then we turn toward the School. There, we catch up with the boys from the garden who are bringing with them the rations. We quickly run away from work and look forward to the rations. Our joy is in vain because the rations consist of small strawberries and several leaves of kohlrabi and cauliflower. Schwarzbart should really be ashamed of himself. On the way to the garden we learn that there will be a punishment because we played hooky from work. However, it doesn't happen. At noon, I go to Mother's. Nowadays, I don't have any time to enjoy either Mother or Father. I'm so tired that I lie down on the bunk and rest. The afternoon program gets on my nerves. I have a lot to do with the writing of my article for the competition. *Rim, Rim* behaves toward me exceptionally well. Lion keeps buttering me up. I have strong competition in Gans [Ginz?].[91] The afternoon program is dumb. At five o'clock, the Nešarim are playing soccer. I have to decide quickly what to do. I take a paper and pen and go to L313 where I write a note that I will come later and I hurry to the *bašta.* I watch the match and the Nešarim beat the Dragons 4:1. Then I sit down and start writing an article, the title of which is "Sword Tells

---

91. Petr Ginz (b. February 1, 1928), the child of a Jewish father and gentile mother, was separated from his family at age fourteen and deported from Prague to Terezín on October 24, 1942. A couple of years older than the room 7 boys, Petr was assigned to room 1. A writer, poet, and painter, he was the force behind the room 1 magazine, *Vedem.* Petr was shipped to Auschwitz in 1944, where he was killed. Decades later, his younger sister Chava Pressburger, who also had been deported to Terezín when she turned fourteen (1944) and survived to liberation, undertook the publication of a diary her brother had kept for one year, from 1941 to 1942. Ginz's extraordinary work gained wide attention when Israeli astronaut Ilan Ramon took one of Petr's linoprints on the ill-fated *Columbia* space shuttle, which exploded on February 1, 2003.

the Story." It deals with the war. I think it will be quite good. I write about half a page and go to Mother. There I only have dinner and immediately go home to write. I sit on a bench in front of the building and I almost finish it. Afterward, I go to play *německá* with Springer. We have to be home at 8:30 because of the scandal in the garden. At nine o'clock, we have a rehearsal for *nesev* as the performance will be soon. Then I go and get washed and fall asleep.

Friday, 7 July 1944

I complete the article. It is quite long. I forgot to say something about yesterday. Otík and Leo were called in by Rahm. He has not been satisfied with them. They are to be replaced by some German Jew. In the evening, this changes. Supposedly, the father of Bastik[92] will come to us. He is the former leader of the Prague orphanage. I cut Irenka's lessons today. Instead, I go to have lunch at Father's. It is beastly hot. We have garden work and then we play a two-hour match. It is not pleasant because I don't feel much like playing soccer. We're playing against Terezín, which fields only a team of five. Even so, we still lose 2:1. Blecha keeps insulting us. I feel like slapping his face. Without shoes and without shirt, I go home and in this attire I walk around until I go to sleep. However, I first rinse myself and I go with Kalíšek to the garden. Schwarzbart says that he doesn't need us and we can go home. Outside the garden, a *betreuerka* [female child care worker] asks us whether we want to come and water the plants at seven o'clock. We are pleased because we think that we will get something. We go to the *bašta*, where our team plays against Dror. The result is 15:0! Because there is *Apel* at five o'clock, I have to go home. At home, I am punished because I have not put my socks away. I am supposed to sleep without a mattress, but somehow I believe the punishment will go away. Then I go to Father's. Mother is there too. I have supper and, because I have to do the watering job, I go home. There, I have a fistfight with Gustl. Then, I go to the garden again. It is gorgeous there. We are watering several gardens and I take some strawberries. Schwarzbart is as "generous" as he was the last time. At nine o'clock I go home. We have a rehearsal until ten. I cannot feel my feet. I'm happy when I succumb to sleep.

92. "Bastik" refers to Rudla Freudenfeld. The July 10 entry confirms that his father, Ota Freudenfeld, became the new *Jugendleiter* (see note 93).

Saturday, 8 July 1944

In the morning, we get up at five o'clock because our three groups
have races on the *bašta*. I really don't care for it. We are allowed to
stay in bed longer, which I take advantage of. I make up with Kalíšek.
In bed, I copy my article. I'm offered the job of rating the competition. Now I have the feeling as if I am doing everything with a definite
exactness and I am satisfied with myself. I don't skip any days in my
diary and I simply say to myself that I will not leave until I finish what
I am doing. In the morning, we have general choir. It is quite good
considering that we have had only one week's rehearsal time. The
performance in the evening will be for the boys and Otík, Leo, and
their wives. The rehearsal lasts until noon. Outside it is even hotter
than yesterday. We walk around barefooted with no tops. When I think
about it, I must conclude that things have improved a lot in Terezín.
Now, even the access to the *bašta* is open. At Father's, I have lunch
and we agree that I will come to him between four and five. Then I
go home. It is the second anniversary of the School. I go home with
the determination that I want to study. However, it is spoiled because
there is a sports festivity on the *bašta* and Otík wants to say good-bye
to us. I don't feel like going, but I have to. On the *bašta,* I watch a
relay race that Room 7 wins. I am bored and therefore go home. I
sit down to finish my diary. I study English and French and read *The
Chod Rebellions* that I borrowed from Jiří Mautner. When I finish, it is
already five o'clock and I therefore go to L313 but my mother is not
to be found. Then I go to her barracks, where I haven't been for a
long time. My mother is there and she is in a very good mood. I eat
up a storm and talk with my father. Since it is eight o'clock, I have
to go and get washed. At nine o'clock the performance starts, and it
lasts until 10:30. Then I go to bed, where it's awfully hot and the fleas
are really torturing me. Terezín is full of them; tonight, the fleas just
would not let me fall asleep.

Sunday, 9 July 1944

Because I forgot to write my diary for two days I am going to have to
describe this day briefly. In the morning, there is the usual program.
At noon, I go to Father's because my mother has an afternoon shift.
I am angry because the program is in the afternoon too. Before the
program, I correct my competition article. It looks like I will be in sec-

ond place, after Gans [Ginz?], who has written a masterpiece. I forgot to mention that Sasha and I have room duty together and it turns out well. After the program, we have a meeting with Heini during which we talk about different sports. It is quite uninteresting. Then, I go to my father. We are free from 7:30 on and then I have duty. At my father's, I have my dinner and then we go to watch a match at the Dresdner Barracks. At home, we talk with the boys about various Terezín and pre-Terezín events, before falling asleep.

Monday, 10 July 1944

The morning is spent by the visit of our new *Jugendleiter* [youth leader], the "old man" Freudenfeld.[93] He is a pleasant, white-haired, deep-voiced gentleman. I have a violent argument with Kalíšek. At one o'clock, we have an English lesson. Šmudla's lesson is canceled. Then math and history follow. After the program, I go to my mother with my dirty laundry. I don't stay long. This year, I really cannot complain about having a lack of vegetables. The best vegetable I have ever eaten is cucumber salad with a little bit of sugar on it. It tastes like a honeydew melon. Handa brings a lot of vegetables. Today, we are supposed to play soccer at two o'clock with Hagibor. Because the weather is not nice, the match is postponed indefinitely. And, for this reason, we study Hebrew instead. It is a very boring lesson. In the afternoon I write my diary. There are supposed to be school exams, but fortunately they are canceled. I have stopped making notes on what other classes are studying. Therefore, I am glad that the exams have been canceled. In the evening, I go to Father's and, after eating supper, we study French. I am making good progress. After the lesson, we go for a walk. It stops raining and the air outside is clear. We walk throughout Terezín. The *bašta* is opened, from the bakery all the way to the entrance to the east side of the laundry. In the evening, we

93. Ota (also called Moritz) Freudenfeld, born July 27, 1891, was deported from Prague to Terezín with transport De on July 5, 1943; his number was 492. Formerly the director of the Jewish orphanage in Prague, he became the director of the Hagibor orphanage in Terezín and, taking Otík Klein's place, director of L417. Calling him "old man Freudenfeld," Pavel distinguishes him from his son Rudla, who had been deported to Terezín about a week before his father, on June 30. The Freudenfelds held a special place in Terezín history through their connection with the children's opera, *Brundibár* (see notes 83 and 128). Rudla (or Bastik, as Pavel also refers to him) was a gifted amateur musician; he conducted all fifty-five performances of *Brundibár* in Terezín. Ota Freudenfeld was shipped to Auschwitz with convoy Ek (number 2390) on September 28, 1944. He did not survive.

have rehearsal for the choir "The Slaves," because tomorrow it will be performed in front of all the *madrichim* [youth leaders or counselors] and the whole School personnel. Tomorrow, Franta will start a 10-day "vacation."

Tuesday, 11 July 1944

There is *Grunt* and therefore we have to get up very early, at six o'clock. I clean only one of my mattresses. Today is Kalíšek's birthday. I don't give him anything because we are still not on friendly terms. I have a ticket for bathing at 7:30. The bath is excellent! The weather is changeable. For a while it is beautiful and then it rains. The day starts well. There is news that the program has been canceled. It is confirmed that the rumor is correct, and it pleases me. Kohn will most likely leave the School even though I don't believe it. I would be very pleased because he is obnoxious. Because there is no program, I go with Kalíšek and Grizzly to play *německá*. I really cannot take Kalíšek any longer and we even argue during the game. It is Kalíšek's fault. We start pushing and shoving each other. He is very obnoxious. Gustl kicks the tennis ball over to the garden in the Vrchlabi Barracks and we go to get it. Many sick people are lying there. It is so sad. . . . We retrieve the tennis ball and continue playing. At 10:45, I stop and go home. I want to write my diary, but somehow it doesn't happen. I quit. I don't feel like doing anything that has to do with my thoughts. Therefore, we start to gossip about various *madrichim,* particularly about Rudla Weil. I'm in a bad mood and I go to Mother's. I meet her on the way, and she tells me to go to the Hannover Barracks for lunch. I obey, but I am angry for no apparent reason. I feel very lousy. I let my anger out when I am with my parents. Father has a tremendous amount of fleas and therefore I leave shortly. However, I have difficulty saying good-bye to Mother. Seriously, I see her very little now. I'm looking forward to going to the garden in the afternoon. In the *heim,* Franta Graus replaces Franta [Maier].[94] I don't know what kind of man he is. After *Apel,* we go to the garden. I am again assigned to picking linden blossoms. It is dumb. Grizzly has "connections" which allow him to stay always in the garden. We go with Mrs.

---

94. František Graus (b. December 14, 1921) was deported from Brno with transport G on December 2, 1941. He replaced Franta Maier as *madrich* for just a short time. Graus was sent to Auschwitz on September 28, 1944, with convoy Ek and survived to be liberated there.

Kienová to the co-op and from there to Seestrasse. It is very boring work. We get a ration of a few raspberries. By five o'clock we pick half a bushel of raspberries. It's quite an "achievement"! At home, we get a ration of several strawberries and peas. I am well satisfied with it. Afterward, I go to my parents. I have dinner, but at 6:45 I have to go to a meeting with Heini. Only three boys show up. Heini goes with us to the *bašta,* where there are good matches being played. I stay there until 8:45 and then return home where I change into a clean shirt. Later, I write my diary. *Nesev* follows. Of the fifty invitees, only twenty come. Several leave during the performance. However, Franta is very satisfied with us. Then, I go to bed and soon fall asleep. Kalíšek got a notebook and therefore he is writing his diary.

Wednesday, 12 July 1944

Franta Graus wakes us up in the morning. Because there is some kind of an exam in the gym with Franta Maier, the first part of the program is canceled. Today we give out laundry. We go to the gym where all the *heims* are assembled. With Franta, we rehearse the Hatikvah and Techrahun[95] for Sunday's Herzl celebration.[96] It will be a real comedy. We are supposed to be riding a bike and I really don't know how it's going to turn out. I don't care for the whole thing. After that, we are free and therefore I write my diary. The program follows. Today, after a long time, I go alone for lunch. I take my lunch to Mother's. We have noodles. I am in a bad mood, and I leave soon because I have an argument with Mother. I'm looking very much forward to the match with Hagibor. Tutinek is not playing because of illness. I don't know what the outcome will be. Outside, the weather is changeable, but it is very good for the match. After the first few minutes, there are goals and then goals are scored like crazy. The match ends with a score of 8:2. Because I promised yesterday to Heini that I would make a list of boys who want to sing, I have to leave early. Unfortunately, Heini doesn't show up and I am mad. At 4:30 I go for an English lesson that is quite good. Then I go to Mother's, where there is a continuation of the noon activities. Kalíšek has mentioned that I haven't given him anything. Therefore, I ask Mother to give me something. She very laconically refuses. I get angry on account of her egotism. There will

95. Hebrew songs. "Hatikvah" became the Israeli national anthem.
96. Theodor Herzl (1860–1904), founder of the modern Zionist movement.

be no talking to me any more. She wants to give me a *buchta,* but I throw it into a pail of water. Mother starts crying. I feel sorry, but nevertheless, I go home, where I study Hebrew because tomorrow is an exam. My mind is not on it, however. I lie down on the bed, thinking how obnoxious Gustl and Kalíšek are to me. I fall asleep. During the night, the fleas are biting something awful. I apply a wet cloth on the bites and I am up for a long time. Only later I fall into a wild sleep. I sleep under Kalíšek's eiderdown and then under mine.

Thursday, 13 July 1944

After the bad beginning, I have a good night's sleep. I wake up very late even though I have to go to the garden at 7:30. I don't air my bedding at all and hurry to L410. I think it's unjust that Grizzly and Kalí always stay in the garden and I have to go to pick linden blossoms. It happens again today. We go to Backerstrasse. The thought keeps occurring to me that I no longer enjoy being in the *heim.* The boys keep pulling my leg and I keep fighting with them. I would prefer to live with my parents. Today, there is another commission and a new *Verschönerung* is taking place. While we're picking the blossoms, we can see the commission. It consists of six men, four of whom are in civilian clothes. Soon, we have a full basket of blossoms and therefore we return to the garden. We are dismissed until 3:30, at which time we are supposed to come for rations. We have childlike expectations. I return to the School and I keep arguing with Kalíšek. I read for a while, but nothing pleases me. I don't want to study French because I would be neglecting English and vice versa. Finally, I go for lunch (liverwurst and "*bosnak*"[?]) and I take it to Mother's. Of course, the mood is as bad there as yesterday. Handa brings cabbage, cucumbers, etc. I must not rib him so much even though he is so obnoxious. After *Apel,* I read. I have to learn Hebrew for the program. We have it as a first lesson and I am tested. Zebulon gives me an A. Then I go for the ration and it is very poor. We get kohlrabi and parsley and some leaves which are faded. The program is boring. There are rumors that there will be a yearly exam. I will have to take an exam for the second-level subjects, which I don't know at all. After the program, I go to a soccer meeting that is called off, and then I go to Mother's, where the mood is again bad. We have a vegetable dinner and I'm so mad that I leave. At 7:30, there is supposed to be a rehearsal for the Herzl celebration but I do not go. Instead I go for a walk with Jila.

We walk along the *bašta*. We throw the ball around with a woman and a man. When we arrive at the bakery, Porges is playing there with a ball and we join him until 8:45. My tennis shoes are paying the price. Kalíšek is keeping away from me and I also don't pay any attention to him. Afterward, I air my bedding so the fleas won't bite me so much and, after a wash, I fall asleep.

Friday, 14 July 1944

Last night the fleas didn't bite me at all. Before I get up I want to read, but Franta Graus comes and gets us out of bed. During house-keeping I somehow get into an argument with Kalíšek. It is entirely his fault. It comes to it that he doesn't want to make up beds to-gether so that each makes up his own. After the usual *Apel*, there is program. Because the first hour is free, I finish writing my diary and underlining the headings in my notebook. The second hour is his-tory. Zwicker dictates to us three full pages about Žižka.[97] The third lesson is physics. What is [not: PW] noteworthy is that during the lecture, Schleissner fell asleep on the bench. After the program, I don't feel like doing anything. Again, I feel as if I don't know any English at all. I don't know whether it's true. I go for lunch and I bring it to my father. I completely forgot that my mother has a shift. Father is in a good mood and he walks with me. Today we go to the garden again. It would be dumb if I had to go yet again to pick the linden blossoms. However, my fears come true. I am having bad luck and, therefore, I go with Mrs. Kienová to the co-op. Today we are as-signed to Bohušovice tree alleys. We go there and again we can see the outside civilized world. The Aryans are on the road. The gen-darmes are amazingly good. They very openly talk with the Jews. The clouds appear in the sky. It is getting ready to rain, and then it comes. The gendarmes send us home. I quickly run to Mother. I heard that there was a fire in the barracks, but I find out it wasn't true. I don't catch my mother home. At the School I write in my diary and, when it stops raining, I go and ask Schwarzbart whether he needs us. He doesn't. At home they are getting ready for *Apel*. I'm mad on account of the garden. They have it better in Kavalierka! I get washed and change my clothes for *Apel*. Afterward, I go for supper and then to

97. Jan Žižka (1360–1424), a Czech general and follower of the Protestant reformer Jan Hus, and a key figure in the Hussite wars (circa 1420–34), famous for his military inven-tions and strategies.

Mother's. I have already made up with her and we talk normally. Now we have vegetables every day; today, it's cauliflower. It is wonderful. It is rumored that there is a revolution in France, but it doesn't appear to be correct. The rumor probably came about because today is the French national holiday. I eat cucumbers with condensed milk and sugar. It is a real delicacy! Because my parents go to listen to the writer Lederer, I go home to read. At 8:30, I go to the Herzl celebration, which is directed by Franta Maier. It is taking place in the gym. It is a tremendous hall and it's crowded. The entertainment is obviously infiltrated with Zionism and therefore I don't like it. Today, the results of the competition were supposed to be announced, but they are postponed until tomorrow. I leave my bed linen to air out and talk with Zwicker about politics. Because I'm sleepy, I go to bed and soon fall asleep.

Saturday, 15 July 1944

The wake-up call today is not before nine. We do the usual housekeeping. I am on good terms with Kalíšek and Gustl for a change, but soon we get into an argument. The morning *Apel* is called off. I look forward to the afternoon, to the end of the *Rim, Rim* competition. Meanwhile, another competition has started, but it involves sports. We have to guess the outcome of the cup matches. Immediately I put down bets on the first round. After *Apel,* I write an article for myself titled, "Alone." After lunch, I go to Mother's where a bad mood prevails. Therefore, I soon leave. I'm eagerly awaiting the results of the competition. At *Apel,* Gans [Ginz?] wins the first prize, which is a picture of the School and also a special issue of *Rim, Rim.* I win the second prize, and so I will get the next three issues of *Rim, Rim.* And then comes Sasha. He'll get a special issue. So far, I am on good terms with Lion. After *Apel,* I don't know what to do and therefore I lie down on the bunk where I study French and English. Then Kalíšek comes to me and asks whether I would like to go for a walk with him. I agree. We go to the *Bahnhof* [train station] and then we return through the block back to our parents. In one of the houses, I see Pepík Ganz, who is sitting with an invalid, wiping his forehead. Pepík has really come up in my esteem. At Mother's, there is again a bad mood. I invite my parents for the *nesev,* titled "The Slaves," which will be performed today for parents. At home, I clean up and wait for my parents to arrive. *Nesev* begins. Father is bitten by a flea and he scratches something awful. I could jump out of my skin. Otherwise, the entertainment is quite good.

Sunday, 16 July 1944

I wake up with difficulties. I have a headache and throbbing in my ear. I keep arguing with the boys. I feel lousy and have diarrhea, perhaps from the cucumbers. This will stop now because SS Officer Haindl is soon coming to the *Landwirtschaft,* at which time Handa will not be able to bring home vegetables. It is now sure that there will be psychotechnical tests. Math will be my downfall. Most likely there won't be any school starting Thursday. Today there is supposed to be the Herzl celebration on the *bašta* but most likely it will be canceled. I don't feel like doing anything in the morning because I feel lousy. I cannot find my notebook, but during the program, I remember that I lent it to Krulis.[98] The first lesson is Czech. Gustl, as always, makes fun of me because I like Czech and Professor Eisinger. We cover geography at a rapid speed. We have completed all of the Balkans. Then comes the news that there are some races going on and we have to help out on the *bašta.* Of course, I don't go on account of my aches. Then the uncertainty goes on, whether the celebration will or will not take place. Because we have to prepare questions for the meeting with Heini, I go to my mother's and write them there. Everything is normal with my parents. I don't mention anything about my health to them. When I finish the questions, I return home and I learn that the celebration has been canceled by Dr. Eppstein. I go with the boys to Heini. I have an awful stomachache, but I go nevertheless. The questions are asked. Tutinek asks and I gain seven points. On the way home, Felix trips me. I get mad at him. We have to leave because it has been decided that the celebration will take place. But when I arrive home, the celebration is again canceled. At home I'm bored and I don't know what to do. At last Tuti and Lion arrive and tell me that there was a derailment of a train near the *bašta.* I immediately hurry there. It is just a small thing, as the train remained in its track. The train is loaded with some kind of military cargo. Afterward I go and sit down on the *bašta.* There is a match between Schild and Rapid, but it isn't very interesting. Then the Nešarim play the combined team of the Beavers. I leave at half-time. I hurry because I have my English les-

98. Krulis lived in room 9 in L417.

son with Sasha, who arrives late. The English lesson is excellent when I take it seriously. I go to Father because Mother has an afternoon shift. I hurry with dinner because I have a meeting with Heini. At the meeting, we make up questions and I win by twenty-three points. I feel lousy though and most likely have a temperature.

Monday, 17 July 1944

My earache has stopped. Mrs. Mautner doesn't feel well and therefore we can sleep longer today. It is rumored that three boys have escaped Terezín. They are Sklarek, Pfeffer, and Kohn. So far, there are no consequences. Overall, there seem to be a lot of scandals taking place right now in Terezín. In the afternoon, I learn that the painters Ungar, Haas, Fritta,[99] and two others were arrested and, with their families, taken to the Small Fortress. It is probably because they painted pictures showing Terezín people and then sold them. All of Terezín is full of it. SS Officer Haindl is really doing a "good job." He has already arrested one horse driver for smuggling letters out of Terezín. Handa is now really worried. During the morning *Apel*, Franta notices that I have a dirty neck. It is really the result of my sore ear. The program follows. I have a dreadful stomachache. Tomorrow starts our ten-day vacation from lessons, during which we will have the so-called psychotechnical exams. I am second in the exams. Because I was already tested in Hebrew, I have the afternoon free. For the moment, I just laze around, but then I go with Kalíšek for a walk. Something falls in my eye and I feel a pressure. Gustl joins us. We go to look at L721, where there is a warehouse of books. Our boys have brought piles of books from there. However, I don't steal anything.

99. Pavel refers here to the notorious "painters' affair" of 1944. Otto Ungar, Leo Haas, Fritz Taussig (known as Bedřich Fritta), Norbert Troller, and Ferdinand Bloch were assigned to the *Zeichenstube* (graphics department). This gave the artists access to art supplies and license to visit nearly all parts of the Ghetto. They created a pictorial record of the misery of Terezín daily life and sold some of these works to František Strass, formerly a department store owner, with gentile family connections. Strass added captions and, passed through gendarmes, drawings traveled to the outside world, where they came to the Germans' attention. Ungar, Haas, Taussig, and Bloch were brought (July 17, 1944) to SS headquarters in Terezín for interrogation. They and their families were sent to the Small Fortress, which functioned as a Gestapo prison. Strass and his wife were sent there as well, and Troller followed. Bloch was beaten to death in October 1944. Accused of distributing atrocity propaganda to outside countries, Haas, Taussig, Ungar, Troller, and Strass were shipped to Auschwitz. Taussig and Strass perished. Ungar died of dysentery in Buchenwald shortly after liberation. Haas and Troller survived, as did many of all five artists' works.

It is evident that Kalíšek prefers to go with Gustl. They go to "Mit-teilung"[?] and I return to the School. Afterward, I play *německá* with Jirka M. and Jila. I feel somehow sad. After playing, I go to Father because Mother is again on the afternoon shift. I have an argument with Father about some lard. I feel I should clear out and go home. I want to go with the boys for the books, but they don't want to go. I cry. Out of hopelessness, I go for a walk and I run into Huppert. We go on the ramparts and stop by Holzer's. He is also sad. At nine o'clock, I come home and for a while we talk with Mrs. Mautner, who announces that Franta M. will start again tomorrow and that we will do a big cleanup to prepare. I still feel pressure in my eye and there-fore I go to the clinic, where the nurse flushes my eye out. It doesn't help. Then, in bed I fall asleep.

This is the end of VOLUME 2 of my diary.

Volume 3

Tuesday, 18 July 1944

Today we get up very early because of *Grunt*. The dust in my eye still hurts me. I try to go to the clinic, but I cannot get there because of the cleanup. Franta is starting his duty with a new verve for cleanliness. We have to beat our mattresses and clean the inserts. It is eight o'clock already and we are not finished. Good weather is starting. We also have to clean our clothes. We have the whole morning to finish cleanup because our "vacation" has started. I am assigned to be a water carrier for scrubbing. In my free time, I write my diary. After scrubbing, we clean our clothes and shoes. Because all people who work are not in, there are a lot of clothing and shoes left to clean. These items are distributed during *Apel*. *Apel* lasts until 12:30, and at one o'clock there will be another one. Of course, everybody is mad. But we're supposed to wait. I go for lunch and take it to my parents. After lunch, I pick myself up and attend *Apel*, during which Franta gets all excited because the workers are not there. He says that at 5:30 everybody must be present, including the boys who work. Afterward I go to the garden. Again, I'm assigned to linden blossoms. Milka has recovered and has returned to the garden. She's our leader. We go to Backer Gasse, where we start picking blossoms. It is pretty entertaining, but nevertheless I'm looking forward to returning home. During the garden assembly, Schwarzbart tells us to pick up our ration after work, which we, of course, do right away. I'm lucky; I get half a head of cabbage and cauliflower leaves. I clean up at home and then go to my parents. On the square, several *Ghettowache* stand in front of the *Komandatura*. Apparently, they are there because of the two men who have escaped from Terezín. Everyone is getting ready for a big punishment. Presumably, Sklarek, one of the escapees, had his hair dyed by the barber Lavecky. The barber was arrested and beaten. It doesn't look good for the painters either. I don't have the patience to stay at Mother's as I keep looking at the *Ghettowache,* who are still standing there. I cannot make it to the meeting because I have to get my shots against whooping cough. It doesn't hurt at all. Then I go to the *bašta.* Several gendarmes stand below us at the Jaeger Barracks and the barracks are closed. Inside are SS officers Haindl and Burger from Prague, as well as the gendarmes. They are looking for the paintings.[100] I find out that they search other places too. There is a match going on between Skid and Greater Pilsen (score 2:2). Then, I watch Elektra play and, following that, I go home with Pudlina. In front of the school, I run into a scared boy who says that a gendarme had spanked him. At home, there is *Apel* and Franta sets forth the rules.

Thursday, 20 July 1944

In the morning, Franta wakes us up furiously and immediately we have to go to the bathhouse. I must hurry to get to the garden. At 7:30, I am already at L410. I have bad luck and I am assigned again to pick linden tree blossoms. However, we go to the Bohušovice Lane outside of the Ghetto, and it is a pleasant change. The boys keep making fun of me. Soon we pass the gendarme and we are in the fields and can see the Aryan highway. It is something entirely different. We see free people, buses, fields, and houses. Right nearby is a little house belonging to some gravedigger. We go inside to pick up a ladder and he is very pleasant. I can hear a radio coming from inside that little house, something I haven't heard for a very long time. The gendarme talks to us very calmly. What's interesting to me are the pro- and anti-Jewish scribblings I see in the gatehouse; they have been written by the gendarmes. The gendarme deliberately turns away so that he won't see us reading these words. We pick until eleven o'clock. The gendarme tells us that there was an air raid on Western Germany. After a short conversation with him, we start toward home. As we approach, an air raid occurs. We quickly run to L313, but the raid doesn't last too long. In the meantime, I have lunch at Mother's and then I go home. Just then the fifteen-year-old girls are being tested; they don't know a thing. Afterward, I return to Mother. I have been angry with my mother for several days. She continues to slave away cooking and does not get any fresh air. Soon

---

100. The Terezín artists had hidden their works in all manner of places: in secret compartments behind walls, buried in a tin receptacle in the ground, stowed away in an attic.

I go home. Yesterday, I registered for exams. I am in group N with Springer. During the afternoon *Apel*, Franta asks us who would like to go with him to sit on the *bašta*. Before we go, there is an argument about soccer. Pudlina, who has an inflatable ball, and Lappert want to play. Franta will not allow it and sends März[101] with a notice to Berl asking him to postpone the match. Then we go to the *bašta*. The boys keep making fun of me because I take a pillow with me to the *bašta*. Franta is reading us an essay on sociology about work done by various people. Yesterday, we sat in the same place and he read to us about Edison and today he reads about Rockefeller. He was a man who gained his property through swindles. His life story is very educational and interesting. It is awfully hot today. I return home and write my diary in this new notebook that I brought yesterday from my father. Soon Franta arrives and asks März whether he has delivered the notice to Berl and he says "no." Franta very angrily asks whether he was persuaded by other boys not to deliver it. März, with tears in his eyes, says that it was Bäumel who talked him out of it. I've never seen Franta so furious as today. März and Bäumel have to move out. Franta very angrily paces the room while I finish writing my diary. I go to Mother's, where the mood is dreadful. We keep arguing about her cooking. Finally, I've had enough and I leave. But I soon return. At last we go for a walk and everything is forgotten as we walk along the *bašta*. We meet the Freunds[102] and we talk for a while. Because it's getting late, I kiss Mother good-bye and go home. We then hear the decision on the punishment: März will most likely not have to move but Bäumel is going to the attic.

Friday, 21 July 1944

Today, we have our first exams. In the morning I'm supposed to take a written exam in Czech from Arna.[103] I still don't know at what time

---

101. Gideon Arnošt März (b. September 6, 1931), nicknamed Gida, was deported from Uherský Brod to Terezín with transport Cp on January 31, 1943; his number 358. Assigned to room 7 in Terezín, Gida was shipped to Auschwitz on October 19, 1944: prisoner 1318 on convoy Es. Gida did not survive.

102. Family friends from Prague.

103. Born March 20, 1922, Arnošt (or Arna) Ehrlich (later changed to Erban) was assigned number 270 and deported from Plzeň to Terezín on transport R on January 18, 1942. He served as the L417 room 9 *madrich*. Shipped to Auschwitz on September 28, 1944, with convoy Ek (his number: 2193), Arnošt survived and was liberated in Jaworzno. He immigrated to the United States after the war.

and I'm impatient. I cannot get into the room because the girls have exams there. Finally, it is ten o'clock and I go to Room 9, where boys from Q609 and some girls are waiting. I don't have any serious competition. We have dictation titled "The Spring Blossom." It is easy and most likely I will have no mistakes. Then I have to write a composition on the theme "My Friend." Because it seems silly to me, I write about a man who is all alone in the world. I think it will be good. Most importantly, I am not at all anxious. At noon, I go for lunch and take it to my father's place. Mother has a morning shift. Father had his tooth pulled and it is still hurting him. As a result of the *Ghettowache* scandal, only men over fifty can become *Ghettowache* now. Today, all officers have to report. I don't know what value it has. I come late to my father's place because there is an air raid. Today it is serious. People say they saw American airplanes, and it is true. The raid lasts for a long time and one can even hear shooting. It seems that all political events are coming to a point. The Russian and Italian fronts are advancing. My father is given a "ticket" by one of the *Ghettowache* because he goes out during the raid. The raid lasts for an hour and a half and after it I go home. There is *Apel*. Mrs. Mautner is on "vacation." In the afternoon, we again have exams: geography, history, Judaism, and natural science. Lichtwitz[104] finally arrives and gives me a test on what I know about Africa. In history, I'm tested about Charles IV. I do well in both. Then I go to Room 5 for a test in Judaism. They test me a little and I'm also doing excellently and I am pleased. Then, I go to the natural science exam and I get a "weak satisfactory," equivalent to second grade. I really don't know how I was supposed to know all that. Because I have to report to the garden, I must leave. I am assigned to do watering. It is extremely tough. Then, I return home and get washed and changed for the Friday *Apel*. The *Rim, Rim* boys give out strategic questionnaires on whether we can contribute or whether we have interest in the magazine. It seems like everybody has to say "yes." Then, I go to my parents. Since Mother is not cooking, we hurry so that we can go for a walk as soon as possible. We watch the soccer matches for a while with my father and we lie down on the *bašta*. Because it is late I return home to sleep.

104. Leo Lichtwitz (b. December 1, 1919) was deported on December 4, 1941, with transport J from Prague to Terezín, where he taught geography. Shipped to Auschwitz with convoy Er on October 16, 1944, Leo Lichtwitz did not survive.

Saturday, 22 July 1944

I wake up at 5:30 because we have gym with Heini on the *bašta*. Obviously, I don't feel like getting up. Heini is already on the *bašta*. We do gymnastics and then we learn how to start running. I have to go to the bathroom very badly because I have a tremendous stomachache. I feel lousy. After watching some soccer, I return home. There I lie down on the bunk. Kalíšek continues to be very obnoxious to me because he favors Gustl. Soon, I get bored lying down, and I get up to write my diary. The morning is overall uneventful. At noon I go to Father's and have lunch. I return home and don't know what to do. Out of boredom, I lie down on the bunk and I try to write a poem. I'm doing quite well at it. Soon, however, I lose interest and get into an argument with Beran about the correct usage in English of "shall you" and "will you." Out of boredom, I go with Franta Springer for a walk. We want to *schlojs* some fruit. We try to shake some fruit off a tree but nothing falls. I realize that it is easy to flee from a *sicha* [old, sickly person] who is almost crippled. Afterward, we go to L120, where some fruit finally falls off. Later, we go to the Dresdner Barracks, from where I soon leave. I bring my dinner to eat with my parents and I study French with my father. Because there is a match of Jugendfuersorge vs. Kadr, I go back to the Dresdner Barracks. Jufa wins 6:4 and advances. I go to my mother's barracks. Today, it has been one year since the death of Tetanka [Aunt Trude (Gertrude) Stein]. My mother lights a candle and is sad.

Sunday, 23 July 1944

Because we have our "vacation," we can stay in bed longer. My stomach feels upset. In bed, I write my English lesson. Because I don't feel well, I get up and immediately have to throw up. I lie back down on the bunk. Because of *Apel,* I am forced to get up again. I'm missing my left shoe. In the afternoon, there is supposed to be a ceremony observing Herzl. Franta says that whoever doesn't want to attend doesn't have to go. I have to think about it. At noon I go to Mother, who seems to be worrying about me. She doesn't have to. During *Apel,* I find out that tomorrow the opera *The Bartered Bride* will be performed for the entire School! It is announced that tomorrow we will also have mathematics and Czech oral exams. I am afraid of the math. I already feel much better though. At 1:45, we go to an assembly in the small yard. Franta again reminds us that we don't have to go to the ceremony unless we want to. For this reason, Kalíšek and I leave the group on the *bašta* and sit down on a hill from where we have a good view. The playing field is in good shape for sport and other events. After a short time, the groups start assembling. It gives a nice impression. The ceremony starts with a speech about Herzl. Later on, anthems are sung. The girls do some gymnastics and dances, followed by a soccer match between L417 and L414 that ends with a score of 3:4. Then there are several relay races through the town. The races prove that the Germans are superior runners. Afterward I go to two cup matches—the Bohemians vs. Rapid and Sparta vs. Spedice. Kavanictz and Kohn are playing for the Bohemians. In spite of their presence, the Bohemians lose 5:1. The second match is very interesting, with Spedice winning by a score of 4:2. Later, I meet with my father and hurry to L313 so I can learn about fractions and the calculation of interest. I do well but, because it is already nine o'clock, I go home. Blecha teaches me about ratios. I now feel ready for tomorrow's exam. Before going to sleep, Franta tells us interesting news that Hitler has died.[105] This would be tremendous!

Monday, 24 July 1944

When I wake up in the morning, I don't feel well. I have a headache and also a sore throat. I feel chills and hot at the same time. The morning is spent unexcitedly. I am still preparing for the exam. At eight o'clock, I go to Room 6, where Bastik is testing us. The problems are fractions, ratios, percents, and geometry. The fractions are easy, but I make errors. Overall, these are my only mistakes. I am soon finished. Because I am not allowed to be in Room 7 due to exams there, I go to Mother's to take my temperature. I first go to the barracks for a thermometer. I have 36.9 degrees and I feel worse. With my lunch, I go to L313, where I take my temperature again and I have 37.2. I am immediately the center of attention. I lie down on a bed but then I go home and I have the shivers. Because I have my Czech oral exam in the afternoon, I don't go to bed. After *Apel*, I go to Room 9 and Arna is reading our grades. I have two "ones" [highest grade]. He says that my composition is a bit shaky. I am the second one to be tested and he asks me something about [illegible word], something from literature and to name some inflexible words. I get

105. Pavel refers here to the failed assassination attempt of July 20, 1944, by German military officers who, by that point, saw no good end for the nation with Hitler as chancellor.

an "A." Overall, I have an "excellent" for the third level. I'm forced to lie down in bed. My temperature has gone up to 37.4! Then they test the girls, namely Eva Steinová and company. They are doing very badly and the boys throw pillows at them. I feel quite lousy. My temperature is already 37.6 degrees and I have an earache. I don't know what to do. Mother, of course, has left work to see me. Father brings me porridge and bread for supper. Feeling feverish, I fall asleep. I am awakened by a noise in the room. The boys think that there is a fire somewhere. All the Terezín SS officers have gone to Litoměřice for an assembly. Everything points to a quick end. With Hitler, it looks as though the assassination did not succeed. I cannot fall back asleep. I again throw up and my fever is 38. My ear hurts me. I close my eyes and finally, in about half an hour, I fall asleep.

Tuesday, 25 July 1944

The other boys have to get up because there is *Grunt*. Kalíšek doesn't behave very nicely to me. In the morning, I don't have any temperature. Today is like any other day when one is sick; my temperature keeps climbing and I feel very hot. Supposedly, I have pharyngitis. I am given aspirin and a compress. The rumor about Hitler is again disclaimed. However, the front is advancing. The Soviets are already near the Czechoslovak border. I don't know what to do and yet I have so much to write about. I don't feel like doing anything though. My parents continue to jump around me bringing food. I'm glad, however, when I am overtaken by sleep.

Wednesday, 26 July 1944

Overall I feel better, but I still have an earache. At the clinic I'm examined by Dr. Klein, who says I have a light case of eardrum infection. My mother is very worried about me and gives me compresses on my ear, which is very unpleasant, but it has to be done. I continue to be very hot, but in the evening I have only 37.2 degrees temperature. I hope that tomorrow I can get up. Now it is definite that the news about Hitler is not true, but the Russian front is advancing. They are already near Warsaw, and in France the Allies are advancing also. The circumstances point to an early end. I get a notice from the *Jugend-fuersorge* to see Mrs. Geisinger about studying piano. I am very much looking forward to it! Somehow I had an argument with Mother and she got so mad at me that she will not visit me today. I am unhappy. When Father comes with supper, I don't feel like eating anything. I am unhappy that Mother didn't come and I walk around the room sadly. With Kalíšek, I am finished. I put my stuff on his bunk and he gives me hell. I take my own blanket; I will never talk to him again. Gustl comes home and takes my blanket. I get mad and throw things off his shelf. We start fighting. Gustl doesn't care that I'm sick and even pulls down my scarf. I fight with him on the bed. Somehow, the fight stops. I'm very agitated. I feel so alone; I am lonely without my mother. Then I fall asleep. In the middle of the night I wake up and I feel like I'm on fire. I cry for my mother to come. I'm thirsty and I find some water. Kalíšek complains that the fleas are biting him. I feel really lousy but eventually I fall back asleep.

Thursday, 27 July 1944

I'm looking forward to getting out of bed today. But at the clinic, I'm told that I still have to stay in bed. I'm very mad, and yet I'm looking forward to Mother's arrival, which happens soon. She is very calm. Kikina is also in bed so that I have company, but not a very intelligent one. I want to write something, but I can't. It is rumored that we will have oral exams in math. In the evening, I have again diarrhea. When Mother arrives in the evening, I sit down at the table with her. She helps me to arrange my things so that fleas won't bite me. I don't speak with either Gustl or Kalíšek. The fleas don't bite me at all so I sleep quite well through the night.

Friday, 28 July 1944

I'm glad that I can finally get up today. It is an entirely different feeling. Immediately after housekeeping I sit down and write my diary. Later, I join Kokošek and Mautner for a walk. We sit in the small park behind L504 and give each other questions. We try to shake down fruit off the trees but we don't succeed. Looking into Sokolovna,[106] we hope they will let us go on the terrace, but they won't. Therefore, we just walk around. Upon returning to the School, I again go out with

106. Sokol was, and still is, a Czech sports and fitness movement. The organization's clubhouse before the camp was created, the Sokolovna initially became a hospital and then (end of April 1944) a coffeehouse and cultural center used for lectures and concerts during the camp era.

Kapr and walk behind the brewery. I go barefooted because I cannot find my other shoe. It worries me a lot. I'm sad that my mother is working. I go with my lunch to Father, whom I meet on the way. He is angry on account of my lost shoe. After lunch, I go home and then to the garden. Because it has rained they send us home. I sweep in front of the church before we are released. In the afternoon, I do nothing. In the evening, I go for a walk with Mother. It starts raining, so I go home and chat with the boys. Then I go to bed where I soon fall asleep while listening to Franta's reading.

Saturday, 29 July 1944

In the morning I have to get up early because I have a meeting with Heini on the *bašta*. Of course, I don't feel like getting up. On the *bašta*, we play with the ball. It is pretty good. At eight o'clock I go home. Kohn starts trouble because the boys did not get up to make the room ready for exams. I have to take my orals in math. I go to the attic, where Irenka is to test me. She asks me about the Pythagorean theorem, which I don't know at all, and about the equation A plus B minus C squared, which I know well. I get a "satisfactory" grade to advance to the third level in math. Because of Kohn's anger about the room, we are forced to work in the afternoon in the basement. I go to my father's place to eat my lunch. At two o'clock, after *Apel*, we go back to the basement. The work there is quite hard. Outside, there is a downpour and we finish at 3:45. Then I go and get washed and I again look for my shoe, but it is to no avail. I forgot to mention that I have room duty with Kalíšek, which means we are forced to talk. At Mother's, I am in a bad mood because I cannot find my nice shoe. I only have high beaten-up boots for rainy weather like today. When I am leaving, Mother tells me that she will come and help me look for the shoes. I go and watch a soccer match for a while. Then I continue to search the whole room back home for the lost shoes. Finally Mother arrives and finds the shoes on my shelf. I am pleased! I go again for a walk. At night, I don't get washed and fall asleep.

Monday, 31 July 1944

I wake up normally. Today I am supposed to have the psychotechnical exam in the attic. First I don't know where to go, but then I'm stopped by Dr. Jelínková. She gives out a little card with squares and then instructions according to which we have to mark the squares. Since I'm doing it with pen, it gets smudged. Overall, I'm not doing a good job. Afterward, I'm supposed to draw something and I'm making fun of it. When I come to the *heim,* I'm assigned to go to the barber. There something unpleasant happens. The barber tells me that I have a dirty head. I feel bad and embarrassed. I immediately wash my head. All excited, I go to see Prager in the Magdeburg Barracks. He tells me to come to see him once more to inquire. Then, I go to Mother's where I confess about my dirty head and I already feel relieved. These days the weather is all the same. In the morning it's nice and then it rains. Today is no different. At noon, I go to Mother's as I always do. I'm not really looking forward to today's match against the Stars, which will take place at three o'clock. After *Apel* I lie down on the bunk. Franta reads to us about the Congo, during which I fall asleep. Then we are called in to go for our ration. I receive cauliflower and kohlrabi today. I am now on better terms with Kalíšek. At three o'clock, I go to the *bašta.* However, the grounds are in very bad shape. Therefore we begin to dig and bring in sand, which takes about an hour. When we're finished, it starts raining and we don't have a ball. Finally, somehow, we get a ball and we play in the rain. We score a goal in the first few minutes. The Stars equalize the score and even lead 2:1. The field is miserable so we are completely covered with mud. We manage to equalize the score and the match has to go into overtime. I am very tired. The Stars score a goal and I think the match is lost. However, in the final minutes, Tuti scores the equalizer. Fortunately, we win the draw and I shout out with happiness! I start talking again to Kalíšek. At home, I get washed and go to Father's. Today writing in the diary bores me, but I must write so that it doesn't fail. Father is not at home, but I find him with my mother in the bakery. For dinner we have *zemlbaba* [bread pudding]. At first, I don't even notice that my father gives me a larger portion. However, when I realize it, I get angry and give my father hell. I pack my things and go away. At home, I finish eating and I go with the boys to play Skid [Room 1 in L417?: PW]. After soccer I go home and I read Kalíšek's book.

End of the month of July

Tuesday, 1 August 1944

We have to get up earlier today because of *Grunt,* which is entirely normal. I have a ticket for bathing, which feels pretty good. After the bath I go slowly home. I stop at the library to finish reading *R.U.R.* [by Karel Čapek], which I borrowed last Sunday. The play is marvelous. I cannot pull myself away from it. In a state of excitement, I stay in the library until 11:30. I take my lunch to my mother's, where it is again boring. In the afternoon, I go to the garden, where I am assigned to digging in the #1 garden. I take one radish and then two carrots. It is very dangerous because Miss Milka and Mrs. Kienová are eagle-eyed and watch us very carefully. A piece of chives disappears into my bag. Because Schwarzbart orders me to finish, I head home. I don't remember well the events at my mother's or what I did at home in the evening, as I am late in writing these lines. But I hear that the news from the war front is good. Also, I'm very furiously studying French and I receive a package containing sardines.

Wednesday, 2 August 1944

When I wake up in the morning, I realize that I have to fetch a package and I don't have any identification. Mrs. Mautner, who started her duty again yesterday, offers that her son Jirka will pay for the package. I am to tell her how many people are in the line. However, I get from my father the identification paper. I hold in my hands this piece of worthless paper and I go for the package, which I get after a lengthy wait. While I'm waiting, I realize how valuable food in Terezín is. The last few days I have been feeling some anger for which I don't know the reason. Mother tells me that Franta has complained about me. Partly I feel annoyed with her, but for the most part I'm angry at Franta. There is *Apel* during which, as always, nothing interesting happens. Franta is lecturing us about good behavior. He is very good at it! In the morning I read a book titled *Out of Malayan Jungles,* which I borrowed from Pepík. Somehow, I feel like going to the library so I make my way there. I like reading Čapek and therefore I borrow *The Makropulos Affair.* I read the first act, but I realize that it is not for me. I return home, where I listen to a discussion about our second and third teams. When I go for lunch, the boys make fun of me, which can piss off even the calmest individual. At Father's, the usual mood prevails. My mother only cooks, which annoys me. In the morning, I also went to Prager, who, however, was not in. After *Apel,* Franta finishes reading to us about the Congo. I'm making lots of plans but during the writing of my diary, I decide that, after a long time without speaking to him, I will go outside with Kalíšek to steal pears and apples. First, we go to L421, where Kalíšek steals some boxes. Later, Jirka Mautner joins us and we search the places we already know, but we don't get anything. At three o'clock, I go for my ration in the garden; today, it's two cabbages. I take them to my parents and then we go to the blocks near the Sudeten Barracks. However, we once again don't find a thing. In one of the houses we actually want to steal some paper used for blackouts.[107] In this respect, Terezín is spoiling us. I cannot imagine a life of this sort in Prague. Finally, I realize what I want to do and give up the idea. However, I cannot resist stealing fruit in L129. As fate may have it, the apples will not fall down. When a poor armless man appears, we very calmly flee. Because it starts raining, we return home, where I'm bored. I go to my parents, where there is some dreadful screaming going on. I am extremely tired and I lie down for a while. This makes my father angry for reasons I don't understand. Then he tells me that I only come to my mother's to snuggle. I really don't know why he said it, but it gets to me. I go home, where I lie down on the bunk and read. Later, I go to Room 9, where they are singing songs by Voskovec and Werich.[108]

Thursday, 3 August 1944

We can sleep longer because we have our "vacation" now. We don't get up until 7:45, even though our garden duty starts at eight o'clock. This is how it's done in Terezín—one reports to work just at the time of the assembly. I'm now completely on normal terms with Kalíšek. In fact, we get along better than before. I don't know how to express it, but the truth is it seems that Kalíšek has changed. I think that he is pleased. We really needed such a change. I go to the garden and, of course, I arrive late. At Dr. Rudniková's[109] offer, we go inside. Whenever I go to the garden, I have the determination to get a good assignment, which means that I will be able to *schlojs*. Such is the

107. On German orders, heavy blue-black paper (among other materials) was used to cover windows at night to avoid detection by Allied planes.

108. Jiří Voskovec (1905–81) and Jan Werich (1905–80) founded the avant-garde, antifascist Liberated Theater in Prague, which was closed by the Nazis. Voskovec and Werich fled to the United States in early 1939. Voskovec remained in America after the war and he enjoyed a successful career. Werich returned to Czechoslovakia, where he too enjoyed success until the Soviet invasion in 1968; he had many fewer opportunities thereafter.

109. Dr. Gertruda Rudniková (b. November 3, 1909) was deported to Terezín from Plzeň on transport T (number: 310) on January 26, 1942. Dr. Rudniková remained in Terezín (as Pavel's later diary entries indicate) and survived to be liberated there.

real attitude toward work in Terezín. Today, I have bad luck and I
am assigned to fixing up lawns and weeding. The garden has clearly
emptied out. Mrs. Kienová is watching over us very carefully. During
the break, Roth sings both vulgar and clean songs, so the half-hour
break passes by quickly. Afterward, we don't work and we carry the
already filled cases to the garden cooperative. We are in a good mood
because we can expect good rations out of it. People are looking at
us as if we are wealthy and one old woman even comes to me for some
greens. I refuse to give her any. We carry the cases down to the basement, when a cart loaded with beans arrives. Some beans fall off and
we throw ourselves at them. While other boys manage to take ten
beans, I take only two. Then, out of nowhere, Kienka flies in and slaps
me (from now on, I will refer to Mrs. Kienová with this nickname).
I am startled and become so angry that I throw the beans under her
feet. Out of spite, I take the case back. We get enough vegetables
back. In the garden, we get a ration of cabbage and some greens. I go
home feeling good and I take my lunch to Mother's. It is again very
"dumb" there and I return home. I want to go to Prager, but he is not
there. It makes me mad. I don't find my mother either and therefore
I go home, where I just lie around. We hold a nature science seminar
which I don't like very much. I am determined to finish my diary and
I set out to do so. After finishing, I go for supper and then back to
Mother's. In her barracks they have torn down one bunk and moved
it somewhere else. As a result there is more space to sit. I leave because the place is now very messy and I also have another run-in with
Father. At home, I lie down and read before falling asleep during
Franta's reading.

Note: The *Ghettowache* have now changed their uniform. Instead
of the yellow band, they now wear blue and white bands. It is better
because it doesn't remind us of the Ghetto. This change took place
two days ago.

Friday, 4 August 1944

A new day is beginning. I have now been in Terezín for over two
years and the still-unresolved problem keeps going through my head.
What annoys me the most is that two years of my life have been lost. If
I were in Prague, I would be going to theaters, I would read, I would
write, but here I have no materials, no opportunity, and no freedom.
Freedom symbolizes life and everything that is alive needs freedom.

This is an introduction to one of my days spent in Terezín. I have decided that I will write my diary entirely differently. I will write about my feelings so that I can benefit from it in the future. I will start leading a new life. I will no longer keep my head down, and I will study, read, and study more. Today, I act accordingly. In the morning, I wake up and dash out of the building as soon as possible. Since our floors are being scrubbed, I take with me a book titled *The Savages of Malayan Jungles* and a French book, which I have been neglecting for a long time. I write my diary. The weather is quite nice and I feel somehow more free. I sit down on the bench behind L504 and study. After writing vocabulary from twenty-two lessons, I read my book. I realize that one of my problems is that I read too slowly. I stare longingly at the ripe apples and pears, but fortunately I control myself not to *schlojs* any. I must change my seat because a sick gentleman joins me. At eleven o'clock, I return home. I feel rather cold. While I'm at home, Bäumel comes from the garden and brings some cucumbers. Everybody gets one. In Terezín, one gets joy out of every little swindle. I take my lunch to Father's place, where a bad mood prevails. Mother is at work so Father and I are alone. To be honest, my father really gets on my nerves. Accidentally, I tip over my plate and Father gets angry. I don't know why he is angry, but I soon leave. I am panic-stricken about today's lice control. At one o'clock, a "doctor" arrives and examines us. Very adroitly, I step out of line so that I'm not examined. I'm glad that I got out of it so easily. In the afternoon, I go to the garden. During the assembly, I am assigned to water the #1 garden. We have agreed not to *schlojs*. Instead, we only will pay attention to how the female instructors are stealing. Today we could *schlojs* as much as we wanted, but out of principle we don't take a thing. After the break, we soon finish and go home. I get washed and hurry to the *bašta*, where the Nešarim play Rapid. Išík saves two goals and we win by a score of 5:3. After the match, I go to Mother's, where the mood is good. While we take a walk, we meet Mrs. Geisinger, who tells me that starting tomorrow I can practice piano. I am so pleased to be able to play! In the evening, there is a meeting about which I'd rather not say anything, because it is dreadfully dumb. By 11:30 I fall asleep.

Saturday, 5 August 1944

Felix wakes me up because I have a meeting with Heini on the *bašta*, and I jump out of bed when I see all the boys getting dressed. Yesterday, I didn't think I would want to get up early. Felix set the alarm at the wrong time so that we overslept by fifteen minutes. I arrive at the *bašta* at 6:30. Our search for Heini was in vain because Heini quite correctly already left. We therefore return home. I go back to bed because today we are allowed to sleep until 8:30. Then I hear about the *pruser* involving Blecha, Palounka, Eisner, and Echstein, who *schlojs*-ed fruit above the bakery. The *Ghettowache* brings in Palounka and Blecha. Mrs. Mautner arrives and we must get up. We have some new housekeeping rules. Namely, after we wake up, four boys will be assigned housekeeping duty. The time assigned to housekeeping is firmly set. It is the dumbest arrangement because the rest of us have to go out while the housekeeping is being performed. Still, I can use this time to write my diary, which I do today. When I finish writing, I read my book. I go for lunch because it is getting late. At my father's it is pretty good, but I have to leave because there is *Apel* at 1:30. I am already looking forward to this afternoon. At three o'clock, I can practice the piano and then I will watch the soccer match Rapid vs. Jugendfuersorge. I place a bet on Rapid. Until three o'clock I do nothing, only get washed and change my clothing. After picking up mother, we go into the basement in L410. The coldness of the basement and the warmth of the music welcome us. I cannot get to the piano because it is not yet my time. I have a bit of stage fright lest I forget the notes. At last, it is 3:30 and I sit down behind the piano. First, I play the scales, which I do well. Then I play the "Turkish March" for Professor Weiss.

I completely forgot to mention what happened on Sunday, 30 July, the day I saw Mrs. Geisinger about the piano. She was very kind and wrote out a ticket for times I could practice—Saturdays from 3:30 to 4:00, Mondays from 1:00 to 1:30, and Wednesdays also for half an hour. She told me that I will be instructed by somebody named Professor Weiss, a Dutchman, whom I immediately contacted. He is pleasant and I could see that he knows his stuff. He said that he would be glad to instruct me, but first I have to practice and then play something for him. That's why I have practiced the "Turkish March" and "Melodies" by Beethoven. Then I play some little things. I am lucky that I can practice for a full hour. At home, I learn that I have a meeting at 5:30 with Heini during which the details for Scout Day will be discussed. It is supposed to take place tomorrow from six o'clock in the morning until six o'clock in the evening. During the meeting, I learn about the program about which I will write tomorrow. Because there is soccer, I stay at Mother's only a short time and immediately rush to the Dresdner Barracks. The match is quite interesting and its score is 5:2. I cannot stay until the end because Handa gives me a ticket for the opera *Bastien and Bastienne,* which will take place at eight o'clock in the Magdeburg Barracks. Even though I have a ticket for standing, I am able to sit in the first row. It is amazing! Bastien becomes unfaithful to Bastienne and falls in love with the Countess. Bastienne cries and Bastien soon forgets about the Countess. They make peace with each other and get married. It is by Mozart. One can see that it is ageless art! When the performance is over I go home, wash up, lie down, and soon fall asleep. I realize I should start worrying about a gift for Mother's birthday. Most likely Špulka will carve something for me. I fall asleep feeling that I have spent this day in luxury.

Sunday, 6 August 1944

In the morning I wake up, but I don't feel like getting up. It is six o'clock and at 6:45 we are supposed to be at L410. I am mad about the whole comedy involving the Scout Day festival. But nothing can be done about it. We wear blue shirts. In L410 there are lots of kids. Then we go in groups of three to the *bašta,* and we camp behind the moat. Many people, mostly German Jews, are already there. We assemble for *Apel,* and someone is talking about [illegible word]. The oath is given and anthems are sung, but I don't participate in either. I don't feel so "progressive." The German Jews are given prizes, which I find funny. Joint gymnastics follows, which I find so dumb that I won't even write about it. Afterward there is food, which is the best part of the whole day. I don't remember some events that followed. In soccer our team places well. Later there are some choir rehearsals for singing. We were supposed to sing, but since Heini doesn't know how to conduct, we skip it. We all go for lunch, which is against my principle because I won't be able to eat at Mother's. After lunch, I go to Mother because we don't have to be back at the *bašta* until 12:45. It's unbearably hot and I am tired, bored, and testy. At Mother's, I take a piece of cake, which is delicious, and then I hurry back to the *bašta.* Afterward, I shower and then follows a half an hour of Hebrew. I have never seen anything so dumb. For a while, we lay out in the sun. Then we line up for a scout game. We are divided into tribes, and I am in the tribe of Juda. We receive a written description of a man who is somewhere on the *bašta* and we are to find him. After we find him he gives a letter with instructions for two boys from our team to run to L414 where additional instructions are hidden. Meanwhile, we go behind Ovčín. I get disgusted with the game and decide not to participate. For a long time nobody from L414 shows up, until finally the two boys return with instructions. There are some questions in it, but I don't participate. Additional questions are more intelligent, but I don't answer them either. I am teed off. Then we go to the *bašta* and watch the match between the *madrichim* and the boys (the score is 2:4). It was a funny match. Afterward, some running events take place, followed by various performances. I like in particular the German girls as they sing several foreign songs, and even some in Czech. It is 6:30 when everything is over. I want to go in time for the semifinal match between Elektra and Spedice, and I bet on Elektra. I drop my things off with my father, go for supper and then head straight to the soccer match. It is a tremendous match. Elektra wins 1:0 which means that the finals will be between Jugendfuersorge and Elektra. After the soccer match, I meet with Father to go to L313, where I wash myself in warm water. After eating supper, I go home and go to sleep.

Monday, 7 August 1944

The morning is spent cleaning up. Housekeeping is being done in accordance with the new rules. My mother comes to me in the morning and, because I have to give out my laundry, she changes my bed linen. Springer and Bäumel are obnoxious to me. In all, I don't like the whole *heim*. After the morning *Apel,* I sit down at the table and finish writing my diary. It occupies the whole morning, but I'm glad to sacrifice it. Today, we are supposed to play the semifinal match with Aseum at four o'clock and we don't even have a ball yet. For this reason, Jirka and I go to the shoemaker, Meyer, whom we know. He lets us wait, but then he gives us the repaired ball. I have to hurry home because I can practice the piano from 1:00 to 1:30, which means I have to be there fifteen minutes earlier. I go for lunch, where there is a long line, and then to Mother's. I have stage fright because of the expected presence of Luci Horowitz[110] during my playing. My nervousness affects my overall mood, which comes to a boiling point

---

110. Pavel's distant relative; a cellist from Austria.

while I am with Mother. I need to leave to avoid something serious. At home, I am nervous and, already at 12:45, I am at L410. After waiting a while, I sit down at the piano. I play the sonatina quite well when I play it alone, but soon my mother arrives with Luci. He is a professor of the conservatory and he points out certain arm movements that are essential. I learned them in Prague but have since forgotten them. After a half-hour of practice, I learn what Luci has shown me. I return home for *Apel.* Franta is reading to us and we just chat. We are taught how to guard gardens during the nature science seminar. My duty will be between seven and eight o'clock. After, I change my clothes and go to the *bašta.* It is unbearably hot. Soon after the start of the game, we lead 1:0 and then they tie the score and soon pull ahead. It is half-time and I'm awfully hot. Water just drips off of me. The score mounts 3:1, 4:1, 5:1 and that's how it goes until the match is over. Even though I'm completely exhausted, I stay for the match between the Falcons and the Dragons. I have not mentioned the reforms in our teams. Two boys switched from the Hawks to the Nešarim and Tuti transferred from us (Nešarim) to the Hawks. We also got Grizzly. It is 5:30 already when I go to Father, who, however, is not there. I go for supper and then from there again to my father. I walk barefooted and half-naked. I have to go home soon because I have guard duty. During the duty, I read until eight o'clock and then I play *německá* with Kalíšek. I have a peek into the house where the gendarmes live. They have moved in from Kořina. We finish after nine o'clock and I am fed up with all this soccer. I regret spending so much time with it. I receive a ration of cabbage and some other greens. I think we have been swindled. Afterward, I change my bed and get washed. I sleep very well in the clean linen.

Tuesday, 8 August 1944

We get up early because of *Grunt.* I'm pleased with the rumor that Kraków has fallen and that fighting is going on in Warsaw. Everything points to an early end, but the Germans will not give up. In France, they want to cut off Bretagne. After *Grunt* I realize that I am missing pillows. It pisses me off and I decide not to go to the washroom. While putting things in order, I read and write my diary. This morning the program should restart. However, in place of the usual program, it will include more "entertainment," provided by Franta and Vera. Today we are supposed to continue with natural sciences.

I cannot take part in *Apel* because Šmudla takes us to the small attic to put the luggage storage in order. It is rumored that the School will be evacuated. This is an assumption based on yesterday's German visit, which didn't end exactly in the best way. When we are finished with the luggage storage, I go down to join the program. We learn about apes and Vera reads to us about the conditions of Indians in Mexico. I'm so sleepy that I have to lie down. Later I go for lunch and through a little trick we jump the line. It is again so hot and I don't feel like going to the garden. Something interesting happens at my father's. I say something that Father obviously doesn't like and he scolds me. It really gets to me and I jump away from my food and literally fly out of the room. At home I lie down on my bunk and I am very unhappy. There is *Apel*, during which it is determined who will go to the garden and who will go to [*hlášky?*: PW]. I am assigned to the garden. Immediately I go to the meeting place, but we have to wait for a long time for Mr. Schwarzbart. There are only four of us in the garden with Dr. Rudniková. We water the first garden and seed strawberries. It goes slowly and Schwarzbart doesn't like it. I ask him whether he could release me to have a mid-afternoon snack and he lets me go. I then continue to water the #1 garden. Upon leaving, I realize that I succeeded to *schlojs* a cucumber, several apples, a carrot, and parsley. At Mother's, a bad mood prevails as always. I have a good excuse for leaving this time, because I have a meeting at 6:30. Heini doesn't show up in time and so I go instead with the boys to the *bašta*, where the elimination match is under way. Overall, it is an interesting match. At the end I get into an argument with Brena. We chase each other on the *bašta* and throw stones at each other. I didn't realize the consequences it will have. I go home but Brena continues to throw. We walk along Langestrasse and then to Hauptstrasse. When we approach the School, Brena starts again throwing. I promise to fight him, which we actually do in the hall. He applies a stranglehold and I fall down straight on my face. He releases me, but I tell him that I could have freed myself even though I know I could not. As I get washed, I meet a boy who used to go to school with me in Prague. He arrived in Terezín just fourteen days ago. He tells me about the conditions in Prague, like how Jews are not allowed to walk along the main streets. At home, *Rim, Rim* is read to us as we lie down. It is truly hopeless because it has no new contributions. Now they are begging, with Franta's help, for contributions. I soon fall asleep. Tonight, for the first time in a long time, I'm dreaming about something.

Wednesday, 9 August 1944

The morning is entirely uninteresting. After the program we are free. My relationship with my parents does not improve, just the contrary. We receive a ticket to go for ice cream in the dining hall today. First, however, we chat with Franta about the magazine. He urges us to exert ourselves mentally. He feels that no one is doing anything and he asks me what I have been doing lately. I tell him that I study and I read. For example, just today I was in the library and I read [Shakespeare's] *The Merchant of Venice*. As far as the magazine is concerned, I have more important things to do than to write. I don't have the time or subject matter to inspire me. I also have to worry about a gift for Mother for her birthday. After the meeting we go to the dining hall. We show childish joy! After some wait, we are let in. We sit down and are served a cup full of ice cream. I gulp it down in a minute and then we are kicked out. So, this is the way the famous ice cream feast ends up. Afterward, I go home and nervously await six o'clock, the time of my piano practice. Since no one is there when I arrive, I can start practicing. But soon my mother arrives with Luci. He is not quite satisfied as yet with my playing. He keeps bugging me about the positioning of my hands. At 6:30 even my father arrives. When I finish playing, I am somewhat disturbed. I give hell to both my parents. I behave like a crazy guy. I cannot stand it too long and leave. At home I lie down and spend the whole evening talking with Kalíšek about a great variety of interesting things.

Thursday, 10 August 1944

I wake up at seven o'clock. I can stay in bed until 7:30 since I don't have to be in the garden until eight o'clock. I'm now on very good terms with Kalíšek. In the bunk we joke and chat. At 7:30 I get up quickly and go to the garden. After attendance, I sit down on the bench and wait for my assignment. I'm assigned first to put away cucumbers and to weed out yellow leaves. I take this opportunity to *schlojs* two cucumbers. I eat one in the garden, but with the other I have some bad luck. On the main street the cucumber falls out of my pocket and immediately Mrs. Kienová starts after me. Fortunately, Sasha kicks it off to the side path and Kuli picks it up and gives it back to me. An incident like this could never have happened to me in Prague. Overall, the matter of *schlojs* in Terezín intrigues me

greatly. Afterward, I do various jobs in the garden. Others deliver
stuff to the co-op, while several of us stay in the #3 garden cleaning
up the ground. As we are completely alone, we devour about twenty
apples and pears, in addition to onions. I am overtaken by the *schlojs*
fever! Two boys throw apples over the fence, hoping that nobody will
pick them up. Suddenly Milka comes back from delivery and catches
the boys just as they are eating the apples that were thrown over the
fence. Fortunately, nothing big comes out of it, but we get scared nevertheless. On account of all this, I am in a bad mood and grouchy. I
go to Room 9 for a ration consisting of a dilapidated lettuce, which I
bring to Mother. The mood at Mother's place is already better as the
problem has solved itself. I leave with the hope that I will get some
time to pay attention to my things. I still have to stop at Heini's and
talk about the meeting. Afterward I read a book. After *Apel* we again
have a boring program. I excuse myself because I have to go to my
English lesson, which is quite good. After the lesson, Vera is reading to the boys, but I come only at the tail end. When the program
ends, I go to the *bašta* to watch soccer. I leave a message for Mother
that she should go alone to Professor Weiss. On the *bašta* I watch the
match between the Nešarim and the Schild (4:1). I hurry for dinner
at Mother's, from where I depart for a meeting with Heini. We criti-
cize the Scout Day and discuss plans for an evening program. After
the meeting I go back to Mother's, where I spot my parents sitting on
a bench. I talk with them very nicely until we get into an argument.
I maintain that Turks are Mongols, but my father says they are Semites. We bet a sausage and then we ask several people nearby. While
my father walks me home, even Professor Hoffmann maintains that
the Turks are Semites. I am convinced already that I have lost my bet
when I ask Franta for his opinion. He looks into a book and confirms
that Turks are in fact Mongols! After resolving the argument I get
washed, lie down next to Kalíšek, and soon fall asleep.

Friday, 11 August 1944

We are allowed to sleep later today and I stay in bed until 7:30. Then
I do my housekeeping. During *Apel*, I'm told that I have to be inocu-
lated in the evening against diphtheria. In the morning we have the
usual program. First Vera reads several stories and we have to summarize one of them. Then we have economic geography, which I like
less. Afterward I go only to my father because my mother has the

morning shift. I have figured out the gift for Mother and it's partly ready. I had Špulka carve out a turtle and then I will write something to her. I don't think that it will be too bad, but nevertheless it worries me what to write. I don't stay too long at Father's. At home, I am told that the Dutchman came to visit me—the one who will teach me piano—and that he will come back around 1:30. Because the Dutchman doesn't show, I go to the garden at two o'clock. In the garden there is a big commotion because fruit is being collected in the presence of the Aryan Altman.[111] For this reason, we are not allowed into the garden and have to wait outside. This obviously doesn't please me. While we wait the boys make fun of me, which is becoming a daily occurrence. Only at three o'clock does Schwarzbart let us into the garden. We have to prune and, in the meantime, I tidy up in the corner. I see Aryans who are filling cases of big yellow apples. I envy them a lot. My greatest desire in the garden is to *schlojs* but today it doesn't go so well. I feel lazy and I don't feel like doing a thing. Mrs. Kienová is watching us so that nobody will steal and she controls the garden. I take only two carrots and one apple. I'm so bored that I go to the #3 garden, where I hope to take something. In the #4 garden I bite into an onion, only to put it down. Before I leave I ask Schwarzbart whether he can give me some flowers, but he says "no." I am angry and go home. On my shelf I have a ration of a pear, an apple, some parsley, and celery. It is unjustly divided. Then I go to Mother's, where the mood is good. Mother sends Father and me to the barracks to bring some rhubarb and a baking tray. After we finish, I walk my father home and I show him the turtle which I have already bought for 5 dkg of margarine. I don't return to Mother's because I have to write in my diary and think about something good to write for Mother's birthday. I write the diary, but I can't come up with a suitable theme for my mother. At home, I wash myself and fall asleep.

Saturday, 12 August 1944

In the morning I'm awakened by somebody pulling on my sheet. It is Felix, who is waking me up because we have a six o'clock meeting on the *bašta.* It is not six o'clock yet, but Tuti wakes me up for good. We stroll slowly to the *bašta.* Heini arrives shortly after us. We have to

111. Pavel refers to a German civilian (first mentioned in the May 20 entry) who occasionally supervised groups working in the gardens. According to others who were there, he did not treat the boys kindly.

take our boots off and the stones hurt me, particularly when I run. The boys are laughing that I cannot run well and this annoys me a lot. After running, we learn how to fall, which is not much fun. Working on the parallel bars is not exactly the most interesting. I'm glad when it's over. Now a big job is ahead, namely, to write something for my mother. Meanwhile, in the morning I still have to go to Heini and help in organizing the Pacific Entertainment Evening. At home, I learn the unpleasant news that today I have room duty with Kalíšek. I really needed it like a hole in the head but I have to suffer through it. It is not a very difficult duty, but it spoils my day. The boys stay in bed a long time and I use this time to write an article for my mother. I don't know how the subject came to me, but I know that it is good. It deals with the following: I am at a crossroads of Fate and I don't know which way to go. One old man advises me to go on a thorny road and I take it. I reach a house that is rundown, but it is also the center of a kingdom of justice. I don't finish the article because there is a wake-up call. Four boys are assigned to me for housekeeping duty. Everything goes smoothly. It is good that *Apel* is called off. I still have a chance to study my French vocabulary. Lion wants to put together some kind of a celebration for the anniversary of the twentieth issue of *Rim, Rim*. It will include some kind of a play and an orchestra led by Holzer. I'm supposed to play the recorder. I cannot refuse, but I know that it will not work because harmonica and recorder together do not harmonize well. I go to the attic, where the first "rehearsal" takes place; it is awful! I am lucky that I can leave soon because I have to meet with Heini. I take with me the half-finished article so that I can finish it in the library. At Heini's we discuss what to put on the program of the Pacific Entertainment Evening. Then I go to the library, where I finish the article. I think the ending is particularly successful. I'm ending with the sentence ". . . I would bring you a bouquet of sweet smelling roses picked in a paradise garden of justice and freedom." I like it very much! At home, I start rewriting it into the final form. I have to quit so that I can eat lunch with my father, at which point I remind him to bring me some cotton and a little case to pack the gift. Today I have the opportunity to deal with a big problem, namely the observance of a family event in Terezín. I am spending the entire day in a fast-moving, festive tempo. I'm in a constant hurry and I like it. The house duty turns out well, even with Kalíšek, which is surprising. We divide our duties evenly. From 2 to 3:30 I am on call but I excuse myself because I have to go with Špulka, who [illegible words]. Mr. Spitz has a very nice cubicle. I go home in order to finish rewriting the article. It is not written in the best handwriting but the main thing is that its content is nice. I want to go to Father for the little case and cotton, but I realize that it is getting late and therefore I simply return home. I have a piano lesson from 3:30 to 4:00. It is dumb that next door the harmonium is playing and that Mother comes without Luci. I don't know what to play. I'm somewhat angry and take it out on Mother. Almost instantaneously, my good mood has changed. When we walk out of the basement, we meet Professor Weiss. He wants me to play something for him. Considering what consequences it will have, I don't even have a big stage fright. It will turn out somehow. From his behavior I can tell that Professor Weiss is a serious artist. He seems to be conceited about his artistry. I'm asked to play some scales for him, which I do quite well. I also play chords and finally a sonatina that I don't finish. He feels my fingers expertly and tests my finger span on the keyboard. He tells me that I will do and that I may take lessons with another student (a Dutch girl) and that he will tell Mrs. Geisinger about my lessons. So it turned out pretty well for me, but I am still nervous about whether he will take me. I am again on good terms with Mother and I go quickly home. There the boys advise me that meat soup is being given out in the butcher's place. Even though I don't really want it much, I want to get some just out of greediness. It is egotism on my part. The soup is not very good. I stay home until five o'clock because I am on duty, but then I have an hour free. I go for supper and take it to Mother's. An incident causes the mood to change from good to bad. Mother drops a pot of rhubarb on the floor and part of its content pours out on the floor and into the bedroom slippers. For my mother, this is a tragedy. Unhappily, she starts to scrape the rhubarb off the floor and put it back into the pot. This really gets to me and I lose my temper. I swear and complain. Mother answers in the same way, which only fuels my temper. I scold and complain. I go home determined not to give her the gift. The gift is ready, as Father has brought me the promised little box. But now I don't feel like doing anything, not even writing in my diary. Out of boredom, I start to wrap the gift. I don't know why I am doing it—perhaps as a safety measure. What will happen if . . . ?

Felix takes over the room duty for me and I go to watch soccer. It is very boring, and therefore I leave at seven o'clock. I go to Mother's to have dinner. The situation there is even worse and it culminates with

Mother saying that my love is only superficial! It convinces me without any doubt not to give her my article, because I now feel embarrassed about it. Again, I don't know why I'm doing it, but I keep rewrapping the gift and I even ask Kalíšek whether the gift is good and he nods. I wonder about myself, why I am asking him, since I know that I will not give the gift to Mother anyway. Then it all comes out! I relate to Kalíšek the whole confrontation with Mother and I explain that this is the reason I don't want to give her the gift. "And what would you think," I ask him, "if I were to give her the gift anyway?" I arrive at Mother's, who happens to be doing something in her closet. I slip the present into her hand. Mother is obviously very pleased and she likes it! All the anger is forgotten. We go to the bench, where I read my article to her. She likes everything, particularly the ending. She wonders how I come upon such themes. Then I change over to a clean jersey and, in a good mood, run in front of the barracks, where Kalíšek is waiting. In good spirits we stop at Father's and I bring with me the "unfortunate" rhubarb cake, which we eat together. At home I wash up and listen until 10:30 to Professor Zwicker's storytelling. Tired from today's really rich impressions, I fall asleep.

Sunday, 13 August 1944

The whole day is spent in preparation for the finals between Elektra and Jugendfuersorge. I bet on Jugendfuersorge. Nothing unusual happens during the morning. Before noon, there is a program that I want to skip very badly. The first hour we have Georgi Schubert, whose material I could easily live without. We all make fun of him, but he will not leave; on the contrary, he wants to give us a repeat lesson at three o'clock, which, I can say with certainty, will not take place. The second lesson is by Vera. She talks to us about Čapek and about other writers between the two wars. I finish writing my diary of last Friday, but I don't have time for Saturday. At noon, I go to Mother's, as today is her birthday. She has had a tooth pulled and is in quite a bit of pain. It doesn't look like there will be a birthday lunch. We talk a little bit about my article, which I had written for her. I still have to go to Professor Weiss to inquire about my lessons. I go there before *Apel* but the professor is sleeping! In a bad mood, I go to Mother's, where I accomplish nothing. On the way home I meet Lappert, who is going to the soccer match. The weather is nasty and it is uncertain whether the match will take place. I arrive at *Apel* but nothing of importance takes place. I go with the boys to the library, where I finish *The Merchant of Venice*. It is 4:45 when I leave the library. First, I stop at my father's, who is not there. In fact, no one at all is in the barracks. I'm quite frustrated and, when I return again to my father, I want to write a note and leave for the match. But fortunately I run into Father. We agree that I will go to the match and he will join me and we will meet in our usual spot. I quickly eat supper and go straight to the match. The match between Rapid and Spedice for third and fourth place is not interesting and its score is 3:1. The Dresdner Barracks are overcrowded when the final begins. Both teams (Jugendfuersorge and Elektra) are greeted with applause. During the game, blue pieces of paper are thrown to the ground. The Jufa team is cheered on boisterously. At half time, Jufa is ahead one to nothing. During the second half the goals start to pile up. Passer is playing very roughly and when he kicks Franta, he is thrown out for the rest of the game, which ends in a score of 5:1. Jufa wins the cup! On the way home we meet a boy who, as a result of a bet on the game, must walk around with a muzzle and a leash of a Great Dane.

Monday, 14 August 1944

I don't exactly remember the time I got up and it really doesn't matter a great deal. What is important is that I am assigned to housekeeping duty today, which turns out well for me. The usual *Apel* follows. Franta checks our ears and mine are dirty. If I didn't know that everybody's ears are dirty, I would worry. Afterward is the program, which I don't like much today. We have history and then arithmetic with Franta. I can see that there is not much that I have missed. Professor Weiss comes to me before the lesson to tell me that he has already spoken with Mrs. Geisinger and moved the piano lesson from 4:30 to 5:00 and that I can have a piano lesson today. I'm looking very much forward to it! After the program, I fool around with Sasha, who chases me in the staircase. I slip and bang my head, my hand, and mostly my knee. I am quite upset and I am visibly limping. Afterward, I go for lunch and the whole afternoon is uninteresting. After *Apel* we sit around and then suddenly the cleaning brigade arrives to scrub the floors. Franta makes assignments; mine is from three to four. Until then I lie down on the bunk and write my diary. After finishing my house duty, during which I really don't do a thing, I go to the library, where I again write my diary. I'm happy that my diary is so long now. While I'm in the library, I want to do some reading but I don't have time because I have to go to practice. At home, I wash up and soon I sit down to practice the piano. It's very noisy there because of some small kids. The professor arrives fifteen minutes late. I am told to straighten out my chair and then I play scales in the following manner: first four octaves, then backward and up and back. He is a forgetful professor as he doesn't realize that the woman who is accompanying me is my mother. For practice he gives me two pieces from Schutze [presumably German composer and organist Heinrich Schütz, 1585–1672] and a scale; tomorrow I am to come back for the études. I practice until six o'clock because nobody else comes. At six, I go to my father's, and we eat supper together and talk with Handa about Professor Weiss. After supper, I walk Handa home and go with my father to the *bašta* to watch the match between Sparta and Skid (7:11). The boys are yelling at me without noticing my father's presence. I hear Passer talking badly about Franta, who has a wrenched thumb. After the match I go to Mother's, who, however, is not in and I go home. Kalíšek is somehow teed off and won't talk to me. It is obvious that he favors Gustl because he is spending time with him right now. I really can't blame him; it's just his unfaithfulness that upsets me. When we are going to bed in the bunk, I speak my mind and he admits his shortcomings. Now we are again on good terms. *Rim, Rim* is read to us. News from the front: Orléans has supposedly fallen!

Tuesday, 15 August 1944

Yesterday, Sasha and I agreed that we would get up early in the morning so that we can write our English lesson. Our lesson is from 8:30 to 9:30. Today *Grunt* is skipped because we had no wake-up call. After finishing our homework, we go to our lesson, which is quite good. Jelínková's main flaw is that she doesn't finish dictating the vocabulary at the end of the lesson. At home we have *Apel*, followed by the usual program. The first lesson is English, during which Kopperl keeps making fun of me. It seems that in our *heim* there is a group of boys who have nothing else to do but play soccer and make fun of someone! The second lesson is natural science. I like this subject the most. After the program I go to Mother's, and then I go for lunch with my father. Father spoke with the daughter of a French minister who later became the mayor of Le Havre. She said that she would like to give me lessons, but the only problem is that she speaks only French and English. It probably won't work out. At Mother's, it is not too bad. Father will most likely have to move but not before the filming. At one o'clock, I remember I have to go to Professor Weiss to get the sheets of music. I find the professor asleep, but then he wakes up and stares at me as if I was a stranger. Finally he recognizes me with some difficulty and then gives me the music right away. It is "Études" by Duvernoy, and it looks easy. It is primarily a finger exercise. Afterward, I go to Mother's, from where I return home. After *Apel,* I go to the garden, where it is quite boring. I fetch some manure and I see cows and pigs. On the way home I stop to see Mother. In the afternoon I rake in the #1 garden. At three o'clock, I have to leave because I have a ticket to the pool. It is quite bad in the pool again, because the big boys are jumping all over. I return to the garden when everyone has a break. It doesn't appear that I can *schlojs* anything today. I water the #3 garden. I am saved when it is five o'clock and I can go home. I carry a ration of apples and pears, which are half rotten. I am supposed to split them open. I am nervous because I am not good at it, but finally I succeed. Suddenly I realize that I am missing my white jersey. I know for sure that I left it on my bed, but still I fear that I might have lost it somewhere. I'm also missing my washcloth so that I cannot wash myself well. I take another shirt and, all excited, I go tell Mother about my losses. Of course, Mother scolds me and says I must have forgotten the jersey in the garden. I maintain that I have not. When I return home, I first think to write my diary, but instead I continue to look for my jersey in my room and also in the garden. I can't find it in either place. However, Hermann finds my jersey on the top of the bunk bed, which makes me very happy. Immediately, I feel like writing my diary and, as soon as I finish writing, I go to bed. I notice that I'm starting to get impetigo on my nose and it worries me. Tonight the blackout begins already at nine o'clock and therefore all the lights must go out.

Wednesday, 16 August 1944

The morning passes uneventfully. There is *Apel* and then a program. The first lesson is math and I realize that I don't do well in reasoning problems. The second lesson is literature and we talk about Čapek. Then suddenly the sirens sound for an air raid. We notice that the English planes usually fly at noon. Today, they are making a film, for which SS officer Haindl selects people who look like "typical" Jews. It is a masquerade directed by Gerron, a former film director.[112] After the program, I cannot go to Mother's because the air raid is still on. I go through the washroom to the kitchen for the children. Franta is not there but just while I'm waiting at the exit, three Germans appear who yell out "make room!" and the exit empties out. It only takes three ruffians to scatter twenty Jews. Soon the air raid is called off. At Mother's it is not at all good. She receives an admission ticket to the cabaret, but she refuses it. That really gets to me and I think that Mother is opposed to entertainment. I pack up and leave. Anyway, I have guard duty in front of the garden with Kalíšek from one to two o'clock. The purpose of the guard is to prevent people from stealing. The guard duty turns out quite well. During *Apel* (which I missed), it is decided that as a penalty we must be in bed by eight o'clock. I really don't care. I pack up and go to the library, where I borrow *Echoes of Czech and Russian Songs* by Čelakovský. I finish reading it; it is plain but nice. At 4:30 I go with Sasha for my English lesson, which is quite good. Afterward, I quickly go for supper at Mother's, who is not at home. Soon, I leave because I practice piano at six o'clock. The practice turns out quite well. Afterward, I return to Mother's, where I have supper. We hear what appears to be authentic news that the English and the Americans have landed in the south of France. It is marvelous! Now, the end must be pretty near! At 8:30, I return home. I completely forgot about the punishment, but nothing happens. I wash up and go to bed where, after talking with Kalíšek, I fall asleep.

Thursday, 17 August 1944

I have made up my mind today that I will not go to the garden. Because my impetigo has gotten worse, I have to go to the clinic. There is a long line there and boys are pushing ahead. My turn doesn't come up until nine o'clock. Then I'm free because there is no *Apel*. After I finish writing my diary, I go to the library, where I borrow a book on the history of French literature. People in the library are laughing at me a lot because they claim that the book is too difficult for me. They may be right, but they do not have to laugh at me. It spoils my mood. I feel that I suffer from being too conceited about

112. Kurt Gerron (b. May 11, 1897), movie actor (he starred with Marlene Dietrich in *The Blue Angel*) and director, was deported to Terezín from Westerbork on February 26, 1944. A German Jew, he had sought safety in the Netherlands, but the Nazis caught up with him there. He was shipped to Auschwitz on October 28, 1944, where he was killed.

my intelligence, which does me harm. The news from the front is excellent! The Allies are just thirty kilometers from Paris! The mood at my mother's is good as a result. At home is *Apel* followed by the usual program, for which I don't care. Since I don't know what to do, I decide to go with Pedro to practice my piano assignment. I can stay there because nobody shows up for the lesson. In the evening, I take my supper to Mother's. After a walk on the ramparts, I return home. I go to bed and soon fall asleep.

Friday, 18 August 1944

Franta comes to wake us up. I get up and I put my things in order. My impetigo is already better but not completely healed. Nevertheless, I go to the clinic. I bring along a book to read because there are five boys ahead of me. At the clinic, they open up the impetigo and put a bandage on it. They want to give me only one because they claim to have very few, but then they give me another one anyway. Then, as usual, we have the program. Today it is natural science and literature. After the program, I go to my father's. I am alone with him, as Mother has her shift. The mood is bad and it really comes to a head in the evening. I have to depart early because I have guard duty in front of the garden. I climb up the hill but I decide to read and not pay any attention to guarding because it is entirely useless. At two o'clock I go to the garden. I am assigned to Dr. Rudniková in the #1 garden. This is good because it is possible to *schlojs* with her and this is all that counts. However, I am mistaken. Due to my awkwardness, I can hardly *schlojs*. I manage to *schlojs* only one onion. I have difficulty in lifting a full watering can. When I go to the #4 garden during recess, I take one apple. It doesn't make much sense to try for more because we will receive apples as a ration. In fact, we receive five apples. After recess, I return to work. When we're finished, I'm alone in the garden with Schwarzbart. I pick a big, big pear, but I get scared and I return it to Schwarzbart as if it were an apple that had fallen off a tree. When I see how the other boys make out, I feel sorry about that one lousy pear. Afterward, I quickly wash myself because at six o'clock we have *Apel* with inspection. I put things in order and then I go for supper. It is quite good: white baked goods and sausage! At *Apel,* Franta does the inspection and those who pass receive one-quarter kilo of fruit picked from the garden in front of the School. I'm afraid that I will be dirty, but I pass! To be sure, Franta doesn't consider me to be the cleanest of the boys. This is why I find Franta obnoxious. For a long time now, Franta has not been what he used to be. After *Apel,* I go to my parents and bring them my fruit ration. This brings about a big incident. For a long time now my father appears to me so old-looking. He keeps doing things that somehow get on my nerves. For example, when he eats an apple, his face becomes somehow distorted. It makes me angry! Such are our family's problems. My parents go for a walk after accompanying me home. At home, I don't feel at all like writing in my diary and I am mentally depressed. Out of boredom, I lie down and soon fall asleep.

End of Volume 3

Volume 4

Sunday, 20 August 1944

My relationship with Franta keeps getting worse. It is evident that he is angry at me. I don't know why, but I think he feels that I act smarter than others and that I am conceited. He is so wrong. I would like to see him in my place. The best part of it is that he keeps urging me now to do mental work, but earlier he laughed at me and at my articles in *Nešar.* I already have come to terms with the thought that Franta has turned against me. I'm now on good terms with Kalíšek, but I still maintain that he is insincere. With Gustl, I haven't exchanged a single word lately, but I made up with Brena. Now the events of today . . . these days are awful for me. I am in continued conflicts with my parents. Yesterday I watched a soccer match and I was supposed to go to Mother's, but I didn't go. I feel badly about it. Now the biggest enemies in Terezín are fleas. Last night they bothered me terribly. On average, I catch two fleas a night. Today also starts the program. I look forward to it quite a bit because I'm concerned about my diary, which I have not been doing regularly. I ran out of ink so that I cannot write. I try to fill my pen with other ink, but the pen immediately gets plugged. In the morning I go to the program. The first lesson is, as usual, Professor Eisinger with Czech. We study the Czech renaissance of Joseph II. It is more interesting than with Vera. The second lesson is free and I use this opportunity to write my diary entry for Friday. The third lesson is geography, where we study Hungary. And then we have Hebrew. I don't like to study Hebrew because I know that it will not help me if I become proficient in it. After the program ends, I have to hurry because Mother has an afternoon shift. Unfortunately, there are lines for food and when I arrive at Mother's I am greeted with a cleaned-up table. This means that Mother has left and is angry at me. However, she doesn't have very much time for that because I soon leave and go home. Today, assignments are made for filming as spectators in *Brundibár* [the children's opera]. By chance I'm assigned. This whole filming is a comedy, as is everything in Terezín. It is terribly hot. I go to Heini's with Tutinek where we take a German book entitled *Der Weg Zuruck* [*The Road Back*], from which we translate. Heini has a nice attic occupied only by the Zionists. I can see that the Zionists understand what collectivism is all about. For example, they give us a piece of cake to taste as if we are one of them. Who else would do something like this? We translate about three pages and afterward we go home. Because of the awful heat, I lie down and read a book. However, I don't have great patience and instead walk over to the Dresdner Barracks, where people are playing handball: Kadr II vs. Fortura. Heini plays for Kadr II. However, I have to return home soon because I have an English lesson with Sasha. The lesson is excellent, although I admit that Jelínková proceeds slowly. After the lesson, I go quickly for supper and then to meet Mother, who is in the bakery. For a short while I cuddle with her and then I go with Father to L313. I quickly finish my supper and then I am off to soccer, where a speed tournament and ladies' handball is taking place. There is a final between Jugendfuersorge and Sparta. Franta's reputation has gone down because, when he was hurt on purpose by Passer, he complained to the referee. Now all the spectators are screaming at him "Au! [ouch!: PW]." After the soccer match, I return home, where I air my bed linen and get washed up. The boys want to sleep in the yard but Franta will not allow it! Therefore, I go to bed and soon fall asleep.

Monday, 21 August 1944

The morning becomes one big problem. At first, it didn't appear to be a big deal, but it developed into something large. Last night, someone made a dumb joke by throwing everything off one of the shelves in our room. Among these items was Franta's book, which tore. I find out about this after my guard duty in front of the garden, which turns out well. During *Apel*, Franta supposedly announced that there will be other *Apels* today at 1:30 and at 5:30 in order to find out who did the throwing. I don't attend my first lesson today because of guard duty. However, I attend my English lesson. Jelínková assigns me to read from an English textbook, pages 21 to 31. It is marvelous! We have Šmudla for the second period. Even though I know it is not useful, I'm doing very well. Afterward we have arithmetic and I am quite amazed that I haven't forgotten everything. For the last period we have history. Zwicker dictates to us two full pages. Then I go to Mother's, where I stay only a short time. I have an argument with her on account of soccer. She says that our team shouldn't play soccer when it's so hot. I insist on playing even though Mother is really right in not allowing me to play. I see that Mother is annoyed because I don't pay any attention to her orders, but nothing can be done about it. I go home, where I announce that I cannot play because I realize that I have a piano lesson at 4:30 and the match starts at 4:00. It is awfully hot—about 31 degrees. In the afternoon I am bored. We have our usual food distribution. I go to get it together with Schwarz from Room 9. It (*fašung*) [rations] is quite poor; just several pieces of lettuce, one fourth of a tomato, and one fifth of a cucumber. In the evening, I throw out the so-called "cabbage" and eat the rest. Afterward, I go for my piano lesson. The professor is already there and I realize that I have forgotten to bring pencil and paper. I run home and then quickly back. A girl who also takes lessons from Professor Weiss practices before me. She plays quite well. The professor appears very indifferent. Then it is my turn. The scales come out quite well and the professor seems satisfied. Even with the other pieces, he is satisfied and he assigns more études and rondos. Afterward, I quickly go to Father's place and then to my mother, from where we bring our dinner. I can spend only fifteen minutes because next, I have a meeting with Heini. I take my dinner with me. Heini has asked a boy who lives with Handa to explain to a few of us world history starting from the French Revolution. I have also enrolled in a French course, so I quickly go to L216, where the class is being held. I find out that the woman who is our instructor is Mademoiselle Meyer,[113] who doesn't explain things well. It is unfortunate that the course is attended by boys from Room 6 who always make fun of everything. We have to be home at 7:30 on account of the scandal earlier today. Franta asks which one of us is the culprit. I suspect Hermann. Franta is very obnoxious to me. At 8:30 there is another *Apel* and the purpose is the same. Then we go and get washed and lie down. I recognize Kalíšek to be a false friend. I sleep naked, but the fleas keep biting. At long last, despite the heat, I fall asleep.

113. Denise Meyer (b. 1896), daughter of Léon Meyer (1868–1948), taught French in Terezín. Her father had been mayor of Le Havre (from December 7, 1919, until France fell to the Germans in June 1940), a Radical deputy, and minister of the merchant marine. He was one of the more protected people at Terezín, which helped his daughter. She survived.

Tuesday, 22 August 1944

Today is housekeeping. I get up slowly and therefore I am already behind in my housekeeping. There is pus in the impetigo and, therefore, I sign myself in for the clinic. In the morning, we have the program. The first lesson is Czech grammar, but the second period is free and I spend it by doing nothing. Afterward, we have geometry, where we cover two Euclidean theorems. Next is physics, which I enjoy to a point. During lunch nothing of importance happens. At two o'clock I go to the garden and I am assigned to a group with Aninka (which means going to garden #3). The work is quite good for a *schlojs*. The problem is that I have to keep going to the bathroom and the only means of wiping myself is with leaves. The tomatoes, plums, and apples are already quite good. During recess, we get a ration of fruit. This I like the best! After the work in the garden, I wash up. At home there is another *Apel*. This useless event must be the result of yesterday's scandal. Franta thinks that, by doing this, he will find the culprit. I think he should just let the whole matter drop. Today, Nešar is playing a semifinal match with Slavie. Franta warns that if things are not in order, he will cancel the match. Fortunately, the match does take place. I have a quick dinner at Mother's place and then I run to the *bašta*. It is an interesting match. First, Slavie is ahead but we even it up by half-time. We form a cheering section and vigorously cheer our team. It helps! Our team wins 2:1! Upon returning home, I air my bed linen. At night, Nora Fried[114] comes to our place with a guitar and sings to us songs of various nations. I am awfully tired so I lie down and soon fall asleep.

Wednesday, 23 August 1944

Sasha wakes me up at seven o'clock because I have guard duty in front of the house, which turns out quite well. I want to do my English lesson and we sit down on the bench. I leave to go to the bathroom and, in the meantime, Sasha sits on the bench and doesn't pay much attention. When I return I see some kind of a gathering and I receive quite a scolding. Guard duty is followed by the program. The

114. Norbert (or Nora) Fried (Fryd after the war; 1913–76), cabaret, theater, and film writer, was deported from Prague with transport Dh on July 8, 1943. He was shipped to Auschwitz with convoy Ek on September 28, 1944, and survived to be liberated in Allach. He returned to Czechoslovakia after the war.

first lesson is Czech followed by a free period. I take advantage of the free time and go change my meal ticket because it is torn. On the way home I find out that I have received a 20 kg package! I'm very happy! Afterward, we have English. It always seems to me that I am not learning enough English. I also neglect French. Somehow, these days I don't get to do everything I want to do; I don't even get to write my diary. The fourth lesson today is geography, where we cover Slovakia, the Nazi's puppet state. We joke a lot about that state. At the end of the lesson, Zwicker explains to us the status of the war front. On the west, in France, Paris is surrounded and it is expected to capitulate. As of now, the Allies are holding Normandy and Brittany. However, they still don't have Brest. The front goes from St. Nazaire to Orléans and from there to Paris. In the south, Toulon is surrounded. On the Russian front, there is a standstill. After the program, I go for lunch and then to Mother's. It is interesting that Mother has also received a package, containing eggs and many other things. There are no sausages in the package because it is again awfully warm and they would get spoiled. In the afternoon, I look forward to studying and writing. Then I remember that I have to go to Heini to translate. Today there is supposed to be *Apel* again at six o'clock but I will not go because I have my practice lesson at that time. I know that if I don't excuse myself I will be in trouble, but I really don't care. I finish writing my English homework for today's lesson. Perhaps they will forget about the translation . . . but, unfortunately, Heini comes and reminds us to go. I don't like it very much but I stay until 3:45. Afterward I go to the English lesson with Sasha. He pays for the lesson with a quarter of a loaf of spoiled bread. It makes me laugh and then, in the course of the lesson, we think about it again and both of us start roaring with laughter. Jelínková is helpless. It is already five minutes before six and I have to hurry! Grizzly makes a dumb joke and locks me up. I get delayed by crawling over the doors and I want to fight with Grizzly, but I don't have the time for it. I notice that I lost my letter of recommendation and I have to have a new one issued. Then, I quickly go to L410. I have bad luck though, because about thirty persons come to the adjacent room. They are dancing and playing accordions. I can hardly hear my own playing and therefore I leave. At home I find out that Franta has only written my name down. I don't pay much attention to it. At Mother's place, there is nothing of interest. At home I decide that I will move to the table to spend the night. I am almost completely moved, but then I decide that I would prefer to sleep in a bed. I find that to replace the slats is quite difficult and I call Kalísek to help me. First he does it with a lack of enthusiasm and, after the second call, he doesn't want to come at all. Suva helps me and soon both Kalísek and I lie in the bed. I start the discussion by blaming him for his behavior. I ask him whether he likes me more, the same, or less than he does Gustl. He doesn't answer and I understand. I ask him whether he wants to remain my friend and he says that he does. I blame him for his false disposition. We talk long into the night and in fact we don't decide on anything, but at any rate it was important. After some more chatting I fall asleep.

Thursday, 24 August 1944

Today I have to work in the garden and I go there with Kalísek at eight o'clock. I am already in a better mood. With my bad luck, I am assigned to Mrs. Kienová to water garden #4. Fortunately, though, Mrs. Kienová works on cucumbers with her back turned. I *schlojs* plums, apples, etc., but mostly tomatoes. In the garden there is suddenly great commotion. There was some account of a *schlojs*, and also an Aryan is in the garden pruning trees. After the break, I roam around the garden with Kalísek. Afterward, we go home and I carry out only one tomato. At home, I realize that I have not finished my long math assignment. Even though we are supposed to do housekeeping in the large attic, I first wash up and then spend part of my time writing my assignment. Afterward I go for lunch. When I am at the exit of the bank, the sirens sound. Immediately, I run to Father's place so that the chain of the ghetto guards doesn't stop me and send me to some house nearby. I manage to get there just in time. Soon after my arrival, Father comes as well. However, Mother is caught in the street. Meanwhile the streets empty out. Not because of the *Ghettowache* effort, but because people themselves are afraid to remain outside. Of course, the funniest part of it all is that it's OK for the Germans and the Aryan gendarmes to walk outside. I sit at the windows and watch SS officer Bergel, the German girls, and others. In the room there is a special glee that intensifies when we hear in the distance the roar of airplane motors. Yes, after about five minutes, Mr. Kusy notices very high up silver dots. Yes, there are the planes and I can see them too. How dignified and beautiful are these birds of the air. Best of all is that they are our friends. Again and again, about thirteen airplanes appear above L318. Passing gendarmes point to the sky and laugh.

People crawl out of the front of houses to watch. All the "golden" Czechs are smiling and they have to smile. The residents of Victoria [Germans] stand in front of the building and stare at the sky. Suddenly, along Rathausgasse a German appears in uniform on a bicycle. When he passes by L414 and sees all the people in the doors and the windows, he starts screaming something awful. We quickly shut the windows and watch. The German passes by L408 and there he also screams. All the *Ghettowache* are on their feet. Then the German passes by us and we quiet down. We conclude that about three hundred airplanes flew by at a height of three kilometers. They flew from a northeast direction to the southwest. Only at 1:30 is the raid called off. Soon Mother arrives all worn out. She says that she had been standing at the apothecary. She is angry that I ate my lunch. The good mood is gone. I eat some dumplings and return home. Franta is mad again. He says that until things are put in order, we cannot go to the program. Finally, there is *Apel*. I couldn't have realized of what importance it will be to me. However, I soon find out. Franta asks where I was last night during *Apel*. I respond that I had a lesson. And then I lie, telling Franta that I had looked for him. He asks where I had looked, and I answer in his cubicle in the attic. I realize that I'm lying. I don't even remember that on the way I had excused myself to Mrs. Mautner. Franta tells me that I have house arrest and that my parents cannot come and visit me. It is apparent that my action hasn't changed anything. On the contrary, I add to the other boys' guilt. I maintain that Franta is hysterical. I think it over whether I should leave the *heim*. Perhaps not. I arrive just as the Hebrew lesson is ending. During the physics lesson, I'm not in the mood for such idiocy; it doesn't interest me. The third lesson is mathematics. With Šmudla, we hardly learn a thing as he talks to us instead about soccer. Thus the whole lesson is killed. After the program, I go for dinner. From the garden we get a ration that only resembles fruit and vegetables. For supper is cabbage. I'm furious at Franta and I call him bad names. At six o'clock we have the traditional *Apel*, during which Franta doesn't learn a thing. Franta already lost my confidence and he is angry at me. During *Apel*, he says to me, "And you, Pajinko, don't forget it." And he asks me what I have for [illegible word] so that he can embarrass me in front of everyone. After *Apel*, I write my diary. I don't get too far along though, because Heini arrives and we have a meeting. In the meantime, I send Kalíšek over to tell everything to Mother. Heini explains to us the geography of Palestine, which is great stupidity and I

have to laugh. Then we play a game that I win. I don't enjoy it any longer. What do I have to gain from my cleverness???——Franta's anger!
When we finish, Mother arrives and, despite the "boss'" [Franta's:
PW] prohibition, she brings my supper: bread with eggs and cheese
and a tomato and *vanočká* [Christmas cake]. She wants to give hell to
Franta, but I send her away. Tonight at 8:30 there is supposed to be
the celebration of *Rim, Rim*. I'm supposed to play the recorder, but
I make fun of it. Lion rehearses some play and therefore I go into
the hall where I write my diary. I don't feel like doing it. After the
rehearsal, I put myself in order and then the performance begins.
Holzer's band surprises me; it is relatively good. After Lion's play, I
play three pieces: "Zelení Hájove" [Czech folk song], "March of the
Comedians" [from Bedřich Smetana's opera *The Bartered Bride*], and
another piece. The whole evening surprises me. Afterward, I lie down
and I'm soon overwhelmed by sleepiness.

Friday, 25 August 1944

In the morning, Beran wakes me up because I have guard duty at the
garden. Today, I will pay more attention. I sit in the corner and study
French. I'm afraid the boys will not put my name in for the clinic and
I will not be able to go. My impetigo has worsened considerably and is
full of pus. At home, I find out that no name is on the clinic schedule
and therefore I go to the clinic, fill out a form, and hand it over to
Mrs. Eppstein. Soon my turn comes. I catch hell because I don't go
there often enough. The female doctor tears off the bandage with
tweezers. It's full of pus. She bandages it very "thoroughly" by simply
putting some kind of glue on my leg. It is comical. The first lesson
today is free and I utilize it for writing my diary from Wednesday.
Now my writing seems to be falling off, as I write only every other
day. I really don't feel like writing at all. The best I can do is to say the
hell with Franta and do whatever I wish. The second period we have
history and we cover the Italian Middle Ages. Then we have physics
and we cover electricity, which I don't like much. The fourth period
is free. I'm concerned about the marmalade ration. It seems petty,
but it is a worry nevertheless. After lunch I have to find Tutinek, who
is translating by himself at Heini's. Together we translate until 12:30
and finish one whole chapter. I don't feel like going to my father and
I return home. Soon Handa comes and he brings me food and calls
me names. Today I have to work in the garden. After, there is a new

[word missing] arranged for six o'clock. Nowadays Franta has nothing better to do than making [word missing]. L410 is being disinfected and we have to wait at the side entrance. At two o'clock Schwarzbart comes to get us. Fortunately, Kienová is sick. Aninka and Dr. Rudniková are against Schwarzbart and permit us to *schlojs*. Schwarzbart doesn't assign me to any work. I still manage to carry out one radish and one apple. When we're through, I go to the gazebo. By chance, Schwarzbart is also there. He notices a garden hose spread on the lawn. Schwarzbart starts screaming that I'm not doing anything and, as far as he is concerned, I can go and fly a kite. I don't really care. Soon we have a break which lasts for one hour. We receive a ration of a few fallen-down apples. During the break we entertain ourselves at Mr. Schwarzbart's expense. This gives us confidence to *schlojs* during the next work period. When I walk out of the garden, I carry in my pocket plums, cucumbers, apples, and an onion. I am delighted with myself! When I return home, I wash up and go to Mother's place with the apples. Somehow I get into an argument with Mother. It happens quite frequently nowadays, but this one is particularly bad. I argue with Mother and she very excitedly tells me: "You and Handa have lost my love and my whole personality [?]." Her words touch me and tears come out, but soon my tenderness changes into anger and I leave. At home I'm distraught. I go for a walk, but in front of the School's cornerstone, I sit down and cannot go any farther. What I do afterward I cannot remember.

Saturday, 26 August 1944

I'm half asleep as I sense somebody pulling on my bedsheet. Only after the second pull, I realize that I have a meeting on the *bašta*, which is why I must get up. But I'm very hoarse and I don't feel like getting up. Last night Springer took the bench on which I put my clothes and this morning I can't find it. Now everyone will think that I did it on purpose. Anyway, it is getting late and therefore I go back to bed. I can spend my time better this way. I take my diary and start writing. I'm in a good mood because my diary is so long. As expected, the boys return and Tutinek, in his usual tone, says: "Don't you think I knew you had hidden them [the clothes: PW] on purpose?" I forgot to mention that before I went back to bed earlier this morning I noticed my clothes in the corner behind the closet. Now, however, I keep it a secret. After a fake search, I find my clothes. Afterward, I

go to the clinic, where I am told that I still have some pus. Today is
Bäumel's Bar Mitzvah. It is a comedy that lasts for one hour! I prefer
to laze around at home. I go for marmalade, about 40 dkg. Tuti tells
me to go to Heini to translate. Heini, however, is asleep and I cannot
find the book. Later I go there with Tutinek to translate, and we do
quite well. At home I go for lunch. Tutinek comes to me and tells me
that I have room duty. Kalíšek and I claim that this would mean three
Saturdays in a row. We agree that I will take care of housekeeping
during lunch. I fulfill my duty diligently. During *Apel*, Franta asks who
has room duty. When Franta hears that there is no one, he wants to
assign Tutinek, but Tutinek excuses himself by claiming that nobody
would listen to him. Franta then assigns Kalíšek and me to two days
of room duty. We agree that we will do nothing! Franta is not satisfied
with the housekeeping and we have to take out all the shelves. When
all the things are off, Franta gives us permission to leave. I spend
the entire afternoon doing nothing. The long diary has gotten to
my head. Also, the heat wave causes me to do nothing. Until 3:30 I
do nothing and then I practice the piano. However, near the church
I can see that there is disinfection going on in L410 and I cannot
enter the building. When I pass by L414, I remember an event that
occurred at noon: at the post office, the film people are filming Jews
as they walk out with packages. When the filming is over, Gerron, who
is directing it, tells the people who are carrying packages: "Bitte es tut
mir leit aber die Paketen geben Sie zuruck [I am sorry but please return the parcels]." I am enjoying it. At home, however, I do nothing.
Mainly, Kapr and I play with a rag ball. Kalíšek is not feeling well. He
has a fever and he lies down to rest. At home I say the hell with the
whole room duty. At six o'clock I go to Mother. The mood there is the
same, if not worse. She doesn't want to take back anything she said.
She says she will give me only what is essential. Therefore, I am trying
to get out of there as quickly as possible. I feel unhappy, but at home
I play for a while with a rag ball. In fact, I don't like it and I want to
go somewhere, but I don't know where. Just when I am walking out of
the door, I notice Mother. She is looking for Franta. Fortunately, she
doesn't find him. She wants to complain about me. Father wants to
go for a walk with me. I really don't want to, but I go anyway. I swear
like hell. We stop by the *Stadtkapelle*. Mother says that I'm dressed im-
properly. I can see that it annoys her. I say good-bye to her, but I stay
and stare searchingly into her eyes. I laugh sarcastically. She says that
I am dumb. Mother departs and I also leave. I don't know what is driv-

ing me to it, but I go and change my clothes and then I go to look for Mother on the *bašta*. Even though I don't like her as [illegible word], but still I have to go. Unfortunately, I don't find her and I return home feeling unhappy. Distraught, I lie down and soon fall asleep. In the morning we are supposed to play Skid III. When I'm getting washed, I'm unhappy. But then the news I hear is marvelous. Peace with Romania; even the Hungarian front is advancing and martial law has been declared in the Reich and in the adjacent lands!

Sunday, 27 August 1944

I am writing up this day on Monday. Since Monday is the beginning of a big thing, the description of Sunday's events will be short. In the morning, I wake up at 5:30 and immediately go to the *bašta* for a match. I have a bad cold, but I play all positions. The match ends with a score of 15:5 so we make fun of it. At home, I go to the clinic and then to the program, which is overall uninteresting today. I take my lunch to Mother's, where the mood is unchanged. Today, it must come to a boil and that indeed is what happens. I argue with Mother. I want to go home and Mother goes with me. I say good-bye to her. When I am at L315 my mother calls to me and tells me to come to her. She says good-bye. I leave, but then I remember that I could also say good-bye to her. I call back to her and she asks me to come to her. I tell Mother that I will not change until she repudiates the fateful sentence. She says that she will not. After a long discussion, we don't come to terms and I leave. When I am at the intersection, I can see my mother in L313 with a pail in her hand. I put my things at home and I want to still go to Mother's in order to discuss things with her, but I decide against it. Today we play a new game. The rules are as follows: one has to look for three people and he himself is being looked for by three others. The winner is the one who first finds all three. I do my English lesson until three o'clock, but then the lesson is called off. After going for an identification card, I get changed for the game. On Hauptstrasse [Main Street] I catch Lappert with a [illegible word] and Springer with a night pot, but then I'm caught by some girl who already had caught two others. She is the winner and goes with me to the finish. I go home, write my diary and then go to Father's place. I meet him as he walks out of the bakery. I have my supper and we go for a walk. Because I'm on duty, I sit down on the grass and write my diary. We get a ration of half a kilo of fruit. Then, I go to sleep very tired.

Monday, 28 August 1944

One doesn't have any peace in Terezín, be it a scandal in the Ghetto or a transport or whatever. Today, we get news about a move. At noon it's just a whisper. Someone says that tonight it will be decided whether the School is going to move. Nobody knows why or where. It is felt that perhaps Střešovice[115] will move in. It is rumored that the bank will move into L318. Be it as it may, there is a big confusion. As far as I'm concerned, I lie down on the bunk and write my diary because I have a very bad cold. Franta has become a raging madman. He runs around like a maniac and then goes with Grizzly to the Magdeburg Barracks to get some information. Grizzly is the son of Mr. Rindler, the manager in the *Raumwirtschaft* [housing department]. Suddenly, Špulka brings the news that the School is moving to L313. However, it is not definite. It would be funny, but at the same time tragic, if Father would have to move out for me to move in. It will be a real pity if we have to move. We are all settled in and now we will have to move out. When I realize this, I lose my appetite for writing. I pack up and ask Father to find out where the matter stands. Father doesn't know anything about it and therefore I send him to inquire at the *Raumwirtschaft*. When he comes back, he confirms the news. For sure, my mood has not improved; in fact, it has worsened. I go to ask Professor Weiss what will happen with the piano lesson, which cannot take place now because L410 is being disinfected. The professor is not there and I leave a message. Disheartened, I return home. All kinds of things are happening there. Our main worry is that the fruit must still be picked. Everybody is happy that we will get such a big ration. I spend the time until six o'clock discussing the move. There is an apparent calm before the storm. At six o'clock, I go to meet Mother in the bakery. Father is there too. We also hear rumors about some kind of a work transport. Most likely it is just a rumor. My mother, when I tell her everything, is very upset and I can sympathize. She is worried about all of us. However, nothing can be done about it. On the way home my wooden shoe breaks. For dinner we have potatoes. Outside it's raining cats and dogs. I don't have much patience to stay at Father's place. At home, I want to go to bed for the last time in the School, but I can't because I get to talking with the boys. I don't even start packing yet. We get a ration of pears. Only then do I lie down.

---

115. A reference to the Central Office for Jewish Emigration, which Eichmann had established in a villa formerly owned by a Jewish family in the Prague suburb of Střešovice.

At least I will have a theme for my diary. My stomach is upset though. When I finish writing my diary, I go to the bathroom to throw up. It is possible that I have the habit of getting sick whenever I must move. I made a mistake by eating that one pear. I keep the others. Franta arrives and announces tomorrow's program: wake up at six o'clock, go for luggage stored in the *Kofferlager*, and bring it all to our *heim* where it will remain during the disinfection. Everything is packed up and at eight o'clock we all depart for the attic in the Magdeburg Barracks where we will live while L313 is put into order. In anticipation of tomorrow's event, I fall asleep.

Tuesday, 29 August 1944

Franta's voice wakes me up. Now then, this is the last time I will sleep here. I get up with difficulties, aware it will not be repeated. Immediately when I get up I throw out the bed linen and go to make the bedroll. I pack it into the red blanket. Then, I have to go again to the bathroom to throw up. The day is not starting very well, but it does not matter. However, I will not get rid of this feeling for the whole day. I have to go to the small attic for the luggage. I know what it means to carry down four heavy suitcases. I didn't prepare them right, but this is how it is. In the small attic there are about eighty people and everybody is going for his suitcase. Inside, it goes relatively well and I soon find what I want. With difficulty, I carry down the luggage and then again upstairs to Room 7. When I finish, I start sorting things out on the shelf. I realize that I don't have a suitcase with enough space for all my belongings. Finally I find a coat, into which I pack everything. However, I have no place for food. We get a ration of four pears. Fortunately, Mother arrives and takes my things home with her. My father doesn't have to move yet. I don't show my joy, just the contrary. My mother doesn't like anything. At last, at eight o'clock, I take down my bedroll in front of the School. I take along with me only my serving dish, a spoon, and the pears. The rest I'm keeping with my father in the warehouse. At long last, everything is packed and I get on the cart and triumphantly depart. Deep inside me I think: "Farewell to the site of so many eventful things, so long." Soon, however, I don't think about it and I'm in a good mood. On the way, everybody stares at us. And then we make it to the Magdeburg Barracks. We stop right in the first yard. I jump off to give my father the serving dish and the other things. When I return, I see that everybody else has carried their own bedroll. Therefore, I quickly grab it and run upstairs to the attic, where I catch up with others. I can see that the leadership didn't give us the best spot. It is the same spot where my mother slept half a year ago. There is no window here and lots of bedbugs. We are in a relatively good mood. I lie down next to Brenner. My spot is fairly good. Afterward I go and help Mrs. Mautner with her luggage. For the time being, I am not aware of my tiredness. We even have a table and a bench. We make use of it by playing a game. I have nothing to do and therefore I go for lunch and find out that the *Kinderkuche* may be also moving. Only then I can see that I am not in the best shape. I feel like a bird that fell out of his nest and doesn't know where to go! I remember my own words: "I will go home!" Now I cannot say them because I don't know where I would go. Father is looking for a place to stay. Perhaps he will get a room in L407 (The Sun).[116] However, it is not certain. I am very sleepy. I would prefer to lie down somewhere and go to sleep. I feel like a blind [illegible word] when I go to Mother's for lunch. I don't stay there long because there is some kind of *Apel* at two o'clock at the School. It was announced earlier this morning. Kalíšek and other boys are staying with their mothers. During the afternoon *Apel*, it is agreed that [illegible words] the guarding of the School will be under the direction of Rudla Weil, and the *heims* will help during housekeeping. Today, Room 10 will be on guard duty and Room 7 will guard tomorrow from six to twelve. From *Apel*, I go to my father to get my diary and I hope that I will be able to write at Mother's place. Instead, I lie down for a while and I immediately fall asleep. I sense Mother covering me up and then . . . I wake up at 5:30. All sleepy-eyed, I go for a supper of *geback*. There is a notice in the children's kitchen that from tomorrow evening on they will be cooking for us at L408. It is dumb. Afterward, I go to Mother, where I find out that her move has been postponed by forty-eight hours. Later, I learn that she has to move within twelve hours. Naturally there is an argument as to where she is supposed to move but nothing is decided. I keep feeling crummy. I have diarrhea. My father gets the idea that I should wash myself in warm water. I do so and feel better. Afterward, I have to go home because there is another *Apel* at eight o'clock. My parents go with me. We meet the Freunds, who stare at me as if I were a refugee. When I arrive home (to the attic), I'm amazed. Each compartment is lit up and it is quite nice. Mother puts

---

116. L407 got its name from a picture of the sun over the entrance.

things in a little bit of order and I go to *Apel,* during which nothing of importance happens. On the way up I run into Mother and send her a kiss. When I arrive to the attic, I see that my bed is all made up. I am wondering why I have three straw mattresses. I ignore it and quickly undress and lie down in my "bed." Earlier, I arranged my guard duty from six to eight so that I would have the morning free for moving. In bed, I stare at the attic and think about something, but I don't even know what. Then, the fleas start biting me. And they won't stop. I cannot sleep. I'm lying there for an hour when I again feel that my stomach is upset and I have to run to the bathroom. The attic looks eerie. On the way down, I run into a naked Murmulik, or at least I think so. In the hall I can hear Engineer Zucker.[117] After some searching, I find the bathroom. First I have to move my bowels. Fortunately, I have some paper on me. Then, I throw up. It comes out like a current. Obviously, it is everything I had eaten. I am there about three-quarters of an hour. Then somebody shows up who, I believe, is the painter Ausenberg. He gives me hell for throwing up on him. It isn't my fault though. Then I return to the attic, lie down, and fall asleep without any further disturbance.

Wednesday, 30 August 1944

Brenner wakes me up. For a while I forget that I have guard duty and that I have to get up. But it is already late, perhaps 6:30. Quickly, I put my bed in order and go to L417, where I report to Rudla. My late arrival doesn't cause any trouble because there is no one there anyway. I start walking through the garden and many times I must explain to people that the fruit does not belong to them. Only at seven o'clock, Gido and Jelínková arrive. Gido joins me in guard duty. The disinfectors are gluing up the rooms with long strips of paper. Gido asks them for pieces of this paper, and they agree. I ask Gido whether he could give me some and he does. I can see that it can be used for writing. The guard duty is without any purpose and therefore I leave my spot and go upstairs to look. While there, I take an additional ten pieces of paper. Now I don't have to worry any more about paper to write on. Boys come from the attic to tell me that my mother left a message say-

117. Otto Zucker (October 3, 1892–September 29, 1944), deputy to Jakob Edelstein (first chairman of the Jewish Council of Elders) and an ardent Zionist, arrived in Terezín with the second construction crew (AK II) on December 4, 1941, and was shipped to Auschwitz on transport Ek on September 28, 1944. He was killed the next day.

ing to come to Father's place because he has to be out by ten o'clock. I immediately run to L313. Father is not there, but Mother is packing. Father has to move out, together with others, to the Hannover Barracks into some kind of *Kofferlager.* I want to help Mother, but she doesn't need me and therefore I leave. I go to sit at my mother's barracks. It is 9:30. I take my diary and I write about Tuesday's events. I couldn't imagine that I would be moving that day. I write my diary until eleven o'clock. Mother arrives just as I want to leave. I go for lunch and with it, after a long while, back to Mother. She orders me to stay at her place the whole afternoon and to lie down. As it turns out, I'm prevented from doing so. At "home" (that means the attic—I have gotten so used to it that I refer to it as my home) there is *Apel,* during which it is decided that everybody has to help in the School. Obviously, I'm mad and I don't even want to find excuses. At the School we learn that we have to clean up two parts of the attic. I carry down several benches and tables. Franta has thrown out from his private cubicle a lot of stuff and he has given several things to the boys. I get the book *Life of Animals* by Brehm, which is in German. I notice that all the boys have found wooden shoes. I go and look myself and, after a long search, I find some that fit me. The work bores me and I'm glad when I finally can leave for home. To my surprise, it is already five o'clock so I have missed my piano lesson. I feel bad that I don't have an excuse paper. I am told that I can practice, but I don't. The night passes more or less normally.

Thursday, 31 August 1944

Thursday, Friday, Saturday, and Sunday will not be days marked with anything of importance. I don't get to do anything, not even write in my diary. I'm writing this the following Monday. In the morning, I go to the garden. I go there unwashed and with my hair uncombed and I only get washed up passing by a street water pump. The past few beautiful days have been replaced by a series of raw, cold days. In front of the garden, there are boys standing. Today, Anička will be the one in charge, and that's good. I make up my mind not to eat any fruit so that I won't feel bad. I still feel woozy. It is evident that Schwarzbart doesn't like me much. Today he assigns me with the boys to the first garden under Anička's supervision. Anička keeps walking away and I cannot restrain myself from picking pears, tomatoes, and carrots. The following event is of interest: Someone tells Anička to go away. She obeys and we take this opportunity to clean up a little apple tree. There is recess. Most of the boys go to *Apel* but several remain in the garden. It starts raining. We again take this opportunity to fill up Kalíšek's breadbasket with fruit and vegetables. I have all my pockets full. In one I have a cucumber and in the other apples. We are told to leave and we start running so that we will be off as quickly as possible. Then, someone calls Kumerl to return. I look back and I see Schwarzbart standing in the door. It is Kumerl who has the above-mentioned breadbox. I can see that we are in a bind. I immediately try to disappear. Soon Kumerl comes running and says that Schwarzbart confiscated the whole breadbox. In the rain I run to Mother's place, where I empty out my pockets. During lunch nothing of importance happens. After lunch, I return to Mother because we want to go together to see Professor Weiss. We hope that he will agree to some kind of lessons, because I will not be able to practice while L410 is painted. Mother, however, notices that I am dirty and doesn't want to come with me. I don't want to get washed from the head down. I don't even realize what will come of it. After a long argument, I go to the professor by myself. In broken German, which annoys me, I tell him that I will go to Mrs. Geisinger to agree with her on additional lessons. At home, I want to write my diary, but Mother calls me to go to the yard with her. I sit down next to her on the bench and we start arguing again. She says that I'm stupid. This gets me mad and I ask for the article that I had given her. I am embarrassed for its content. Mother doesn't want to give it to me. My ranting is in vain. I'm looking forward to the English lesson at 5:30. It is quite good. We are reading an interesting book, *England, the Unknown Island.* Suddenly, I have the same feeling as I had before I last vomited. I also have to go to the bathroom. Then Father tells us wonderful news. It is confirmed about Paris, and the Russians are advancing in the Danube delta! They are supposed to be already in Dobudse [PW: ?]. In Hungary, there is another democratic non-Communist government. Surely everything now points to an early end. Now my desire for home is even stronger, now when I can almost reach it. I keep thinking about that cart carrying away women to Terezín's Small Fortress. This is something!!! Now, however, what interests me is my diarrhea. I feel awful. I don't even attend *Apel,* and I go quickly to bed. At about eleven o'clock, I wake up and have to run quickly to the bathroom. I was right. I vomit just as I did last time. I feel better and go to bed. At two o'clock, I wake up and have to go to the bathroom once again. I have an awful stomachache. On the way I stop in the washroom to wash up a little. Then I fall asleep.

SEPTEMBER
Friday, 1 September 1944

I don't remember what happened in the morning. I'm sure it was not anything interesting. We have been getting meals in L408 since Tuesday. There is a special window for us. Today there are dreadful lines there. I ignore them and put myself right in the front. I do that all the time. I don't feel like going to the garden, but I have to go. I expect that some kind of a *pruser* will take place. I stand for a while in front of the garden and soon they call us in. We are supposed to sit down. Schwarzbart wants to investigate everything. In the end, he reads the names of those who are permitted to stay in the garden. Of course, these are the ones who are [illegible word] and I'm not among them. Thus, I'm thrown out of the garden. There we stand for a while like dogs without shelter. I set out with Kalíšek to go to the Dresdner Barracks. I see long lines of old people, youngsters, and invalids who are forced to go watch the soccer match, Sparta vs. Jugendfuersorge. It will be filmed and two thousand people will have to watch and scream under the supervision of the SS. It is not funny. In the barracks, I sit down on a bench and wait. In the corners there are cameras manned by Czechs (Aryans) and in the yard walks SS man Valenkho, who is relatively decent. The match ends up as expected, 8:1 in favor of Sparta. I am also filmed. During the intermission, the German screams that we must cheer louder for the players. After the soccer match I go home, namely to Mother's, and I don't do anything until the evening. But the news from the front is marvelous! It is said that the Allies have liberated Belgium. The end is just a matter of days.

Saturday, 2 September 1944

Today is Koko's Bar Mitzvah. Even though I don't feel like it, I have to get up. I go to Mother's to get washed and straighten up my hair. Because the boys want me to, I go to my father to borrow yarmulkes. Afterward, I go to the Dresdner Barracks, where the Bar Mitzvah is taking place. Today I will do it even though it is against my principles. Soon I realize I have done a dumb thing because the following happens: In the hall is a crowd of old women. Rabbi Ferda is very religious and prays aloud. It is hilarious. He notices that one "religious" Jewish woman is very calmly eating her breakfast. This makes him mad and he screams out very loudly in German: "This of course is doubly religious!" After the Bar Mitzvah, I'm looking forward to practicing piano. I'm doing well. I have to leave because one woman there wants to practice for a concert. Regardless, I have to go to Heini in L218 for translation. Tuti promised that he will join me, but he doesn't show up. I'm translating quite well. When I finish, I go for lunch, where there are awfully long lines. The lunch is luxurious today: cucumbers, meat, and potatoes. Of course, I don't stand in the line, but even then it takes a long time. Mother is at work and I eat lunch alone with my father. The mood is good because the news is good. The Germans are actually getting crushed. They admit themselves that Amiens and Roubaix [cities in northern France] have fallen. Marvelous! Soon Mother arrives and brings freshly baked *bábovka* [coffee cake]. It adds to our good mood. We are all looking forward to dinner. I leave my mother's place to practice piano again. Since some man is playing there, I have to wait. I practice for about an hour and then return to Mother's place to wait for my father who arrives shortly. We taste the *bábovka,* which is excellent. Today we have cheese for dinner. It seems that the Germans are trying to butter us up! I go with my parents for the cheese. Its brand is Chalet. We are making jokes about it because when you read it backwards, it spells "Telahc" [probably means something in Yiddish or Hebrew: PW]. I mention this merely incidentally. Father will most likely get an apartment at The Sun. We go to visit the Feldmans to arrange for something and then we go each separately to get our dinners. At home, we finally get to eat and it is tremendous. Immediately after dinner we go for a walk. I joke around with Father. However, I have to return home because we have *Apel.* For a change, there is actually a need for it today: they are announcing tomorrow's evacuation of the school. It will be as follows: at 7:45, we must be in the School and then everybody must pack up things. Further details are not known as yet. I have to stop at Mother's to pick up a label and a piece of string to tie up the luggage. Afterward, I go to the attic. I take a shower and then to bed.

Sunday, 3 September 1944

In the morning, I'm wakened by Franta's voice telling us about the tremendous storm during the night. It is obvious that I had a good night's sleep because I didn't hear it at all. However, now I have to go quickly to the School. I cannot get washed because after the storm there is neither water in the faucet nor any electricity. We set out, therefore, for the School. As always, we have to wait. We arrive into great chaos in the room. One can hardly make a move there. Soon my mother shows up as I expected. She asks whether I need anything. It is very unpleasant for me. She leaves. Meanwhile, I pack up my things. The organization is obnoxious. We are not allowed to leave the room. Mother pays three visits to me, once even with my father. As luck may have it, I also have dreadful diarrhea and I have to run back and forth to the bathroom. We are forced to wait in limbo doing nothing. Everything is for the sake of collectivism. We depart, leaving our luggage in place. However, I take with me my little suitcase containing daily utensils. Mother wants me to also take my rucksack, but I don't listen to her. To my amazement, I realize that it is time for lunch and I go and get it. I'm looking forward to my English lesson later today. Instead, however, I have to go and help out in the School. One should not be pleased or look forward to anything here. Even though I would never imagine that the work will last until 3:30, I am concerned that it may. I'm getting more and more furious at Franta. Until three o'clock I do almost nothing, just roam around in the street. At three o'clock, we carry down our luggage, which is quite heavy. Now I can see that I will not make it to my lesson. After having carried down various pieces of luggage and mattresses, we find out that it was pointless because we have to just take everything back up again. I go with Sasha to cancel the lesson. Jelínková obviously is not thrilled, which I fully understand. When I return to the School, I notice that Franta has carried down everything. Together we load it onto the cart and head for the Jaeger Barracks, where everything will be kept in some prayer room. Then I help out Franta with his things but on the way I leave and go to the barracks. Soon Father arrives and we walk together to the *bašta*. We speak English together. Now I'm really getting interested in it!

Monday, 4 September 1944

In the morning, I wake up and I am again extremely cold. I look outside and I see that the weather is still ugly. I quickly get ready and go to Mother's place, where I have been spending these long days marked with boredom. I'm cold because I am lightly dressed. I come to an agreement with Mother that I will go to my father to change. I find my father sitting at the table dressed in a winter coat and a cap. I get angry and ask him to take it off immediately. He listens to me. I put on a warmer shirt, a sweater with long sleeves, and stockings at my mother's. Today, at eleven o'clock, everybody who works in the garden is supposed to come to L413, where the *Jugendfuersorge* has moved. I have an alibi for not going. Before sitting down at Mother's, I have to go to the warm-up room in the Hannover Barracks. I feel well because I'm warm. Finally, I sit down and write my diary. I can remember the previous days quite well. Soon I get bored with it and go to look in the *Kofferlager* in the Jaeger Barracks to see whether I can take out my soccer boots from storage to use in today's match against Union. It's getting warmer and I slowly take off my clothing. The *Kofferlager* is closed. I'm worried about the boots, but I will leave it to chance. I notice that it is already eleven o'clock. I quickly go to BV so that my fate can be decided. The boys are waiting there. Soon, Prager lets us inside and we sit down. It is agreed that we will be fired from the garden and we should be back to see Schwarzbart at two o'clock. But now the boots worry me. No one wants to lend anything to me. Therefore I go for lunch. Fortunately, Išík is there and he lends me his soccer boots. Even though I don't feel right playing with them, it is better than nothing. Ten boys are supposed to go to the School. Even though I'm assigned, I cannot go. At two o'clock, I go instead to Schwarzbart. We talk and we agree that we are to be thrown out of the garden. I really don't care. I hurry to the *bašta*. Soon we take the field. I don't feel right in my borrowed soccer boots. In spite of that, we win 3:0. It is a good beginning! Then I change and watch the second match. I soon have to leave because at 4:30 I have my lesson. At Mother's, I wash up and quickly go to L410. The professor is already there and is playing. I sit down at the piano and play my pieces. I remember now that I forgot to practice one of the pieces. Just by chance, I manage not to reveal it. Overall, it goes quite well. I feel self-conscious about my long and dirty fingernails. I am assigned two new pieces. After some practice, I go to my father's barracks, where I have dinner. After dinner, we go to the *bašta*. Since there is no game, we return home. On the way, we talk in English, which goes quite well. I go to see my father in the *Verteilungstelle,* where I wash up nicely, study my vocabulary, and write my English assignment. I am very pleased! Only at nine o'clock I go to the attic, where I lie down and go to sleep.

[The following text through September 7 in the diary is crossed out and barely legible: PW.]

I don't write about the next two days. There is only one impression and that is that the end is near. The news is that within forty hours the English have taken Belgium, and are advancing into the Netherlands and into Germany! Köln and Düsseldorf have fallen! The Russian front is at a standstill in Poland. However, Romania is already in Russian hands and there is an uprising in Bulgaria. In Slovakia, Žilina and Banská Bystrica are in the hands of the rebels. There is a rumor that [General Walther von] Brauschitz [commander-in-chief of the German army] is in London and pleads for peace. The German soldiers are no longer fighting, only the SS. In Terezín, for two consecutive nights, Bergel and Rahm have been in the crematorium burning documents. I don't know which ones. The fact is that in the whole protectorate the gendarmes have to give up their arms. During the night, all the Germans in Terezín were called up and went with their arms to Litoměřice and no one is watching the Ghetto. If I could remember it all, I could fill up my whole diary. Some people are saying that the end is already here; some are already packing. I almost believe it, but I think this is just a rumor. I am afraid that in the end the Germans may bomb us.
[Crossed-out text ends: PW.]

Thursday, 7 September 1944

Last night we agreed that we will play a "friendly match" with Hagibor Terezín at six o'clock in the morning on the *bašta*. I am looking forward to it. I don't have my boots but I don't care. I get up early with Mangl,[118] who has moved next to me. When I get dressed properly I go down to wake up Pedro and Gustl and we soon go to the *bašta*. The Hagibor team tells us that we most likely will not be able to play much. The field is not free at first and therefore we play next to it. Soon we manage to get the field. The Hagibor are very rough. We play only for ten minutes because the Hagibor team claims that it has to practice. We give them hell for making us get up so early at 5:30! We manage to win by a score of 10:1. I scored once in our team's own goal and one real one. We continue to argue among ourselves. It's

118. Pavel's friend Mangl (full name unknown at this time) did not survive.

caused primarily by Eisner and Palka, who always want to butt in. After a short while playing with a rag ball, I return home with Mangl. We make our beds and agree that today we have to find a coach. We like Soridek from Hagibor, who also owns a ball. We go to look for him at the Jaeger Barracks, but then we change our mind. We shoot the ball with Palka, who now wants to transfer to another team. I know that he will not do it. In a bad mood, we go back to the *bašta* and watch the match. We decide that we will pick Mr. Weider to be our coach. We are mad at Lion because he would not let us play. We stay at the *bašta* for about an hour. Full of anger, I go to Mother's. I cannot refrain from showing my bad mood and I can already feel that it will end with a big crash; this is exactly what happens. Very angry, I leave. For a while, we talk at the *heim* and then I suggest to Mangl we go for a lemonade at Sokolovna. However, nobody is at Sokolovna. We sit for a while on the terrace, but because there is no lemonade, we go to look over the building. It is luxuriously equipped, including two pianos. I want to play something, but I can't. There are two balconies and large halls with easy chairs. We agree to return at three o'clock to get some lemonade. Now we go and look for Mr. Weider, who is working in the blacksmith shop. On the way, I talk with Mangl, with whom I get along very well. We are in luck as Mr. Weider is in. Now we have to figure out what to say. Mangl decides to ask Uri. He is very polite but unfortunately he has to decline because of too much work. Then we confront Weider but he soon disappears in the house and we have to look for him. We sit at L218 and don't know where to go from there. We can see how difficult it is to get a coach who also owns a ball. We therefore leave for Sokolovna, where we sit down under a sun umbrella and order lemonade, which is handed to us in a dirty jar and with only a little bit of sugar. We finish drinking it and we get ready to leave for home. We agree that we will go to the captain's meeting at six o'clock. I don't find Mother at home and therefore I set out for *šance* [the entrance to the *bašta:* PW] because I know that I can find her there. Suddenly, little Míša[119] attaches himself to me and I take him for a walk. I see Mother, but I don't pay much attention to her. With little Míša, I go to the carts, where I let him off. I show him the tracks and the carriages at the Sudeten Barracks. We return home as

---

119. Pavel apparently uses "little" to distinguish this Míša (who has not been identified) from Míša Gruenbaum.

it's getting late. At home I'm already in a better mood. I quickly finish supper and go to the captain's meeting, which I like quite a lot.
We are to play the next round on Wednesday at four o'clock against
Alijah II. We have a good chance for a win! I go directly to the *bašta*,
where I find Mangl and Kovanitz, who could coach us. There is a
match between Plzeň and Fortuna, which, however, doesn't interest me much. It's getting close to eight o'clock and Kovanitz goes
home. We stop him in front of the Jaeger Barracks. He's again nice
and says that he doesn't have time, but that he would arrange to get
someone for us. We are to check with him in a week. We are not very
satisfied with his answer but nothing can be done about it. I go to
Apel. Franta reads the names of the boys who are to move to Room 6.
Kalíšek is among them. On the surface it annoys me, but actually it
is not a great loss. Franta wants to get rid of twelve boys but I am not
among them. It is evident that I was wrong in thinking that Franta is
angry at me. Later on, I spend some time at Father's place. I talk to
him about our coaching situation and he refers me to Mr. Heller. I
give this news to Mangl and we agree that we should sleep on it until
tomorrow morning. Feeling good about the wonderful news, I fall
asleep.

Friday, 8 September 1944

I wake up and notice that it is already 8:30. We can stay in bed a bit
longer. After the wake-up call, Mangl and I go to look for Mr. Heller.
On the way, Grizzly joins us and together we go to the *Materialverwaltung* in the Kavalier Barracks. We don't find him there. We go to the
office at the Vrchlabi Barracks, and we are told that Mr. Heller works
there but isn't in right then. We set out for the "Brewery," where he
lives in an attic. We go to attic #1, where there are many cubbyholes
and even someone by the name of Heller, who is not our man. Finally,
someone tells us that we should look for him in attic #2. At last we locate a cubicle where we find Mr. Heller in the middle of shaving. He
says that he would very much like to coach us but that he has no ball.
However, he would check with Spedice. Hoping that we will have a
coach, we depart. We go to the *bašta*, where we borrow a rag ball and
then we play with a tennis ball. At noon we go home. I have lunch at
Mother's. I have a bad cold and cough. Since there is no *Apel*, I can
stay at Mother's. I wash up because I discover that I am awfully dirty.
After a long lapse, I write my diary. I go for milk and then to the

bašta, promising my mother that I will come back soon so that we can study French. At the *bašta,* there are no games and I return soon. I sit down with Mother on a bench and study French personal pronouns. I go quickly for supper. After a long observation I can conclude that our food has improved significantly. Every other day we have cucumbers. We have so much sauerkraut that I can't even eat it and sometimes I even give it away. Yesterday, many Dutch people arrived here and now the whole of Terezín is full of "Joods" ["Jews" in Dutch]. At eight o'clock, I go to *Apel,* which doesn't take place because there is some kind of a Viennese cabaret. Whenever one man finishes singing in German with a sound like a cock-a-doodle-doo, boys from the School whistle and make fun of him. I am staying neutral, but I am on the side of the Czechs. Then, I go to the attic and talk and read a book with Mangl. Franta arrives and says that we have to go to bed because tomorrow we will do housekeeping at L313. I'm mad and I don't move for awhile when suddenly Franta screams out: "Now, Mr. Weiner, wouldn't you want to get up?" I keep my thoughts to myself and go to bed. In a while, Rudla Weil arrives and confiscates our light bulb because we have exceeded our time limit for having the light on. Old times are returning and we are regressing.

Wednesday, 13 September 1944

Mangl is now my best friend. We will lie next to each other in the bunks. I think that I will find in him a better character than in Kalíšek. With Kalíšek, I confine my conversation to the merest necessities. This morning it is really cold but during the day it warms up. I continue to have a cold and cough. Today we are supposed to go to L313 to beat and carry our mattresses. First, I go to Mrs. Fried to borrow a mattress beater and take it to L313. We go by cart to L414 for mattresses. Afterward, again with a cart, we go to L218 to load the mattresses that we take to L313. On the way something happens with Franta and he has a run-in with one of the boys. I look for my mattress. Finally, I find it and I beat it. There is relatively little dust in it. We have our sleeping spots assigned. But first, I have to say something about our room. It is a large, high-ceilinged room adjacent to a big hall, which will now serve as a nursery. One can see on the ceiling the remnants of a former stage. It has central heating and four high windows. The room is quite bright. The bunks are assigned as follows:

[Diagram is shown in the text: PW.]

Diary entry from September 13, 1944, showing diagram of bunk assignments

All the boys are already present except for Mangl and me. We cannot get an upper bunk and we don't want a middle bunk. We, therefore, are assigned spots at the bottom, next to the cupboards. It is not exactly the best. We pull away the cupboards. Just when we put the mattresses in place, the siren starts howling. It is now a common occurrence because air raids are now every day at noon. Sometimes we can even see the airplanes. I'm not even surprised. By chance, this air raid doesn't last long. Just when I'm ready to leave I notice that I'm missing the mattress beater. Furiously, I look for it and finally Beran finds it in between the cupboards. Satisfied, I go to Mother's. I don't know why, but I'm in a good mood. I go for lunch. I have to go first home because I still have to write my English lesson. I finish it. Today at 3:45 we are supposed to play against Alijah II. Now all the boys who are staying at BV are what one may call "soccer nuts." We have nothing else to do but to play. I spend the whole day on the *bašta*. In the meantime, we manage to get Mr. Heller to be our coach. On Monday, we had a practice session. All the boys liked him enormously. We are playing the Hawks and they lose 1:0. I play with borrowed boots that are too big for me. It is better than nothing. From the beginning, I realize that we are the better team. The referee keeps interrupting the game,

which annoys us. In the beginning of the second half, Eisner scores
a goal. Spizl says something to the referee, who then throws him out.
We are very angry! We defend ourselves furiously and are happy when
the game is over. I learn that Sasha will not go to our lesson today and
therefore I have to go alone. All heated up, I fly to the attic and then
quickly to the lesson. It is already 4:30 and I am late. I like the lesson
even without Sasha. At Mother's I have supper and quickly go to practice. It goes quite well. The evening proceeds as usual.

Friday, 15 September 1944

We are awakened at 5:30. Franta doesn't care about us any longer; he
lies quietly in bed. We have to pack up our bedroll. I'm having difficulties with mine because I have a poor string. I'm nervous but finally
I succeed and I carry it down to the third yard, where other luggage
is already piled up. It is being loaded onto a cart and brought to the
Entwesung. I am very uncertain while waiting for the departure to the
Entwesung. Koko and Lion bring me very bad news: my bedroll has
come apart and is now only skimpily tied together! It turns out to be
a needless worry, though. As my bad luck may have it, I still have to
bring some luggage to the *Entwesung.* At home, I catch the boys just
when they are leaving for the washroom. In front of the *Entwesung,* we
line up and I'm in the back. I have bad luck being first in the second
group. I am led into the change room, where I take off my clothes
and put it into some kind of a crate. Then, naked, I wait for bathing
with the other boys. In about half an hour, my turn comes. It is nothing special. Then, they give me a bathrobe and I go and sit down
with our boys. The air there is awful and the waiting is boring. Only
at eleven o'clock does the clothing of the first group come out of the
gas. Unfortunately, mine is not there and I have to wait for another
hour until my clothing arrives. I quickly get dressed and hurry to the
barracks. I go for lunch. I don't enjoy having lunch without Mother.
At last, I go to the attic and I pack up my things that I will bring for
the interim to Mother's. Father seems to be too concerned about me
and I behave toward him quite rudely. Soon Mother arrives. I intend
to start a new life in L313 and I want to start it right today. *Apel* at two
o'clock interferes, during which it is advised that the boys of Room 7
will cart two by fours from Magdeburg's attics. I stare idly at the yard
and I just barely catch something from an argument between Franta
and Rudla Weil. I'm now very good friends with Mangl. I think that

this friendship will be better than between Kalíšek and me. Occasionally, I go upstairs. Finally, we are told that we are supposed to go with the cart to BV for the two by fours. Many of the boys play hooky. At L313 we have to wait for the bedrolls which are arriving from the *Entwesung*. Mine is not in the first group. Finally the second one arrives and I find my bed linen, which is in perfect shape. We are not allowed to use them and they are stored in the large hall. I say the hell with the others and go to Mother's. I pick up my dinner on the way. The mood at Mother's is good. I go home and want to write my diary. Unfortunately, I don't get to it. I take advantage of the nice washroom and get washed up with Mangl in warm water. I brought a blanket and a pillow from Mother, but I remember that I don't have any pajamas! Mother comes to visit me so I go with my parents to get them. After returning home I lie down and after a brief talk with Mangl, I fall asleep.

Saturday, 16 September 1944

It was very cold during the night. In the morning I wake up and even though we can stay in bed longer, we get up and go to Merz's Bar Mitzvah. It is in the Kavalier Barracks. I like the service reasonably well. The men act very religiously. However, I am bored just staring into space, and I am glad when it's over. In the afternoon, there is a meeting and several details are being decided. I go to practice the piano. It is obvious that I am progressing well. News arrives that there was a big robbery in Terezín's *Kartoffel Lager* [potato storage building] in the Kavalier Barracks. About 700 kg have been taken.

Wednesday, 20 September 1944

I have my makeup piano lesson. It doesn't turn out well because my hands are frozen. After the lesson, I practice. On Sunday, a sports festivity took place which involved league matches, a match between the Nešarim and the Beavers, the cup final, and then an assembly of all the teams. I watched the matches with Mangl. During the match between Jugendfuersorge and Vienna (4:4), it was announced that Franta will most likely quit the team because Gonda[120] has blamed

120. Egon (called Gonda) Redlich (b. October 13, 1916), formerly a law student and vice principal of the Prague Youth Aliyah school, served as the head of the youth welfare

him for the match ending in a tie. The match between the Nešarim and the Beavers followed. It was a suspense-filled match with the Nešarim scoring twice in the first half. We then had to move behind the moat but Franta called us right back to cheer our team on. We furiously screamed "Rim Rim Rim Tempo Nešarim"[121] and it brought results. The lead kept changing, and at the twenty-second mark before the end of the match, the Nešarim scored the equalizing goal. The match went into overtime and while everyone was screaming louder and louder, the Nešarim scored twice and we were ahead 6:4. Just before the end, the Beavers scored another goal which, however, was meaningless. I left with my father and the whole day we talked about the beautiful match.

On Tuesday evening, I had a big argument with my parents. It reached a point that Father even spanked me. The cause of all this anger has been my father's dreadful nervousness [illegible words]. At home, I was so upset that I started to cry. On Tuesday, a new library was set up in our *heim*. I borrowed a book titled *In Archduke's Court*.

Today Mother has been transferred from the bakery to *Glimmer* [mica].[122] She is awfully excited, and rightfully so. Her nervousness partly contributed toward the big upset of last night.

The program is starting today. However, one wouldn't know from the way we get up. We stay in bed until 7:30. Mrs. Mautner gets mad and we have to quickly get up and have everything in order in fifteen minutes. During *Apel*, Franta is furious and warns us that in the afternoon we will remember our waking up late this morning. We have program until nine o'clock in the room where there are no bunks. It is quiet there. We have Czech, and Eisinger is lecturing to us about Czech poets. Toward the end of the lesson, I excel in front of Kohn.

department in Terezín. A member of the Zionist organization Maccabi Hatzair, Redlich remained dedicated in Terezín to providing a general and Zionist education for the incarcerated children to prepare them for a future in Palestine. As he wrote in his diary on January 7, 1942, "Our work is like that of the Youth Aliyah. There we brought children to freedom. Here we attempt to save the children from the face of death" (Saul Friedman, ed., *The Terezín Diary of Gonda Redlich* [Lexington: University Press of Kentucky, 1992], 4). Redlich sought to protect the youngsters at every turn in Terezín. Gonda was transported to Terezín from Prague on December 4, 1941, and sent to Auschwitz with convoy Et on October 23, 1944. He did not survive.

121. "Rim Rim Rim Tempo Nešarim" (something like: "Go, go, go, Nešarim!") was the "war cry" of the boys of room 7 (the Nešarim) to inspire them to play their best at soccer matches.

122. Splitting mica (*Glimmer* in German) was deemed essential to the war effort. It was terrible work, but the women who held these jobs (at one point, some thirteen hundred) were protected from deportation. Pavel was covered by his mother's protection.

I'm asked whether I'm really interested in the subject and I say yes. The second period is free. The third lesson is English followed by history, where we talk about King George of Poděbrad.[123] Recently, *Dienstelle* [the SS office][124] moved into the bank. It is quite awkward. I go for lunch and then to Mother's. I behave entirely uncaring and soon leave. Mother goes already to work. At 1:30, there is *Apel*, at which we find out that we have house arrest for the rest of the day. Franta won't even allow me to go to the clinic. He says that my shelf is in bad shape even though everybody can see that it is in perfect shape. The program for the afternoon is as follows: we are going to the *bašta*, then we will count, then a free lesson, and at eight o'clock to bed where night rules will apply. I raise my hand saying that I have an English lesson between 4:30 and 5:30. Franta claims that my shelf is messy, but I look straight into his eyes and say that it is all right. He allows me to go to my lesson but otherwise I have only half an hour free. I have to cancel piano practice. Sasha and I continue to argue about our lessons. On the way to the *bašta* we both call Franta names. At four o'clock, I leave and then go to the lesson. There we talk about life in Terezín, of course in English. I don't find my father in the barracks and therefore I leave a note for him and go home. I want to write my diary, and yet I don't feel like it. I just waste my time. I go to get washed and soon fall asleep.

Thursday, 21 September 1944

[There is only one line for the day which is crossed out: PW.]

Friday, 22 September 1944

The only thing of interest about Thursday was the afternoon, namely soccer. We again played the Hawks. I had my usual boots and therefore I played marvelously. I particularly excelled in volleys. However, it was to no avail as we were losing by a score of 2:0. I was mad at everyone and particularly at Grizzly, who was playing very badly. Even though we scored a goal, the opposing team scored also. The match

---

123. George (or Jiří) of Poděbrad (1420–71) was king of Bohemia from 1458 until his death. A Hussite leader during the Hussite wars, he fought papist forces and sought a moderate course in the Hussite camp.

124. The word *Dienstelle* connotes a government office or department, and reflects the Nazi propaganda that Terezín was a "normal" town.

ended 3:1. After soccer, I realize that when I play a match at 2:30 my whole afternoon is gone. The impetigo doesn't hurt me anymore because I go regularly to the clinic. I only talk the merest essentials with my father. I want to spend the evening by reading the book *In Archduke's Court,* which I like very much. I can't do it though, because we have a scheduled meeting with Heini, which, however, doesn't take place. In the evening, Franta tells us a story during which I fall asleep.

Today, there is supposed to be some kind of an inspection and everything has to be in order. As my bad luck may have it, I have room duty with Lappert. The program is canceled, as it was yesterday afternoon. The reason for the inspection is that some German control is expected.[125] The Germans are looking for escape routes from Terezín. They were already at L410 and found school benches there. After housekeeping, Zwicker arrives and lectures about adventurous journeys. The electricians are installing lights for us and they make a tremendous mess that we have to clean up. I stop at L216 for lunch and then I go to Mother's. I am now on very good terms with Mother, but not with my father. I soon leave, as Mother again has an afternoon shift. Yesterday's news about a transport completely dies down. It was a rumor apparently. *Apel* doesn't take place, but at six o'clock is the Friday inspection. Immediately, I go to practice the piano, but I cannot stay long because another boy arrives. At home, I sit in my little corner and study. Then we must do housekeeping again. Lappert is not there because the Nešarim are playing again and the score is 10:2. Finally the electricians depart and I have to sweep up. I am pissed off. Just before *Apel,* I go to the washroom to take a shower. I arrive just in time for *Apel,* during which nothing of importance happens. Then, I go to Father's. The road past the former *Komandatura* is now open. It feels somewhat unusual to be walking there. This is what habit does to a person. I can imagine what the feeling would be to enter freedom and a normal life. At my father's, I eat supper. I am on somewhat better terms with him. At home, I sit on the bunk and read. I then lie down and listen to Franta's storytelling, during which, unfortunately, I fall asleep.

End of VOLUME 4

---

125. German authorities inspected Terezín for many reasons, and each time the boys cleaned up their quarters in anticipation of the visit.

Volume 5

Saturday, 22 [23] September 1944

I look forward to sleeping longer, but this pleasure is denied to me because the inspection is expected today. Unwillingly, I get up. I am on good terms with Mother and in the afternoon we have a good talk. In the morning, I read and I feel quite well. I go for lunch where I get more [food: PW]. After lunch, there are the sirens of an air raid. Indeed, we go to the windows and listen to the approaching roar of the planes. We are all extremely happy. It takes a while until the raid is called off. It's nothing special; almost every day this spectacle repeats itself. I go to my mother's. I take with me my music sheets because I plan to go from there to practice. I get some water for my mother and on the way I meet Mrs. Beran.[126] I want her to tell Leoš something about the books, but Mrs. Beran's words shock me: "Do you know that Leoš's father is dead?" I feel as if somebody has shot me and I cannot say a word. Immediately, I go tell the news to my mother. I lose the desire to practice and Beran walks with me to L313. On the way I ask him all kinds of questions. Mr. Beran died at 12:30 a.m. and he had tuberculosis for six months. Recently it attacked his intestines, which were infected, and he could not stand the pain any longer. However, he died peacefully. I feel very sorry for Beran. In our room the news has a tremendous impact. One cannot do anything about it so I go practice the piano, but I don't feel like playing. I am in a bad mood, but at Mother's a good mood is maintained for future's sake. Late at night, Mother and Father accompany me home. On the way, I look at my father's shabby topcoat and get angry. Obviously, my father is annoyed, and when we part he says, "Go to sleep feeling that you are a little scoundrel." I don't take him seriously. At home,

126. Leo Beran's mother.

I lie down on the bed and enjoy the beauty of Jirásek's[127] book, but what is it good for? Suddenly, Špulka runs into the room bringing dreadful news. Freudenfeld[128] has announced that all men in the age group of eighteen to fifty must leave in a transport for a work camp in Germany. Even though it does not concern my family, I am somehow moved. I don't feel like reading anymore and I go with the boys for a walk through the Terezín streets, which are already full of talk about the transport. Even though I am also anxious, my selfishness keeps me calm. After all, that's all that counts. I keep remembering my mother's words and with this thought I fall asleep.

Sunday, 23 [24] September 1944

Mrs. Mautner wakes us up today. Her first words are: "Do you know that the age bracket has been increased to sixteen to fifty-five?" I feel as if someone has shot me. I think of my father and of my brother and their inclusion in this new bracket. This news gets me very anxious and I quickly set out to my mother's. I go crazy when I am told that my mother is at work. I feel entirely abandoned. I quickly run to my father, whom I fortunately reach at the table. As far as he is concerned, he is reconciled with the idea that they will leave. I am consoling him by saying that everybody will leave. After all, this is the truth. Whomever I run into says that he is in the transport now. I go with my father to the attic, where there is a big commotion. My father quickly picks up some shoes. He gets them for Handa as well. Everyone is saying good-bye to someone. In the hallways people are standing, perhaps because of *reklamace*. It makes me nervous and I urge Father to go and see Dr. Bergmann[129] to get out of the transport. My father, however,

127. The renowned author Alois Jirásek (1851–1930) focused on the Czech national struggle for independence in his numerous historical novels and plays.

128. Pavel probably refers here to the younger Freudenfeld, Rudolf (also called Rudla or Rudi), one of the L417 educators. Rudla Freudenfeld (1921–85) was deported from Prague to Terezín with transport De on July 5, 1943. A gifted amateur musician, he conducted all fifty-five performances of Hans Krása's opera, *Brundibár*. Rudla was deported from Terezín to Auschwitz with convoy Ek on September 28, 1944, and survived to be liberated in Gleiwitz. He returned to Prague.

129. The Weiners' family friend Dr. Rudolf (Rudla) Bergmann (b. June 15, 1910) was in the first transport (Ak) from Prague to Terezín on November 24, 1941. He served as head of the financial department in the first Council of Elders appointed by the Germans; Jakob Edelstein was the chairman. The Germans removed Edelstein as Elder in January 1943 and appointed a German Jew, Paul Eppstein. By September 1944, the Germans wanted to get rid of Eppstein and he was summarily arrested and shot. Benjamin Murmelstein, a Viennese Jew, succeeded him; Bergmann remained on the council as a representative of the

is against it. He is trying to assemble some useful articles. I'm trying to console my father, but I'm not succeeding. Several unclear rumors have already spread. For example, the *Schleusky* will be in the Hamburg Barracks. There will be 5,000 people called. The transport will be divided into 2,500 people each. The first will be the men living in the blocks (my father) and the second will be those living in the barracks. The first transport will assemble tomorrow and depart the next day. The second will go later. The destination is Dresden, where the work camp will be built. I cannot think of *reklamace,* because of the 3,000 men in the *Wirtschaftsamt* [business office], only 151 will remain; my father will certainly not be one of them. The men in Spedice will be protected because women cannot do their work. On the way to the barracks my father tells me to behave well toward my mother and that I should not anger her. I feel terribly sad. On the way, Handa joins us. He adds to the confusion, which is not small! In the barracks, there is great commotion. All the husbands are leaving (Mr. Brody, Popper, Roubíček, and others). I am anxiously waiting for my mother. We go for lunch and then I go for a little walk. We discuss several family problems and complications that may result from the departure. At two o'clock, we wait for my mother at the *Leichenkammer* [morgue]. Of course, I couldn't attend Mr. Beran's funeral. Zucker is in the transport, and it is being decided whether Bergmann or Schliesser[130] will leave. Mother arrives all upset and she is already crying. When I tell her to calm down she gets angry. This makes me mad. Mother scolds my father for not knowing for sure whether he is in the transport or not. We are trying to calm her. It is just the beginning. My mother immediately starts packing. We go to my father's place, The Sun. Sasha's father, who is also in the "mess," is there. I chat with Sasha because I see that I'm only in the way during packing. I go with Sasha to the School. Of all the *Jugendfuersorge,* only four people remain. All counselors go, which means so will Franta. The whole education program

Czech Jews. Bergmann had protected the Weiner family from inclusion on transports; now he and his family were among the many Jewish leaders deported from Terezín to Auschwitz in the weeks thereafter. The Bergmanns went with transport Ev on October 28, 1944. They did not survive.

130. Deported from Prague to Terezín on November 24, 1941, Karel Schliesser (b. May 24, 1899) was a member of the first Council of Elders appointed by the Germans and he remained as head of the *Wirtschaftsabteilung* (economic and supplies department) through the reorganizations in October 1942 and January 1943. He was shipped to Auschwitz with convoy Ek on September 28, 1944, and was last seen standing on the train ramp at Auschwitz upon arrival, handcuffed to Otto Zucker. Both men were killed.

will collapse because Zwicker, Kohn, and Eisinger are going. I am completely distraught. Everything has been derailed from its normal track. Women now give out food in the kitchens. At my father's, there is packing chaos. Father is taking with him a knapsack, a bedroll, and a small suitcase with food. We agree that when the war's end comes we should all write to our relatives, the Schinkos.[131] Everything resembles a funeral wake. The departure would not be as awful if there was not this dreadful uncertainty whether or not there will be any air bombardment in the places where the transports will go. Mother goes to Handa to pack and I remain with Father in the barracks. We are awfully nervous, especially my father, who is anxious as to when Mother will return. It's dark outside and it's raining heavily. The nasty weather certainly doesn't help our mood. In the barracks the mood is terrible and the women are nervous. My mother still hasn't come and therefore I decide to go with an umbrella to Handa in L218. Soon my socks get wet. I cannot see one step ahead. Mother is pleased that I have come. Only twenty-seven boys will remain in L218. I soon go back to my father's. When I tell him that Mother will not be back for an hour, he is completely beside himself. Soon, Father tells me to go home. I do so because I am very dirty. I take a shower and go to bed. I forgot to mention that when I return home, the boys are sitting around the table with Franta, who is saying good-bye to us. I can't stand it any longer and I shed a few tears.

Monday, 24 [25] September 1944

After waking up, I hurry to my mother. The whole morning, in fact the whole day, I spend helping with final packing. My father and Handa think their luggage is too heavy and they keep repacking. This is being done at my father's place. If I were to name people who are in the transport, I would have to fill up this whole thick notebook. I really am not quite aware of what is happening. In the street I see only teary-eyed faces. I pay no attention to others. My parents and I agree on [illegible]. I get into an occasional argument with my parents, which is of no great significance. Father keeps telling me that after he leaves, the whole responsibility will rest on me. I'm amazed that he is so blunt. I can't wait until they start loading because I want to have

131. Relatives of Pavel's mother; Else Schinko (also mentioned at the end of the diary, in the entry for April 22, 1945) was Valy's first cousin, and thus Pavel's first cousin once removed. The idea was to contact the Schinkos as a way to find each other after the war.

all the farewells behind me. They were supposed to load in the morning, but now all will load in the evening. "Our" people, however, will not load so late because it would be very dark. I am concerned about my father. He prefers to keep saying good-byes. He has already said good-bye three times to the people in the barracks and he keeps returning. Also in the street everybody says good-bye. Everything looks so sad. It is interesting to note that today my stupid but simple good luck charm which I kept on a window in the Magdeburg Barracks disappeared. It is difficult to describe the transport briefly. The situation keeps changing and so do my emotions. Sometimes I would be happy if the whole thing was already behind me and sometimes I would like that it be delayed. I am sorry that my father is not in the second transport. First of all, his friends are there and secondly there is a greater possibility for *reklamace*. Finally, the time comes for entering the *Schleusky*. "Our" luggage is too heavy. I couldn't carry even one. The bedroll is packed in a horribly awkward manner. There is a big crowd in front of the *Schleusky*. We exchange a few kisses while in tears, and soon they enter the gates that engulf them. My mother and I are left alone. My duty as a Good Samaritan is about to begin. I go and ask where our people will stay. Finally, I find out it is the room on the first floor where the numbers are 801 and 802. By chance, I know someone there who calls for them. Handa makes a tremendous fuss that the luggage is too heavy and that he has to throw out half of it. This doesn't help our mood and we sadly return home. I try to cheer up my mother, but I'm not too successful. I bring supper to her and we go to L218, where we pack up the things we need. We put them together and then we return to the *Schleusky*. We call for Father and Handa to come down and we talk a little. Then comes the second phase of the farewell. With my father it goes well, but when Handa comes I don't know why, but I start crying and so does my mother. Fortunately, I am hidden by the darkness. Afterward, we go sadly home. I slowly calm down. The railroad cars are not there yet. I say good-bye to my mother. Franta still wanted to say good-bye to us, but I was not there. Now, we have to write a farewell letter, which I sit down to do. For a while we discuss the *bonky* and I fall asleep.

Tuesday, 25 [26] September 1944

Even though I want to stay in bed, something is telling me that I should be going to the *Schleusky*. It is rumored that the transport is postponed. [Illegible word] has not arrived yet so it is definite that the transport will not depart today. Yesterday, my mother received a summons to go back to the bakery. Outside, it is raining and it is raw. I go to the barracks, where I am told that my mother has already left for work. I want to cut some bread, but I can't find it. I'm annoyed that the women in the barracks are already considering me a half-orphan. I'm in a quandary as to whether or not to go to my father. I really do not want to say good-bye again. I return home. I need to go to the barber, but I don't feel like it. At home, I don't have patience and something is telling me to go to my father. The ghetto guards are standing around the Hamburg Barracks and they don't let anybody near the window. Fortunately I find my mother there, all upset as she waits for my father to appear in the window. I ask that he be allowed to go near the window. My mother wants to bring him something to eat. I don't remember any details at all. We both are sorry that our men are not in the second transport. Rumor has it that the second transport will not leave. Even the departure of the first transport is not certain. All through Terezín, there are rumors about transports, such as that there is a general strike of workers and the railroad people and the railroad tracks are not usable. Also, there are rumors that the railroad cars are not available. With this news I try to console my mother. We spend the time going from the *Schleusky* to the barracks, bringing tea and food. We envy those who are in the second transport, and deep inside we wish that if the first transport leaves, the second one will depart as well. My mother is trying to reach Rudla Bergmann, but she doesn't accomplish anything. Mother has a terrible tendency to think that everything bad is going to happen and to ignore anything good. Handa and Father already repacked their luggage, particularly their bedrolls. They took out only sandals. Some fast-thinking people knocked out the bars in one of the windows so that one can crawl through. In the evening, I am able to get into the *Schleusky* to talk with Father and Handa, perhaps for the last time. In the whole Ghetto there is a terrible disorder. For example, in the [illegible] young children are scolding me. Mother is terribly nervous. It is very difficult to console her. Tonight is the eve of Yom Kippur. Everywhere candles are lit. All the people come out of the *Schleusky* and are allowed to sleep at home tonight. My brother does the same. Only late at night I return home. Soon Franta arrives and announces that tomorrow morning the transport will most likely be dissolved. With the good news, I run to CII,[132] where the rumor is accepted with some skepticism. Hoping that the transport will not depart, I take a shower and then go to bed, where, very tired, I fall asleep.

The next evening, Wednesday, I learn that the railroad cars will arrive in the morning and that at six o'clock they will be loading. I will probably say good-bye to my father for the last time.

Thursday, 26 [28] September 1944

Even though we are allowed to stay in bed longer, I get up and run to the *Schleusky*. The ghetto guards and the gendarmes are all over. In vain I try to look into the window. "Our people" do not show up. In the crowd of people, I see my mother, who is tearful. I try to console her rudely. Mother is taking it very badly. The gendarmes form a chain and, despite their politeness, they tell the women to go away. My mother is very concerned because she forgot to tell Handa where his cap was. Even though I understand her anxiety, I won't admit it and instead I scold her very badly. Mother keeps on crying, which disturbs me and I tell her off. I keep telling her to wise up, but it only reminds her of my presence and she starts crying again. I'm sad, and so I go home. From there, I go to get the sardines which I received yesterday but couldn't pick up until now. I go together with Mangl, who has a big package. Even before that, I run to my mother for [illegible]. Mother blames me that all the other children stood on the *bašta*, but I was not there. It makes me feel very sad. But despite that, I argue that it would not help anyway. On the contrary. Our conversation is overheard by Mr. Popper, who is leaving today, and he asks what message he should give to my father. My mother answers in place of me and says that I make her angry. These undeserved words make me also angry. I am extremely mad. I go for the sardines.

At home I start writing my diary. There are rumors that Eppstein will go with the transport. It is certain that he is locked up in the *Komandatura*. Schliesser is also in the transport.

In the Ghetto, it looks so sad without the men. I have difficulties thinking that I may now live several months without my father and Handa. I go for lunch. I keep looking at the chairs where my brother

132. Typically central European, Terezín architecture consists primarily of attached buildings that run the length of a town block. The rows on each street were designated with a capital letter and, in ascending order from south to north, a Roman numeral. Thus, CII was the second along the C row.

and father used to sit. God only knows when I will see them again. Mother goes to work in the afternoon. Deep inside, I am pleased that I have a free afternoon all to myself. This idea, though, vanishes very quickly. On Friday, I find out that it will be quite difficult to get used to this new life. At home, I lie down on the bunk and start to read. After an hour or so I get bored and I ask Mangl to go for a walk with me. We look into L218, my brother's attic, to see whether any of his books are left. I take several French and English books. One of them is called *How Should a Man Defend Himself?* The books are neither valuable nor good. Soon I go for supper. They serve "Ghetto Soup," which I take. As long as my mother is not around, even this soup is good for me. The men are saying good-bye there. I am beginning to form my own views and that's better. I'm looking forward like a child to having half a can of sardines. My mother must have divided it badly and I am angry. I visit Mother in the bakery. She comes out very sore. I feel sorry but not because of this. Mother is in a hurry and we make up. I return home, hoping to spend a quiet evening, but I cannot resist and play two games of chess. This season I am not in the best form. All this will pass . . . only without my father!!!

I go under a warm shower. My robe comes in very handy now. I spend a long time looking for books tonight and then I read until 10:30. I forgot to mention that Professor Nobel is our new *Jugendleiter.*

Saturday, 30 September 1944

Yesterday, a new problem arose. A new transport of five hundred will consist of both volunteers and non-volunteers. My mother is firmly convinced that we should not volunteer. I think it would really not be too bad to volunteer. But then I change my view and I tell her that the only obstacle is that we could not take too much luggage with us. It is for this reason that we completely discard the idea of leaving. I feel very grown up! Occasionally, Mother and I get into an argument because she tends to take smaller portions of food. It comes to a point this afternoon over some pudding. I cannot control myself and leave.

At home, a chess league has been formed. The first round I played against Tuti and the match ended in a draw. The second round I played yesterday against Pudlina. I played from nine o'clock until almost two and from three o'clock until 4:30. Then I lost the game. I don't mind—it's sufficient that I know how to play chess.

It's Saturday; that means we can stay in bed until eight o'clock. Then, as I have just described, I played chess, which made me very excited. I go for lunch, and then I go with Beran for a walk. After, I go to meet my mother and run into her on the way. I give her my promise to come back very soon, but first I have to finish my game of chess. It turns out that the game goes on until five o'clock. I go to my mother's, and find her cleaning up. We go together for a walk and we think about my father and Handa. I return home, where I am determined to do something. Instead, I play *sprtec* [game simulating hockey played with buttons]. I stay up quite long, until 11:30.

OCTOBER
Monday, 2 October 1944

I am getting a new taste of life. Slowly, I must heal the wound caused by my father's departure. Even if the wound heals, there is much sorrow within me. I do not know how long it will last. The whole Ghetto is so sad; there is no news about where the men are now. We are forgetting about freedom. I think about my home in Prague most frequently when I read some book containing a description of a civilian and normal life. I keep thinking that we managed in the past, we manage now, and perhaps we will manage in the future. Such fatalism is protecting me from definite disaster. I hate to think that the state I am in today may lead to my mental collapse. If I were to return to Prague, I certainly would want to study. If I stayed the same way I am now, studying would be difficult. Something keeps telling me that I am smarter than other boys, but I prefer to keep it to myself. This is fate, isn't it? In the morning we wake up and put our stuff in order. I run to Mother so I can still see her before noon. Afterward, we have a program. We study English with Dr. Jelínková. We read the history of English literature. I understand it fully and therefore I feel that I know English. I am recommended to go to Prof. Nobel and ask him to give me the book that we have read. He is reluctant, however, to give me the book because supposedly I would not understand it. All this is the result of my being so short. I go for lunch and I spend the afternoon at Mother's place. Then something awful happens. I hear a voice coming from the barracks: "Do you know that tomorrow fifteen hundred women married to the men who had been in previous transports will depart?" It seems as if lightning has struck. At first we don't believe the news. But it is almost certain that we will go. Everybody thinks the same way. It's not the time to mull things over. We hurry to Rudla [Rudolf Bergmann] but we can't find him. As far as I am concerned, I don't care at all. Actually, I'm looking forward to leaving. Soon Mother's bed has changed, as did the whole barracks, into a rummage warehouse. Mother sends me to the brewery to see whether I can have my laundry dried. This is the first thing on my mother's mind. I don't know whether to laugh or cry, but I do what I am told to do. I feel [illegible word]. It is unbelievable how fast the news has spread in only five minutes. Now, everybody believes it. For the time being, I don't know what to think about all this. We'll see. In the meantime, I am running around telling myself that we are in the transport. Our only hope, actually I don't know what to call it, is Mother's work in the *Glimmer*. It is said that this will protect us. Everybody, however, says something different. So, we will let fate work it out. Now I must go to get the suitcases. There is a big mess everywhere. This is what the transport is all about. One can suppose that it will be without crying and bitter farewells. In the attic, I cannot find our knapsack. Surprisingly, I am not strongly affected by the transport and I think that somehow it will work out. I discuss the transport with the boys. They keep telling me that I will not go. I go to my mother. She is all agitated. Her real concern is that we will have to leave behind 75 percent of our belongings. Now everything focuses on what we will take with us. I will carry a knapsack, a bedroll, a little suitcase with food, and a breadbox. We hear that we will also be allowed to take with us a *Mitgepack* [carry-on]. Let us see! Mother finds the knapsack and furiously begins to pack. Actually, I feel ashamed that my mother acts like a madwoman. At last I must get dressed for the transport. It is an awful situation and yet Mother keeps on scolding me. The biggest problem is just beginning: Mother will not allow me to take my personal belongings (my diary, *Nešar* magazine, etc). Later, I am able to put it in my knapsack. The bedroll is heavy. I can't get the sudden change into my head. I don't feel comfortable in this state of affairs. One thing I would not have to worry about is company. I keep thinking that I will not be in the transport of *Glimmer*—and this thought is getting stronger. But I commit a big error: I'm angry with Mother because she is packing while at the same time I'm telling the boys that I'm going. This is a real mistake. I'm trying to help, but I'm not succeeding. It is fortunate that we got off the daylight savings time and that the watch at half past one was moved to half past twelve. We therefore have more time. The transport will depart tomorrow at eleven and the loading will start at midnight. We'll see. I'm running around as one says, a "sheet in the wind." It is my fault that I feel sorry for myself. I reason that if I go, I'll be glad because I'll have the opportunity to see my father. We'll see. I'm doing a few errands. It is sort of a strange transport because it hasn't been officially announced. We are trying to reach Rudla, but we cannot find him. I am quite sleepy, and as a result I am impatient and I am getting angrier with Mother. I feel that the situation will erupt. I can't take it any longer and I start swearing. Mother tells me that I'm the worst son under the sun, but this doesn't insult me. At last, some strangers tell me to shut up and I obey. I'm angry at the whole world. I feel ashamed. In fact, I worry that the boys will laugh at me. I'm partly right. Mother gives me [illegible word]. Even though we know that we are not in the transport, we must figure on the possibility. I feel as if I have come out of a hot shower. I feel that peculiar feeling of hiding my anger and fear and shame. So, at eleven o'clock at night, I march through the empty streets alone and cry. I'm so unhappy. This is my reward. If I had my diary on me at that time, I would have certainly thrown it away. I would be capable of anything. The Germans are to blame. I stare at the lit-up windows of the *Komandatura*. Perhaps the people there are worse off than I am. At home, I crawl into an [illegible word], recognizing that I can fall asleep without [illegible word] and without bedsheets. I know it already; Mother knows it but unfortunately doesn't want to admit it.

Tuesday, 3 October 1944

I wake up and the first sentence that I hear is, "You see, you panicker, you're not going." I feel as if someone has stabbed me. I defend myself saying that we had to be packed. Mangl says he kidded me because he could see how distraught I was. I have a tremendous anger toward Mother. I don't even notice that it is only half past six. It's already light outside and everybody is packing. I have changed my view about wanting to leave in the transport and now I am looking forward to the next day. I try to fall asleep again, but I can't. I keep thinking of different things. My biggest worry is how I will change my clothes. It is not naive of me to think that everybody would laugh at me if I went out in my boots. The impetigo hurts me very much. I feel that I have to get up and go to my mother's place. In the street, things are in turmoil. I have a horrible confrontation with Mother. Under no circumstances would she give me the key to the little bag where I keep my diary. Really, I do not understand it. Mother feels that I can only open the bag after the train departs. If my mother is always right, this time she is not. I realize the situation is tragic and therefore I decide to leave in order to avoid an even bigger argument. At home, I'm on edge and therefore I decide to play with a tennis ball and do so until eleven o'clock. I spend the entire day writing and learning. In the evening, I make up with Mother and at home I fall asleep very tired because of the previous sleepless night.

Thursday, 5 October 1944

Today, another transport is being put together. Included in it are light invalids. This transport will again be "stupid." The whole family of Bretisu is included. From our room the following have been summoned: Gansalka,[133] Gustl, Brenner, and Seiner. We bum around the room, which turns out to be ominous because Sister Fischer, the nurse, catches me and tells me that we have to help pack the invalids. I'm very angry. We report to the Magdeburg Barracks. Afterward I go to my mother. I am being stubborn and I make Mother angry. She is working the afternoon shift. I'm looking forward to the afternoon. I change my plans and want to go for a walk. I meet Beran and suggest that we go to look for books in the nursery. I'm looking forward to some excitement since we can reach for the books through a broken window. We talk a little and then we dare. I'm disappointed because I realize that the only book we can easily reach is a foreign dictionary. I'm, however, caught up in this adventure and will not give up. I reach for another book. It is better! I reach for a French-German dictionary. Emboldened, I reach again for two books. The first is some kind of a prayer book and, while I reach for the other, I tear my coat. I decide that it makes no sense to continue. However, I look inside and I spot *The Little Lord* in English. I try to reach for it but can't make it. At home we boast about our *schlojs*. I don't know how it came about, but somehow I return to the nursery, this time with Jila and Furcht. Jila manages to take a bunch of books, among them *The Little Lord*, which I grab at once. Otherwise, there are only French books, which we give back. On the way home we agree that at night we shall

---

133. Petr Gans (b. April 21, 1930), nicknamed Gansalka, was deported from Plzeň to Terezín with transport S on January 22, 1942, and assigned to room 7 when it was established in July that year. Evidently, Gansalka avoided transport for another fortnight: he was sent to Auschwitz with convoy Es on October 19, 1944. He did not survive.

return and Valtr and Jila will crawl inside. We are looking forward to it. Nothing can really happen to us. I eat my dinner at Mother's place and then go home, where I read *The Little Lord*. At last, it is eight o'clock and the boys arrive. We leave into the dark night. We are getting ready. If I think about what we are planning, I realize that it is a plain burglary. We enter the yard. We encounter a big obstacle. The doors are lit up and in the yard there are lots of people. The two boys who are scheduled to crawl inside are visibly fearful. I feel the same way and therefore I don't try to make them change their minds. I am sure that nothing will come out of this adventure. We go back in the street and see a man approaching us. He is loaded with clothes and on his head he has a weird-looking hat. He starts talking to us. We very cowardly back away. We recognize that he is some kind of a *Getak* who is on a night shift. This only adds to our fears. We stand at the intersection for a while and then turn around and leave. Thus ended my first night of adventure! I return home as my leg hurts very much. In general, I feel lousy. I come home and for a while I sit around. I feel that something is not right and therefore I take my temperature. I have 37.3. I lie down quickly and read in English. I have the shivers and when I go to the bathroom I almost fall down the stairs. I feel that my fever has gotten worse. I put the book away and try to sleep. In a short time, I succeed. Mangl and others go to help out in the *Schleusky*. I wake up during the night to go to the bathroom, but I don't feel any better. I feel feverish and fall asleep.

Friday, 6 October 1944

In the morning I already feel better. Nevertheless, I stay in bed. The doctor comes to see me and says that I may get up. I stay in bed a while longer, though. When I get up I feel awfully upset because Hermann has lost my suspenders yet he maintains that he hasn't done it. I get very angry and we start to fight. We continue to argue for a while and we end it when we find another pair. I feel lousy the whole day. Mother is also angry with me because I didn't come to meet her. Finally, after a long argument I tell her that I was sick. In the evening we make up. Today the transport is leaving.

Saturday, 7 October 1944

As was agreed last night, today is a sort of *Grunt*. Even though *Grunt* is always unpleasant, it is needed. Everything is scrubbed and cleaned.

Since I am not showing much interest, I leave and decide to read *The Little Lord* at Mother's place. At half past ten, I go for lunch and then return home. I go and meet Mother only to find out that she has already left. Later I find her all upset because somebody has told her that the men who left in the transports have lost their entire luggage. I have also heard that they were bombed. We must leave everything to fate. Rumors just follow rumors. Tomorrow's transport is the worst ever. The Germans are angry and have forbidden people to take along bedrolls, [illegible word], or washbasins. The transport has to load at six o'clock tomorrow morning. We need not be afraid. We are well protected. All day, however, I am in a bad mood. In the evening, Lion and Išík get the summons. It is awful. With this feeling, I fall asleep.

Sunday, 8 October 1944

I feel as if someone is waking me up. However, I see that it is still night. I hear the voice of Mangl: "You see, we are in it, the transport." At night the human brain doesn't fully register and, without truly realizing what was said, I fall asleep again. At six o'clock, Mangl wakes me up and asks whether I can get for him an improvement. Without questioning I get up and go with Mrs. Mautner to the *Schleusky*. Really, one can see a friend when one truly needs one. I feel very sorry that Mangl is leaving. I have bad luck when my best friend has to leave. We hear dreadful news about the people who had departed earlier. It is said that they are in Birkenau[134] suffering from bombing and that everything has been taken from them. I better not tell all this to Mother. The whole morning I sit with Mother and read *The Little Lord*, which is my best entertainment. After lunch, I go to meet Mother again. These days nothing in particular happens. The same song repeats itself—transports and rumors. I am in such an awful state that I cannot do anything. In the evening I go for a walk with Mother and we think about the events of the past few days. Then, I go again to the *Schleusky* to see Mangl. Only late at night I return home and fall asleep.

Monday, 9 October 1944

The transport is the talk of the day. It no longer interests me. How could I have thought just a few weeks ago that there would be only

134. Nearly all Jews who were deported to Auschwitz and passed through the selection process were quartered in the subcamp Birkenau, also called Auschwitz II. The purpose-built gas chambers and crematoria were sited in Birkenau.

twenty thousand people left in the Ghetto? It is unbelievable. I see that the Mautners are very serious-minded people. They treat me the same way as I treat them. When I hear in the morning that Eli spent half the night at the *Schleusky* (with the Mautners), I go there immediately. I spend a few pleasant hours with them. In the morning a woman shows up who is supposed to be our *betreuerka*. Her name is Karla Hradecká[135] and she is a professor of Czech. This is welcome news to me. I am very interested in her and, as the expression goes, I try to do a little "ass kissing." Certainly, it cannot do any harm. Her opinions are different from Franta's but this doesn't really matter to me—just the contrary. We have a little chat and I immediately recognize that she is a "genuine Czech." I appreciate this quality the most. Later on I go to Mother, but unfortunately she is at work. I am facing a big problem all alone. There is an opportunity for me to get into MTL [*Materiallager*, supply warehouse]. On the plus side, I would like to earn some money so that Mother doesn't have to work so hard. But, on the negative side, I would have to stop learning. Since a professor is now staying with us, there will be good opportunities for learning. I have to think about it. I expected this day to be pleasant, but I was wrong. Mother wrote me a note not to eat the potatoes, but I forgot and I ate them all up. Mother arrives angry, and my having eaten the potatoes only makes her angrier. She starts complaining and swearing, asking why the dinner isn't ready and so on. I boast, I think inadvertently, that I ate the potatoes "on purpose." This would make even the greatest *klidas* [Czech slang for a calm person] furious! I run out of the house. I meet Beran and Kalíšek, who are on the way to *schlojs* books. I join them. Kalíšek crawls in and pulls out several books. He repeats it several times and pulls out a French textbook. Two boys from Room 10 arrive and one of them crawls inside. Since he is a bit mentally retarded, he doesn't pull out anything good. I feel badly that I have wasted the whole afternoon. As far as Mangl is concerned, I feel very sad. Kalíšek is moving back with me. My friendship with him will not have deep roots. I no longer have any strong relationship with him. I intend to learn, but I decide to go to the *Schleusky* to see the boys. I accompany them to their grandmother. We're having a fun time. Then, suddenly we learn that railcars are in Bohušovice and loading will start in thirty minutes! This is too sud-

135. Professor Karolina Hradecká (b. November 4, 1909) was assigned number 879 on transport Bg from Prague. She taught Czech literature in Terezín and remained to be liberated there.

den a change to keep us calm. We say good-bye quickly, the boys go to the *Schleusky* and I go home, where I announce the news. I feel sorry that I cannot go into the *Schleusky* because I don't have the pass. To make things worse, it starts to rain and the weather looks menacing. Soon it becomes dark and I don't feel like doing anything. My bad mood persists throughout the evening.

Tuesday, 10 October 1944

This day will be the turning point in my life. The reason is my talk with Professor Hradecká. I start to recognize that I am assessing my life correctly. Yesterday Professor Hradecká told us that she will study with us. I am determined to continue learning so that I can study later. In the morning Hradecká comes to us and asks who would like to talk with her. I volunteer. I can see that it will turn out well. She suggests that I show her some of my literary creations. It occurs to me that I could show her *Nešar*. It's worth a trip to Mother to get the key. I have a sharp exchange with Mother because I had said the words "on purpose" the previous day. I pull out *Nešar* and bring it to the professor. She examines it very carefully and I can see right away that she is an expert. It seems that she likes it, especially my articles. She concludes, to my great joy, that she can see some talent in me. She asks me all kinds of questions which I answer faultlessly. I am overjoyed. I feel very good, but I don't boast about it. Another serious matter concerns my mother. I keep my distance from her and I am outright fresh with her. I feel that I am in the right. I stick to my guns and I will not change until Mother apologizes. She appears very excited, but I am completely calm. I'm very angry at my mother and this spoils the joy of the day. The whole afternoon I study. At five o'clock, Petruška offers to go for a walk with me. I accept. We talk about various things, about Englishmen and about Americans and current relationships. I see in Petruška half fanatic and half thinking person. I don't know which half prevails.

Today, yet another transport is being put together. I am completely indifferent to it. On the contrary, it gives me satisfaction to see others suffer the same way as my father does. It seems that his transport is not doing well, as there have been no clear reports on my father or his transport. The rumor has it that they are somewhere in Germany and some are near Birkenau and altogether no one knows anything. In the evening, there is a meeting with Hradecká. She is surprised that *Nešar* is so sentimental. She asks whether this is my individual thinking or that of the group. I confess, but I'm hiding it. She is also interested in the boys' plans for the future. My turn comes. I'm stupidly silent. I'm awfully ashamed for not knowing what I am going to be in the future. It bothers me only superficially because I am sure that I will study at a *gymnasium* [academic high school]. There is a lot of time left for that! In spite of it, I am annoyed. I am angry at all the boys, and with this feeling I fall asleep.

Wednesday, 11 October 1944

I had an ugly dream about Mother last night. It's telling me that I should make peace with her. Even though I don't believe in dreams, in this case I do. Truly, I cannot stand this kind of state much longer. I get up quickly and there is awful news. Hradecká is going in a transport. It is awful. Again, there will be a change. Just awful! I go to Mother determined to come to terms with her, but I don't succeed. Mother scolds me for not having been to the barber, even though I try to convince her that I'll go at eleven o'clock today. It's pointing to still another conflict. It ends with my agreement to go have my haircut, and I hope that this will lead to an easy reconciliation. I come to our home and I'm told that my haircut appointment was changed to ten o'clock. I am angry at the whole world. I go to the barber, where my fears become reality. I am told to come back tomorrow. I want to scream at the whole world, but I control myself. With some trepidation, I go to Mother's. She acts strangely and wonders why I haven't had my hair cut. I am really amazed at her. I cannot control myself and we start arguing. I walk Mother to the bakery. On the way, something moves me and soon I give her a big kiss and everything is OK. We sit for a while in front of the house and then take a walk. Then I am alone. I don't worry about the transports. The rest of the day I study.

Thursday, 12 October 1944

Today the transport is departing. Unaware, I go to the Hamburg Barracks hoping to see Mangl. In the yard I see a big commotion and I spot the railroad cars. I dart upstairs and see Mangl. They are just being loaded. I'm glad I can offer last assistance. I carry his luggage down. With a little trickery, we manage to get in front. We chat for the last time. Suddenly an announcement comes: "everybody on board." Quickly we say good-bye, perhaps forever, perhaps for only a few weeks, perhaps for a few years. I don't know—nobody knows. The last look and we quickly run so that we can watch as they are being loaded into the railcars. I no longer can see Mangl. SS man Haindl is calm because he is not beating anybody. For a while I stare at the train and then I walk to the main floor where I jump through the window. I go to my mother's place, where I spend the rest of the day. I am so sad without Mangl. I hardly talk with Kalíšek—just a little bit, for old time's sake. Even then we get into an argument when he admits that he would have preferred to bunk next to Furcht. Since Furcht left in a transport, he might as well lie next to me. However, I tell him that by all means he is free to move away from me. I hope it will happen.

Friday, 13 October 1944

Tomorrow's transport looms on the horizon. The scope of the transport is immense. Everyone in the Jewish administration must register and most likely will leave in the transport. I don't feel at all sorry for them because they have never really tasted a transport before. All *Hausalter* and *Gebäudealter* [house and building chairmen] will be included. We, however, are sufficiently protected so I don't care. No news from my father though. When will it come? When?

Saturday, 14 October 1944

The transport has not been put together as yet, but everybody thinks that he is in it. I am staying longer in bed. When I get up the first summons arrives. Bäumel and Eli are the first victims and others follow: Götzlinger, Koko, Kopperl, Eckstein, Lappert. It is awful. From the whole room, only fifteen boys remain. It is outright ridiculous. In the streets all that one can see is crying. It is evident how all the Jewish higher-ups are arranging it. It is almost unbelievable that all the cooks are going, all bakers, all warehouse people, all *Hausalteste* [building supervisors or chairmen], Mr. Fleischer among them. I feel as if I were the "Last of the Mohicans" who is remaining after the storm. I don't know what they are going to do with us. It is rumored that the mixed marriages will arrive. Everything is so sad. Many people from the barracks are leaving, including Mr. Popper. The streets are so dead and empty. It is an awful state to be alone with my mother, who will soon be without friends here. Her last friend, Mrs. Fleischer, is now leaving. I can fully understand her state of mind and her problem but I cannot help her. On the contrary—I'm so upset from all the happenings that I act as a madman unaware of what he is doing. I cannot control myself. During the day I can stand it, but in the evening I am obsessed by malaise and cockiness. I really cannot call it cockiness. It is something different, something that I have never experienced before and yet it is so familiar to me. It is the Terezín madness. The impact of the circumstances affects one so much that one doesn't know what he is doing and tends to vent one's feelings to the nearest person—in my case, it is my mother, even though I love her. For example, I scold her in a vulgar manner because her dishes are dirty even though I realize that she cannot help it. This argument quiets down shortly because love toward Mother overtakes me and I calm down. Saying good-bye to her has a nasty effect on me. Again, I cannot control myself and again I take it out on my mother. At least, there is a pretext—bad [illegible word] which were not so bad after all. Later, perhaps after an hour, I calm down. I see in my mother the only friend I have. I realize that I cannot go to sleep feeling at odds with her. Therefore, I'm not ashamed to ask her to make peace and not to be angry with me. I have acted similarly five years ago, but not recently. My mother walks along with me and as we stop I confess to her. She also recognizes that my behavior is unusual. We say good-bye on good terms and now we can both go to sleep feeling better. I am very pleased.

In the afternoon, an unpleasant thing happens to me. I go for a walk with my mother under the *bašta* and I notice chestnuts falling next to us. I look around and I spot on the ramparts Jila, Kapr, and Kalíšek, who are trying to hit us. After each throw, they hide behind bushes hoping that we will not see them. In fact, Kalíšek is not throwing but laughing. I am furious! These are my so-called friends! I have lost whatever remaining faith I had in Kalíšek. I'm ready to give Jila a few smacks. I look at the *bašta*, but they are no longer there. I must wait until this evening. I will be even angrier by then. This incident, and what happened with Mother, have intensified my anger. At home, I look through a book and soon Jila arrives, coming directly toward me. I ask calmly: "Jila, what was it all about with the chestnuts?" "What chestnuts?" asks Jila innocently. I raise my voice. Jila immediately remembers and my slap wakes him up. I start fight-

ing with him. We roll over on the bed and we are fighting until he
starts to cry. As a good-bye present, I give him another slap that really
smacks. I will definitely move away from Kalíšek in the bunks. The
boys are blaming me that I did not attack Kapr (who is a taller boy),
but I'm satisfied with Jila.

Sunday, 15 October 1944

I have a good night's sleep. I feel as if I had earned the day yesterday.
Unfortunately, it is just wishful thinking. With Kalíšek I don't talk
at all and I am seriously considering moving away from him in the
room. I cannot count as a close friend a boy who has insulted my
mother. He doesn't seem to care at all. He is so without character because, as soon as Gustl Stein departed from Terezín, he immediately
found other friends, Jila and Kapr. He is with them constantly and
they walk together all the time. Really, why am I writing about them?
After tidying up, I feel as if I were in a new world. In fact, I very
proudly depart to Mother's place. I sit down and read. Then, Mother
arrives all nervous, but she is pleased that I look so well. I feel sorry
for her that she works so hard. In the morning she goes to the bakery
and in the afternoon to *Glimmer*. When I think that I don't see my
mother the whole day, I feel sad and [illegible word]. How precious
is the hour when I can be with Mother, how I am thankful for it.
The time of my departure comes and I can see how sorry Mother is.
Helpless, I head for home. I still don't know what I will be doing in
the afternoon. I think: "I will go out, perhaps something will amuse
me." I walk with my head down through the empty streets. In Terezín
it is so sad. One doesn't see anyone but the Dutch and the old and
the sick. I am mad at the whole world. And in the future I can see
only the present. I cannot help it. I think of my dad and Handa and
I feel like crying. I think of Mangl, my friend, whom I miss so much.
Because of their departure, I must go for walks by myself. Because of
it, I go to bed without being able to talk to someone warmly and in
confidence. I can see only darkness and in this darkness there is only
one bright spot and that is my mother. Still farther in the distance
something shines and that is my dad and Handa and Mangl. By a
detour, I return home. I begin to play. I cannot concentrate on studying or reading. I go to my mother's. After supper, I read for a while
and I am amazed that I am able to do it. On my return home, I hear
the same old boring tune that, however, fills everybody with anxiety. I

hear the sound of the wheels of a locomotive. The train arrives. Only the sick will be in this transport. I run upstairs and announce that perhaps it is the train. Big commotion. Nobody wants to believe me. I go to convince myself and I see that I am wrong. Nothing but darkness. I go home and again I laugh, again I frown, again I cry, and then I smile and look forward to seeing my mother tomorrow—will I? I go to bed. The home is empty. Only fifteen remaining boys are in their beds. The light stays on for a long time. Nobody orders us around. There is nobody around. Confusion.

Monday, 16 October 1944

I'm looking forward to seeing my mother. I am indifferent about the *heim*. Because there is a terrible mess in the room, I get up early and go to my mother's. I am looking forward to talking and studying. But my mother swamps me with tasks which we have to do together. I do what I am told and Mother cooks. We must take care of the transfer of suitcases to the attic in the Hannover Barracks. We enter the barracks, which are almost empty of people. This is to say, I don't consider the Dutch to be normal people, just human beings. The barracks are teeming with them. They don't tell us anything. We go to the *Wachestube* [guardhouse] to ask for information and we spot three *sichy* who are playing chess. They claim to be *Kuchenwache* [kitchen guards] and cannot help us. At last, after a long search, we find the luggage warehouse and an old German man who is repairing a suitcase (or at least he is supposed to be doing that). Everywhere is such a sleepy and dead atmosphere. We are entirely lost and we don't know what to do. In spite of it, we proceed to L404, where we encounter the same situation. No one we know, no Czechs. We find some German Jews who are supposed to help us. We return to the Hannover Barracks. I converse with the wife of a blind man. Everybody seems to be looking out only for himself and doesn't care that other people are so unhappy. And, in fact I do the same thing. I'm glad when I return home. I go to the Magdeburg Barracks for lunch when the siren starts. I quickly run home. The street is emptying out. In the distance I hear the sound of airplanes and shooting. This no longer pleases me because I shudder with the thought that Father and Handa must suffer through this, an air attack in the true sense of the word. I run into the yard to watch the German airplanes pass in the air. It has a beautiful impact on me. The air raid lasts for two hours. I go to meet

Mother. She purposely gives me jobs so I won't be bored. How nice it is of her. I return home and again there is the sound of the sirens. Again an air raid. This one doesn't last too long. I return to Mother. I take care of a few things and then sit outside on a bench entirely relaxed. I start writing my diary. I feel pleased. Finally, I can put in writing my innermost thoughts. Now I know that some things can be experienced only through misery! In the evening I study. I go back home with Beran. I tell him the contents of *The Little Lord*. At home I'm pleased with the thought that today I have accomplished and learned something. All the rest, particularly Kalíšek, can go to hell. I fall asleep. What are my father and Handa doing? Are they falling asleep the way I do? They must.

Wednesday, 18 October 1944

Yesterday, a new transport was announced. I take it very calmly. From our home the following people are summoned: Petera, [illegible name], März, Springer, and Pedro, who, however, gets out. There are only eleven of us left in the room. It gives us a feeling of emptiness. Otherwise, I am leading a life as if nothing has happened. At nine o'clock I get up. I tidy up and go to my mother's place. She is not home and therefore I study different things. I finish reading *The Little Lord*. I take care of my lunch and afterward I study again. At two o'clock, I go to meet Mother. We show our love for each other and I return home. In the afternoon I am bored as usual. I go with Mother for a walk (this doesn't always happen). I study French, which I'm starting again, when Mrs. Ascher disturbs me. Mrs. Ascher is in the transport but hasn't loaded up as yet. She asks if I can carry her luggage to the *Schleusky*. Outside it is dark and it is raining very hard. In spite of this, I set out on my journey. I load the luggage on the cart, but as soon as we start moving it all falls down on the wet ground. Nevertheless, we manage to get the luggage to the *Schleusky* and I return. I repeat the same journey before returning home. The train is just arriving. Upon my return, I play my usual game of *sprtec*. I go to bed and soon fall asleep. Days like these really don't do me any harm. On the contrary, they benefit me but I don't think I can take them for very long. Let's see!

~

The following days are dreadful—perhaps the worst of my life. I feel so awful, so alone that I would like to scream at everything. Yes, at everything. Whatever I do bores me and whatever I do is wrong. I see in front of me today's transport. Again I watch helplessly as Beran leaves me. Now I am really alone. Entirely alone. With Beran, we used to chat about speeches and we would forget about the present. But now? With Mother, it's no longer bearable. She is awfully nervous and she swears and I swear back at her. This tends to repeat itself and it will repeat itself until we return home to Prague. I will no longer write. I would prefer to end everything. I have lost the desire for life, the desire for work, the desire to love, the desire to do anything that the mind of a boy can love. I don't know what else to say. Perhaps it is weakness or hate or loneliness which is the cause of it all. Nobody understands me, not even my own mother. Again I'm ending this volume of my diary which has witnessed the worst things. I hope that the next volume will not have such a tragic ending. Now I only wish for the transports to end and for me to find a boy in whom I could trust!

One who hopes will win!!!

[End of Volume 5: PW.]

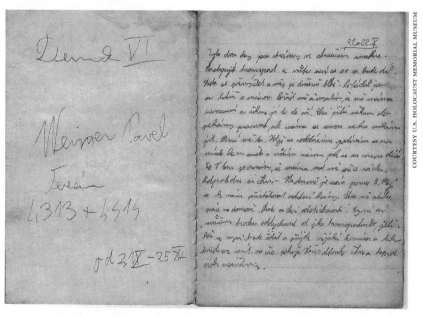

Title page of the sixth notebook, covering the period from October 21 to November 25, 1944

Pavel specified the buildings in which he was quartered during that time: "Diary VI. Weiner Pavel. Terezín. L313 + L414."

Volume 6

[Saturday and Sunday], 21 and 22 October 1944

These two days are spent in a tremendous turmoil. The transport is being loaded and nobody knows what is going to happen. One cannot think and I feel mentally miserable. To be specific, I had another argument with my mother. I keep thinking that my mother doesn't understand me and I tell her this face to face. I want to go to work in the bakery but my mother will not allow me. I feel bad about it. When we say good-bye to each other, I notice her looking back at me. I realize then that perhaps my mother still likes me. In the afternoon I read.

There are now only eight of us left in our *heim*. Some others are supposed to move in. The work in our room annoys me. It is for this reason that I would like to move. Now we can breathe a bit easier since the transports are gone. It is rumored that we will have to do some housekeeping because some kind of a commission will arrive. So, we will live in peace for a while. In the evening, I read for a while and only then I fall asleep.

Everything is now over. A tremendous wave of sorrow has engulfed me and we have not been even touched directly. Yet, when I look into the street and don't see anybody but strange faces, I feel sad. For selfish reasons, I don't see any comfort or pleasure from the end of the transports. Nothing pleases me and I doubt that anything ever will. Everything is temporary and so is joy. These times are really not very interesting and I would like to forget them, but I can't. Nothing is still something. Something that weighs so heavily upon us.

Monday, 23 October 1944

Everything is being cleaned up, which does not please me very much. Different boys have moved into our room and they are small and dumb. This is, then, all that is left from the once famous room of the

Nešarim. I want very much to move out and go to work somewhere. We clean out the warehouse, where we find a library. Immediately, we take it over and in a basket we carry the books to our room. A feeling of joy comes over me, but soon it no longer amuses me. Everything bothers me and I leave for my mother's place. We agree that my mother will inquire at L405 if I could work there. Again, the same temporary feeling of joy overcomes me, but it soon leaves me and again I'm alone. Even my studies no longer please me. I am utterly bored and I can read only detective stories, nothing else. I'm negating my resolve to not talk to Kalíšek. I am realizing again that I need someone with whom I can go for a walk and talk. In a state of confusion, I run away to L313 leaving everything to fate, and I go for a walk.

Today the transport departs. We look for a while at the train and at the last preparations by the poor souls. We agree that we will help each other to look for work. In the evening, I lie down and want to read. It is 8:30 and we are supposed to go to a meeting of trustees. I have attended it several times before, but today I don't want to go. Then our new *Jugendleiter* comes and says that I must go to the meeting. I respond that I don't know why I should go, and I refuse. He says that I have to go there, but I stand pat and so does he. He tries to carry me there in his arms, but I manage to get out and lie down on my bed. Everybody laughs at him because he wants to fight with me, and I start to cry. Then, suddenly somebody comes with the news that the meeting has been attended already for half an hour by one of our boys. We all start to laugh and the *Jugendleiter* is teed off and wants me to go to the meeting anyway. I refuse. We agree that I will have house arrest for two days. I can stay in bed because I know I will not have to stick to it. Then, as I read quietly, the *Jugendleiter* comes to me and says that he forgives me. I expected it. I read and then I fall asleep.

Tuesday, 24 October 1944

In the morning, we have to again clean up. It is a real Potemkin village.[136] Everything on the surface. We made a mistake thinking that the transports are over. On Saturday, another will take place. Well, we'll see. I get into an argument with my mother. To be specific, I'm mad that I cannot go to work at L405. My mother is so strange. I

136. Pavel refers here to the myth that Russian minister Grigory Potyomkin ordered the construction of fake (hollow) settlements in Crimea to impress Empress Catherine II when she visited in 1787. The term "Potemkin village" has come to mean a misleading façade to hide a miserable situation.

really don't know what to think about all this. Perhaps nothing. With a feeling of nothingness, I fall asleep.

Wednesday, 25 October 1944

I make up with Mother. In the morning I go for a walk with Kalíšek. Each of us steals a head of cabbage. I would not normally do it, but now I will. After all, it is common property and therefore I don't care. In the afternoon I'm already looking forward to going with my mother to see Mr. Rössler.[137] This is a good reason to make up. I don't know what gets into my mother, but she doesn't want to go to Mr. Rössler but rather to Mr. Bergmann. By chance, we run into him in the corridor. He responds favorably to our request, namely, that he will put me somewhere, perhaps into the bakery. I am very happy. In just a minute, a letter of recommendation is written and we hurry to the White Bakery. The content of the letter is as follows: "To Mr. Altman, take Pavel Weiner among your youngsters." It really is not a request, but rather an order. I have a 99 percent chance of being accepted. We soon reach Mr. Altman. He reads the letter and says: "Gemacht [Done]." So, I became a baker. On the way, my mother says to be honest. I am very glad and I feel as if I'm in a new world. Everybody admires me with some sarcasm. I fall asleep with a feeling that now a new era is beginning: I will work productively and I will recognize what is work and what is rest. I'm looking forward to it, I'm looking very forward.

Thursday, 26 October 1944

I don't feel like doing anything right now. Everything is so sleepy, but tomorrow's transport will wake us up for sure from this sleepiness. It is noon. I can't wait to see my mother; that is, I can't wait to go to work. The entire morning I am excited about my work. Mother accompanies me all the way to the door. Then we say good-bye—she goes home and I go to work!! I enter the hall. Nothing. Nobody seems to notice me. I report to Altman. He hardly looks at me and tells me to change my clothes. Soon, I'm ready with a baker's cap that really doesn't fit me well and I must look very funny. I walk into the room

137. Josef Rössler (b. January 28, 1896) and his wife, Anna (b. June 10, 1909), were friends with the Weiner family. Josef was deported to Terezín with one of the first transports, on December 4, 1941, and put in charge of the *Materiallager*. Anna was assigned number 24 on transport AAt from Prague on July 23, 1942. The couple remained in Terezín and survived to be liberated there.

where they are making *buchty*. I stand there for a while and I don't know where to start. Finally I dare to ask one woman what I should do. Slowly everything sinks in. Špulka is there also. I feel bashful, like an apprentice. I'm supposed to carry trays to some kind of stand. I am embarrassed when I cannot reach the top shelf. Later on, I realize that I worried needlessly. Everybody behaves very politely toward me. I make yeast. This amuses me. I place the *buchty* into the oven. And later on I clean up. Slowly I'm getting used to my work and I start liking it. It is strenuous and awfully hot but I don't care. Time passes by quickly, and I am not hungry. I go to fetch coffee for everyone. On the way I meet Kalíšek, who announces that he was called into the transport. Another friend is gone. However, my thoughts are in the bakery. I steal two *buchty*. One I eat and the other I hide. In the afternoon we make three orders of dough. It really is not too hard. At nine o'clock, we have to go home. I receive a ration of one more *buchta*. I shower and get dressed. After cleaning up, we say good night and set out into the darkness. I have a feeling of a working man who goes home to rest. I feel very important! On the way home, I think about my experiences. I want to show my mother my earnings, but when I arrive there everything is in darkness and Mother is asleep. I put down the *buchty* on the table and hurry home. No lights are allowed. I shoot the breeze for a while and then I crawl on my bed and with good feelings, I fall asleep. I think it is because of my work!

Friday, 27 October 1944

When I wake up, I see my mother in front of me. Her first words are that four boys are in the transport. I find out that Hermann is one of them. In the morning, I wait eagerly for my afternoon work. Today, my work goes even better, even though I get scolded while carrying the trays of cookies. We get a ration of several *buchty* and *geback*. At eight o'clock I return home. I still have a little time to read. Today the transport was loaded. It consisted of both young and old people. The rest of my friends are leaving. I feel so sad, without anything and with no word about my father. I am writing about this day five days later so I'm not describing the events in much detail even though they are important.

Saturday, 28 October 1944

Today is supposed to be the famous 28 October [Czechoslovak Independence Day], the day meant to be celebrated, but instead it is so ugly. Rainy weather and in Terezín one sees only crying and sadness. The transport is leaving. Again, a little spark of a big flame is gone. Where to? Nobody knows.

Monday, 30 October 1944

Yesterday, I agreed to work the morning shift. I got an alarm clock and I set it to 5:30 a.m. During the night I kept waking up because of bad blackout and also because I'm excited lest I oversleep. Finally, I get up and get dressed. Outside it's raining and dark. Still, I step out bravely and soon I'm in the bakery. I get dressed and I start working right away. The whole morning we are making salty cookies, gingerbread, and *buchty*. I still do only lowly work such as carrying trays, cleaning the machine, and carrying water. I get along well with the German boy. I keep worrying that he will think I am awkward. Partly he's right. On principle I don't steal, even though I have the opportunity to do so. Finally, I receive a ration consisting of two *buchty*, two salty *geback* and pumpernickel. Proudly, I bring it all to my mother. For the time being I have no feeling of guilt. At my mother's, I explain to her my stealing rationally and with some levity. Only then, my weariness hits me even though I maintain good spirits. I make fun of my mother, often to excess. The whole evening I am in very good spirits. The drawback of working in the bakery is that I don't have time for studies and for writing my diary. In all, I neglect too many things. In the evening, my mother and I go visiting. Wherever we come, wherever we go, we don't find anybody, everybody is gone. We go to see the Horwitzes and Mrs. Bergmann. All are gone. It's dreadful. In the evening, I have to go to bed early because I have to get up at six o'clock.

Tuesday, 31 October 1944

I wake up at four o'clock and I have a headache. Soon, however, I fall asleep again. The ringing of the alarm clock wakes me up, which tells me it is five o'clock and I must get up. Again outside it's dark and raining. I feel dizzy and not well. I didn't get enough sleep. I arrive at the bakery and I have to fetch coffee. I don't feel like doing it, but I have to. Then I change my clothes and again with the German boy, whom I like, we take care of all tasks.

In the afternoon, we make five trips carrying coal from the basement, which is quite heavy work. Otherwise, the work is not difficult but to be there eight hours is quite demanding. While we are making

buchty I try to *schlojs,* or to "appropriate," some *buchty.* The first time it
is difficult and obviously I don't know how to do it, but soon I learn.
I feel ashamed. I keep trying and still I am not doing it well. I hear
them talking about me as being a typical Jew. I would like to say something to them, but I don't. The whole time we don't do anything,
only sit near the oven and occasionally we add fuel. The time passes
by slowly. At long last they come to relieve us and we can go home.
I stole two *buchty* and two *geback.* Very proudly, I carry them home. I
sleep for an hour. I don't feel well, but I don't let on. In the evening I
try to write my diary, but it doesn't go well. I go home to lie down, but
I cannot fall asleep until quarter to ten. We are supposed to be moving very shortly to L419. It occurs to me that perhaps I should move
to my mother's. Perhaps it would be better.

NOVEMBER
Wednesday, 1 November 1944

I already feel better about having to get up at five o'clock in the morning. The bakery is still locked up and I have to wait for Czapla[138] with
the keys. I will try now to describe life in this bakery—the description is based on my thinking and my impressions. The whole bakery
consists of four or five rooms. Right at the entrance is a room with
the oven. It holds about thirty-six trays and it is fired with coal. Sometimes I stoke the oven. In the room there is also a table and a shelf
for the trays and for the big pots. Also, the oven is always hot. From
there, one goes to the office where Czapla sits, formerly a fireman but
now the boss. He is quite nice, but he does not really run the bakery
well. His fault is that he speaks German with a Hamburg dialect so
that I cannot understand him very well. From the office there are
doors into the warehouse, which is always full. Today I turned the
buchty over and I could *schlojs* but I didn't. From the room where the
oven is one can also go to the workroom where everything is being
made. Inside is a big table at which the women work. Also inside
is a machine to which dough is added. A movable lever divides the
dough into thirty equal pieces that are then thrown on the table. For
me, the machine is somewhat of a mystery into which I threw a piece
of dough only once, but I was called off immediately. The pieces of

138. The head of the bakery, Bruno Czapla (b. January 24, 1922) was deported from
Hamburg, Germany, with transport VI/3 (his number: 5) on February 26, 1943. He remained in Terezín and survived.

dough are thrown onto the table where they are put into forms of either gingerbread, *buchty*, or into various shaped cookies. [Shapes of cookies are shown on page 6–14 {i.e., page 14 of volume 6} in the original: PW.] I am content with carrying the finished trays onto the appropriate shelves. At the end of my work, I always clean up the machine or scrape the dough. From the room where the oven is one can also go into the bathroom, where there is water and a dressing room. This is a literal description [diagram of the bakery is shown on page 6–15 {i.e., page 15 of volume 6} of the original: PW]. Now about the work: the first thing I do is to look whether the reservoirs are filled with water and I go to fetch more water. We carry coal from the basement and put on the fire in the oven and in the stove. We must make sure that all the pots are filled. Then we make margarine-spreaded toasts. Then, for about three hours, we don't do anything while the dough is being prepared and allowed to rise. During this period, I sometimes carry trays or do errands. The work is somewhat repetitive. When my work is finished, I take a shower. I always become nervous about what I should steal. This is just a short description of my life in the bakery.

Cookie shapes

November 1, 1944: Pavel recorded the cookie shapes, perhaps reflecting the importance of food.

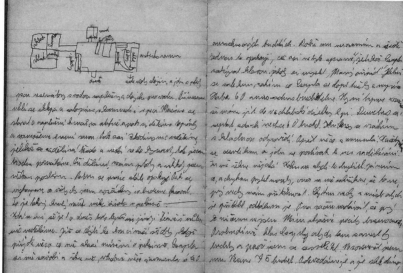

November 1, 1944: Layout of the bakery in which Pavel worked

It seems that today it is better than at other times. We do hardly anything. It is coming close to the end of the shift when something happens which spoils my opinion about the bakery. Czapla calls me and says (actually whispers): "sixty off-quality *buchty*." I don't understand him well and I repeat it, which probably was not correct because Czapla nods his head as if he thought: "Hopeless case." I become scared while Czapla grabs a pencil and writes in German that sixty off-quality *buchty* were produced. Now I finally understand that I'm supposed to go to the Vrchlabske Dietary Kitchen to ask Mrs. Deweles if she wants sixty *buchty*. I soon return with a positive answer. Again, he mumbles something. At any rate, I change and go to see what the dough is doing. Suddenly, someone by the name of Mrs. Kohn calls me and tells me to move. I don't know why and I grab a sack of flour. She starts screaming that this is not it, that I should bring the trough. I grab the trough and, instead of bringing it to her, I move it away. She starts scolding me that I'm good for nothing. I have an awful feeling of uselessness. I hear Czapla telling me to bring the *buchty* and asking why I have changed my clothes. I don't understand him. I carry and deliver the seventy-five *buchty*. They find out that there are only seventy-four. This is really bad luck. Czapla, however, doesn't say anything.

It is being rumored that kids under sixteen years of age will be thrown out of the bakery. I would be ashamed in front of others. My mood is completely spoiled and I don't say a thing. I don't even wash up, I only get a ration of three *buchty*. I feel that I am a mess and dirty. At my mother's, I hardly say a word and Mother immediately senses that something has gone wrong. I feel awfully tired. I also feel that this will be my last day in the bakery. In the evening I go to bed late because we talk about the boys who have left. Tomorrow, I'm supposed to move to L419 and therefore I put some of my things together.[139] In an awful mental turmoil, I fall asleep.

Thursday, 2 November 1944

Outside it is unpleasantly cold. Everything looks so gloomy and lonely. The yellow leaves lying in long rows in the streets only make a child whose beloved have left even sadder. I don't even realize that it is the end of the transports and those who have left are forever separated from us or at least for the time that we will be in Terezín. When I am happy, I only have to remember St. Wenceslaus Day[140] [September 28, the day of the transport: PW] and immediately I become quiet. When will the time come when I can see my father and Handa again? I don't know whether anybody in this wide world of ours knows it. This consoles me a little.

In the morning, I continue packing my stuff. I go to the railroad station to get a cart. I load my possessions and I am moving to a building where there are only boys I don't know who speak different languages. I am already getting accustomed to this life, so I don't care anymore. I don't care that I don't have a spot to sleep picked out—it really doesn't matter. It will end somehow, yes or no? I am becoming an egotist. I care only about *my* luggage. I beat only *my* mattress and so on. I come to the hall but before that I have to go through some kind of a vestibule. The room is rather large and the black bunks don't appear nice. The walls are all cracked and there are no light bulbs. Dirt is everywhere. I look around for a while to find a spot that would best suit me. Finally I conclude that a spot in the single block appears to be most suitable.

[Plan of the room and the vestibule shown in the original: PW.]

139. With so few children, *madrichim,* and *Betreueren* (child care workers) left in Terezín after the fall 1944 deportations, the children's homes were consolidated.

140. Wenceslaus I, duke of Bohemia from 921 until his murder in 935, was canonized after his death and revered as the patron saint of the Czech people.

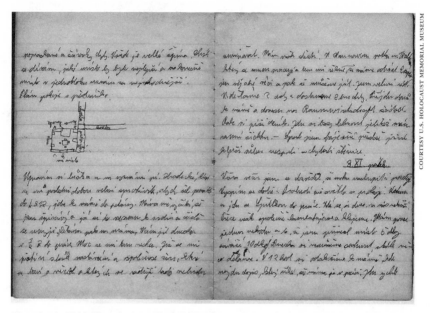

November 2, 1944: Plan of room and vestibule

I make up my bed and Mrs. Hradecká, who is lately obnoxious to me, asks me to help out at L313. Instead, I go to see my mother in the bakery. My mother keeps blaming me that I'm dirty and I take it to heart and wash up. I then wait for my mother. I'm supposed to go to work at 1:30. I don't feel like it very much. I tend to get into arguments there. The women in the bakery talk about things which I would rather not mention here. However, I'm lucky. At the Hannover Barracks I meet Walter, who works with me, and he tells me that we have to do just a few things for Czapla and then we will be dismissed. I am very pleased. We make two trips and get two *buchty*. I arrive home to my mother and bring a petition to the *Raumwirtschaft*. Then I write my diary. I go to bed because I have a morning shift. I sleep well even though other boys don't sleep at all. They are too busy catching bedbugs.

Friday, 3 November 1944

Last night, I found out that I can start working later. I sleep very well. The light in the room wakes me up and I go to work with Špulka. It appears that today we will not be scolded. Still we complain and gossip. I have only one mishap and that is that I brought only 5 dkg of *zavari* [??] instead of 10 dkg. Today we are not allowed to sit down; we are always doing something. At noon I run off to Mother's place, where I find a note saying that she is at work. I return quickly. The boys bring me a full pot of goulash, which we divide up. Then, I tend to the coals. We can already see that we will be working longer. First misfortune: three buns got "lost" in the warehouse and Špulka and Beni stole them (nobody, of course, knows this). Czapla is furious and this is not very pleasant. Second misfortune: we already have two containers filled when Czapla notices that some dough is missing. As a result, all the buns must come out and Czapla becomes more furious. It is already 2:30 and my head is spinning. I am looking forward to going home. At last I can go. I take a bath and then we go for our rations. I can't believe my eyes—for nine hours of work, only two *buchty*! I am awfully angry. Out of spite, I eat both *buchty* right away. After I confess to my mother that I have eaten them, I feel better. In the afternoon I'm very tired and I have an argument with Mother. But soon everything is made up. At home, there is some kind of meeting that is supposed to start our new life. I don't know what this is all about. I change my linen and, feeling clean, I read for a while and then fall asleep with healthy dreams.

Monday, 6 November 1944

In L419, it really isn't so bad. This morning I wake up late. Last night I wanted to steal some potatoes, but instead I found a little kitten. I took it home and played with it. I found out to whom it belonged and early this morning I intend to return it. But first I want to show it to my mother. On the way there, the kitten pees on me and therefore I quickly go and take a bath. I leave the kitten with Majošek. On the way I meet Špulka, who is stealing potatoes, and I join him. We watch the *Ghettowache* until they are safely far away and we crawl with the suitcase onto the railroad car. We are disturbed by the presence of *sichy*, who undoubtedly will attract the attention of the *Ghettowache*. Our suitcase is already filled when Špulka screams out: "Watch out!" I want to close the suitcase but unfortunately it falls down and all the potatoes spill out. The bloodthirsty *sichy* swarm over us and I escape from the guards, saving only a few potatoes. This is how my big *schlojs* of potatoes turned out! But I am gripped with the desire to *schlojs* some more. In the afternoon, I go to the bakery early because hamburgers are being made, which means good "earnings." Right in the beginning, Beni gives me one and then Walter gives me another one. Then we receive a ration of two more. Everything is festive and everybody is in a good mood. I'm helping out and I not only carry trays but also wheedle and grease the hamburgers. Today is the first time (except for my first day) that I really enjoy the bakery. I take some more while the hamburgers are being cooked. When I am finished, I tell the boys to go and take a shower. I get three hamburgers from Mr. Furth and then I get four additional ones. The full count is eleven hamburgers, which I bring home, and eight, which I have already eaten. I have a wonderful feeling which I always have whenever I feel like a boy who earns his way. However, one thing bothers me after eating two additional hamburgers which I found on a plate at home and which I split with Špulka. Walking in the street I realize they probably belonged to some woman who wanted them as much as I did. I worry about it even before I go to sleep. Nevertheless, sleepiness overtakes.

Thursday, 9 November 1944

I'm already getting used to the present. Only when I think about it, I'm getting disgusted. I go to work, which I don't enjoy. Various insults thrown at us get me very angry. I don't enjoy writing the diary. It is evident from the missed days. In the afternoon, I occasionally study but mathematics doesn't agree with me. Last night, I was summoned to go for chestnuts. I can see it is a step toward being fired. I am rather indifferent to it so that I can sleep easily and I think that it will turn out somehow. It is the truth. In the morning I wake up and decide to go to Czapla and to the bakery with the boys. I arrive and various things are already in progress. I find out that four boys from Spedice are allowed to stay, but we have to go gather chestnuts. On the way I meet Kapr, who tells me that he is not going to gather chestnuts. I quickly tell it to Špulka and we both run to work. They welcome us coolly and order us and another boy to go to the cellar to sort out coal from the coal dust. It is a narrow cellar chock full with coal. We consider it impossible to work for three hours in such dreadful dust. We are told that if we don't do good work we will not get our ration, and that we have only until 1:30 to do this work. Indeed, we are good enough to do this kind of work for them! We spit black saliva and we look like Negroes. We go upstairs to get some fresh air into our lungs.

However, the work does not go on and it cannot go on because we no longer have the strength to lift the shovel. The last hour we spend swearing and complaining. We decide that we will cover one pile with dust and another pile with coal. It is approved and we are allowed to get washed up. We are still dirty, but we don't care. We really worked hard this morning and they are not even ashamed to give us only two *buchty* as our ration. We are dreadfully angry. I feel like stealing some potatoes. The railroad cars are full of them. When I return home I ask Akim whether he would like to go with me to get some potatoes. He says that he would and we go. Fearlessly, I crawl on top of the railroad car and throw potatoes down. Aki doesn't even have time to pick them up but the *sichy* help him, albeit placing them into their own pockets. One old man, when I won't give him potatoes, wants to report us and therefore we have to crawl down. We repeat this maneuver once more. Then a *Getak* notices us and we have to hide in an alcove. These days are filled with many adventures; however they do not fill my knapsack. This time I get all excited. The boys help me out and we soon have our knapsack full. It all lasts only one hour. It is not even worth it. I hurriedly go to my mother's. I can't wait to steal potatoes with my mother. She is very afraid and therefore she does not help me. I'm furious! I tell my mother off so badly that even I am amazed. I am determined to steal something. So I go very nonchalantly past one of the cars. I look into it and I see that it is filled with potatoes. I am caught with a frenzy to steal! I climb on top of the car and very calmly I fill up completely my knapsack. I do this maneuver three times. After the third trip, I take one more [illegible word]. I am immediately in a better mood and so is Mother. Soon, I say goodbye to my mother and go home. I read and then I fall asleep.

Saturday, 11 November 1944

Today is a famous anniversary. A year ago today we were in the meadow.[141] So, another year has gone by and we are still stuck in Terezín. Really, I wouldn't have thought so!

---

141. Pavel refers here to the census of November 1943. The day after the Germans arrested Jakob Edelstein, they ordered the entire ghetto population, some forty thousand people, to assemble in a field outside the walls. Surrounded by armed Czech police and SS men with machine guns, the inmates stood, forbidden to break ranks. Numerous attempts to count them ended in failure. The prisoners were allowed to return to barracks near midnight; several hundred elderly and ill people died that day.

I'm in a hurry to be on time at my work. While I'm leaving I have mixed, strange feelings. I don't enjoy my work at all. They are making a servant out of me. For example, once when I went for lunch I had to stand in line for half an hour and with my bad luck my serving dish fell into a mud puddle. It is also apparent that Czapla doesn't like me. First, he tells me to go to pick up something and then he mumbles about my awkwardness and calls somebody else. Even though I'm trying to be pleasant to everybody, I am not succeeding. An unpleasant episode occurs to me with *particka* [?]:—I see that there is some goulash in my serving dish and I empty it onto my plate. Mrs. Fantová then asks me who has done it, as it was her goulash. She blames me for borrowing things from her. I feel very bad about it. I'm also upset that Ruza had given me less goulash than to anybody else. Otherwise, everybody is nice to me except for Czapla. I stay only for a short while at my mother's now. I hardly see her. I'm already very tired when I leave work at five o'clock. We get two *gebacks* and two *buchty* as a bonus today. I am looking forward to going to sleep. At my mother's, I eat and quickly go home. I think about my father and Handa in the evenings when I don't see anybody. In the evenings, everything is dark and I don't see anything but darkness. It makes me feel better and teary-eyed at the same time. When I return home, I get into a better mood. I read and then I fall asleep.

Sunday, 12 November 1944

At seven o'clock I go to work. I can see that I did a stupid thing by going to Ruza for potatoes. Today the whole bakery wants me to do it for them. I find excuses that I don't feel like doing it. This makes me unpopular. During the shift an interesting event takes place. Czapla tells me to bring him wood shavings. First I have to fill up the pots and then bring them inside. Czapla thinks it takes me too long and sarcastically asks me what my father's profession was. He tells me that I am sleepy. I feel very annoyed. However, I take it all in. I am summoned to go to *Jugendfuersorge* because I did not report to pick chestnuts. I can feel that something stinks. The whole *Jugendfuersorge* is obnoxious to me, especially the leader, Frau von Stengel. Based on past experience, I can see that we will be let go. They will not allow us to work. I go to tell my mother, who is not pleased to hear it, but I don't care much. I expect that there will be a decision tomorrow. I return to work. I get annoyed by several sarcastic comments. I work without any enthusiasm which becomes obvious. But it's nothing serious.

I work until five o'clock. Again, I'm dreadfully tired and look forward to going to bed. At home something special happens—yesterday, four boys from L218 moved over to our home. Somehow today two of them have gotten into an argument with Willy.[142] I arrive just as the situation becomes very grave. A big fight starts, which Willy loses. We are all tremendously overjoyed.

I'm on very good terms now with Hradecká. We get along well and she always gives me advice. I feel very blue though on account of my birthday being tomorrow. I have a premonition that something will happen.

"My Birthday"—Monday, 13 November 1944

It is always the dumbest thing to be congratulated on one's birthday. I get up nervously. Finally, I am at my mother's. I can already see her preparing gifts and it seems that she has not finished yet. My mother throws herself at me crying and I watch her calmly on the surface. Inside, however, I feel lousy. I have my eyes on the presents. First I spot a large *bábovka,* a plate of vegetables from the Roubíčeks, a small bag of candy, and little *kuličky* [candy balls]. I regret that I did not get any practical things. However, I'm satisfied. My mother promises that she will make it up to me. Now I recognize for the first time what really my mother means to me. I am already thirteen years old. It sounds so strange. How vividly I remember Handa's Bar Mitzvah in Prague. What a festive and joyous occasion it was and how I looked at him with deference. However, I am still a child of Terezín, just a child, who is in Terezín.

> Perhaps a day will arrive
> When the farmer returns to his work
> When again everyone will return
> When a dream returns to the child
> I am thirteen years old, I can be called a man
> The time has come when one's life must change a little
> However humanity will win
> The fourteenth year will be a merry one.

---

142. Possibly Willy Groag, who had been the *madrich* of L410, a Czech girls' *heim.*

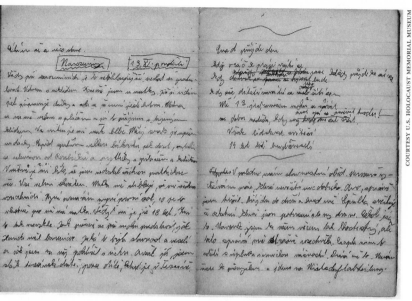

Poem written by Pavel on his thirteenth birthday, November 13, 1944

At noon, I have a festive lunch. I nervously wait for the work to finish and I feel something ominous is about to happen. Yes, my fears were justified. I enter and immediately Špulka announces that all boys can stay, but he and I must leave. I expected it. On the surface I am indifferent to all these things, but his news has made me terribly jittery. Czapla gives us this news with sarcastic seriousness. I feel insulted. I don't have time to think about it and we go to the *Wirtschaftabteilung* [business department]. The fact that I will not work in the bakery doesn't bother me much. But it's the principle that's disquieting. It looks as if it were my fault that I was let go. In the Magdeburg Barracks we find out that we will no longer be allowed to enter the bakery. We are offered jobs in the *Materialverwaltung*. I feel ashamed in front of others. We work without any enthusiasm. Both Špulka and I are angry at Czapla, whose fault it is. He looks for pretexts such as my sitting on the table. At five o'clock there is a crisis. Czapla starts a long speech saying that we have been behaving badly, that all the women have been complaining how badly we have worked. He makes many false accusations. However, when I think about it calmly, he is right that we goofed it all up. I'm curious what my mother will say to all this. It reminds me of stairs descending into a tomb. However, anger and helplessness dominate my feelings. My main worry is about my future. This is the real problem: I am not suited for a trade and yet

I have to go to work. How will I go about it? The answer must come from my mother's mouth. We get a ration of five hamburgers today. I dare to *schlojs* one more. I don't know why. Upon my return home I am very mad so I eat all the hamburgers, potatoes, candy, apple, pear, milk, and water. Thus, my helpless anger is somewhat calmed down. But it is replaced by a different feeling, namely pity. So this is how my celebrated thirteenth birthday/Bar Mitzvah has turned out! What will the next year bring? Now I know what it is to celebrate a birthday only with my beloved mother, without my father, and without Handa.

[The following page there is an illustration: PW.]

COURTESY U.S. HOLOCAUST MEMORIAL MUSEUM

November 13, 1944: Pavel's drawing of a vase with flowers in honor of his thirteenth birthday

Tuesday, 14 November 1944

This day reminds me of a child who stands in the middle of a maze and doesn't know which way to go. I am confronted with a very difficult question, namely how to get work. I am very unhappy and I ask everybody for advice. Several jobs come to mind. For example, *Ordinance* [messenger boy] but this seems too demeaning. Then perhaps there is *Hausdienst* [house duty], which is not great either. And so I stand there and don't know what to do. Today I don't go anywhere and I tidy up my room and then I read. I'm ashamed to go to my mother. In vain I strain my brain over how to go about it. Finally at two o'clock I go to lunch and then directly to my mother's.

I am curious how it will turn out with my mother and it turns out differently from what I had imagined. My mother, when she finds out, immediately concludes that everything is my fault. I defend myself in vain. At last, we make up. We go to the Magdeburg Barracks. It would suit me fine if I didn't have to work at all. At the *Arbeitszentrale* [central employment office] there is nobody in and therefore we go to ask at *Wirtschaftabteilung*. We are determined to meet Mr. Rössler with the hope that he will accept me at the *Materiallager*. We go there and right in the door we spot the man we are looking for: Mr. Rössler. He listens to us and he agrees that I can work there. I am glad, very glad, that I have found work so soon! Everybody is kind to me. Then, I go with my mother for a walk. In the evening, I boast everywhere that I have already found work.

I have a feeling of joy because all has turned out so well.

Wednesday, 15 November 1944

With strange feelings I set out at eight o'clock in the morning to go to the *Zentrallager* [main warehouse]. Right at the door I spot Mr. Rössler. I report to him and he immediately takes me to the warehouse and tells me to rewrap a bundle of papers. I can see that it will not be too bad here. Everybody is very kind. I'm trying to have a better beginning here than in the bakery. Slowly I familiarize myself with my surroundings. In addition to Mr. Rössler there are two other men: a *sicha* and a Dutchman. Definitely this place will not be all fun! The first room is an office, the second room is a warehouse, and the remaining six are also warehouses. Inside there is an unbelievable variety of things ranging from matches to electric machinery. All around are cases and bundles. I can see that it will be interesting here and that something good will come out of it. That's very important. I occupy myself by carrying packages of soap powder to the end of the warehouse where all the things are sorted out. There are the following sections: plumbing and heating, cleansing products, office supplies (paper, etc.), cooking utensils, and iron. I crawl into all corners so that I get oriented and know where everything is. Slowly I get accustomed to my new environment. Before I realize it, it is eleven o'clock and I can leave. I go for lunch.

In the morning there were four air raids. I hardly have time to talk with Mother because I have to return to work. In the afternoon, the work is the same. I work until five o'clock. I am reading a very interesting book entitled *Vyzvedac* [*The Spy*] by J. F. [James Fenimore] Cooper. In the evening, I read until eleven o'clock under a night lamp.

Thursday, 16 November 1944

I go to work more lightheartedly today. Everybody is praising me that I work so well. This gives me more appetite for my work. First, I go for coal with some old man. Then we rest, and I ask that old man what his name is. His name is Van der Zyl. It is a funny name! Afterward I carry broomsticks and the brooms themselves to the top floor. I finish at 11:30 and I can work on something else. In the *Lager* [warehouse] everyone is very nice to me and I even like the work better than in the bakery because I see that I'm needed. I can go home for lunch. At home I realize that I didn't get enough sleep. I hardly exchange a word with my mother because I have to return to work. This afternoon, I work very hard. On a little cart, we are moving big containers from one warehouse to another. We are cleaning out one warehouse so that there will be enough space for storing goods that are expected to be delivered. I'm doing acrobatic feats on the crates that we are straightening out. I work until 5:30. As the opportunity arises, I "take" (I should not call it "steal") several reams of paper that can be used as toilet paper. At Mother's, I have dinner and at eight o'clock I return home. I go to bed very soon thereafter.

[Layout of the main warehouse is shown on
the next two pages of the original: PW.]

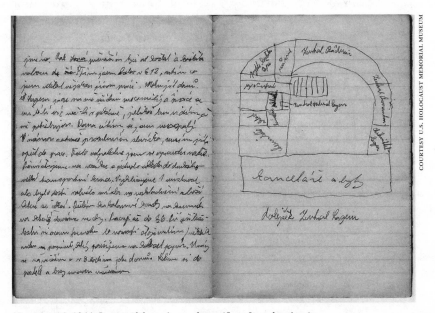

November 16, 1944: Layout of the main warehouse (first of two drawings)

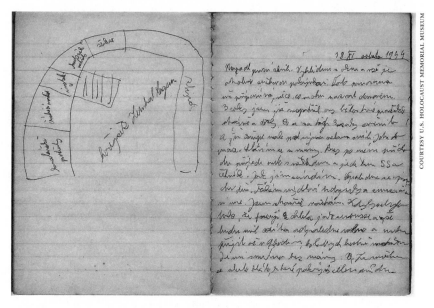

November 16, 1944: Layout of the main warehouse (second of two drawings)

Saturday, 18 November 1944

We have our first snowfall today! I look out the window and everything is covered with snow. This panorama reminds me of something which I could call homeland. For three years I have not seen the white hills and [illegible word] of Prague. I wonder what has changed in those three years! I hear the snow crunch under my feet. I go to work, but first I stop at my mother's. At work an SS man and a gendarme bring in a truckload. How I envy them. In the afternoon I really work hard. I pull cases of soap and [illegible words]. It would have made me very angry if it were not for the extra half a loaf of bread I receive and for permission to start work at nine o'clock tomorrow with the afternoon off. I'm sad without Mother. The snow has turned into mud which is all over the ground. I'm so sad that I feel like crying.

Saturday, 25 November 1944

I don't feel like doing a thing. For seven days I haven't written my diary. I would prefer to quit writing forever. By chance many interesting things did happen in these last seven days. I was sick but nothing serious. I continued going to work. I had an argument with Hradecká. There are great changes in our room. For example, common meals, etc. We get a ration of [illegible words]. I go to the *Arbeitszentrale* for confirmation. But what is of most interest this week? It's my mother. During my sickness, I loved my mother. She appeared to me as an angel of goodness. We are supposed to move together. We frantically search for a place to stay, but we cannot find anything. How can people be so indifferent? One evening I feel so sad and I would be so pleased if I could live with my mother. Now I'm giving up all hope that we will find a room. And there is another reason why it is impossible to live together—we have another argument. It was a horrible argument for which I must be blamed. It started yesterday when my mother couldn't understand something and I started to give her hell. Today I do everything to spite her and to make fun of her. While peeling potatoes she grabs her head and lies down on the bed. I don't know what to do and I am afraid that she will faint. When I see that it is nothing serious, I regain my calm, but the incident still leaves an impression on me. I fear that my mother could harm herself. It is a thought that is ridiculous and sad at the same time. My fear intensifies when Mother wants to take all her photographs with her. I feel that I have to step in. I walk my mother home and I change the conversation to another topic. I succeed and manage to forget somewhat the incident. When saying good-bye, I give my mother a kiss. I hope that this will do.

END of VOLUME 6

Volume 7

Thursday, 30 November 1944

These days are marked both with pleasure and sorrow. I don't know which prevails. I am starting to realize that the work in Terezín does me good. It doesn't matter what type it is, but rather whether I am courageous and able to overcome the first hurdles. Right now, I am in the second half of my struggle. Do you think that I will win? I get to know people as they really are and I'm learning. I am ashamed, thinking that in the past I could not even make a fire. I get to know many people who have high positions. This by no means can do any harm. The other day I helped Engineer Beck move. As he is in charge of importing goods to Terezín, he has one of the highest positions here. He is a Czech and a very pleasant young man. When asked, my poor father always helped out when he was here. Consequently, everyone knows him and that means they know me too. I wonder where my father is??? The same day I met Eng. Beck, I got to know Mr. Epstein, who also worked with my father. I explain to him, as I do to everyone, how much I would like to move with my mother. This is what I feel. Everyone is touched and so is Mr. Epstein, whom I ask whether he could intervene with Mr. Rössler. My audacity borders on being fresh. Now, I must wait. I feel very conceited. This, of course, is my shortcoming!

Yesterday, I persuaded Mr. Van der Zyl to take me to the so-called Powder Tower, which is outside of the Ghetto limits and I like to go there. Mr. Van der Zyl is a very ordinary man who is a warehouseman but he is also my boss. He thinks very highly of himself. He works hard and scolds others when they don't do anything. He doesn't like what I do, but he always shows me how to do it correctly. It is good even though sometimes it annoys me. He is hungry and he always begs for a piece of bread. I usually give him a piece without him even asking. He smokes a lot and he cleans his nose in his hands. Occasionally, he sends me for water and sometimes he sends me for personal errands, which I don't like. So, this is the accurate characterization of a man who used to be named Adolf and now must call himself Abraham, and who now goes with me to the so-called Powder Tower. We stop at the Magdeburg Barracks, head toward the Dresdner Barracks and then we leave the Ghetto. I look above, on the ground, and all around. I look at the horses, at the bicycles, at the mud, at the German signs, at the sky, at the buildings, in short, at everything. Even then, I cannot grasp it all. Freedom is something else than sitting around in the Ghetto. Freedom is something one fights for and dies for! And when I look around I feel so strange—so free. We reach [illegible], the key rattles and we find ourselves in a cavernous room about forty meters long. Along the walls there are barrels and sacks. A gendarme is accompanying us. I can see that there is Czech blood in him[143] because his interests are the same as ours. When we ask the gendarmes when the end will come they answer that they are waiting for it as eagerly as we are. I ask the gendarme all kinds of questions because it interests me so much to find out how the outside looks. After half an hour we go home. On the way we meet the prisoners from the Small Fortress. They have an appearance of yellow wax. I am afraid to look into their worried faces. When we are back in the Terezín Ghetto, I keep remembering this disturbing procession.

Afterward, I do some tidying up in the warehouse. I go for lunch. At two o'clock I return to work. Just when I am ready to start the fire, Eng. Beck calls to come and help him. I immediately go there with my cart. Again he is very kind. We go together to the Hamburg Barracks and then to the attic. We open the storage cubicle with a passkey—it is very messy. We move some kind of a bed. We enjoy talking to each other and with some difficulty we take the bed down. Then we go to the Magdeburg Barracks. We take the bed into the warehouse. He thanks me and I return to work again. I am in a good mood. In the evening I still take some dishes into the Jaeger Barracks. When I arrive my bladder starts hurting me. I hope that nothing will come of it. Soon, I go home, where I read poems. Recently this has been my entertainment. I borrow from Mrs. Kollinerová a sheet of poetry mostly with communist and socialist content. I enjoy it very much. At eight o'clock I have to go home. I don't know what's happening, but I don't have time to do my own things. I have band rehearsal. At 10:30 I fall asleep.

143. Pavel distinguishes here between Czech and German blood.

[DECEMBER]
Friday, 1 December 1944

In the morning it was confirmed that today I will again go to the Powder Tower, except for a different reason—I will be the only one going
from the whole warehouse. I have some misgivings. I cannot converse
very well with Mr. Van der Zyl and Mr. Bergen, who are Dutch, which
leads to occasional misunderstandings. I take along with me the necessary tools and already at 1:45 I go to Room 116 in BV. Right from
the start, I have bad luck because nobody shows up for a long time. I
am getting angry and want to go home, when in the hall I meet the
doctor. We head toward the Dresdner Barracks, where a one-armed
gentleman is already waiting for us. We go past the gendarme and I
already see a cluster of people who are waiting for the door to open.
The gendarme is the same whom I met yesterday. "So give us the
key," they tell me. I look at them in disbelief because I have no key.
Again I messed something up. It was really Mr. Van der Zyl's fault, but
I bear the brunt. I am the target of jokes and insults. I start running
quickly to get the key. I am awfully ashamed. I see that I can't keep up
running all the way and I slow down to a walk. I am just about near
the church when somebody shouts to come to him. I look up and see
that it is the driver of the tractor, which also waited at the outer tower
for chemicals and now he has driven to fetch me. I quickly jump up
and we soon go clickety-clack on the pavement. I feel as if I were in
heaven. Soon we are at the *Zentrallager* and I quickly jump off the
tractor. I fetch the key and then sit again in the tractor. I feel as if all
the children's eyes are fixed upon me. I feel great! I no longer think
about the forgotten key and soon we arrive. The tower is opened. I
start talking with the gendarme. Occasionally, I roll a barrel toward
the car. We start talking about forbidden things: about how children
must work here, about the conditions in the Ghetto, about Prague,
and Velká Opereta,[144] and so on. All this blends in my mind into an
endless chain of unforgettable things. The mere thought makes me
so sad because of two related memories: my father and Handa, and
my home. Neither memory is fulfilled and there exists a big, I mean
gigantic, precipice between them. Again, we see the prisoners from
the Small Fortress. I ask the driver if I could hitch a ride with him

144. The Velká Opereta (Great Operetta) opened in 1929 in the arcade of the building
where Pavel lived in Prague. The theater presented performances for children and youth
from the 1930s until 1995, when it expanded its target audience.

and he agrees. When we are ready we get on, I sit on the barrels, and we drive off. We go through unknown territory, around the Ústecký [Aussig] Barracks. We see two German soldiers talking to two girls. We pass across an intersection from which the highway leads away or out of town and along the road there are signs reading "Dienstelle Theresienstadt" [Theresienstadt SS office], and others. We stop in front of the *Kasino* [officers' mess hall] and the gendarme departs. Then we drive through Terezín and I feel like a king. Childish! This is Terezín, I must remember.

There are awful things happening in the *heim*. Starting tomorrow, we have to eat together. I immediately go and complain at *Jugend-fuersorge*, but I don't succeed. It is really impossible and Hradecká is awful. I don't want to make up with her.

Tuesday, 19 December 1944

I don't feel like doing a thing, not even writing my diary. Really I can't do anything about it. I'm at work the whole day and afterward I'm either so happy or so sad that I don't feel like writing my diary. This month I start to think very wisely. I don't know whether it *is* wise, but I *feel* wise. My mood is so changeable like the weather. Perhaps it feels this way because life is so symmetrical on the surface. In the mornings I get up on time and wander into the Hauptstrasse. I stop at my mother's. I am sleepy and not in a pleasant mood. I go to work. Small details interest me as I walk. For example, is the mud frozen or melted? Or is it closer to go this way or that way? I'm really dumb! At work, I feel happy. I have arranged everything quite well. I don't argue with anybody and everyone likes me. I feel so superior and my behavior seems to insult my mother.

The end of war is supposed to be near. It is *supposed* to be, but it will not be. I no longer believe. Whenever I allow myself to laugh like a crazy guy, I see my father and Handa in front of me and I become sad again. I talk a lot with Aryans, who ask me whether my father is in Terezín. I say "no" and they ask whether I know where he is. In reply, I only shake my head sadly. God knows if they know where our dear ones are and are reluctant to tell me. I don't know.

At the *heim* things are impossible. I go there only to sleep and even that annoys me. I would prefer to live with my mother. I continue to live in hope that we will find a flat, but somehow we don't succeed. I don't like the boys in the *heim* now at all. The time I spend there is dreadful. I'm glad when every day I walk out into the gray morning. My thoughts are elsewhere. This time of the year, around St. Nicholas Day, the stores back in Prague are full of beautiful gifts where everything smells of incense and one can hear the noise of firecrackers. As a small child, I used to walk with my parents through the streets and with great interest peep into the lit-up stores. *That* is peace.

Last night I didn't get enough sleep. Somehow things are in a mess today. I feel the need to complain to my mother and get straightened up. I have to confide in someone that I am filthy. I wash up and then I go to work and again follow the same routine. Making fire comes easy to me now, and since yesterday our work is split up. I work with Mr. Veigl, who is extremely lazy. That's why Mr. Van der Zyl doesn't talk to him at all. We really are doing some heavy work. We sort out cases of cleansing powder that weigh about twenty kilos. Today Mr. Veigl is for a change working. I am no longer working alone: a Dutchman works with me. His name is Rolf. We get along quite well. I feel pain in my stomach. I'm afraid that something may happen. I make up my mind that I will not strain myself so much. At ten o'clock we have a short break. Then we toil until 11:30, at which point I go home. At my mother's I behave, as one says, like a "teenager." My mother is annoyed, but we like each other nevertheless. I go for a walk with her and then I return to work. Today we must finish the affair with the cases and indeed it happens. While we carry the cases to the top floor, I take two pieces of soap. Then, as always, I am afraid that someone might have seen me. Because I want to take a bath, I go home. A dreadful old woman has moved in with us. Her name is Larche. One can tell from the name that she is some kind of a witch. I don't know why, but I seem to dislike all old German women at first sight. In the evening one can hear one of them gargling merrily in the *baráky* [barracks]. One can get used to everything. The bath is marvelous. Then I have dinner. On Sunday we got a ration of butter and today when I am alone I spread it on thick. I'm sure that I'll get sick. Something tells me that I have to start writing my diary again. And this is exactly what I do. Even though I don't enjoy doing it, I know that later I'll be glad that I did.

Wednesday, 20 December 1944

I wake up in the morning and sleepily I ask what time it is. I do want to get to work a little bit earlier today. It is a way of ass-kissing, which is expected. At work, I make up my mind that I'll sweep well. And this is exactly what I do. Van der Zyl tells us that we are going to Ovčín, where they store cement and gypsum. I don't feel like working; my feet are cold. We are emptying bags. It is boring work. At 11:30 we go home. I am completely white and my lungs are full of cement dust. It no longer feels strange when the siren sounds at noon. It happens every day now. I would not care if I knew that our dear ones don't work in an area where it is rumored that the bombs are falling. But I don't know.

I'm sleepy and I'm able only to read some dry history. I prepare lunch and then I notice my mother's tired face. We kiss good-bye and I run again to work. A good mood prevails there. We are putting Room 8 in order when the news comes that a wagon of toilet paper is on the way. Everything turns upside down. I am not supposed to participate because I am called off to tidy up the picture warehouse with Mrs. Benišová. Tomorrow Dr. Marzbach is scheduled to come. I converse nicely with Mrs. Benišová. On the way we meet my mother and Mrs. Benišová praises me to her. At 4:30 we're finished, but I still help to store papers in the *Zentrallager.* Then I return home with Van der Zyl. He asks me to accompany him. He tells me about Veigl's laziness. Obviously he enjoys telling me. They don't say a word to each other. I am in a good mood, but at my mother's it drops to a freezing point. In the barracks, news arrives from the first departed transport [from the fall: PW] that some man in Buchenwald is asking for a towel and a handkerchief. The whole evening I think about my father and Handa; I wonder how they're doing. My mother feels the same. I am writing my diary. At home I am tired. A few weeks ago we got a new female counselor in the *heim* named Irma Senecká.[145] She also works in the *Glimmer.* She's quite good. Now we are all alone in the *heim.* Mrs. Hradecká has left us. I don't regret it. Irma is telling us about racism. However, I soon fall asleep.

Thursday, 21 December 1944

I wake up during the night and feel cold. In the morning, I wake up at 6:45, which is late for me. Quickly I get to work. I am in a bad mood. I worry about a Christmas gift for my mother. At about 9:30 we

145. Irma Senecká (b. February 16, 1926) was deported from Prague to Terezín on March 6, 1943. She remained and was liberated there.

are called in to move children's goods. It does not interest me much. It is too lowly a work for me. But I keep reminding myself—as lowly as the work may be, it is the work itself that counts. When people ask me if I would prefer to work with food, I answer "no." I am determined to remain at the *Materiallager* as long as I can. While we move goods, at least I manage to steal a nice cap. In the evening, I go from work to *Arbeitszentrale* for a work permit. Every time I go there, I get the runaround. Today it is no different. I am registered in the male *Hundertschaft*[146] and now these crazy people want to switch me over to the *Jugendsamt* [youth office]! I try to get out of it and tell them that I will go and discuss it with Eng. Nathan, who is the head of the *Arbeitszentrale*. I am curious how the whole thing will turn out. But, before I can start explaining, Nathan appears and interrupts me to tell me that I am already confirmed. I am very surprised and overjoyed! I am supposed to come and get the work ID tomorrow. On the way home, I feel like screaming out with joy: I can work!

Friday, 22 December 1944

It is freezing outside. It's the first time this winter the weather looks like Christmas. Dry frost makes romantic flowers on the windowpanes. How wonderful everything looks and yet I must go to work. I have a request from Mrs. Kollinerová to bring her some glue. It creates quite a worry for me because at the same time I have to get a gift for my mother. I have to sacrifice half a day, namely to work in the chemical warehouse so that I can earn the glue. It is very unpleasant work because I get very dirty. At the end I ask for the glue, and with no trouble I get it. I am in a good mood because I was in L405 and I got [illegible]. After work I go and get the work ID. It pleases me greatly! I get it and I boast about it. In the afternoon there is nothing special at work. I go with two cases to BV to Mrs. Strauss, who is a widow of a [member of the] Ältestenrat [Council of Elders]. She is having some kind of a party and she offers me to have some tea and a piece of cake. After some formal refusals, I accept. On one hand it bothers me, but at any rate I get to warm up and that's the main thing.

---

146. Work units tasked with unskilled, menial labor: cleaning without the proper supplies to do the job, farmwork, pushing carts. Newly arrived deportees were routinely assigned to *Hundertschaft* details. It is unclear whether these units consisted of one hundred (*hundert*) persons (the more probable case) or if they had to do one hundred hours of work.

In the evening, I decide that I'll go to Mrs. Benišová to get her advice concerning the gift for my mother. The answer is as I expected. She promised she would look for something. Namely I wanted some [illegible]. I'm pleased with my success, and even at my mother's I spend the whole evening joking with her. These evenings we both think about my father and Handa. We go to Mrs. Klementová and there we talk. My mother walks me home. We talk about how nice it would be if we lived together.

Saturday, 23 December 1944

In the morning it is apparent that I went to sleep late the night before. An unpleasant thing happens to me today—Van der Zyl and Veigl hate each other and I am once again in the middle. Due to my diplomacy I usually manage quite well, but today I am not successful. The following happens: Van der Zyl does not allow anyone to bother me, especially when I eat breakfast. I always take advantage of it. In the meantime, Veigl is working with some chemicals during the break. He needs help and therefore he calls for me. Van der Zyl says "no." The women stay seated. In the meantime, there is a great going-on in the room and I completely forget about leaving. Suddenly, Veigl barges in. Why didn't I come? Van der Zyl probably doesn't hear it and therefore I go with Veigl. I don't like the work at all. When he asks me why I didn't come, I tell him that I had breakfast and that Van der Zyl prohibited me from going. When he hears this, Veigl's face turns red and he runs like a tiger to Van der Zyl. They are ready to go at each other when Mr. Rössler walks in. I have been looking at all this from a distance. Mr. Rössler quiets the commotion and we all go to our work. Soon, Mr. Rössler comes to us and in fact correctly blames Mr. Veigl. Then he asks me to tell my side of the story. I tell him that I had just finished half of my breakfast and I would not have cared if I had to leave, which is the truth. Mr. Rössler does his nervous tick, as is his habit, and leaves. I sense that the situation is getting serious. To add to the confusion, I hear Van der Zyl being called to come to Mr. Rössler. There I have to translate everything from German and I make a mistake in confusing the words *mussen* [must] and *wollen* [want], which results in a great tragedy. I feel like crying. By chance I run into Van der Zyl, who tells me my behavior is not very nice when I don't speak the truth. I realize then that Van der Zyl wants to get out of it and puts the blame on me. I feel so sorry. My mood is spoiled.

We receive the usual ration consisting of a loaf of bread. At my mother's, I am cranky and my mother immediately recognizes it. She shows her concern by asking whether I am sick. Unfortunately, the reason is different. But one tends to forget everything and by afternoon I don't even think about it, mainly because something pleasant happens—Mrs. Benišová tells me to come to her to pick up the present. I go there and what I see is beyond my dreams! I see a tastefully packed small box of the finest Parisian powder, trademark Coty. I'm overjoyed! Everything is back to normal. Even though Mrs. Benišová promises not to tell anybody, I cannot hold back and I boast about it to the boys. I decorate the gift with some green branches. I am without any worry—the gift is ready. I am still trying to get hold of a key for sardine cans but it is useless.

Yesterday a transport of Hungarians and Slovaks arrived; today it is said that gentiles were also among the transport from Hungary. There is an air raid every day now.

Christmas Eve—Sunday, 24 December 1944

I think this will be the saddest Christmas Eve in my life. It is without my father and without Handa. We used to have nice Christmases in Prague. We had a beautiful Christmas tree decorated with candy and such good spirits. Today I feel so sad. As soon as I start laughing a little, I remember my father and I become sad again. This day is *štědrý* [generous],[147] not in joy but in sorrow and suffering. The greater the misery, the more I turn away from Jewishness. This is somewhat irrelevant, but this thought comes to my mind while I am writing these lines. Since it is Christmastime I don't want to write in a sentimental manner, but nevertheless I have to write the way I feel.

When I wake up, I'm very dizzy. Outside it's dreadfully cold. The frost is bitter. It is only the weather that reminds me of the way Christmas should be. Does it matter? I don't feel well. But mother's gift warms my heart. I worry about how I'm going to give it to her. At last . . . I feel so confused that I drop the present. When I give it to her, she shows real pleasure. We are both enjoying it. I receive a box of candy. I'm awfully cold. I take my top off and sit next to the stove and there I sit idly until noon. I still don't feel well. We have a so-called festive lunch. We keep thinking about my father. Before my mother's shift starts, we go for a walk on the *bašta*. It is gorgeous outside. Every-

147. Christmas Eve is referred to in Czech as Štědrý Den, which means "generous day."

thing is covered with silver frost. Everything glitters with whiteness. The nature is so dead, so beautiful. Behind us we can see the red sun. I'm cold. Finally, I get angry with my mother and I go to work. I hope that I can sit down on the box and rest. I am very mistaken. The door opens and the order is out. I am supposed to help Engineer Beck with a move. I cry with anger! What am I supposed to do? We go with a wagon all the way to Building 601 and there I guard the wagon while the others bring down the luggage. I am freezing. Even though I cry inside, on the surface I appear to be helpful. I wait for one and a half hours and finally we go back to the Magdeburg Barracks. I think that I will have to start again and guard the wagon outside, but fortunately I can go upstairs and warm a little. When the work is finished, Eng. Beck asks me if I want something from him. Very coyly, I ask if it were not possible for him to get us an apartment. He says that this is not possible, but if I want something else I should come to him. Perhaps on account of the cold, I don't feel too disappointed. I go with the cart to the *Zentrallager.* Soon I go home. I agree with Mrs. Kollinerová to go to a concert. It reminds me of the old times but now everything is different and not very festive. At home though, I am pleasantly surprised. Irma gives everybody a present. I get an English book and a clothes brush. I'm trying to get a gift for her. I feel so sad. I fall asleep with the feeling that this is my worst Christmas. The evening air raid, however, pleases me very much.

Christmas Day—My Father's Birthday—Monday, 25 December 1944

Today is my father's birthday. How beautiful it used to be when in Prague we made the rounds giving best wishes, and how pleasant it was even last year when we sat in the *Verteilungstelle,* the whole family together. These were the times. Where is my father? How is he doing? Is he thinking of us? I'm sure he is. What a sad day.

It is beautiful outside. Frost, the sun is shining; typical Christmas weather. I go to work. We get a ration of sugar and margarine. The Dutchman is telling me about things in Westerbork.[148] It seems that people were treated there much better than here. In the afternoon

---

148. The Dutch transit camp of Westerbork was established to house German Jewish refugees and was run by the Dutch Jewish community. After the German invasion of the Netherlands, Westerbork became a transit camp to which Jews were sent and from which they were deported, most to annihilation camps. Some five thousand Jews (primarily Dutch nationals) were sent from Westerbork to Terezín in nine transports between April 1943 and November 1944.

I'm free but I don't know what to do. I feel even sadder when Mother has to leave for her shift. First, I'm trying to locate my savings book, which seems to be lost. Today is also a Christmas celebration for the young people. I try to get in without a ticket but to no avail. I am mad at all of Terezín. Finally, I go to the warehouse office and sit down for a while there, and then I go back to the barracks. I eat dinner and write my diary. At eight o'clock I return home. There I see the boys (the electricians), whom I envy. It's quite nasty on my part. I fall asleep. Again another Christmas Day passes by. Where will the next one be?

New Year's Eve—Sunday, 31 December 1944

Today we have to work because tomorrow there is a free day in all of Terezín. I work upstairs in the paper department where I take inventory. This morning I count sewing utensils. It is rather interesting. Today everything is in festive anticipation of the new year. I feel so sad when I don't have my mother with me. I don't feel so comfortable among strangers. The whole afternoon I work upstairs. By six o'clock my work ends for the year 1944 and in 1945 new, uncertain, and peculiar work will start. I go to the office and I wish everyone all the best for the new year. They are pleased. We obtain a ration today for a festive dinner: cabbage, gravy, meat, and two *buchty*. Indeed luxurious, and we get a bonus ration of bacon, butter, and salami. I have a wonderful dinner and I also have a good conversation. It is snowing outside. The ground is almost all covered. Everything looks like a fairy tale for the new year. I keep thinking about "ours." I miss them very much. On the way home, I think about what good Terezín has done for me. I'm only thirteen years old and I can already independently form my views about the world. I have grasped what life is about, which is the principal matter and also the most difficult one.

I come home and there is nobody in. On the walls I see New Year's posters. By chance, I find out that everybody is in Sokolovna for some festivity. I immediately set out to go there and I arrive while it is in progress. The hall is overcrowded and I don't feel well there. I am glad when I get outside. I go home with two boys. All the young people are outside. It is so pretty, and so sad. In our room we are starting to get into a New Year's mood. We decide that we are going to visit the German girls' *heim*. Our boys are already there. There is entertainment there. We sing and so on. At approximately 10:30, we go upstairs to Irma's. We are not having such a good time there. The remaining boys from Room 7 are there and together we reminisce about Franta and about all the boys and our friends. At exactly midnight, the mood picks up. We joke while we burn the tree. We are barely aware that it is the end of 1944; what is awaiting us? But what is the sense in mulling over it? It's not worth it. Now we go triumphantly to all the *heims* and we wish everyone a Happy New Year. Then we return to our room, where Irma reads us *The Good Soldier Švejk*.[149] I am thinking of going to sleep when two boys from our room bring about ten seventeen-year-old girls over! Of course I no longer want to go to sleep! Soon, Irma arrives with another grown-up. We decide that we will dance. At first I am bashful, but soon I find one girl and we start dancing. I enjoy it enormously! And soon I start with another girl. Others join in. Holzer plays a drum and everything is very merry. After dancing, we just circle around. Only after an hour we have enough and rest. Then we play "*fanty*," which is fun. For example, I give and receive a lot of kisses and smacks and various other dumb things. Afterward, we dance for the last time and go to bed. Really, if entertainment is considered, this has been one of my best New Year's Eves, but——un-fortunately . . . . So long old year; I spent one of my worst moments in it, but, nevertheless, I want to thank you for this year. I hope that your successor will be a good one. I am sorry that I have to say farewell to you, but I am forced to do so because nothing lasts forever, not even the year 1944, and therefore with the hope, that is, with a happy hope that everything has its end, Happy New Year.

New Year's Wish—1945   [Blank page in the text: PW.]

New Year's Day—Monday, 1 January 1945

After the evening out, I wake up at eleven o'clock. I'm pretty sleepy for the new year. Soon, I get up and put things in order. Outside there is a lot of snow and it is still snowing. Real New Year's weather! It is not cold. Just as I am cleaning my coat, my mother bursts into the room. She seems to be very upset. She asks me why I haven't come to her. I explain everything from A to Z. Mother is not angry at me on account of my dancing, but because I stayed up so late. Angrily I show her the door. Then I get dressed and go for *zusatz* [meal seconds] in the Kavalier Barracks. Afterward, still fuming, I go to Mother's. How-

---

149. In his satirical novel *The Good Soldier Švejk*, the Czech writer Jaroslav Hašek shows the futility of war.

ever, after lunch we make up. Then we go with the Zentners for a walk
in the snow. It is beautiful. At times like these, I think a lot about my father. Where is he?! The whole afternoon, we sit with Mrs. Kollinerová
and play solitaire. Later, we have supper. At nine o'clock I go home,
and in bed I listen to Irma's storytelling, during which I fall asleep.
Tomorrow, the work will be waiting for me. Work is what offers me the
only means of forgetting.

Wednesday, 3 January 1945

The frost has eased off. However, there is still a lot of snow outside.
A new woman named Mrs. Kreisl has come to the *Zentrallager*. She was
interned at a camp in Svatobořice.[150] I'm learning some interesting
things from her. She is quite nice. Van der Zyl is getting more obnoxious every minute. He sticks his nose into everything. Nevertheless, I
like him better than the other bosses. The bosses only give orders and
let us boys work like hell. When it comes to some food ration or *zusatz*,
they are usually given to the grown-ups, who don't do a thing, and we
youngsters who work so hard get nothing. It is a glaring injustice. We
have to do everything and the others, with the exception of Van der
Zyl, just keep looking at us. Van der Zyl is different; he always takes
our side and argues fiercely. This alienates him from others. In the
morning, I help doing inventory. Mother will start overtime work dry-
ing potatoes in the bakery. It's at least something! In the afternoon,
we are assigned to carry correspondence cards to the second floor.
And there are a lot of them. We work very hard the whole afternoon
and, of course, others are just looking at us. At 5:30, I go to Mother's.
Unfortunately, I argue with her the whole evening on account of some
half a loaf of bread which got lost. At 8:30, I go home. There is *Apel*,
indicating that there will be a restriction on lighting. The Germans
are really giving it to us. Their anger, I hope, is useless.

Saturday, 6 January 1945

I am tired from all this constant work. I'm angry at everything. I hate
people because of their malice and unfriendliness. Everyone only
wishes that something bad will happen to his fellow man. Van der Zyl
and Veigl are perfect examples and I act just as their intermediary. It
is awful to work in such an environment.

---

150. A labor camp near Kyjov, Moravia (Czechoslovakia).

I find work distasteful. Today, the situation again comes to a point. Everybody wants me to work for them and others don't want to do a thing. Now I could read the poems of Bezruč[151] and Wolker and I would understand their meaning. All people are lazy, and when they work it is just for the sake of competition. I hate the whole world . . . only if my mother can remain. She is my only and endless happiness. Yesterday, I was at a concert, Beethoven. The hall was overfilled and there was good reason. I could hardly have found concerts of this type in Prague. I can guess my mother's feelings: she must be lonely and she must be missing our loved ones. It took some doing on my part to drag her to the concert, but later she gave me a kiss out of thankfulness. In the evening, she was so excited that she couldn't fall asleep.

And now something concrete. In the course of the morning I feel discombobulated. I don't know which way is up. I want to take the cart, but unfortunately someone has borrowed it ahead of me for business. I need it for suitcases that I'm supposed to move from the luggage storage in the Hannover Barracks. Van der Zyl is always on my side and wants to protect me. He has a very loud voice (and no teeth) and he even yells at Mr. Rössler. He is really getting on my nerves. Finally, I get the cart and soon all is settled.

My mother is now preparing very good lunches. She is fattening me up. I'm getting so fat that I weigh forty-five kilos. Awful!

In the afternoon there is no work. We just keep sitting in the warmth. And this is not to my liking. I keep blaming myself for not having learned a trade. I made a big mistake.

Friday, 12 January 1945

I oversleep today. I expect an explosion to take place at work or something that will make the situation worse. I don't like at all being in the company of old people. Veigl is not doing a thing, but nevertheless I prefer to work with him rather than with Van der Zyl. The only decent man is Mr. Rössler. It appears to me that Van der Zyl is a false, egotistical man. I cannot figure out his character. On the one hand, he tries to embarrass me and on the other he praises me. Nevertheless, he is obnoxious. By chance, I go with one boy to Q905. I am happy that I get a fabulous piece of cake, which, however, I must share with three people. I am not an egotist. Today I have a *zusatz*.

151. Petr Bezruč (1867–1958) was a Czech poet and short story writer. He is most famous for a series of poems written in 1899–1900 about the people of Czech Silesia. For Wolker, see note 18.

With Mother, it is still the same. In the afternoon, I go again to work.
The snow of yesterday, which covered the ground to about half a
meter, is quickly melting. The weather is entirely springlike. I go with
Rolf to work at Mrs. Benišová's. There we are carrying things and
we are looking already forward to a reward. We can choose. Out of
many things, I choose a really beautiful and artistic quartet [?]. I'm
extremely pleased. This was quite a decision. Thank God. In the evening, we chat very nicely with Mrs. Kollinerová. I cannot grasp how
a glass can tell fortune. We talk about the conditions in Terezín and
then I return home. Irma managed to get out of working in *Glimmer*.
She intends to start a new regime in our *heim*. She wants to introduce
a regular program. I think it will be quite good.

Sunday, 14 January 1945

I think that I should stay in bed longer whatever is the result. The
first thing I hear today is that there has been a theft in the *Proviantura*
[food storage], a barrel of marmalade and a box of sugar. A kitchen
patrol searches the back windows and the warehouses. At work, I have
to get coal and coke [?]. Then, calmly, I bring a set of chess and play a
game with Mr. Veigl. While we play, we see Murmelstein,[152] Prochurka,
and Koralka searching the warehouse. Everyone seems to be very
anxious. After a two-hour game, I win with a beautiful move. I am in a
good mood and, to add to it, I receive a *zusatz* of a *buchta* with cream.
Even before lunch, I decide that I will take a bath. I am making plans
of how nicely I will get dressed up today to please my mother. As
bad luck may have it, there is no bathing, but instead I decide to get
washed in warm water. This I do. I scrub myself clean and change my
underclothes, I put on my new suit, and I shine my boots. And so, by
two o'clock, I really look nice. My mother is pleased. Meanwhile, I
go for some cookies. I am sorry that I am not working at the bakery.
Then, we go for a walk. Outside, it's again awfully cold. We stand in
line in freezing weather to get some gloves. We have to stand outside
and I don't care for it a bit. I bang at the door and it is a miracle that

152. Benjamin Murmelstein (1905–89) was deported to Terezín in 1943 and served as
the third and last chairman of the Council of Jewish Elders. An ordained rabbi and lecturer
at the University of Vienna, Murmelstein had been second in command to Josef Löwenherz, director of the Jewish Community of Vienna. These men were the key figures in the
community's efforts first to help Jews emigrate and then to develop the deportation lists
demanded by the Germans.

I don't get into a fight with the saleswoman. My mother is angry at me for my poor behavior. After all this, we don't get the gloves. I am extremely angry. My mother wants to go to the bakery to sell her scarf and I get very angry at her. She goes in the direction of the bakery and I go to the barracks. I almost run. From a distance I can still hear Mother calling, but even that soon disappears. I am dreadfully cold and I immediately take my boots off. In a short while, my mother arrives and announces that I have to go and eat supper. During the rest of the evening we are arguing very badly but then we make up.

Something awful is happening in Terezín which puts me into a panic. At the railroad station, SS man Haindl found cigarettes on the glass worker Taussig, and also a list of his customers. These people were immediately arrested, all seventeen of them. Among them are many people I know. Despite that, we go upstairs to the girls and we play games there. I enjoy that very much. Then Wolfik arrives, saying that his uncle was also arrested. We go back downstairs to our *heim*. These are awful moments. To add to all this, Sidlof is not feeling well; he has diarrhea and there is blood in his stool. They suspect dysentery. I'm scared. There is a lot of talk about today's Terezín scandal. I fall asleep with a feeling of dread, not knowing what will follow and whether this may be fateful. I don't know.

Tuesday, 16 January 1945

When I wake up, I wonder what today will mean to me. It is almost eight o'clock when I go to work. But lo and behold, it is dark everywhere when I arrive. I quickly surmise that Van der Zyl is sick. Veigl is still sick, which means that I will be alone today with the seventy-five-year-old Levit. I say to myself: "Let's see." In the meantime, I am delighted that I will be alone in the warehouse. At any rate, I quickly start the fire. Already the customers are starting to stream in; one wants this and another wants that. Fortunately, Mrs. Kubilova comes to help me and she looks after things. For example, the disinfection people come here for soap powder and also for a roll of paper. Great complications arise, but everything turns out well. Mr. Rössler also helps me. Everyone admires me and I am pleased that I am alone and that I don't have to listen to such an unappetizing man as Van der Zyl. I have my own peace and quiet, which means a lot to me. Everyone criticizes Van der Zyl for his lack of activity. Unfortunately, empty crates arrive from L405 which used to be filled with food.

There are a lot of them. In the meantime, Mrs. Kubilova is in room #5 and we have to go and store the crates, which takes us until 11:30. How surprised I am when I see the room in perfect order. I am overjoyed! I have *zusatz*. In the afternoon, I think we will not have any more work, but then a car [cart] arrives from Pejchor with dishes. SS man Tresnak screams that there are no people here. And then lots of people show up. Now I'm confronted with the touchy task of waiting on customers and at the same time toiling with the dishes. In addition, two railroad cars with stoves arrive. Everything must be done in a hurry, but I manage it all. The SS man tells me to go on top of the truck to help in picking up the wood. I consider this "an honor." When I finish, he tells me something which sounds like "Schni-Schni" [possibly *schnell, schnell,* or quickly, quickly] and I scramble down. At 5:30, we are finished. At six o'clock, I close the store with a feeling of great responsibility. Ridiculous! A thirteen-year-old boy has to do this. *This* is Terezín. Thinking about Terezín, the cigarette affair comes to my mind. The situation has become more critical. Tonight the above-mentioned Taussig jumped out of a window. Awful. I knew him personally. It is clear that the Germans want to find out from which Aryan Taussig bought the cigarettes! They are using the most impossible means. The punishments are as follows: nobody can be out after eight o'clock, the coffeehouse is closed, leisure time and stores, everything is restricted. Some Dane who knew about the cigarettes has also been arrested and, in fact, tortured to reveal the name. There is a threat that if the name is not revealed by nine o'clock tomorrow, Terezín will be for three days without warm food, electricity, and heating. That would not be very pleasant. I have a feeling that all this is like the Middle Ages when there were torture chambers. Today's tragedies are much, much greater.

Wednesday, 17 January 1945

I'm again looking forward to working alone, but unfortunately Van der Zyl got better. I despise Van der Zyl now. He even wants me to get his lunch. Wait, you old man, I'll show you. In the evening, we agree that we will have our fortune told. [Illegible word] is immediately ready and soon we sit down with our hands on a plate. This requires very warm hands and a very warm room which, unfortunately, we don't have. We spend half an hour with our hands on the plate and the plate doesn't move. I am very mad. Oh yes, one more news, the

Dane told everything. Still, we don't know exactly who it was—perhaps a German soldier, or a gendarme, or an Aryan from the road construction. We still don't know. All punishments have been canceled. We have won.

In the evening, we again try the séance with the boys, but it doesn't go well.

[Next entry is April 15: PW.]

15 April 1945—Sunday

I'm starting to write my diary again after a long lapse. I didn't write for two simple reasons: my work and the resulting weariness prevented me from writing, and also my pen broke suddenly so that even now I write with a borrowed pen. During this period a lot of things have changed here. Fortunately, I can say they have changed toward the better. Only what has not changed is that I am still in Terezín and I am still without my father.

I cannot write in detail about what has happened during these two months because I don't remember the events well. At the end of January, the Russian front broke with a tremendous offensive. We thought that the end would come in just four days. But as it turned out, this has not happened yet. The Russians are holding in front of Berlin, near the Czechoslovak border and elsewhere. A bit later, perhaps in the middle of March, the occupation of Slovakia began. There was an uprising there, but after all, the Slovaks have behaved very badly. Even more important was the Western offensive. Now the Allies have occupied almost all of Germany and Austria, all the way to Leipzig. The latest news is the capitulation of Cheb.[153] Now, the end can be expected at any minute. The mood here is marvelous. The Germans are furious. I only hope that they will not take out their last anger on us. On 12 April, I hear the news that Roosevelt has died. I don't know whether there is some truth in it. Now, back to something about Terezín. Every day there are transports arriving from Prague which consist of people who are half Jewish or who are Czech gentiles married to Jews. Terezín is now completely filled with them. Transports have been arriving even from Germany and from Slovakia and Hungary. Now the most improbable mix of people has met in Terezín. Obviously, it does not have a good effect. In the streets one sees a Polish

153. A town in western Bohemia (Czechoslovakia), near the German border.

Jew who is picking up something in a trash can. The Czechs from mixed marriages behave very badly here. I think that if all the Czechs behave that way, I will not think twice and will move abroad when I am free. The weirdest transport ever was the transport to Switzerland. Out of nowhere, the news spread that twelve hundred people from Terezín will go to Switzerland. My mother and I were not even given consideration because only whole families or singles could go. About fifty-one hundred people received summonses. Most of them, however, didn't believe the Germans and didn't expect anything good from them. More have refused than have accepted.

[Now the diary switches from pen to pencil: PW.]

I am personally thrilled. The concept of freedom means something very beautiful. For freedom I would even risk my life. Several days after the transport to Switzerland left, a cable arrived in Terezín saying that they have arrived happily. Later, many cards were received from St. Gallen [Switzerland] describing the beauty of their lives. We all envy them.

There have been many air raids regularly between noon and two o'clock. It is awful to think that our Prague must be badly destroyed and to think of the uncertainty of whether Father and Handa were victims of the bombardment. I better not think of it . . .

Spring has now arrived. Spring, the most beautiful thing in the world! A week ago, nature was completely barren and empty. And now, we have a perfectly summerlike day, allowing us to walk out in shirtsleeves. The trees are budding and getting new leaves. How enticing is the rich green color that floods the whole surroundings. The flowers are growing and everything is waking up to a new life. They are alive, they breathe, and they rejoice that they can look again at the world. Why can't I? I am now locked up on two accounts—it is not only Terezín, but my work as well. I'm getting to know people. I hate them all. They all would let me work doing the most demeaning tasks and others benefit from it. This cannot go on. I want to rebel, but I cannot. Something does not let me. I think it is a superiority complex. Everybody likes me and therefore they exploit me. I am a slave to my work. I don't have any time to study. The following happens to me on my free day . . . The whole week I have been looking forward to studying. On my free day, I start reading but then I don't feel like it; I start writing but then everything bothers me. When I go home in the evening, I become very angry when my mother tells me that I am lazy and that I only laze around. I start crying. Mother is concerned and asks me what the matter is. I say it's nothing, because being so sad I will not confide in anyone.

Now, unfortunately, I have to skip over several important events: moving to L313, the *Entwesung*, spring, evening walks with Mother, Mother's move to Room 31 in the Dresdner Barracks, rumors that the transports that had departed in October will return, and I almost forgot to mention *Verschönerung* and the commission, which I cannot just skip over lightly. The commission, similar to that of last spring, took place in March. It was even more thorough than the last one. Much depended on it. Again the sidewalks were scrubbed and swept. It disgusted me. Finally, the day of the commission arrived. Again, the same spectacle repeated itself. Outside there was a line of automobiles from which stepped out several elegant people, of whom only approximately four were foreigners. They looked into everything. "Our SS men," Rahm and Company, were nowhere to be seen. It had been rumored that Rahm was in the hospital with a serious case of pneumonia. But as it turned out later, it was all made up simply because he did not get along well with the commission. Of course, the commission did not turn out well. They asked primarily about the people who had departed in October. In the pharmacy, they asked where the drugs are that they had sent to Terezín.[154] Yes, I remember also that shortly prior to the commission, eight cars belonging to the Swiss Red Cross arrived. They were filled with foodstuffs: chocolate, rice, lentils, powdered milk, etc. At any rate, the commission ended with a failure. Now, as I am writing these lines, it all reminds me of a fairy tale. It is obvious that everything is closing in on the Germans.

This is what happened on 13 April . . . how it happened, I don't know. I am quietly sunning myself on the bench when I hear the world-shaking news: the Danes are going home at eight o'clock this evening.[155] The news spreads over Terezín like an avalanche. It stops by me and can't go any further. With a heavy heart, I run outside into the yard of the food storage building, where I find the Danes. I am flushed with the feeling of freedom. The entire Terezín is immediately turned upside down. To add to the situation, a tremendous

154. Paul's footnotes indicate that the Germans had confiscated these drugs.

155. Protected by their government and the Danish Red Cross, the 456 Jews deported from Denmark were privileged in comparison with the other Terezín inmates. Most important: they received Red Cross packages, they were not shipped to the east, and the 423 still alive and in Terezín were evacuated by the Swedish Red Cross with the now-famous white buses on April 15, 1945, as Pavel reports.

spring thunderstorm blows in. Lightning flashes back and forth in the stormy sky. The downpour slowly subsides, but the sun doesn't come out yet. The trees look even greener. Everything smells of spring. People are almost crazy. Rahm, Haindl, and Murmelstein stand in front of the Danish houses conversing in a lively manner. What a turn-around on the part of the Germans. How angry they must be!

Sunday, 15 April 1945 [later that day]

Today all of Terezín has a day off. I am looking forward to sleeping longer. The sun is already on the horizon when I decide to get up. Everything seems so strange. In front of the building Viktorka 20, white buses are standing which are supposed to take the Danes away, perhaps to Sweden. All this does not seem to sink into my head. There is a great comedy being enacted in the *Schleusky*. They can take food with them. When we look out of the window, we see Swedish soldiers. They are all smiling and one of them waves a closed fist at us indicating that we should not despair. I am delirious with joy! I run into the street. On the corner of the *Komandatura* there will be a band playing as a farewell to the Danes. People are already gathering there. Such a spectacle Terezín hasn't seen yet. The buses pass by. I take a place in the first row and the band starts playing. Through the [illegible] go two Germans. It is said that the Germans are the biggest pigs who now must watch the five hundred Jews depart, and the world will find out about what has been happening in Terezín. They are entirely power-less. At last—a motorcycle appears and then a car with Rahm. The band is playing. The spectators roar with joy. The first bus passes. It is luxuriously furnished. In the middle there is a case full of chocolate and cigarettes, a Swedish driver who nods at us pleasantly, and the happy Danes. All this blends into one image, an image of Freedom. Everybody screams, "Ahoj! Nazdar!" [a salutation] and the Swedes answer back. After the twenty buses, there are trucks and in the last car on the runners there are the Germans. While the crowd cheers, the buses disappear on the state highway and we are left behind. I feel sort of sad; they are gone.

Monday, 16 April 1945

In the afternoon, Dr. Salomon sent me for milk. As I go to fetch milk today, I see a crowd of people in front of L419. I go to see what's happening and find out that there is another commission in Terezín. Soon, I am going to see it. It consists of Rahm, SS man Guenther, two civilians, and Murmelstein. When they come out, the whole crowd streams behind them. I join them. The Germans must be awfully ashamed. The commission stops at the end of the pavilion.

There is the sound of a preliminary air raid alert. Suddenly a tremendous explosion is heard and a sound of falling [illegible??]. One can hear the noise of airplanes. In the distance, an air fight is going on. How many helpless victims?! The Germans are keenly observing it. After awhile, the noise stops. It is quiet. The end of the raid, but these minutes must have brought sorrow to many people.

Tuesday, 17 April 1945

Rumors continue that the Red Cross will come in and the SS will leave. The front is approaching nearer. It is said that not only Cheb has fallen, but now also Podmokly and Teplice.[156] At any rate, the Germans are in a bind. Today, I also go to the Ústecký Barracks and I can see cars crowded with soldiers. They are heading toward Prague. I see passenger cars full with luggage and officers. Also, our SS men are getting ready. The entire *Komandatura* is packed up. Unfortunately, they will take with them everything they can. They are even killing pigs and horses, and they are emptying the food storage building and all of the Ústecký Barracks. Today, SS men Haindl and Vostrel come to our warehouse by car and they take away foodstuffs.

This afternoon there is another big air raid. The whole day the sirens are howling. It is evident that they are not too far away. At noon, one can see hundreds of airplanes in regular formations. It is a beautiful sight. Everybody says that these are Russians. They have such characteristic tactics; they circle around and then they split, followed by a meeting at some other place. Occasionally, we hear bombs detonating.

In the evening, I am determined to write my diary again. Suddenly, someone announces that a commission is at the corner. I feel like somebody has shot me. It is the same thing as yesterday. The people are delighted and run after the commission. This time there are two civilians, Rahm, and Murmelstein. They go through [illegible ???] and the "Grand Hotel." Haindl continues riding around in a car and

---

156. Pavel is following the liberation of Czechoslovakia. Podmokly is much nearer Prague than is Cheb, and Teplice, a city north of Prague, is very close to Terezín.

even talks with the Jews. It is unbelievable. About five hundred people follow the commission. One member of the commission looks Jewish. He has black hair and glasses and keeps smiling at us. I later find out that he was indeed a Jew—someone named Dr. Kessel from Bratislava. There is tremendous rejoicing going on in Terezín. Every night, we wait for the Germans to depart and in the morning we hope there will be a flag flying high on the *Komandatura*, a flag of peace, the flag of the Red Cross. I personally cannot believe it and I expect the departure to take place not before Friday. While we are all waiting, something else happens . . . . During the night, between Tuesday and Wednesday, a great mistake occurs. Somebody comes from the Magdeburg Barracks with the news that the SS is gone. Obviously, there is chaos and shouting of joy. Everybody (namely the Czechs) rushes into the streets and shouts slogans praising the Republic of Czechoslovakia and the SSR [Soviet Union]. It is actually a demonstration. Just in the middle of things, ten SS men arrive with Rahm in the lead, armed from head to toe and carrying one machine gun. They station themselves around the city barracks. Something similar is happening at the Hamburg Barracks, where the Germans go to all the houses and call everybody down. However, it turns out well as Rahm makes a speech indicating that the situation is not as yet ripe to make all this merriment and telling everybody to go back to their jobs quietly. So, this is the way Terezín's St. Bartholomew Night ended.[157]

Thursday, 19 April 1945

Again there are big air raids. The mood after last night's events is not as good as it has been lately. In the afternoon, I go to Dr. Porges for something and find out that another transport will go to Switzerland. The transport will consist of the Ghetto leaders, including Murmelstein. It is hard to believe that the Red Cross would commit such an injustice! Now, when the end is near and the situation becomes critical, the "big shots" are allowed to depart. They want to leave because they are afraid that, after the war is over, the Jews will have their revenge. This arrangement must have been thought out by Jews themselves. Everybody is upset. As yet though, nothing definite is known about the transport.

157. St. Bartholomew Night refers to the mass murder, timed to coincide with the feast of Bartholomew the Apostle, of French Calvinists in Paris in 1572.

Friday, 20 April 1945

Today is one of the blackest days of the calendar. It is the birthday of a man who has made so many people unhappy. His name is Adolf Hitler. No need to say anything more. Everyone expects that on this ugly day something significant militarily will occur, such as Berlin falling or something similar. In the afternoon, something happens but it is something dreadful. It is only the beginning and when it ends, everybody will breathe easier. A transport is expected from Celle.[158] Nobody knows when. How surprised I am when, at about four o'clock, a long cattle train steams in. From the small barred windows, yellow skinny faces look out. All of the people wear prisoner garb. I step out for a while, but I am very restless. A big crowd is assembling and everyone stares at the dreadful theater. These people have been on the road for two weeks and have eaten nothing. They are from various camps, but primarily from Buchenwald. They are being unloaded: 40 percent are stretcher cases. They look awful, unshaven, dirty, and thin. Chaos begins in Terezín. All the departments are mobilized. My inside is revolting. What injustice. Why all this suffering, why? They are mostly Hungarians and Poles, in whom I am not personally interested, but what is happening with my father and my brother? Now, my fear is only intensified.

At 6:30, I return home. My mother is also very upset. I fully understand. I cannot eat a thing. Immediately, I run with Mrs. Kollinerová in the direction of the *Schleusky*. Just as we arrive, the sick are being unloaded, individually on stretchers or en masse on carts. It is a sight I have never seen before and never want to see again. The bodies seem close to death. The mouths of some of the poor people are trying for a deep breath, begging for a piece of bread. When somebody throws them a lump of sugar, they start to fight for it with whatever strength they still have; others can't even do that. They are apathetic to everybody. Whoever sees them must be very anguished. A great disaster is threatening Terezín: the danger of disease and hunger. Several women arrive who had left Terezín before. I am already sure that I would not recognize my father in such a state. If the Germans didn't succeed in anything, they did succeed in maiming the Jews. I realize that now every able person has to work. We cannot stand look-

---

158. Pavel refers here to Bergen-Belsen concentration camp, located about ten miles north of Celle, Germany. Force-marched from camps in the east, thousands of emaciated and ill Jews were crammed into Bergen-Belsen.

ing at it any longer, so I go to visit the Piesingers[159] for a bit of cheer. One cannot find consolation anywhere because everybody is equally disturbed. My mother doesn't want to allow me to go help, but I tell her that I have to. They need me in the *Zentrallager* so I go and ask Mrs. Rössler if I can help. For a while, we both cut bread. When we run out of bread, Anni [Rössler] doesn't need us any longer. She takes me to a back room and gives me a parcel. Without looking at it, I give it to my mother with these words: "Give it to my father when he arrives."

Saturday, 21 April 1945

I ask to be awakened at 6:30 so that I can go and help out. I am almost dressed when Mother appears at the window saying that all people in the Dresdner Barracks must move. Another blow. I go to the warehouse to be excused and also to borrow a cart. Soon, my mother arrives with Mrs. Kollinerová and we go to the *Raumwirtschaft* and then to the Dresdner Barracks. Mother starts packing. It is rumored that everybody will have to move to the attic. I don't believe it and somehow feel that my mother will get a nice flat. We move two loads of suitcases and then I am waiting for Mother's instructions. Supposedly, she is assigned to some "hole" in Turmgasse No. 9. Mother is very unhappy.

The worst thing about all this is that a commission is expected. So that the commission won't see people moving, we are allowed to move only from six o'clock on. I go and have a look at the "hole" where six people are supposed to live. I find out that it is really not a hole, but it is unsuitable for six people. Therefore, Mother and Mrs. Kollinerová keep running to the Magdeburg Barracks, where they succeed in convincing the officials that the place can only house three people. And then, by means of a small trick, it is arranged that for the time being only two people will stay there. On one of our trips to Turmgasse, we see many people running toward Seestrasse. I am told that a transport is arriving that traveled for one hundred kilometers on foot. I am ready for anything. However, the transport consists of men who seem to be in a better condition than those who came off the train, or perhaps I have already gotten used to it. Again, they are mostly Hungarians, Poles, Dutch, French, Italians, Germans, and only a few Czechs who had been in Terezín. One man yells out in Czech, "This mother I know. I did lie next to Handa in the hospi-

---

159. Weiner family friends in Terezín.

tal," and keeps moving on. Their striped uniforms have an indelible marking, "K4," on the back which is a horrible identification. They all open their mouths: "Hunger!" We keep telling them that they will all get something and that they don't have to be afraid. Someone in the crowd calls to one of them to come to the window so that he can give him something to eat. A whole bunch of men rush in. They break windows and then one of them, who is particularly furious, tries to throw others out so that only he can get inside. Only with difficulty is he separated. Then come the women. They are not too bad. The procession is over and we return home.

At six o'clock, we start moving. Everything turns out well, and by 10:30 we are finished moving.

Sunday, 22 April 1945

I am not enjoying my work. There are many "mixed" people from gentile/Jewish marriages working with me. They are extremely obnoxious. Their attitude toward all this ugliness is indifference, as if it did not concern them. If I acted as they do, I would probably go crazy. This morning, another transport arrived. Almost all are Hungarians and Poles. Last night another transport arrived with young girls. They look very well. Among them, it is rumored, is Zuzka Beranová,[160] but Leoš [Beran] and his mother are not with her.

The people from the transports have brought with them some awful news which we cannot believe: All children twelve years and under and all people sixty-five years and older have been gassed. Only those capable of work were not killed. What are our grandmother and grandfather doing, and all the boys from Room 7? This is supposed to be the twentieth century, when innocent children are being gassed and killed? If all this is true, it is up to us who survive to make the appropriate revenge. What's awaiting us will be the worst possible thing—the aftereffects of the war.

It's raining cats and dogs. Even hail is coming down. Poor people! Among the arrivals are people who are the worst murderers and robbers and they are hungry to boot.[161] The *Zentrallager* has changed.

---

160. Zuzana Beranová (b. March 8, 1927) was assigned number 284 (Leo, younger than she, was 285) on transport Av and deported from Třebíč to Terezín on May 18, 1942. She and her brother and mother were shipped to Auschwitz with convoy Et (her number: 637) on October 23, 1944. She survived to be shipped back into Terezín, where she was liberated.

161. Common criminals were among the prisoners arriving from camps in the east.

The gates are closed and the fire hose is ready. Everything is being barred. Five hundred people have run away and stolen all that they could. There is a great danger to Terezín. Four people murdered each other. At my mother's, in the yard, there is a quarantine. During mealtime, they are fighting and shouting and I feel sorry for them. In the afternoon, I sleep. The sleep does me good. In the evening, we go to Mrs. Klementová only to find out the shocking news that Else Schinko has arrived. She used to be in the Small Fortress but was transported to some place in Germany. Now she is lying sick in the hospital quarantine, L206, and probably has typhoid. Then we hear some good news: from now on, the Red Cross is officially taking care of us! It is official. Someone by the name of Mr. Durand is in charge. Immediately, the mood improves and one tends to forget about today's misery. We think that we are again a little bit closer to freedom.

Slowly, one gets used to everything, even the awful pictures of today. The gates of the concentration camps are opening up, and into the outside world come skeletons who are closer to animals than to people. Unfortunately, not many of them come out.

[Diary ends: PW.]

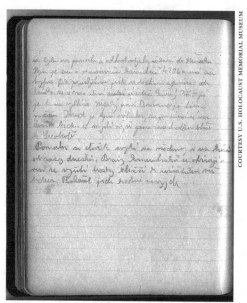

Last page of Pavel's diary, April 22, 1945

APPENDIXES

Boys in Room 7 Mentioned in the Diary

NAME	NICKNAME(S)
Bäumel, Erich	
Beneš, Jiří	
Beran, Leo	Leoš
Bloch, Jiří	Blecha
Brenner, Hanuš	Brena
Furcht, Valtr	Duch
Gans, Petr	Ganzolka, Gansalka
Götzlinger, Felix	
Götzlinger, Pavel	Pudlina
Gruenbaum, Michael*	Míša
Heller, Petr	Kokošek, Koko
Hermann, Jan	Mustang, Kuzma
Herz, Robin (Robert)*	Biblu
Holzer, Hanuš*	Extraburt
Huppert, Pavel*	
Jilovsky, Arnošt	Jila
Klein, Karel	Kalíšek, Kalí
Kopperl, Rudolf	Krysa
Lamm, Bedřich	
Lappert, Heinz	
Lederer, Petr*	Pedro
Lekner, Jiří†	Išík
Lion, Pavel	
Mangl (nickname only)	
März, Gideon Arnošt	Gida
Mautner, Jiří	Jirka

Mautner, Pavel	Palka
Mayer, Martin*	Majošek
Mühlstein, Gabriel	Eli, Elihu
Repper, Jiří*	Kikina
Rindler, Petr	Grizzly
Ruzek, Jiří*	Kapr
Schweinburg, Alexandr	Sasha
Seiner, Jindřich (possibly Steiner)	
Spitz, Erich*	Špulka
Springer, František	Franta
Stein, Gustav	Gustl, Gusta, Gustla
Strebinger, Jan*	Gorila
Weiner, Pavel*	Pajík, Pajínko
Witrofsky, Petr	Witr
Zweig, Gustav	Tuti, Tutinek, Suva

*Survived

†Jiří (called Išík) Lekner, born May 18, 1931, was deported on December 10, 1941, from Prague to Terezín with transport L (his number: 312). He was sent to Auschwitz as number 424 on transport Ep on October 9, 1944. Išík did not survive.

Pavel's Family

Valy Weiner	Mother, survived
Ludvík Weiner	Father, died in Kaufering, December 1944
Hanuš Weiner (Handa)	Brother, died in Kaufering, January 1945
Zikmund and Hermine Stein	Maternal grandparents, died in Auschwitz, probably March 1944
Eric Stein	Maternal uncle, refugee to the United States; survived
Gertrude (Trude) Stein	Maternal aunt, died in Terezín, July 1943
Otomar and Olga Sušický	Paternal uncle and aunt, died in Auschwitz, July 1944

Persons Mentioned Frequently in the Diary

Bergmann, Rudolf (Rudla)

Weiner family friend; brother of Mrs. Knobloch, a close friend of Valy's from Prague. His position as head of the financial department afforded him influence in the camp, and he protected the Weiner family from deportation for as long as he could.

Berman, Karel*

Bass-baritone; key figure in the musical life of Terezín and Pavel's singing teacher in Terezín

Czapla, Bruno*

Head of the bakery at Terezín

Demner, Leo (Leošek)*

Assistant to Otto Klein

Ehrlich, Zebulon

Formerly a teacher in the Jewish school in Prague; a *madrich* in L417

Eisinger, Valtr

Madrich for room 1 in L417; taught Czech

Eppstein, Paul

Second chairman of the Council of Elders; executed in the Small Fortress in 1944

Fuchs, Katerina (Kata)*

Assistant *madrich* to Franta Maier

Hradecká, Karolina*

Instructor of Czech literature

Jelínková

English teacher

Klauber, Arnošt (Šmudla)*

Madrich for room 5

Klein, Otto (Ota, Otík)*

Director of L417

Kohn, Antonín

Mathematics teacher

Maier, František (Franta)*

Madrich for room 7 in L417

Maier, Heinrich (Heini)

Hebrew instructor

Mautner, Marie

Assistant to Franta Maier

Murmelstein, Benjamin*	Third and last chairman of the Council of Elders
Rahm, Karl	Third and last commandant of Terezín, executed in 1947
Rössler, Anna and Josef*	Family friends; Josef ran the warehouse in which Pavel worked
Schwarzbart, Julius	Squad leader and Pavel's boss in the garden
Seidlerová, Irena	Assistant *madrich* to Franta Maier
Van der Zyl, Adolf†	Pavel's boss in the *Zentrallager*
Weil, Rudolf (Rudla)	Temporary *madrich* in room 7
Zwicker, Bruno	History and geography teacher

*Survived
†Possibly survived

Glossary of Camp Terms

Words are from Czech, German, and Hebrew (or a fusion of several languages), and appear as spelled in the diary.

Ältestenrat   German-imposed Council of Jewish Elders

Apel   assembly

Arbeitszentrale   central employment office

bábovka   coffee cake

bašta   grassy area atop the town walls used as playing fields

betreuerka   female child care worker

bonky   rumors (slang)

bordel   mess or uproar

buchta (pl. *buchty*)   bun or roll, usually filled with jam

česka   boys' version of handball

dekada   food ration

Elektra   Electricians (soccer team)

Entwesung   delousing station

geback   pastry and other baked goods

gendarmes   Czech rural police

Getak   slang for *Ghettowache*

Ghettowache   Jewish ghetto police

Glimmer   mica

Grunt   general cleanup

heim   home (for children)

Jugendfuersorge   youth welfare department, also a soccer team (Jufa for short)

Jugendleiter   youth leader

Kinderkuche   the kitchen where the children's meals were prepared

Kofferlager   suitcase storage room

Komandatura   SS camp headquarters

L410 (address)   Czech *heim* for girls, counterpart to boys' L417

L417 (address)   Czech *heim* for boys

Landwirtschaft   agriculture department

madrich (pl. *madrichim*)   counselor or youth leader

Materiallager (MTL)   supply warehouse

Materialverwaltung   supply department

Menagedienst (pl. *Menagedienste*)   mess service

menášek   serving dish

menaška   meal ticket

Nachschup   additional food serving

německá   a ball game

Nešar   magazine founded by Pavel; one of two written in room 7

nešarim   room 7 group name

nesev   Hebrew-language entertainment program

okenka   a children's game

pruser   scandal (slang)

Raumwirtschaft   housing department

reklamace   attempts to get out of a transport

Rim, Rim, Rim   magazine written by boys in room 7; complete set of issues has been saved. The diary refers to the magazine as *Rim, Rim* or just *Rim*

Schleusky   processing center for incoming or outgoing transports

schlojs   to purloin from communal property

School   L417, the Czech boys' home

sicha (pl. *sichy*)   old, sickly person (slang)

Small Fortress   site of Gestapo prison adjacent to the camp

smelina   trickery for personal gain

Sokolovna   formerly the Sokol club gym, the building served a series of functions during the ghetto era

Spedice   Haulers (soccer team)

sprtec   game simulating hockey played with buttons

Stadtkapelle   town orchestra

Theresienstadt   German name for Terezín

tunke   watery gravy of no nutritional value

Verschönerung   beautification of Terezín for visit by the International Red Cross

Verteilungstelle   distribution center

Wirtschaftabteilung   business department

Zentrallager   central or main warehouse

zimmerka   room cleanup duty

zusatz   meal second helpings

air raids, 45, 72, 97; by Allied planes, 99, 123–24, 132–33, 152, 158, 178–79, 207, 210–11, 223–24; blackouts against, 107, 123
Akim "Aki," 193
Allach (subcamp), 130n114
Allies: invade France, 63, 64, 102, 124–25, 131, 143, 145; invade Germany and Austria, 148, 219. *See also* air raids; Soviet Union
Ältestenrat (Council of Elders). *See* Jews
Altman, Mr. (German gardener), 56, 117
Altman, Mr. (heads bakery), 183
Anička, Aninka (squad leader), 130, 135, 142–43
Apel (assembly), 10, 68–70, 96, 110, 111, 136, 140, 155; announcements at, 17, 20, 44, 64, 100, 114, (concerning escape of two boys) 23, (concerning evacuation of School), 145, 150, (concerning torn book) 128–30; canceled, 12, 32, 43, 45, 54, 92, 118; as "gateway to new life," 54–55; and German restrictions, 214; with inspection, 125; outdoor, 19; Pavel castigated at, 72, 74, 79, 82, 83, 94; Pavel misses, 24, 35, 39, 133, (fears being absent from) 28, 31, 33, 57, 66; "worthless," "boring," 22, 25, 56, 59, 65, 73, 106, 120, 141, 157
"Arna." *See* Ehrlich, Arnošt; Meisl, Arna
artists' work. *See* "painters' affair"
Ascher, Mrs., deported, 179
Auerbacher, Inge: *I Am a Star,* xxxix note 1
Auschwitz-Birkenau, xxvii; deportations from Terezín to, xiii, xviii, xxiv, xxvi–xxviii, xxxviii, 7–36nn1–60 passim, 50n64, 53n67, 57nn69–70,

67n75, 71n80, 76n85, 78n87, 82n89, 84n91, 88n94, 94n99, 98n101, 98n103, 99n104, 124n112, 130n114, 141n117, 159n128, 160nn129–30, 169n133, 171n134; Germans abandon, 10n12
Ausenberg (painter), 141
Austria: Allies invade, 219; Jews from, xix

bakery, 70; mother works at, 35–37, 53, 69, 71, 79, 104, 109, 145, 163–64, 181, 214, 217, (afternoon shift) 20, 86, 94–95, 127, (morning shift) 64, 99, (night shift) 73, 81; Pavel works at, 181, 183–92, *illus.,* 188
Bar Mitzvah observances, 37, 136, 144–45, 154, 195, 197
The Bartered Bride (Smetana), xxii, 78n87, 100, 134
Basser, Mr. (food officer), 68
Bastien and Bastienne (Mozart), 111
"Bastik." *See* Freudenfeld, Rudolph
bathing: bathhouses, 11, 19, 20, 67, 79, 97; bathing tickets, 7–8, 24, 34, 77, 88, 105; delousing, 67, 109, 153–54
Bauer, Dr. (camp doctor), 45
Bäumel, Erich, 19, 22, 29, 45–46, 98, 109, 112, 136; deported, 175
beautification campaign, xxvi–xxix, 64–65, 69–70, 73–76, 182, 221
Beck, Mr. (engineer), 202–3, 211
Beethoven concerts, 8, 10, 215. *See also* music
Belgium, xviii; liberated, 144, 148
Belov (escapes from camp), 22–23
Beneš, Edvard, xv
Beneš, Jiří, 32, 44, 48
Beni (bakery worker), 192
Benišová, Mrs., 207, 209–10, 216

Beran, Leo "Leoš," 19, 20, 31, 79,
    100, 134, 152, 179; deported, 180,
    (does not return) 227; grandmother
    deported, 47; at library, 22, 30;
    magazine contributions by, 10–11, 17;
    moved, 82; parents of, 158, (father
    dies) 158, 160, (mother does not
    return) 227; schlojs-ing books, 169,
    172;
Beranová, Zuzka, 227
Bergel, Karl, xxix, 74, 132, 148
Bergen, Mr. (Dutch worker), 204
Bergen-Belsen concentration camp,
    225n158
Bergmann, Dr. Rudolf "Rudla," xvii,
    xxiv, 159–60, 163, 167–68, 183
Bergmann, Mrs., deported, 185
Berl (in charge of soccer schedule), 98
Berman, Karel, 16, 56, 58–59, 64–65,
    70–71, 80
Bernadotte, Count Folke, xxxi
Bezruč, Petr, 215
"Biblu." See Herz, Robin
Birkenau, 171, 173. See also
    Auschwitz-Birkenau
Bloch, Ferdinand, xxx, 94n99
Bloch, Jiří "Blecha," xlii note 36, 67, 85,
    101, 110
Bohemia, xv, xvii, xix, 219n153. See also
    Czechoslovakia
Brauschitz, General Walther von, 148
Bremschová, Mrs. (friend of family), 71
Brenner, Hanuŝ "Brena," 8–13, 17, 24,
    27, 36–38, 60, 75, 114, 127, 140–41;
    deported, 169
Bretisu family deported, 169
Brody, Mr., deported, 160
Brundibár (Krása), xxiii, xxix, xxx, 74,
    128, 159n128
Buchenwald, 94n99, 207, 225
Bulgaria, uprising in, 148
Burger, Anton, xxx, 15n29, 97

Čapek, Karel, 65, 72, 74, 120, 123;
    R.U.R., 106
Catherine II, empress of Russia,
    182n136
Čelakovský, František Ladislav, 124
census of November 1943, anniversary
    of, 193
Chamberlain, Neville, xv

children: born at camp, xx; children's
    home (Kinderheim), xx–xxi; children's
    kitchen (Kinderkuche), 45, 124, 140;
    child welfare in Terezín, xx–xxi;
    statistics regarding, xxxix note 1. See
    also games and sports; room 7 and
    room 7 boys
Christmas, 206, 207–8, 210–12
cigarette scandals, 68, 99, 217–19
clinics, xix; Pavel's use of, 95–96, 102–3,
    130, 134, 136–37, 157, (long line at)
    124–25, (not allowed to go) 156
clothing, xxvi, 15, 17, 22, 31, 62, 147,
    154; delousing of, 153; gloves and
    scarf, 216–17; laundry and cleaning,
    34, 61, 75, 87, 89, 96, 112, 167; shoes,
    15, 51, 53, 56, 63, 91, 96, 100, 104,
    (soccer boots) 72, 82–83, 147–48, 152,
    156, (wooden) 142, (wooden shoe
    breaks) 138; socks, 61, 85
Columbia space shuttle, 84n91
Communist party, 11n18, 81
Cooper, James Fenimore, 198
Council of Elders. See Jews
culture. See education; library, camp;
    music; "painters' affair"
Czapla, Bruno, 186, 190–92, 194, 196
Czechoslovakia and Czechs, 151;
    Communist Party, 11n18; Czech
    Aryans, 144, 205; Czech language
    and literature lessons in camp,
    93, 127, 130–31, 155–56, 172–73,
    (exams for) 98, 100; and Czech
    nationality, xiv, (Czech vs. German
    Jews) 51n65; Czechs from mixed
    marriages, 219–20; Czech songs, see
    music; founding of country, xxxiii;
    Hitler invades Sudetenland, xiv–xv,
    xvii; Jews annihilated, 69n78; Jews in
    Prague, 114, (deported from) xvii–xx;
    rural police, see gendarmes; Soviets
    approach border, 102, (invade)
    107n108; Terezín chosen as transit
    camp, xix–xx (see also Terezín); as war
    ends: (liberated), 223n156, (Republic
    of) 224
Czechoslovak Independence Day,
    184–85

Dachau, xxxix
Demner, Leo "Leošek," 53, 85

Denmark, Jews from, xix; released, xxxi–xxxii, 221–22

deportation. *See* transport, deportation

Deutsch, Peter, 69n77

Deweles, Mrs. (kitchen worker), 188

diary, title, cover, and first pages of (*illus.*), 3, 5, 6

Dietrich, Marlene, 124n112

Durand, Mr. (Red Cross representative), 228

Dvořák, Antonín, 12

Dwork, Debórah, 4

Echstein, *schlojs*-ing by, 110

Eckstein, deported, 175

Edelstein, Jakob, xx, 73n81, 141n117, 159n129, 193n141

Edison, Thomas A., 98

education, xxi–xxiii, xxiv, xxxiii–xxxv, 70. *See also* library, camp; Weiner, Pavel

Ehrlich, Arnošt "Arna," 98, 101

Ehrlich, Zebulon, 30, 76, 79, 90

Eichmann, Adolf, xxvi, xxx, 69n78, 138n115

Eisinger, Professor Valtr, xxiv, 57, 93, 127, 155; deported, 161

Eisner (soccer player) 149, 153; *schlojs*-ing by, 110

"Eli," "Elihu." *See* Mühlstein, Gabriel

English Sunday (Whit Sunday) observed, 75

entertainment program, Hebrew language. *See nesev*

Epstein, Mr. (friend of family), 202

Eppstein, Mrs. (runs clinic), 134

Eppstein, Professor Paul, xxix, 73, 74–75, 93, 159n129; transport rumor, 164

Fantová, Mrs., 194

Feldman family, 145

Ferda, Rabbi, 144–45

"Final Solution," xviii

"Fire-Flies" (Karafiát), xxiii

Fischer, Sister (nurse), 169

Fleischer, Mr. and Mrs., deported, 175–76

food, 11–12, 15, 19–21, 24, 33, 36, 46, 138; during beautification campaign, xxvii–xxix, 74, 75–76;

bread, 57, (stolen), 83; *buchty* with cream, 22, 32, 58, 61, 65; from camp garden, 78–79, 84–85, 89–91, (vegetables) 87, 90, 92, 96, 105; children's kitchen (*Kinderkuche*), 45, 124, 140; commission orders for, 70; cookie shapes recorded (*illus.*), 187; "dreadful," 78; food ration (*dekada*), 66, 72, 73, 90, 96, 105, 107–8, 113, 116, 125–26, 129, 133–39 passim, 184–93 passim, 210, 212, (butter) 206, (stolen) 54, 61; "Ghetto Soup," 165; importance of, xxxiii, 13, 106, 119, 187n; improves, 151; long lines waiting for, 8, 34, 50, 53, 127, (Pavel jumps line) 114, 144, 145; "luxurious," 145; meal ticket (*menaška*), 22, 26, 45, 56, 67, 68–69, 131, (ice cream ticket) 115; milk, 82, 150, 222; mother prepares, 41, 62, 66, 71, 75, 80, 106, 111, 119, 178, 215; packages from friends and strangers, 37, 59, 63, 72, 78, 79, 106, 131; as payment, xxxiii, 23, 35, 55, 78, 117; purloining, *see schlojs*-ing; second helpings (*zusatz*), 53, 213, 215; storage buildings robbed, 154, 216. *See also* bakery

France: Allied invasion of, *see* Allies; French Jews, xix; French lessons, *see* Weiner, Pavel; French Revolution studied, 129; Germans in, 113, 129n113, (fall of Orléans rumored) 122; rumors of revolution in, 92

Frank, Karl Hermann, 70

"Franta." *See* Graus, František; Maier, František; Springer, František

Freudenfeld, Ota (Moritz), xxiii, 74n83, 85n92, 87

Freudenfeld, Rudolf "Rudla," "Bastik," xxiii, 85, 87n93, 101, 159

Freund family (friends from Prague), 98, 140

Fried, Mrs. (friend of family), 51, 68, 151

Fried, Norbert "Nora," 78, 130

Fritta, Bedřich (Fritz Taussig), xxix–xxx, 94. *See also* "painters' affair"

Fuchs, Katerina "Kata," 57, 63

The Führer Gives the Jews a Town (propaganda film), xviii, xxx–xxxi

Furcht, Valtr, 19, 169–70; deported, 175

games and sports: chess, 165–66, 178, 216; gymnasium, gymnastics, 53, 56, 100, 101, 111, 118; handball (*česka*), 19, 27, 42, 53–54, 60, 64, 128; *německá* (ball game), 85, 88, 95, 113; "new game," 137; *okenka* (children's game), 51, 53–55, 57; playground, rumors of installation, 15; playground equipment, 70; rag ball, xxxvii, 46, 49–50, 136, 149–50; scout game, 111–12; "Smelina" (board game), 81; *sprtec*, 166; swimming, 28–29, 83; "Treasure Hunt," 26–27; volleyball, 35. *See also* Sokol, Sokolovna center

Gans, Petr "Gansalka," "Petera," 84 [Ginz?], 87 [Ginz?], 92 [Ginz?]; deported, 169, 179

Ganz, Pepík, 92, 106

gardening, 36, 37, 55, 60, 61, 109; food from, *see* food; harvested crops sent to Germany, 79n88; Pavel barred from, 63, 64, 144, 147, (returns to) 66–68, 76–79, 91, 99, 134, (*schlojs* from) 78, 106–8, 114–16, 123, 125, 132, 142–43; picking linden blossoms, 84, 88, 90–91, 96–97. *See also schlojs*-ing

Geisinger, Mrs. (piano teacher), 102, 109–10, 119, 121, 143

gendarmes (Czech rural police), 68, 79, 91, 97, 113, 132, 164, 203–4; at census, 193n141; and "painters' affair," xxx, 94n99; relinquish arms, 148

George, king of Poděbrad, 156

Germany, xix; Allied forces in, 148, 219; food from Terezín gardens sent to, 79n88; martial law declared in Reich, 137; surrenders, xxxii, (escape route from Terezín) 157, (leaves) xxxix. *See also* Gestapo; Hitler, Adolf; Nazi party

Gerron, Kurt, xxx–xxxi, 124, 136

Gerron, Olga, xxxi

Gestapo, xix, xx, 65n74, 94n99

Ghettowache. See Jewish police

"Gida." *See* März, Gideon Arnošt

Ginz, Petr, xlii note 35, 84 [?], 87 [?], 92 [?]

girls, 16n31, 101, 112; girls' *heim* (L410), xli note 25, 195n142, 212; at New Year's dance, 213; tested, 97, (exams) 99, 102; on transport, 227, (back to Terezín), 227

Gleiwitz (subcamp), 8n4, 76n85, 159n128

Glimmer (mica processing): Irma works at, 207, 216; Pavel's mother works at, 155–56, 159, 167, 177, 210, 212

"Gonda." *See* Redlich, Egon

The Good Soldier Švejk (Hašek), 213

"Gorila." *See* Strebinger, Jan

Götzlinger, deported, 175

Götzlinger, Felix, 29, 49, 93, 109–10, 117, 119

Götzlinger, Pavel "Pudlina," 29, 34, 49, 54, 83, 97–98, 165

Graus, František "Franta," 88–89, 91, 94

"Grizzly." *See* Rindler, Petr

Groag, Willy, 195

Gruenbaum, Michael "Míša," xlii note 36, 29, 52, 54; grandmother deported, 48

Grunt. See housekeeping duties

guard duty, 31–33, 113, 124–25, 128, 130, 141

Guenther, Hans, 69, 223

Gustl, "Gustla." *See* Stein, Gustl

gymnasium and gymnastics. *See* games and sports

Haas, Leo, xxix–xxx, 94. *See also* "painters' affair"

Hácha, Emil, xv

Haindl, Rudolf, xxix–xxx, 68, 74, 93–94, 97, 123, 175, 217; as war ends, 222–24

haircuts, 21, 28, 36, 37, 39, 105, 174

Hašek, Jaroslav: *The Good Soldier Švejk*, 213n149

head soccer (*hlavicky*), 28. *See also* soccer

Hebrew language entertainment program. *See nesev*

Hebrew language studies, 57, 79, 87, 90, 94, 127, 133

Heine, Heinrich, xxxv

"Heini." *See* Maier, Heinrich

Heller, Mr. (soccer coach), 150, 152

Heller, Petr "Kokošek," "Koko," 23, 26, 33, 52–53, 103, 144, 153; deported, 175

Henry VII, Holy Roman Emperor, 59n71

Hermann, Jan "Hanuš," "Mustang," "Kuzma," 14–15, 46, 51–52, 82, 123, 129, 170; deported, 184

Herz, Maček, 14n27, 46

Herz, Robin "Biblu," 10–12, 15–16, 19, 23, 25–26, 29, 39; deported, 46, 49, 53; Pavel's fight with, 18, 46, 53
Herzl, Theodore, celebration for, 89, 90, 92, 93, 100–101
Heydrich, Reinhard, xix
Himmler, Heinrich, xix, xxxi, 34n56, 74
Hitler, Adolf, 74n82; birthday of, 225; comes to power, xiv; invades Czechoslovakia, xiv–xv, xvii; rumors of death of, 101–2
Hoffmann, Professor, 116
Hoffmeister, Adolf, 74n83
Holocaust Memorial Museum, xxxix
Holzer, Hanuš, xlii note 36, 35, 43, 95, 118, 134
Horowitz, Luci, 112–13, 115, 119
Horwitz family, deported, 185
Hosková, Helga, xlii note 36
housekeeping duties (Grunt), 37, 45, 64, 72, 77, 102, 121, 130, 170; canceled, 9, 10, 122; early rising for, 7–8, 11, 13, 31, 34, 52, 82, 96, 105, 113, for inspection, 157; new rules, 110; Pavel in charge, 118, 136
Hradecká, Professor Karla, 172–73, 190, 195, 205, 207; in transport, 174
Hungary: Hungarian front advances, new Hungarian government (1944), 137, 143; Hungarian Revolution (1956), 55n68; studies of, 127; transport from, 210, 219
Huppert, Pavel, 25, 29, 34, 37–38, 45, 53–54, 95
Hus, Jan, and Hussite wars, 91n97, 156n123

I Am a Star (Auerbacher), xxxix note 1
identification card, 137
ink supply, 11, 37, 45, 127
Ilse (squad leader), 55, 82
I Never Saw Another Butterfly (Volavkova), xxxix note 1
"Irenka." See Seidlerová, Irena
Išík. See Lekner, Jiří
Israel: immigration to (1949), 13n22

Jaworzno (Ehrlich liberated in), 98n103
Jelínková, Dr. (English teacher), 55–56, 61, 104, 128, 141, 146, 166; Pavel dislikes, 17, 30, 64, 67, 122; payment for lessons, 23, 78, 131

Jewish Community of Vienna, 216n152
Jewish police (Getak; Ghettowache; Ordnungsdienst), 35, 71, 75, 96–97; during air raid, 132–33; change in uniforms, 108; cigarette scandal, 68, 99; and schlojs-ing, 110, 170, 191, 193; during transport, 48, 163–64
"Jewish Question," xvii
Jews: Central Office for Jewish Emigration, 69n78, 138n115; Czech, annihilation of, 69n78; Czech vs. German, 51n65; Danish, see Denmark; deportation from Prague begins, xvii–xx; dispossession of property of, xviii; Dutch, xix, 151, 211n148; French, xix; instruction in Judaism, 58, 69, 81, 99; Nazis take power over, xv, xvii, xx; Soviet Union murders, xviii; in transit camps, xviii–xx, (Council of Elders) xix, xx, xxix, 15, 73n81, 159n129, 160n130, 208; as war ends (Jews-for-sale deals), xxxi, 34n56. See also Jewish police; Zionism
Jilovsky, Arnošt "Jila," 26, 90, 95, 169–70, 176–77
Jindra (friend), 58–59, 66, 70–71, 78
Jirásek, Alois, 159
"Jirka." See Mautner, Jiří
Joseph II, emperor of Austria, xix, 127
Jugendfuersorge, xxiii, xli note 23, 77, 102, 147; established, xxi; members deported, 160; Pavel dislikes, 194, 205; soccer team (Jufa), see soccer

"Kalí," "Kalíšek." See Klein, Karel
"Kapr." See Ruzek, Jiří
Karafiát, Jan: "Fire-Flies," xxiii
Kaufering (Dachau), xxxix
Kessel, Dr. (member of commission), 224
Kienová, Mrs. "Kienka," 82, 89, 91, 106, 108, 115, 117, 132, 135
"Kikina." See Repper, Jiří
Klauber, Arnošt "Šmudla," 76–77, 79, 87, 114, 128, 133
Klein, Dr. (camp doctor), 41, 102
Klein, Karel "Kalíšek," "Kalí," 15–17, 24, 26, 29, 65, 67, 73–74, 77, 85, 101, 113, 120; contributes to magazine, 25, 36; deported, 184; moves, 140, 150; moves back, 172, 175; Pavel shares bed, 21, 35, 58, 75, 116, (friendship cools)

9–14, 44, 53–54, 59, 61, 76–91 passim, 95, 100, 102–3, 129, 132, 151, 154, 176–77, 179, (Pavel makes up with) 86, 92, 94, 105–7, 115, 122, 127, 133, 182–83; shares duty with Pavel, 64, 104, 118, 124, 136, 143–44

Klein, Otto "Ota," "Otík," 12, 33, 44, 55, 57, 62, 73, 85–86; assistant to, 53n67; and garden assignments, 64, 67, 76–77; replaced, 87n93

Klementová, Mrs., 209, 228

Knobloch family, xvii, 59

Koff, B. (pianist), 10

Kohn, Mrs. (bakery worker), 188

Kohn, Professor Antonín, xxiv, 20, 57–58, 67, 88, 104, 155; deported, 161

Kohn (escapes from camp), 94

"Kokošek," "Koko." See Heller, Petr

Kollinerová, Mrs., 203, 208, 211, 214, 216, 225–26

Kopperl, Rudolf "Krysa," 14, 28–30, 36, 45, 122; deported, 175

Koralka, Mr., 216

Kovanitz (soccer coach), 150

Krása, Hans: Brundibár, xxiii, xxix, xxx, 74n83, 128, 159n128

Kreisl, Mrs., 214

Krulis (of room 9), 93

Kubilová, Mrs. (warehouse worker), 217–18

Kudowa labor camp, 50n64

Kuli (friend), 115

Kumerl (friend), 143

Kürschner family, xvii, 27

Kusy, Mr., 132

"Kuzma." See Hermann, Jan

Lamm, Bedřich, 9, 27; deported, 46, 49–50

Lappert, Jindřich, 22, 29, 40, 45, 98, 120, 137, 157; deported, 175

Larche, Mrs. (moves into the heim), 206

Lavecky, Mr. (camp barber), 96

Lechner (worker), 52

Lederer, Petr "Pedro," 9, 15, 125, 148, 179

Lederer (writer), 92

Lekner, Jiří "Išík," 49, 53, 54, 72, 109, 147, 232; deported, 171

Leošek. See Demner, Leo

Levit, Mr. (warehouse worker), 217

library, camp, xix, xxxiv–xxxv; new, 73, 155; Pavel's use of, 10, 12, 20–27, 30, 34, 37–38, 106, 115, 118, 121–22, 124, (library closed) 8, 13, (library discovered in warehouse) 182

Lichtwitz, Leo, 99

Lion, Pavel, 8, 15, 54, 66–67, 149, 153; deported, 171; and Rim, Rim, 14, 23–24, 60, 67, 84, 92, 118, 134

Löwenherz, Josef, 216n152

Luxemburg, Jan, 59, 61

Maier, František "Franta": as boys' supervisor, xxi, xxvii, xxxii, 8, 11–13, 16, 52, 70, 115–16, 121, 135, 145, 153, (assistants to) 7n2, 30n51, (boys' reminiscences about) 213, (gives exams) 9, 64, (holds Apel) xxii, 20–21, 68–69, 79, 82, 96–98, 133, 136, 155, (and inspection) 125–26, (and moving of boys) 81–82, 138–39, 142, 146, (and punishment) 62, 83, 128–30, 150; directs Herzl celebration, 92, 100–101; entertainment provided by, 113; girlfriend of, 50n64; Pavel's relationship with, xxxvi, 18, 23–35 passim, 38, 54, 57–59, 67, 72, 74–75, 79, 106, 126–34 passim, 146, 150–51, 156; receives food package, 63; in soccer match, 121–22, 128, 154–55; tells stories, reads to boys, 14, 24, 27–28, 55–56, 65–66, 71, 76–78, 83, 98, 104–8 passim, 113, 157; and transports, 44, (deported to Auschwitz) xxiv, 50, 160–62, (parents deported) 54; on "vacation," replaced by Franta Graus, 88–89, (returns) 95–96, 114

Maier, Heinrich "Heini," 31, 35, 47, 133; meetings with, 56, 59–60, 67, 72, 83, 87, 89, 104, 109–10, 114, 116, 129, 157, (gymnastics with) 100, 117–18, (preparation for meeting with) 93–94, 118; (translating sessions) 131, 134, 136, 145; and Zionism, 60, 128

Majošek. See Mayer, Martin

Mangl (friend), xxxvi, 148–54, 164–65, 168, 170; deported, 171–72, 174–75, 177

Maria Theresa, archduchess of Austria, xix

März, Gideon Arnošt "Gida," 98; (Gido) 141; deported, 179

Marzbach, Dr., 207

Masaryk, Tomás: photo of and article about, xxxiii

Mauthausen concentration camp, 57n69

Mautner, Jiří "Jirka," 65, 86, 95, 103, 106–7, 112; deported, 7n2, 44, 46, 172

Mautner, Mrs. Marie, 43, 65, 67, 74, 83, 94–95, 133, 140; deported, 7n2, 44, 171–72; rouses boys, 7, 9, 11, 61, 155, 159; on "vacation," 99, (returns) 106, 110

Mautner, Pavel "Palka," 149; deported, 7n2, 44, 46, 172

Mayer, Martin (Majošek), 56, 82, 191

Meisl, Arna, 66

Merz, Bar Mitzvah of, 154

Meyer, Denise, 129

Meyer, Léon, 129n113

Meyer (shoemaker), 112

Milka, Miss (squad leader), 96, 106, 116

Míša. See Gruenbaum, Michael

Míša, "Little," 50, 149

morality, reshaping of, xxv–xxvi

Moravia, xv, xvii, xix

Mozart, Wolfgang Amadeus, 50: operas produced in camp, xxii, 78n87, 111

Mühlstein, Gabriel "Eli," "Elihu," 13, 17, 34, 172; deported, 175

Munich appeasement effort, xv

Murmelstein, Benjamin, 159n129, 216, 222–24

music: during beautification campaign, xxvii–xxviii, 69–70, 73–76; concerts, xxii, 8–10, 63, 80, 215, (by Stadtkapelle) 69, 76, 136; operas produced, xxii–xxiii, 74, 78n87, 128; Pavel plays recorder, 134; Pavel practices flute, 56, 63, (performs) 65, 70–71, 78; Pavel's piano lessons, 102, 109–25 passim, 129, 138, 142–47 passim, 154, 158; singing, 9, 35, 73, 101, 107, 109, (choir) 82, 86, 88, 111, (Czech songs) 76, 81, 112, 124, (German songs) xxvii–xxviii, 70, (Hebrew songs) 89

"Mustang." See Hermann, Jan

Nathan, Mr. (engineer), 208

Nazi party, 74n82, 107n108; comes to power, xiv, (power over Jews) xv,

xvii, xx; Jewish community relations with, xix; Jews-for-sale deals, xxxi; Nazi commandant at Terezín, xxix; propaganda of, 156n124; propaganda film produced by, xviii, xxx–xxxi, 123–24, 136; and Slovakia, 131

Nebuchadnezar (play), 10, 11, 28

Nešar (magazine founded by Pavel), xxxii–xxxvi, xxxix, 8, 16, 29–30, 62, 173–74; articles for, 9–12, 37–38, 127; cover and pages reproduced, xxxii–xxxiii; neglected, 19, 21–23, 31, 33–36, 39, 67, (folds) 65; Pavel loses interest in, 53, 60, 115; Rim, Rim as competition with, xxxii, 9, 14, 17, 22, 28, 30, (attacks) 23–24, 27

nesev (Hebrew language entertainment program), 76, 89, 92. See also games and sports; music

Netherlands, the, 124n112, 148; Dutch Jews, xix, 151, 211n148; German invasion of, 211n148

Neumann, Mr. (camp barber), 28

Nobel, Professor (Jugendleiter), 165, 166, 182

notebook, title page of, (illus.) 180

"Otík." See Klein, Otto

Pacific Entertainment Evening, 118

"painters' affair," xxix–xxx, 94, 96–97

"Palka." See Mautner, Pavel

Palounka, schlojs-ing by, 110

Passer (soccer player), 121, 122, 128

Passover celebration, 14

"Pedro." See Lederer, Petr

Petruška (friend), 173

Pfeffer (escapes from camp), 94

Piesingers (family friends), 226

Poland: Jewish ghettos in, xviii, ("resettlement") xx; Russian front in, 148

Popper, Mr., deported, 160, 164, 175

Porges (friend), 91

Porges, Dr., 224

Potyomkin, Grigory, and "Potemkin village," 182n136

Powder Tower, 202–3, 204

Prager, Mr. (gardener), 33, 56, 76–78, 105–6, 108, 147

Prague Spring, 35

Prague Youth Aliyah school, 154n120
Pressburger, Chava, 84n91
Prochurka, Mr. 216
"Pudlina." *See* Götzlinger, Pavel

Rahm, "Uncle" Karl, xxix, xxx, 15, 21,
    40, 52, 64, 69, 73–74, 85; as war ends,
    221–24, (burns documents) 148
Ramon, Ilan, 84n91
Red Cross: Danish, 221n155; German,
    xxvi; International Commission,
    xxxix, (visits camp) xxvi–xxix, 67,
    69–70, 73–75; Swedish, xxxi, 221n155;
    Swiss, 221; as war ends, 223, 224,
    (official status) 228
Redlich, Egon "Gonda," 154
Reich Security Main Office, xix, xxvi
Reiner, Karel, xxii
reklamace. *See* transport, deportation
Repper, Jiří "Kikina," 13 , 44
Rim, Rim, Rim (camp magazine), 12, 38,
    53, 61–62, 65, 114, 122; anniversary
    of 20th issue, 118, 134; competes
    with *Nešar*, xxxii, 9, 14, 17, 22, 28, 30,
    (attacks *Nešar*) 23–24, 27; Pavel as
    contributor to, xxxiv, xxxv, 67, 81,
    83–84, 86–87, 92; questionnaires
    about, 99; reproduction of cover,
    xxxiv
Rindler, Mr. (housing manager), 138
Rindler, Petr "Grizzly," 12, 44–46, 88, 90,
    138, 150; friendship with Pavel cools,
    29, 131; mother dies, 82; and *Nešar*,
    22, 24; as soccer player, 113, 156
Rindlerová, Mrs. (Petr's mother), 82, 83
Robin. *See* Herz, Robin
Rockefeller, John D., 98
Rolf (warehouse worker), 206
Romania, 137, 148
room 7 and room 7 boys, xxi–xxii,
    xxxiii, xxxv–xxxvi, xxxvii, 7n1, 8; boys
    move, 23; Pavel leaves, 21; relay race
    won by, 86
Roosevelt, Franklin D., 219
Rosenbaum, Kamila, xxii–xxiii
Rössler, Anna, 183n137, 226
Rössler, Josef, 183, 198, 202, 209, 215,
    217
Roth (garden worker), 108
Roubíček, Mr., deported, 160
Roubíček, Mrs., 15, 195

"Rudla." *See* Bergmann, Dr. Rudolf;
    Freudenfeld, Rudolf; Weil, Rudolf
Rudniková, Dr. Gertruda, 107, 114, 125,
    135
R.U.R. (Čapek), 106
Ruza (food worker), 194
Ruzek, Jiří "Kapr," 9, 12, 136, 176–77,
    192

Salomon, Dr., 222
Schächter, Rafael, xxiii, 78
Schinko, Else, 161, 228; and Schinko
    family, 161
Schleissner (classmate), 91
Schlesingerová, Vera, 50, 113–14, 116,
    120, 127
Schleusky. *See* transport, deportation
Schliesser, Karel, deported, 160, 164
schlojs-ing: books, 169–70, 172, 182;
    food, 183–84, 186, 191, 193, 197;
    fruit, 100, 110; from garden, xxv–
    xxvi, 25n41, 36, 78, 82–83, 85, 106–9,
    114–17, 123, 125, 130, 132, 135,
    142–43; from warehouse, 199
School, the (L417), xx, xxi–xxii, 11,
    15, 32, 53n66, 59, 70, 135, 151, 160;
    Apel for, 12, 61, 140 (*see also Apel*);
    behavior in, 58; boys from, escape
    from camp, 22; commission expected
    at, xxvii, 75; disinfected, 18–21;
    garden in front of, 125; guarding
    of, 140, (Pavel guards) 33; move to,
    43–44, (and move from) 34, 114,
    138–40, 142, 145–46; Pavel assigned
    to, 147; performances before, 88, 100;
    picture of, 92; second anniversary of,
    84, 86
Schorsch, Gustav, xxii
Schubert, Georgi, 120
Schütz, Heinrich, 122
Schwarz family, food package from, 72
Schwarz (boy from Room 9), 129
Schwarzbart, Julius, 36, 56, 78–79,
    84–85, 91, 96, 106, 114, 144, 147;
    chastises boys, 61, 135; and flowers
    from garden, 55, 117; and *schlojs*-ing
    by boys, 125, 135, 142–43
Schweinburg, Alexandr (Sasha), 8,
    10–11, 15, 31–32, 65, 87, 115, 121;
    deported to Auschwitz, diary lost,
    xiii, 7n1; and English lessons, 56, 71,

94, 122, 124, 128, 130, 146, 153, 157, (payment for) 51, 55, 131; father deported, 160; friendship with Pavel falters, 38, 42; moved, 23, 82; wins writing prize, 92
Schwenk (Svenk), Karel, 20
scouting, 28–29, 59; Scout Day Festival, 110, 111–12, 116
Seidl, Siegfried, 15n29, 74n84
Seidlerová, Irena "Irenka," 30, 59, 69, 82, 85, 104
Seifert, Jaroslav, 63
Seiner (possibly Steiner), Jindřich, 82; deported, 169
Senecká, Irma, 211, 212, 213–14; works at *Glimmer*, 207, 216
Shakespeare, William, 41, 115, 121
sichy (elderly sick people), 40, 178, 191, 195
Sidlof (friend), 217
Siechenheim (nursing home), 40
Sklarek (escapes from camp), 94, 96
Slovakia, 131, 148; occupation of, 219; Slovak transport, 210
"Small Fortress," xix, xxix, 94, 143, 203, 204, 228
Smetana, Bedřich: *The Bartered Bride*, xxii, 78n87, 100, 134
"Šmudla." *See* Klauber, Arnošt
Sobibór, gas chambers of, xviii
soccer: Pavel as enthusiast, xxxv–xxxvi, 12, 21, 33, 62, 65, 69, (loses interest) 113, 119, (mother objects) 15, 129; soccer matches, 20, 31, 39, 60, 71–72, 75–76, 81–89 passim, 93, 97–101 passim, 104–5, 109–16, 120–22, 127–30, 137, 147, 150–57 passim, (bets on outcome of) 92, ("friendly") 148, (Jufa plays) 16, 19, 26, 32, (Jufa wins cup) 121, (Nešarim win) 165, (spectators forced to watch and cheer) 144. *See also* clothing (soccer boots); head soccer (*hlavicky*)
Sokol, Sokolovna center, 76, 103, 149, 212
Soridek (soccer player), xxxvi, 149
Soviet Union: Jews murdered, xviii; Prague Spring, 35n59; as war ends, xxxi, xxxviii, 224, (approaches Czech border) 102, (invades Czechoslovakia)

107n108, (Russian front) 99, 131, 143, 148, 219
Spitz, Erich "Špulka," xlii note 36, 118, 138, 159, 184, 190–92, 196; carving by, 111, 117; and gardening, 55–56
Spitz, Mr. (Erich's father), 119
Spizl (soccer player), 153
Springer, František "Franta," 28–30, 53, 57–58, 85, 98, 100, 112, 135, 137; Bar Mitzvah of, 37; deported, 179
Springer, Mrs. (Franta's mother), 30
"Špulka." *See* Spitz, Erich
Stadler, Pepek, 32, 42, 55
St. Bartholomew Night, 224
Stein, Eric (Pavel's uncle), xxvii, 63; *photo, xxvii*
Stein, Gertrude "Trude," "Tetanka" (Pavel's aunt), xxvii, 100; *photo, xxvii*
Stein, Gustl "Gustla," xxxvii, 19, 23–27, 39–40, 44, 49, 56, 60, 77, 79, 83, 88, 94, 132, 148; deported, 169, 177; friendship falters, 11–12, 42, 53–54, 61, 64, 73, 76, 90, 93, 95, 100, 122, 127, (fistfight) 85, 103, (Pavel makes up with) 14–15, 92; and magazine, 13, 36, 38
Stein, Mrs. (Gustl's mother), 27
Stein, Zikmund and Hermine (Pavel's grandparents), xxvii, xxviii; *photo, xxvii*
Steiner. *See* Seiner
Steinová, Eva, 102
Stengel, Frau von, 194
St. Nicholas. *See* Christmas
Strass, František, 94n99
Strauss, Mrs. (widow), 208
Strebinger, Jan "Gorila," 14, 17, 26; deported, 45, 49
Sudetenland. *See* Czechoslovakia
suicide, 31
Sušický, Otomar and Olga (uncle and aunt), xiii; shipped to Auschwitz-Birkenau, xxiv, xxvi, 50–52, 79
"Suva." *See* Zweig, Gustav
Svatobořice labor camp, 214
Sweden: deportation to, xx; Swedish Red Cross, xxxi, 221n155; Swedish troops enter Terezín, 222
Switzerland: deportation to, xx, xxxi, 224; Swiss Red Cross, 221

Taucha (liberation in), 53n67
Taussig, Fritz. *See* Fritta, Bedřich
Taussig, Heinrich, 10
Taussig, Josef (dramatist), xxii
Taussig, Mr. (glass worker), 217, 218
Terezín: escape from, 22–23, 94, 96–97;
    German choice of, xix–xx; German
    myth about, xx, (Nazi propaganda
    film) xviii, xxx–xxxi; paintings of,
    see "painters' affair"; pass system, 52;
    second anniversary of Weiners' stay
    in, 50; SS office at, 156, 205; third
    anniversary of census, 193; as transit
    camp, xviii–xx, xxxix note 1; transport
    from, *see* transport, deportation;
    transport to, xvii–xx, 55n68, 57nn69–
    70, (as war ends) xxxviii–xxxix, 106,
    219, 225–28; visited by commissions,
    77, 221, 223–24, 226 (*see also* Red
    Cross). *See also* beautification
    campaign; children; education;
    library, camp; music
Thein (escapes from camp), 22–23
Theresienstadt. *See* Terezín
Trade Fair Palace (Prague), xvii
transport, deportation, xxiii–xxiv,
    xxvi–xvii, xxxi, xxxvii–xxxix, 43–46,
    47–53, 55, 170–85, 207; age bracket
    increased, 159; back to Terezín, 219,
    225–28; deception of passengers,
    xvii–xx; from Hungary, 210; personal
    gain in, 51; *reklamace* from, xxiv, 45,
    47, 159–60, 162; release of Danish
    Jews, xxxi–xxxii, 221–22; rumors of,
    27, 157; *Schleusky* (processing center)
    for, xx, xxiv, 52, 54, 160–64 passim,
    170–73, 179, 222, 225; statistics,
    xx; to Switzerland and Sweden, xx,
    xxxi, 220, 224; transports end, 189;
    volunteers for, 165; Weiner family
    and, xxiv, xxxvii, 55, 159–69 (*see also*
    Sušický, Otomar and Olga); work
    transport, 159, (rumored) 138. *See also*
    Auschwitz-Birkenau
"Treasure Hunt" (game), 26–27
Tresnak (SS man), 218
Troller, Norbert, xxx, 94n99
"Tuti," "Tutinek." *See* Zweig, Gustav

Ungar, Otto, xxix–xxx, 94. *See also*
    "painters' affair"
Uri (potential soccer coach), 149

Valenkho (SS man), 144
Van der Zyl, Adolf "Abraham," 199, 202,
    204, 206–7, 209, 214–15, 217–18
Vedem (camp magazine), 84n91
Veigl, Mr. (warehouse worker), 206, 207,
    209, 214–17
Velká Opereta, 204
Verdi's *Requiem,* 78n87
Vogel (teacher), 34, 35, 39
Voskovec, Jiří, 107
Vostrel (SS man), 223
Vrchlabi Barracks, 35, 58, 88, 150
Vrchlabske Dietary Kitchen, 188. *See also*
    food

Walter (bakery worker), 190, 192
Warsaw, fighting in, 113
Weider, Mr. (soccer coach), 149
Weil, Jiří, xxxix note 1
Weil, Rudolf "Rudla," 32, 88, 140–41,
    151, 153
Weiner family: deportation of, xvii–xxi;
    Jewish identity of, xiii–xiv, 210;
    photos, xiv, xxvii. See also transport,
    deportation, Weiner family and
Weiner, Hanuš "Handa" (older
    brother): before deportation, xiii–xiv,
    (Bar Mitzvah of) 195; camp life, xx,
    11, 30–37 passim, 43, 45, 58, 75, 122,
    129, 135, (attitude toward Pavel)
    76, 90, 134, (birthday celebration)
    64–65, (ear infection) 73, (and
    food packages) 63, 79, (gives Pavel
    opera ticket) 111, (injures hand)
    40, (with *Landwirtschaft*) 24–25, 82,
    93; deported, xxiv, xxxvii, 159–66,
    177–79, 194, 197, 204–5, 207, 210,
    220, 225, (dies in camp) xxxix, (news
    of) 226; *photos, xiv, xv, xvi*
Weiner, Karen (daughter), xxxix, 4
Weiner, Ludvík (father): before
    deportation, xiii–xiv, xvii; camp life,
    xx, 35, 71, 88, 92, 123, 132, (defends
    old woman) 27, (goes to work) 49,
    (and ink supply) 11, 37, 45, (news
    of war) 143, (rumors of move,
    move takes place) 138, 139–40, 142,
    145, (state of health) 8, 14, 16–17,
    20–24 passim, 29, 32, 43, 62, 73, 76,
    99; deported, xxiv, xxxvii, 159–66,
    168, 173–79 passim, 189, 194, 197,
    204–11 passim, 219–20, 225–26 (dies

in camp) xxxix; Pavel's relations with, 9, 21, 26, 30, 33, 56, 65–67, 75–76, 82–86, 91, 95, 105–26 passim, 136–37, 145–53 passim, 157, (father reprimands, spanks) 46, 155, 158; Pavel studies with, 70, 73, 76, 81, 87, 100–101, 146; and Pavel's illnesses, 38–41, 102, 140; *photos, xiv, xxvii*

Weiner, Pavel (Paul) "Pajík": childhood and early life, xiii–xiv; deportation of family, xvii–xxi; diary begins, xiii, xx, xxi, xxii, xxvi, xxxii, 7; diary pages reproduced, xxv, 5, 6, 80; editorial notes in diary, 4; education of, xxi–xxii, xxiv, xxxiii–xxxv, (Czech language and history) 93, 98, 100, 127, 130–31, (English and French), 16–23 passim, 26–27, 30–35 passim, 50, 58, 62–68 passim, 73, 83–94 passim, 116, 118, 122–24, 128–37 passim, 143, 146–47, 151–56 passim, 165, 179, (exams) 8, 98–105, (homework) 8, 59, 61, 66, 122, (physics and mathematics) 25, 37, 58–59, 71, 77, 79, 91, 93, 100, 104, 123, 130, 133–34, (report card) 16, (resolves to study more) 109, (school supplies) 57–58, (ticket for lessons) 82; founds magazine, xxxii–xxxv, xxxvi (*see also Nešar*); illnesses, 38–42, 93–94, 100–103, 139–41, 143–46 passim, 150–51, 170, (impetigo) 123–25, 130, 134, 136, 157, 168, (inoculations) 97, 116; on Jews-for-sale deals, xxxi; moved, 189, (room plan *illus.*) 190; music studies by, *see* music; as soccer enthusiast, *see* soccer; thirteenth birthday, 195–97, (*illus.*) 196, 197; and transports, 47–48; work assigned to, *see* gardening; guard duty; housekeeping duties; works in bakery, 181, 183–92, (*illus.*) 188; works in warehouse, 198–209, 211, 214–18, 220, 227, (layout *illus.*) 199, 200; "written up" and punishment, 66, 69, 83, 84, 85, (house arrest) 28, 133, 156; writings, 118–20; "Alone," 92; "Beggar," 33–34; "Courage," 24; "Death on the Ship," 8, 35; "Envy," 14; "Modern Story," 25; "My Friend,"

99; "Parents and Children," 73; "Prisoner," 9; "The Sick Man," 8; "Sword Tells the Story," 84–85 (*see also Rim, Rim, Rim* [camp magazine]); *photos, xiv, xv, xvi*

Weiner, Valy Stein (mother), xiii–xiv, xxviii, xxxi; camp life, xx, 8, 11, 12, 14, (caught in air raid, 132–33, (cooks) *see* food; (and deportation) xxiv, 155n122, 220, (illness) 39, 43, 57, 60, (works) *see* bakery; *Glimmer;* husband and son deported, xxiv, xxxvii, 159–65; moved, 71–72, 140–42, 221; Pavel's relations with, xxiii, xxxvi–xxxviii, 14–46 passim, 47–93 passim, 97–126 passim, 127–57 passim, 158–80 passim, 181–201 passim, 202–26 passim; receives food package, 131; returns to Prague, moves to United States, xxxix; *photos, xiv, xxvii*

Weiss, Professor (piano teacher "Dutchman"), 110, 116–17, 119–23, 129, 138, 143

Wenceslaus, I (duke of Bohemia), and St. Wenceslaus Day, 189

Werich, Jan, 107

Westerbork (transit camp), 211n148

White Bakery, 183. *See also* bakery

Witrofsky, Petr "Witr," 71

Wolfik (friend), 217

Wolker, Jiří, 11, 12, 215

World Jewish Congress, xxvi

Yom Kippur, 163

Zebulon. *See* Ehrlich, Zebulon

Zentners (family friends), 214

Zionism, xxi, xxxv, 16n30, 35, 60, 77, 89n96, 92, 128; youth movement soccer team, 72. *See also* Jews

Žižka, Jan, 91

Zucker, Otto, 141, 160

Zweig, Gustav "Tuti," "Tutinek," "Suva," 13, 15, 29, 54, 58, 79, 117, 132, 135, 165; lectures on Judaism, 81; as soccer player, 69, 89, 105; in translating sessions, 128, 134, 136, 145

Zwicker, Professor Bruno, xxiv, 15, 57, 61, 91–92, 120, 129, 131, 157; deported, 161

Paul (Pavel) Weiner (1931–2010) was born in Prague, Czechoslovakia. He wrote his diary when he was twelve and thirteen years old, living through the horrors of the Nazi transit camp Terezín with his parents and older brother. Only Pavel and his mother, Valy, survived; they returned to Prague after the war but, with the help of Valy's brother, Eric Stein, soon left for Canada, following the Communist takeover of Czechoslovakia in 1948. After completing high school in Montreal, Paul moved to the United States to attend university and to pursue a career in chemical engineering; he made his home in New York City with his wife, Elaine (who died in 1992), and only child, Karen. As a proud New Yorker for the last fifty years of his life, Paul pursued his many cultural interests, and he was eventually able to return to his beloved Prague for visits with family and friends.

Karen Weiner, Paul's daughter, helped edit the diary. Paul found the diary only in 1979 among the possessions of his mother, Valy Weiner. He then spent many years translating the diary from its original Czech, and Karen worked with her father to edit the translations. Karen lives in New York City; she is a middle school social studies teacher.

Debórah Dwork is the Rose Professor of Holocaust History and director of the Strassler Center for Holocaust and Genocide Studies at Clark University in Massachusetts. Her award-winning books have been translated into many languages and formed the basis for documentaries produced and aired by the Canadian Broadcasting Company (CBC) and the British Broadcasting Company (BBC); they include *Children With A Star* and, with Robert Jan van Pelt, *Auschwitz* (winner of the National Jewish Book Award in 1996), *Holocaust,* and *Flight from the Reich: Jewish Refugees, 1933–1946.*